EP Sixth R(

Days 91-180

EP Reader Series

Volume 6

Easy Peasy

All-in-One
Homeschool

CONTENTS

ACKNOWLEDGEMENTS

Thank you to Abigail Baia for her beautiful cover art.

Welcome to Easy Peasy All-in-One Homeschool's Sixth Reader Lessons 91-180

We hope you enjoy curling up with this book of books.

This is Easy Peasy's offline version of its assignments for the second half of Reading 6. The novels and poetry included are found in the public domain and have been gathered here along with each lesson's assignment directions. The online lessons from Easy Peasy's website have been replaced with offline lessons found in this book. Care was taken to ensure the children don't miss out on any important lessons or activities.

This book covers Lessons 91 – 180 only. The first half is in the EP Sixth Reader Lessons 1-90.

Lesson 91

1. What do you remember of the book? Let's take a trip down memory lane, or at least through the book's plot points.
    *   What was Black Beauty's life like in the meadow? What was his master like?
    *   Who gave Black Beauty his name?
    *   How did Black Beauty save Squire Gordon and John?
    *   Was Black Beauty happy to see Ginger safe from the fire?
    *   Who's Joe Green?
    *   Why did Black Beauty become sick?
    *   Why was Black Beauty unhappy at Earlshall?
    *   What was good and bad about his home with Mr. Barry?
    *   What problems did Black Beauty have in London?
    *   How does Joe recognize Black Beauty?
        (Questions adapted from teacher resource provided at
        http://www.teachit.co.uk/ks3prose?CurrMenu=9&resource=7796)

Lesson 92

1. Write a book report introduction paragraph including information on the author and a paragraph or two telling the plot of the book.

Lesson 93

1. Write a paragraph about the theme of the book. Include a quote from the book. After the quote write (Sewell, chapter _). Normally you'd write the page number of the book, but you're quoting her, not my book, so let's use her chapter numbers as a reference as to where the quote is found.
2. What's the theme? What is the book really about? It's not really about a horse's life. It's about the mistreatment of horses.

Lesson 94

1. Write a paragraph or two giving your critical opinion. (Critical in this case does not mean negative. It means thinking carefully and analyzing what's good and what's bad about the novel.)
2. You can write about her style of writing, the plot and characters, the way she got her point across. Did she get her point across?

Lesson 95

1. Write a conclusion for your book report.
2. Read your report out loud and edit your report.
3. Publish your book report and share with others.

Lesson 96

1. Read the first couple of pages of "The Time Shop" by John Kendrick Bangs.

OF course it was an extraordinary thing for a clock to do, especially a parlor clock, which one would expect to be particularly dignified and well-behaved, but there was no denying the fact that the Clock did it. With his own eyes, Bobby saw it wink, and beckon to him with its hands. To be sure, he had never noticed before that the Clock had eyes, or that it had any fingers on its hands to beckon with, but the thing happened in spite of all that, and as a result Bobby became curious. He was stretched along the rug in front of the great open fireplace, where he had been drowsily gazing at the blazing log for a half hour or more, and looking curiously up at the Clock's now smiling face, he whispered to it.

"Are you beckoning to me?" he asked, rising up on his hands and knees.

"Of course I am," replied the Clock in a soft, silvery tone, just like a bell, in fact. "You didn't think I was beckoning to the piano, did you?"

"I didn't know," said Bobby.

"Not that I wouldn't like to have the piano come over and call upon me some day," the Clock went on, "which I most certainly would, considering him, as I do, the most polished four-footed creature I have ever seen, and all of his family have been either grand, square, or upright, and if properly handled, full of sweet music. Fact is, Bobby, I'd rather have a piano playing about me than a kitten or a puppy dog, as long as it didn't jump into my lap. It would be awkward to have a piano get frisky and jump into your lap, now, wouldn't it?"

Bobby had to confess that it would; "But what did you want with me?" he asked, now that the piano was disposed of.

"Well," replied the Clock, "I am beginning to feel a trifle run down, Bobby, and I thought I'd go over to the shop, and get in a little more time to keep me going. Christmas is coming along, and everybody is so impatient for its arrival that I don't want to slow down at this season of the year, and have all the children blame me because it is so long on the way."

"What shop are you going to?" asked Bobby, interested at once, for he was very fond of shops and shopping.

"Why, the Time Shop, of course," said the Clock. "It's a shop that my father keeps, and we clocks have to get our supply of time from him, you know, or we couldn't keep on going. If he didn't give it to us, why, we couldn't give it to you. It isn't right to give away what you haven't got."

"I don't think I understand," said Bobby, with a puzzled look on his face. "What is a Time Shop, and what do they sell there?"

"Oh, anything from a bunch of bananas or a barrel of sawdust up to an automobile," returned the Clock. "Really, I couldn't tell you what they don't sell there if you were to ask me. I know of a fellow who went in there once to buy a great name for himself, and the floor-walker sent him up to the third floor, where they had fame, and prosperity, and greatness for sale, and ready to give anybody who was willing and able to pay for them, and he chose happiness instead, not because it was less expensive than the others, but because it was more worth having. What they've got in the Time Shop depends entirely upon what you want. If they haven't got it in stock, they will take your order for it, and will send it to you, but always C.O.D., which means you must pay when you receive the goods. Sometimes you can buy fame on the instalment plan, but that is only in special cases. As a rule, there is no charging things in the Time Shop. You've got to pay for what you get, and it is up to you to see that the quality is good. Did you ever hear of a man named George Washington?"

"Hoh!" cried Bobby, with a scornful grin. "Did I ever hear of George Washington! What a question! Was there anybody ever who hasn't heard of George Washington?"

"Well, yes," said the Clock. "There was Julius Cesar. He was a pretty brainy sort of a chap, and he never heard of him. And old Father Adam never heard of him, and Mr. Methusaleh never heard of him, and I rather guess that Christopher Columbus, who was very much interested in American history, never heard of him."

"All right, Clocky," said Bobby, with a smile. "Go on. What about George Washington?"

"He got all that he ever won at the Time Shop; a regular customer, he was," said the Clock; "and he paid for what he got with the best years of his life, man or boy. He rarely wasted a minute. Now I thought that having nothing to do for a little while but look at those flames trying to learn to dance, you might like to go over with me and visit the old shop. They'll all be glad to see you and maybe you can spend a little time there whilst I am laying in a fresh supply to keep me on the move."

"I'd love to go," said Bobby, starting up eagerly.

"Very well, then," returned the Clock. "Close your eyes, count seventeen backward, then open your eyes again, and you'll see what you will see."

Bobby's eyes shut; I was almost going to say with a snap. He counted from seventeen back to one with a rapidity that would have surprised even his school-teacher, opened his eyes again and looked around, and what he saw well, that was more extraordinary than ever! Instead of standing on the parlor rug before the fireplace, he found himself in the broad aisle of the ground floor of a huge department store, infinitely larger than any store he had ever seen in his life before, and oh, dear me, how dreadfully crowded it was!

The crowd of Christmas shoppers that Bobby remembered to have seen last year when he had gone out to buy a lead-pencil to put into his father's stocking was as nothing to that which thronged this wonderful place. Ah me, how dreadfully hurried some of the poor shoppers appeared to be, and how wistfully some of them gazed at the fine bargains to be seen on the counters and shelves, which either because they had not saved it, or had wasted it, they had not time to buy!

3

Lesson 97

1. Read the next couple of pages of "The Time Shop."

"Well, young gentleman," said a kindly floor-walker, pausing in his majestic march up and down the aisle, as the Clock, bidding Bobby to use his time well, made off to the supply shop, "what can we do for you to-day?"

Nothing that I know of, thank you, sir," said Bobby. "I have just come in to look around."

"Ah!" said the floor-walker with a look of disappointment on his face. ''I'm afraid I shall have to take you to the Waste-Time Bureau, where they will find out what you want without undue loss of precious moments. I should think, however, that a nice-looking boy like you would be able to decide what he really wanted and go directly to the proper department and get it."

"Got any bicycles?" asked Bobby, seizing upon the first thing that entered his mind.

"Fine ones-best there are," smiled the pleasant floor-walker, very much relieved to find that Bobby did not need to be taken to the bureau. "Step this way, please. Mr. Promptness, will you be so good as to show this young gentleman our line of bicycles?" Then turning to Bobby, he added: "You look like a rather nice young gentleman, my boy. Perhaps never having been here before, you do not know our ways, and have not provided yourself with anything to spend. To encourage business we see that new comers have a chance to avail themselves of the opportunities of the shop, so here are a few time-checks with which you can buy what you want."

The kindly floor-walker handed Bobby twenty round golden checks, twenty silver checks, and twenty copper ones. Each check was about the size of a five cent piece, and all were as bright and fresh as if they had just been minted.

"What are these?" asked Bobby, as he jingled the coins in his hand.

"The golden checks, my boy, are days," said the floor-walker. "The silver ones are hours, and the coppers are minutes. I hope you will use them wisely, and find your visit to our shop so profitable that you will become a regular customer."

With this and with a pleasant bow the floor-walker moved along to direct a gray-haired old gentleman with a great store of years in his possession to the place where he could make his last payment on a stock of wisdom which he had been buying, and Bobby was left with Mr. Wiggins, the salesman, who immediately showed him all the bicycles they had in stock.

"This is a pretty good wheel for a boy of your age," said Mr. Promptness, pulling out a bright-looking little machine that was so splendidly under control that when he gave it a push it ran smoothly along the top of the mahogany counter, pirouetted a couple of times on its hind wheel, and then gracefully turning rolled back to Mr. Promptness again.

"How much is that?" asked Bobby, without much hope, however, of ever being able to buy it.

"Sixteen hours and forty-five minutes," said Mr. Promptness, looking at the price tag, and reading off the figures. "It used to be a twenty-five-hour wheel, but we have marked everything down this season. Everybody is so rushed these days that very few people have any spare time to spend, and we want to get rid of our stock."

"What do you mean by sixteen hours and forty-five minutes?" asked Bobby. "How much is that in dollars?"

Mr. Promptness smiled more broadly than ever at the boy's question.

"We don't do business in dollars here, my lad," said he. "This is a Time Shop, and what you buy you buy with time: days, hours, minutes, and seconds."

"Got anything that costs as much as a year?" asked Bobby.

"We have things that cost a lifetime, my boy," said the salesman; "but those things, our rarest and richest treasures; we keep up-stairs."

"I should think that you would rather do business for money," said Bobby.

"Nay, nay, my son," said Mr. Promptness. "Time is a far better possession than money, and it often happens that it will buy things that money couldn't possibly purchase."

"Then I must be rich," said Bobby.

The salesman looked at the little fellow gravely.

"Rich?" he said.

"Yes," said Bobby, delightedly. "I've got no end of time. Seems to me sometimes that I've got all the time there is."

"Well," said Mr. Promptness, "you must remember that its value depends entirely upon how you use it. Time thrown away or wasted is of no value at all. Past time or future time are of little value compared to present time, so when you say that you are rich you may be misleading yourself. What do you do with yours?"

"Why—anything I happen to want to do," said Bobby.

"And where do you get your clothes, your bread and butter, your playthings?" asked the salesman.

"Oh, my father gets all those things for me," returned Bobby.

"Well, he has to pay for them," said Mr. Promptness, "and he has to pay for them in time, too, while you use yours for what?"

Bobby hung his head.

"Do you spend it well?" asked the salesman.

"Sometimes," said Bobby, "and sometimes I just waste it," he went on. "You see, Mr. Promptness, I didn't know there was a Time Shop where you could buy such beautiful things with it, but now that I do know you will find me here oftener spending what I have on things worth having."

"I hope so," said Mr. Promptness, patting Bobby affectionately on the shoulder. "How much have you got with you now?"

5

"Only these," said Bobby, jingling his time-checks in his pocket. "Of course next week when my Christmas holiday begins I shall have a lot—three whole weeks—that's twenty-one days, you know."

"Well, you can only count on what you have in hand, but from the sounds in your pocket I fancy you can have the bicycle if you want it," said Mr. Promptness.

"At the price I think I can," said Bobby, "and several other things besides."

Lesson 98

1. Read the next couple of pages of "The Time Shop."

"How would you like this set of books about wild animals?" asked Mr. Promptness.

"How much?" said Bobby.

"Two days and a half, or sixty hours," said Mr. Promptness, inspecting the price-tag.

"Send them along with the rest," said Bobby. "How much is that electric railroad over there?"

"That's rather expensive," Mr. Promptness replied. "It will cost you two weeks, three days, ten minutes, and thirty seconds."

"Humph," said Bobby. "I guess that's a little too much for me. Got any marbles?"

"Yes," laughed Mr. Promptness. "We have china alleys, two for a minute, or plain miggles at ten for a second."

"Put me down for two hours' worth of china alleys, and about a half an hour's worth of miggles," said Bobby.

"Very good, sir," said Mr. Promptness, with a twinkling eye. "Now can you think of anything else?"

"Well, yes," said Bobby, a sudden idea bashing across his mind. "There is one thing I want very much, Mr. Promptness, and I guess maybe perhaps you can help me out. I'd like to buy a Christmas present for my mother, if I can get a nice one with the time I've got. I was afraid I couldn't get her much of anything with what little money I had saved. But if I can pay for it in time, Mr. Promptness—why, what couldn't I buy for her with those three whole weeks coming to me!"

"About how much would you like to spend on it?" asked Mr. Promptness, with a soft light in his eye.

"Oh, I'd like to spend four or five years on it," said Bobby, "but, of course—"

"That's very nice of you," said the salesman, putting his hand gently on Bobby's head, and stroking his hair. "But I wouldn't be extravagant, and once in a while we have special bargains here for kiddies like you. Why, I have known boys to give their mothers presents bought at this shop that were worth years, and years, and years, but which haven't cost them more than two or three hours because they have made up the difference in love. With love you can buy the best treasures of this shop with a very little expenditure in time. Now what do you think of this for your mother?"

Mr. Promptness reached up to a long shelf back of the counter and brought down a little card, framed in gold, and printed in beautiful colored letters, and illustrated with a lovely picture that seemed to Bobby to be the prettiest thing he had ever seen.

"This is a little thing that was written long ago," said Mr. Promptness, "by a man who spent much time in this shop buying things that were worthwhile, and in the end getting from our frame department a wonderful name which was not only a splendid possession for himself, but for the people among whom he lived. Thousands and thousands of people have been made happier, and wiser, by the way he spent his hours, and he is still mentioned among the great men of time. He was a fine, greathearted fellow, and he put a tremendous lot of love into all that he did. His name was Thackeray. Can you read, Bobby?"

"A little," said Bobby.

"Then read this and tell me what you think of it," said Mr. Promptness.

He handed Bobby the beautiful card, and the little fellow, taking it in his hand, read the sentence: MOTHER IS THE NAME OF GOD IN THE LIPS AND HEARTS OF LITTLE CHILDREN.

"You see, my dear little boy," said the kindly salesman, "that is worth—oh, I don't know how many years, and your mother, I am sure, would rather know that that is what you think, and how you feel about her, than have you give her the finest jewels that we have to sell. And how much do you think we charge you for it?"

"Forty years!" gasped Bobby.

"No," replied Mr. Promptness. "Five minutes. Shall we put it aside for you?"

"Yes, indeed," cried Bobby, delighted to have so beautiful a Christmas gift for his mother.

So Mr. Promptness put the little card aside with the bicycle, and the wild animal books, and the marbles, putting down the price of each of the things Bobby had purchased on his sales slip.

They walked down the aisles of the great shop together, looking at the many things that time well expended would buy, and Bobby paused for a moment and spent two minutes on a glass of soda water, and purchased a quarter of an hour's worth of peanuts to give to Mr. Promptness. They came soon to a number of large rooms at one end of the shop, and in one of these Bobby saw quite a gathering of youngsters somewhat older than himself, who seemed to be very busy poring over huge books, and studying maps, and writing things down in little note-books, not one of them wasting even an instant.

Lesson 99

1. Read the next couple of pages of "The Time Shop."

"These boys are buying an education with their time," said Mr. Promptness, as they looked in at the door. "For the most part they haven't any fathers and mothers to help them, so they come here and spend what they have on the things that we have in our library. It is an interesting fact that what is bought in this room can never be stolen from you, and it happens more often than not that when they have spent hundreds of hours in here they win more time to spend on the other things that we have on sale. But there are others, I am sorry to say, who stop on their way here in the morning and fritter their loose change away in the Shop of Idleness across the way—a minute here, and a half hour there, sometimes perhaps a whole hour will be squandered over there, and when they arrive here they haven't got enough left to buy anything."

"What can you buy at the Shop of Idleness?" asked Bobby, going to the street door, and looking across the way at the shop in question, which seemed, indeed, to be doing a considerable business, if one could judge from the crowds within.

"Oh, a little fun," said Mr. Promptness. "But not the real, genuine kind, my boy. It is a sort of imitation fun that looks like the real thing, but it rings hollow when you test it, and on close inspection turns out to be nothing but frivolity."

"And what is that great gilded affair further up the street?" asked Bobby, pointing to a place with an arched entrance gilded all over and shining in the sunlight like a huge house of brass.

"That is a cake shop," said Mr. Promptness, "and it is run by an old witch named Folly. When you first look at her you think she is young and beautiful, but when you come to know her better you realize that she is old, and wrinkled, and selfish. She gives you things and tells you that you needn't pay until to-morrow and this goes on until some day to-morrow comes, and you find she has not only used up all the good time you had, but that you owe her even more, and when you can't pay she pursues you with all sorts of trouble. That's all anybody ever got at Folly's shop, Bobby —just trouble, trouble, trouble."

"There seem to be a good many people there now," said Bobby, looking up the highway at Folly's gorgeous place.

"Oh, yes," sighed Mr. Promptness. "A great many—poor things! They don't know any better, and what is worse they won't listen to those who do."

"Who is that pleasant-looking gentleman outside the Shop of Idleness?" asked Bobby, as a man appeared there and began distributing his card amongst the throng.

"He is the general manager of the Shop of Idleness," said the salesman. "As you say, he is a pleasant-looking fellow, but you must beware of him, Bobby. He is not a good person to have around. He is a very active business man, and actually follows people to their homes, and forces his way in, and describes his stock to them as being the best in the world. And all the time he is doing so he is peering around in their closets, in their chests, everywhere, with the intention of robbing them. The fact that he is so pleasant to look at makes him very popular, and I only tell you the truth when I say to you that he is the only rival we have in business that we are really afraid of. We can compete with Folly but—"

Mr. Promptness's words were interrupted by his rival across the way, who, observing Bobby standing in the doorway, cleverly tossed one of his cards across the street so that it fell at the little boy's feet. Bobby stooped down and picked it up and read it. It went this way:

```
THE SHOP OF IDLENESS
PROCRASTINATION,
                    General Manager

Put Off Everything And Visit Our Shop
```

"So he's Procrastination, is he?" said Bobby, looking at the man with much interest, for he had heard his father speak of him many a time, only his father called him "old Putoff."

"Yes, and he is truly what they say he is," said Mr. Promptness, "the thief of time."

"He doesn't look like a thief," said Bobby.

Now it is a peculiarity of Procrastination that he has a very sharp pair of ears, and he can hear a great many things that you wouldn't think could travel so far, and, as Bobby spoke, he turned suddenly and looked at him, waved his hand, and came running across the street, calling out to Bobby to wait. Mr. Promptness seized Bobby by the arm, and pulled him into the Time Shop, but not quickly enough, for he was unable to close the door before his rival was at their side.

"Glad to see you, my boy," said Procrastination, handing him another card.

"Come on over to my place. It's much easier to find what you want there than it is here, and we've got a lot of comfortable chairs to sit down and think things over in. You needn't buy anything to-day, but just look over the stock."

Lesson 100

1. Finish "The Time Shop."
2. Time someone the story. What is the story teaching?

"Don't mind him, Bobby," said Mr. Promptness, anxiously whispering in the boy's ear. "Come along with me and see the things we keep on the upper floors—I am sure they will please you."

"Wait just a minute, Mr. Promptness," replied Bobby. "I want to see what Mr. Procrastination looks like close to."

"But, my dear child, you don't seem to realize that he will pick your pocket if you let him come close—" pleaded Mr. Promptness. But it was of no use, for the unwelcome visitor from across the way by this time had got his arm through Bobby's and was endeavoring to force the boy out through the door, although the elevator on which Bobby and Mr. Promptness were to go up-stairs was awaiting them.

"When did you come over?" said Procrastination, with his pleasantest smile, which made Bobby feel that perhaps Mr. Promptness, and his father, too, for that matter, had been very unjust to him.

"Going up," cried the elevator boy.

"Come, Bobby," said Mr. Promptness, in a beseeching tone. "The car is just starting."

"Nonsense. What's your hurry?" said Procrastination. "You can take the next car just as well."

"All aboard!" cried the elevator boy.

"I'll be there in two seconds," returned Bobby.

"Can't wait," cried the elevator boy, and he banged the iron door to, and the car shot up to the upper regions where the keepers of the Time Shop kept their most beautiful things.

"Too bad!" said Mr. Promptness, shaking his head, sadly. "Too bad! Now, Mr. Procrastination," he added fiercely, "I must ask you to leave this shop, or I shall summon the police. You can't deceive us. Your record is known here, and—"

"Tutt-tutt-tutt, my dear Mr. Promptness!" retorted Procrastination, still looking dangerously pleasant, and smiling as if it must all be a joke. "This shop of yours is a public place, sir, and I have just as much right to spend my time here as anybody else."

"Very well, sir," said Mr. Promptness, shortly. "Have your own way if you prefer, but you will please remember that I warned you to go."

Mr. Promptness turned as he spoke and touched an electric button at the back of the counter, and immediately from all sides there came a terrific and deafening clanging of bells; and from up-stairs and down came rushing all the forces of time to the rescue of Bobby, and to put Procrastination out. They fell upon him like an army, and shouting, and struggling, but still smiling as if he thought it the greatest joke in the world, the unwelcome visitor was at last thrust into the street, and the doors were barred and bolted against his return.

"Mercy me!" cried Bobby's friend the Clock, rushing up just as the door was slammed to. "What's the meaning of all this uproar?"

"Nothing," said Mr. Promptness, "Only that wicked old Procrastination again. He caught sight of Bobby here—"

"He hasn't hurt him?" cried the Clock.

"Not much, if any," said Mr. Promptness.

"You didn't have anything to do with him, did you, Bobby?" asked the Clock, a trifle severely.

"Why, I only stopped a minute to say how do you do to him," began Bobby, sheepishly.

"Well, I'm sorry that you should have made his acquaintance," said the Clock; "but come along. It's getting late and we're due back home. Paid your bill?"

"No," said Mr. Promptness, sadly. "He hasn't had it yet, but there it is, Bobby. I think you will find it correct."

He handed the little visitor a memorandum of all the charges against him. Bobby ran over the items and saw that the total called for a payment of eight days, and fifteen hours, and twenty-three minutes, and nine seconds, well within the value of the time-checks the good floorwalker had given him, but alas! when he put his hand in his pocket to get them they were gone. Not even a minute was left!

Procrastination had succeeded only too well!

"Very sorry, Bobby," said Mr. Promptness, "but we cannot let the goods go out of the shop until they are paid for. However," he added, "although I warned you against that fellow, I feel sorry enough for you to feel inclined to help you a little, particularly when I realize how much you have missed in not seeing our treasures on the higher floors. I'll give you five minutes, my boy, to pay for the little card for your mother's Christmas present."

He placed the card in the little boy's hand, and turned away with a tear in his eye, and Bobby started to express his sorrow at the way things had turned out, and his thanks for Mr. Promptness's generosity, but there was no chance for this. There was a whirr as of many wheels, and a flapping as of many wings. Bobby felt himself being whirled around, and around, and around, and then there came a bump. Somewhat terrified he closed his eyes for an instant, and when he opened them again he found himself back on the parlor rug, lying in front of the fire, while his daddy was rolling him over and over. The lad glanced up at the mantel-piece to see what had become of the Clock, but the grouchy old ticker stared solemnly ahead of him, with his hands pointed sternly at eight o'clock, which meant that Bobby had to go to bed at once.

"Oh, let me stay up ten minutes longer," pleaded Bobby.

"No, sir," replied his father. "No more Procrastination, my son—trot along."

And it seemed to Bobby as he walked out of the room, after kissing his father and mother good-night, that that saucy old Clock grinned.

INCIDENTALLY let me say that in the whirl of his return Bobby lost the card that the good Mr. Promptness had given him for his mother, but the little fellow remembered the words that were printed on it, and when Christmas morning came his mother found them painted in watercolors on a piece of cardboard by the boy's own hand; and when she read them a tear of happiness came into her eyes, and she hugged the little chap and thanked him, and said it was the most beautiful Christmas present she had received.

"I'm glad you like it," said Bobby. "It isn't so very valuable though, Mother. It only cost me two hours and a half, and I know where you can get better looking ones for five minutes."

Which extraordinary remark led Bobby's mother to ask him if he were not feeling well!

Lesson 101

1. Your next book is by Louisa May Alcott. Louisa pulled a lot from her own childhood to write her stories. She worked into her stories a lot of her family's ideals. Do you recognize her name? If you used the fifth reader, then you read another book by her, *Little Men*, but her most famous novel is probably *Little Women*. Here's the short biography I included in the EP Fifth Reader.
    - Louisa Mae Alcott was born in 1932 in Pennsylvania and was educated by her father. Her first book was published when she was 22 and before that she had

writings published in magazines. She was very similar to the main character of her most famous novel, *Little Women*.

... young Louisa was a tomboy. "No boy could be my friend till I had beaten him in a race," she claimed, "and no girl if she refused to climb trees, leap fences ..." For Louisa, writing was an early passion. She had a rich imagination and often her stories became melodramas that she and her sisters would act out for friends...

At age 15, troubled by the poverty that plagued her family, she vowed: "I will do something by and by. Don't care what, teach, sew, act, write, anything to help the family; and I'll be rich and famous and happy before I die, see if I won't!"
(from http://www.louisamayalcott.org/louisamaytext.html)

2. Do you know the nursery rhyme about Jack and Jill?
    - Jack and Jill went up the hill,
      To fetch a pail of water.
      Jack fell down and broke his crown,
      And Jill came tumbling after.
3. Louisa wrote this version to go with the first chapter of her book, *Jack and Jill*.
    - Jack and Jill went up the hill
      To coast with fun and laughter;
      Jack fell down and broke his crown,
      And Jill came tumbling after.
4. Based on the title of the book and the nursery rhyme, make a guess as to what the book is about.
5. Read the summary in the Answers section.

Vocabulary

1. Try to match the suffixes with their meanings. Suffixes are added onto the ends of words. If you don't know the meaning, try to think of some words with that suffix and see if you can find something they have in common.
2. Write the numbers and letters of the matches on a separate piece of paper. Some of these are similar to each other, so don't stress about mixing them up. (Answers)

1. -phobia	A. become
2. -able	B. belief
3. –or	C. characterized by
4. –fy	D. without

5. –ism	E. having the quality of
6. –ish	F. state or condition
7. –y	G. notable for
8. –less	H. fear
9. –ful	I. able
10. –hood	J. a person who does _____

Lesson 102

6. Look at the title of chapter 1 of your new book and make a guess about what is going to happen.
7. Read chapter 1 of *Jack and Jill*.
8. Reread the first paragraph. What are the children doing?
9. Who are Jack and Jill? Tell someone about the characters and setting of the story.

Chapter 1. The Catastophe

"Clear the lulla!" was the general cry on a bright December afternoon, when all the boys and girls of Harmony Village were out enjoying the first good snow of the season. Up and down three long coasts they went as fast as legs and sleds could carry them. One smooth path led into the meadow, and here the little folk congregated; one swept across the pond, where skaters were darting about like water-bugs; and the third, from the very top of the steep hill, ended abruptly at a rail fence on the high bank above the road. There was a group of lads and lasses sitting or leaning on this fence to rest after an exciting race, and, as they reposed, they amused themselves with criticising their mates, still absorbed in this most delightful of out-door sports.

"Here comes Frank Minot, looking as solemn as a judge," cried one, as a tall fellow of sixteen spun by, with a set look about the mouth and a keen sparkle of the eyes, fixed on the distant goal with a do-or-die expression.

> "Here's Molly Loo
> And little Boo!"

sang out another; and down came a girl with flying hair, carrying a small boy behind her, so fat that his short legs stuck out from the sides, and his round face looked over her shoulder like a full moon.

"There's Gus Burton; doesn't he go it?" and such a very long boy whizzed by, that it looked almost as if his heels were at the top of the hill when his head was at the bottom!

"Hurrah for Ed Devlin!" and a general shout greeted a sweet-faced lad, with a laugh on his lips, a fine color on his brown cheek, and a gay word for every girl he passed.

"Laura and Lotty keep to the safe coast into the meadow, and Molly Loo is the only girl that dares to try this long one to the pond. I wouldn't for the world; the ice can't be strong yet, though it is cold enough to freeze one's nose off," said a timid damsel, who sat hugging a post and screaming whenever a mischievous lad shook the fence.

"No, she isn't here's Jack and Jill going like fury."

> "Clear the track
> For jolly Jack!"

sang the boys, who had rhymes and nicknames for nearly everyone.

Down came a gay red sled, bearing a boy who seemed all smile and sunshine, so white were his teeth, so golden was his hair, so bright and happy his whole air. Behind him clung a little gypsy of a girl, with black eyes and hair, cheeks as red as her hood, and a face full of fun and sparkle, as she waved Jack's blue tippet like a banner with one hand, and held on with the other.

"Jill goes wherever Jack does, and he lets her. He's such a good-natured chap, he can't say 'No.'"

"To a girl," slyly added one of the boys, who had wished to borrow the red sled, and had been politely refused because Jill wanted it.

"He's the nicest boy in the world, for he never gets mad," said the timid young lady, recalling the many times Jack had shielded her from the terrors which beset her path to school, in the shape of cows, dogs, and boys who made faces and called her "Fraidcat."

"He doesn't dare to get mad with Jill, for she'd take his head off in two minutes if he did," growled Joe Flint, still smarting from the rebuke Jill had given him for robbing the little ones of their safe coast because he fancied it.

"She wouldn't! she's a dear! You needn't sniff at her because she is poor. She's ever so much brighter than you are, or she wouldn't always be at the head of your class, old Joe," cried the girls, standing by their friend with a unanimity which proved what a favorite she was.

Joe subsided with as scornful a curl to his nose as its chilly state permitted, and Merry Grant introduced a subject of general interest by asking abruptly,

"Who is going to the candy-scrape to-night?"

"All of us. Frank invited the whole set, and we shall have a tiptop time. We always do at the Minots'," cried Sue, the timid trembler.

"Jack said there was a barrel of molasses in the house, so there would be enough for all to eat and some to carry away. They know how to do things handsomely;" and the speaker licked his lips, as if already tasting the feast in store for him.

"Mrs. Minot is a mother worth having," said Molly Loo, coming up with Boo on the sled; and she knew what it was to need a mother, for she had none, and tried to care for the little brother with maternal love and patience.

"She is just as sweet as she can be!" declared Merry, enthusiastically.

"Especially when she has a candy-scrape," said Joe, trying to be amiable, lest he should be left out of the party.

Whereat they all laughed, and went gayly away for a farewell frolic, as the sun was setting and the keen wind nipped fingers and toes as well as noses.

Down they went, one after another, on the various coasts solemn Frank, long Gus, gallant Ed, fly-away Molly Loo, pretty Laura and Lotty, grumpy Joe, sweet-faced Merry with Sue shrieking wildly behind her, gay Jack and gypsy Jill, always together one and all bubbling over with the innocent jollity born of healthful exercise. People passing in the road below looked up and smiled involuntarily at the red-cheeked lads and lasses, filling the frosty air with peals of laughter and cries of triumph as they flew by in every conceivable attitude; for the fun was at its height now, and the oldest and gravest observers felt a glow of pleasure as they looked, remembering their own young days.

"Jack, take me down that coast. Joe said I wouldn't dare to do it, so I must," commanded Jill, as they paused for breath after the long trudge up hill. Jill, of course, was not her real name, but had been given because of her friendship with Jack, who so admired Janey Pecq's spirit and fun.

"I guess I wouldn't. It is very bumpy and ends in a big drift; not half so nice as this one. Hop on and we'll have a good spin across the pond;" and Jack brought "Thunderbolt" round with a skillful swing and an engaging air that would have won obedience from anybody but willful Jill.

"It is very nice, but I won't be told I don't dare by any boy in the world. If you are afraid, I'll go alone." And, before he could speak, she had snatched the rope from his hand, thrown herself upon the sled, and was off, helter-skelter, down the most dangerous coast on the hill-side.

She did not get far, however; for, starting in a hurry, she did not guide her steed with care, and the red charger landed her in the snow half-way down, where she lay laughing till Jack came to pick her up.

"If you will go, I'll take you down all right. I'm not afraid, for I've done it a dozen times with the other fellows; but we gave it up because it is short and bad," he said, still good-natured, though a little hurt at the charge of cowardice; for Jack was as brave as a little lion, and with the best sort of bravery the courage to do right.

"So it is; but I must do it a few times, or Joe will plague me and spoil my fun to-night," answered Jill, shaking her skirts and rubbing her blue hands, wet and cold with the snow.

"Here, put these on; I never use them. Keep them if they fit; I only carry them to please mother." And Jack pulled out a pair of red mittens with the air of a boy used to giving away.

"They are lovely warm, and they do fit. Must be too small for your paws, so I'll knit you a new pair for Christmas, and make you wear them, too," said Jill, putting on the mittens with a nod of thanks, and ending her speech with a stamp of her rubber boots to enforce her threat.

Jack laughed, and up they trudged to the spot whence the three coasts diverged.

"Now, which will you have?" he asked, with a warning look in the honest blue eyes which often unconsciously controlled naughty Jill against her will.

"That one!" and the red mitten pointed firmly to the perilous path just tried.

"You will do it?"

"Come on, then, and hold tight."

Jack's smile was gone now, and he waited without a word while Jill tucked herself up, then took his place in front, and off they went on the brief, breathless trip straight into the drift by the fence below.

"I don't see anything very awful in that. Come up and have another. Joe is watching us, and I'd like to show him that we aren't afraid of anything," said Jill, with a defiant glance at a distant boy, who had paused to watch the descent.

"It is a regular 'go-bang,' if that is what you like," answered Jack, as they plowed their way up again.

"It is. You boys think girls like little mean coasts without any fun or danger in them, as if we couldn't be brave and strong as well as you. Give me three go-bangs and then we'll stop. My tumble doesn't count, so give me two more and then I'll be good."

Jill took her seat as she spoke, and looked up with such a rosy, pleading face that Jack gave in at once, and down they went again, raising a cloud of glittering snow-dust as they reined up in fine style with their feet on the fence.

"It's just splendid! Now, one more!" cried Jill, excited by the cheers of a sleighing party passing below.

Proud of his skill, Jack marched back, resolved to make the third "go" the crowning achievement of the afternoon, while Jill pranced after him as lightly as if the big boots were the famous seven-leagued ones, and chattering about the candy-scrape and whether there would be nuts or not.

So full were they of this important question, that they piled on hap-hazard, and started off still talking so busily that Jill forgot to hold tight and Jack to steer carefully. Alas, for the candy-scrape that never was to be! Alas, for poor "Thunderbolt" blindly setting forth on the last trip he ever made! And oh, alas, for Jack and Jill, who willfully chose the wrong road and ended their fun for the winter! No one knew how it happened, but instead of landing in the drift, or at the fence, there was a great crash against the bars, a dreadful plunge off the steep bank, a sudden scattering of girl, boy, sled, fence, earth, and snow, all about the road, two cries, and then silence.

"I knew they'd do it!" and, standing on the post where he had perched, Joe waved his arms and shouted: "Smash-up! Smash-up! Run! Run!" like a raven croaking over a battlefield when the fight was done.

Down rushed boys and girls ready to laugh or cry, as the case might be, for accidents will happen on the best-regulated coasting-grounds. They found Jack sitting up looking about him with a queer, dazed expression, while an ugly cut on the forehead was bleeding in a way which sobered the boys and frightened the girls half out of their wits.

"He's killed! He's killed!" wailed Sue, hiding her face and beginning to cry.

"No, I'm not. I'll be all right when I get my breath. Where's Jill?" asked Jack, stoutly, though still too giddy to see straight.

The group about him opened, and his comrade in misfortune was discovered lying quietly in the snow with all the pretty color shocked out of her face by the fall, and winking rapidly, as if half stunned. But no wounds appeared, and when asked if she was dead, she answered in a vague sort of way,

"I guess not. Is Jack hurt?"

"Broken his head," croaked Joe, stepping aside, that she might behold the fallen hero vainly trying to look calm and cheerful with red drops running down his cheek and a lump on his forehead.

Jill shut her eyes and waved the girls away, saying, faintly, "Never mind me. Go and see to him."

"Don't! I'm all right," and Jack tried to get up in order to prove that headers off a bank were mere trifles to him; but at the first movement of the left leg he uttered a sharp cry of pain, and would have fallen if Gus had not caught and gently laid him down.

"What is it, old chap?" asked Frank, kneeling beside him, really alarmed now, the hurts seeming worse than mere bumps, which were common affairs among baseball players, and not worth much notice.

"I lit on my head, but I guess I've broken my leg. Don't frighten mother," and Jack held fast to Frank's arm as he looked into the anxious face bent over him; for, though the elder tyrannized over the younger, the brothers loved one another dearly.

"Lift his head, Frank, while I tie my handkerchief round to stop the bleeding," said a quiet voice, as Ed Devlin laid a handful of soft snow on the wound; and Jack's face brightened as he turned to thank the one big boy who never was rough with the small ones.

"Better get him right home," advised Gus, who stood by looking on, with his little sisters Laura and Lotty clinging to him.

"Take Jill, too, for it's my opinion she has broken her back. She can't stir one bit," announced Molly Loo, with a droll air of triumph, as if rather pleased than otherwise to have her patient hurt the worse; for Jack's wound was very effective, and Molly had a taste for the tragic.

This cheerful statement was greeted with a wail from Susan and howls from Boo, who had earned that name from the ease with which, on all occasions, he could burst into a dismal roar without shedding a tear, and stop as suddenly as he began.

"Oh, I am so sorry! It was my fault; I shouldn't have let her do it," said Jack, distressfully.

"It was all my fault; I made him. If I'd broken every bone I've got, it would serve me right. Don't help me, anybody; I'm a wicked thing, and I deserve to lie here and freeze and starve and die!" cried Jill, piling up punishments in her remorseful anguish of mind and body.

"But we want to help you, and we can settle about blame by and by," whispered Merry with a kiss; for she adored dashing Jill, and never would own that she did wrong.

"Here come the wood-sleds just in time. I'll cut away and tell one of them to hurry up." And, freeing himself from his sisters, Gus went off at a great pace, proving that the long legs carried a sensible head as well as a kind heart.

As the first sled approached, an air of relief pervaded the agitated party, for it was driven by Mr. Grant, a big, benevolent-looking farmer, who surveyed the scene with the sympathetic interest of a man and a father.

"Had a little accident, have you? Well, that's a pretty likely place for a spill. Tried it once myself and broke the bridge of my nose," he said, tapping that massive feature with a laugh which showed that fifty years of farming had not taken all the boy out of him. "Now then, let's see about this little chore, and lively, too, for it's late, and these parties ought to be housed," he added, throwing down his whip, pushing back his cap, and nodding at the wounded with a reassuring smile.

"Jill first, please, sir," said Ed, the gentle squire of dames, spreading his overcoat on the sled as eagerly as ever Raleigh laid down his velvet cloak for a queen to walk upon.

"All right. Just lay easy, my dear, and I won't hurt you a mite if I can help it."

Careful as Mr. Grant was, Jill could have screamed with pain as he lifted her; but she set her lips and bore it with the courage of a little Indian; for all the lads were looking on, and Jill was proud to show that a girl could bear as much as a boy. She hid her face in the coat as soon as she was settled, to hide the tears that would come, and by the time Jack was placed beside her, she had quite a little cistern of salt water stored up in Ed's coat-pocket.

Then the mournful procession set forth, Mr. Grant driving the oxen, the girls clustering about the interesting invalids on the sled, while the boys came behind like a guard of honor, leaving the hill deserted by all but Joe, who had returned to hover about the fatal fence, and poor "Thunderbolt," split asunder, lying on the bank to mark the spot where the great catastrophe occurred.

Lesson 103

1. Read chapter 2 of *Jack and Jill*.
2. How long is it going to take to heal? (Answers)
3. Tell someone about the chapter.

Chapter 2. Two Penitents

Jack and Jill never cared to say much about the night which followed the first coasting party of the season, for it was the saddest and the hardest their short lives had ever known. Jack suffered most in body; for the setting of the broken leg was such a painful job, that it wrung several sharp cries from him, and made Frank, who helped, quite weak and white with sympathy, when it was over. The wounded head ached dreadfully, and the poor boy felt as if bruised all over, for he had the worst of the fall. Dr. Whiting spoke cheerfully of the case, and made so light of broken legs, that Jack innocently asked if he should not be up in a week or so.

"Well, no; it usually takes twenty-one days for bones to knit, and young ones make quick work of it," answered the doctor, with a last scientific tuck to the various bandages, which made Jack feel like a hapless chicken trussed for the spit.

"Twenty-one days! Three whole weeks in bed! I shouldn't call that quick work," groaned the dismayed patient, whose experience of illness had been limited.

"It is a forty days job, young man, and you must make up your mind to bear it like a hero. We will do our best; but next time, look before you leap, and save your bones. Good-night; you'll feel better in the morning. No jigs, remember'" and off went the busy doctor for another look at Jill, who had been ordered to bed and left to rest till the other case was attended to.

Anyone would have thought Jack's plight much the worse, but the doctor looked more sober over Jill's hurt back than the boy's compound fractures; and the poor little girl had a very bad quarter of an hour while he was trying to discover the extent of the injury,

"Keep her quiet, and time will show how much damage is done," was all he said in her hearing; but if she had known that he told Mrs. Pecq he feared serious consequences, she would not have wondered why her mother cried as she rubbed the numb limbs and paced the pillows so tenderly.

Jill suffered most in her mind; for only a sharp stab of pain now and then reminded her of her body; but her remorseful little soul gave her no peace for thinking of Jack, whose bruises and breakages her lively fancy painted in the darkest colors.

"Oh, don't be good to me, Mammy; I made him go, and now he's hurt dreadfully, and may die; and it is all my fault, and everybody ought to hate me," sobbed poor Jill, as a neighbor left the room after reporting in a minute manner how Jack screamed when his leg was set, and how Frank was found white as a sheet, with his head under the pump, while Gus restored the tone of his friend's nerves, by pumping as if the house was on fire.

"Whist, my lass, and go to sleep. Take a sup of the good wine Mrs. Minot sent, for you are as cold as a clod, and it breaks my heart to see my Janey so."

"I can't go to sleep; I don't see how Jack's mother could send my anything when I've half killed him. I want to be cold and ache and have horrid things done to me. Oh, if I ever get out of this bed I'll be the best girl in the world, to pay for this. See if I ain't!" and Jill gave such a decided nod that her tears flew all about the pillow like a shower.

"You'd better begin at once, for you won't get out of that bed for a long while, I'm afraid, my lamb," sighed her mother, unable to conceal the anxiety that lay so heavy on her heart.

"Am I hurt badly, Mammy?"

"I fear it, lass."

"I'm glad of it; I ought to be worse than Jack, and I hope I am. I'll bear it well, and be good right away. Sing, Mammy, and I'll try to go to sleep to please you."

Jill shut her eyes with sudden and unusual meekness, and before her mother had crooned half a dozen verses of an old ballad, the little black head lay still upon the pillow, and repentant Jill was fast asleep with a red mitten in her hand.

Mrs. Pecq was an Englishwoman who had left Montreal at the death of her husband, a French Canadian, and had come to live in the tiny cottage which stood near Mrs. Minot's big house, separated only by an arbor-vitae hedge. A sad, silent person, who had seen better days, but said nothing about them, and earned her bread by sewing, nursing, work in the factory, or anything that came in her way, being anxious to educate her little girl. Now, as she sat beside the bed in the small, poor room, that hope almost died within her, for here was the child laid up for months, probably, and the one ambition and pleasure of the solitary woman's life was to see Janey Pecq's name over all the high marks in the school-reports she proudly brought home.

"She'll win through, please Heaven, and I'll see my lass a gentlewoman yet, thanks to the good friend in yonder, who will never let her want for care," thought the poor soul, looking out into the gloom where a long ray of light streamed from the great house warm and comfortable upon the cottage, like the spirit of kindness which made the inmates friends and neighbors.

Meantime, that other mother sat by her boy's bed as anxious but with better hope, for Mrs. Minot made trouble sweet and helpful by the way in which she bore it; and her boys were learning of her how to find silver linings to the clouds that must come into the bluest skies.

Jack lay wide awake, with hot cheeks, and throbbing head, and all sorts of queer sensations in the broken leg. The soothing potion he had taken did not affect him yet, and he tried to beguile the weary time by wondering who came and went below. Gentle rings at the front door, and mysterious tappings at the back, had been going on all the evening; for the report of the accident had grown astonishingly in its travels, and at eight o clock the general belief was that Jack had broken both legs, fractured his skull, and lay at the point of death, while Jill had dislocated one shoulder, and was bruised black and blue from top to toe. Such being the case, it is no wonder that anxious playmates and neighbors haunted the doorsteps of the two houses, and that offers of help poured in.

Frank, having tied up the bell and put a notice in the lighted side-window, saying, "Go to the back door," sat in the parlor, supported by his chum, Gus, while Ed played softly on the piano, hoping to lull Jack to sleep. It did soothe him, for a very sweet friendship existed between the tall youth and the lad of thirteen. Ed went with the big fellows, but always had a kind word for the smaller boys; and affectionate Jack, never ashamed to show his love, was often seen with his arm round Ed's shoulder, as they sat together in the pleasant red parlors, where all the young people were welcome and Frank was king.

"Is the pain any easier, my darling?" asked Mrs. Minot, leaning over the pillow, where the golden head lay quiet for a moment.

"Not much. I forget it listening to the music. Dear old Ed is playing all my favorite tunes, and it is very nice. I guess he feels pretty sorry about me."

"They all do. Frank could not talk of it. Gus wouldn't go home to tea, he was so anxious to do something for us. Joe brought back the bits of your poor sled, because he didn't like to leave them lying round for anyone to carry off, he said, and you might like them to remember your fall by."

Jack tried to laugh, but it was rather a failure, though be managed to say, cheerfully,

"That was good of old Joe. I wouldn't lend him 'Thunderbolt for fear he'd hurt it. Couldn't have smashed it up better than I did, could he? Don't think I want any pieces to remind me of that fall. I just wish you'd seen us, mother! It must have been a splendid spill to look at, anyway."

"No, thank you; I'd rather not even try to imagine my precious boy going heels over head down that dreadful hill. No more pranks of that sort for some time, Jacky;" and Mrs. Minot looked rather pleased on the whole to have her venturesome bird safe under her maternal wing.

"No coasting till some time in January. What a fool I was to do it! Go-bangs always are dangerous, and that's the fun of the thing. Oh dear!"

Jack threw his arms about and frowned darkly, but never said a word of the willful little baggage who had led him into mischief; he was too much of a gentleman to tell on a girl, though it cost him an effort to hold his tongue, because Mamma's good opinion was very precious to him, and he longed to explain. She knew all about it, however, for Jill had been carried into the house reviling herself for the mishap, and even in the midst of her own anxiety for her boy, Mrs. Minot understood the state of the case without more words. So she now set his mind at rest by saying, quietly,

"Foolish fun, as you see, dear. Another time, stand firm and help Jill to control her headstrong will. When you learn to yield less and she more, there will be no scrapes like this to try us all."

"I'll remember, mother. I hate not to be obliging, but I guess it would have saved us lots of trouble if I'd said No in the beginning. I tried to, but she would go. Poor Jill! I'll take better care of her next time. Is she very ill, Mamma?"

"I can tell you better to-morrow. She does not suffer much, and we hope there is no great harm done."

"I wish she had a nice place like this to be sick in. It must be very poky in those little rooms," said Jack, as his eye roved round the large chamber where he lay so cozy, warm, and pleasant, with the gay chintz curtains draping doors and windows, the rosy carpet, comfortable chairs, and a fire glowing in the grate.

"I shall see that she suffers for nothing, so don't trouble your kind heart about her to-night, but try to sleep; that's what you need," answered his mother, wetting the bandage on his forehead, and putting a cool hand on the flushed cheeks.

Jack obediently closed his eyes and listened while the boys sang "The Sweet By and By," softening their rough young voices for his sake till the music was as soft as a lullaby. He lay so still his mother thought he was off, but presently a tear slipped out and rolled down the red cheek, wetting her hand as it passed.

"My blessed boy, what is it?" she whispered, with a touch and a tone that only mothers have.

The blue eyes opened wide, and Jack's own sunshiny smile broke through the tears that filled them as he said with a sniff,

"Everybody is so good to me I can't help making a noodle of myself.

"You are not a noodle!" cried Mamma, resenting the epithet. "One of the sweet things about pain and sorrow is that they show us how well we are loved, how much kindness there is in the world, and how easily we can make others happy in the same way when they need help and sympathy. Don't forget that, little son."

"Don't see how I can, with you to show me how nice it is. Kiss me good-night, and then 'I'll be good,' as Jill says."

Nestling his head upon his mother's arm, Jack lay quiet till, lulled by the music of his mates, he drowsed away into the dreamless sleep which is Nurse Nature's healthiest soothing syrup for weary souls and bodies.

Lesson 104

1. Read chapter 3 of *Jack and Jill.*
2. How do they amuse themselves? (Answers)
3. Find a simile in the chapter. (Answers)
4. What does she describe as "delicious?" (Answers)

Vocabulary

1. Write an antonym of each word written below. The words are from what you just read. (Answers)
   - weary, drowsed, sorrow, resent, kindness, sympathy, lull, soothing

Chapter 3. Ward No. I

For some days, nothing was seen and little was heard of the "dear sufferers," as the old ladies called them. But they were not forgotten; the first words uttered when any of the young people met were: "How is Jack?" "Seen Jill yet?" and all waited with impatience for the moment when they could be admitted to their favorite mates, more than ever objects of interest now.

Meantime, the captives spent the first few days in sleep, pain, and trying to accept the hard fact that school and play were done with for months perhaps. But young spirits are wonderfully elastic and soon cheer up, and healthy young bodies heal fast, or easily adapt themselves to new conditions. So our invalids began to mend on the fourth day, and to drive their nurses distracted with efforts to amuse them, before the first week was over.

The most successful attempt originated in Ward No. I, as Mrs. Minot called Jack's apartment, and we will give our sympathizing readers some idea of this place, which became the stage whereon were enacted many varied and remarkable scenes.

Each of the Minot boys had his own room, and there collected his own treasures and trophies, arranged to suit his convenience and taste. Frank's was full of books, maps, machinery, chemical messes, and geometrical drawings, which adorned the walls like intricate cobwebs. A big chair, where he read and studied with his heels higher than his head, a basket of apples for refreshment at all hours of the day or night, and an immense inkstand, in which several pens were always apparently bathing their feet, were the principal ornaments of his scholastic retreat.

Jack's hobby was athletic sports, for he was bent on having a strong and active body for his happy little soul to live and enjoy itself in. So a severe simplicity reigned in his apartment; in summer, especially, for then his floor was bare, his windows were uncurtained, and the chairs uncushioned, the bed being as narrow and hard as Napoleon's. The only ornaments were dumbbells, whips, bats, rods, skates, boxing-gloves, a big bath-pan and a small library, consisting chiefly of books on games, horses, health, hunting, and travels. In winter his mother made things more comfortable by introducing rugs, curtains, and a fire. Jack, also, relented slightly in the severity of his training, occasionally indulging in the national buckwheat cake, instead of the prescribed oatmeal porridge, for breakfast, omitting his cold bath when the thermometer was below zero, and dancing at night, instead of running a given distance by day.

Now, however, he was a helpless captive, given over to all sorts of coddling, laziness, and luxury, and there was a droll mixture of mirth and melancholy in his face, as he lay trussed up in bed, watching the comforts which had suddenly robbed his room of its Spartan simplicity. A delicious couch was there, with Frank reposing in its depths, half hidden under several folios which he was consulting for a history of the steam-engine, the subject of his next composition.

A white-covered table stood near, with all manner of dainties set forth in a way to tempt the sternest principles. Vases of flowers bloomed on the chimney-piece gifts from anxious young ladies, left with their love. Frivolous story-books and picture-papers strewed the bed, now shrouded in effeminate chintz curtains, beneath which Jack lay like a wounded warrior in his tent. But the saddest sight for our crippled athlete was a glimpse, through a half-opened door, at the beloved dumb-bells, bats, balls, boxing-gloves, and snow-shoes, all piled ignominiously away in the bath-pan, mournfully recalling the fact that their day was over, now, at least for some time.

He was about to groan dismally, when his eye fell on a sight which made him swallow the groan, and cough instead, as if it choked him a little. The sight was his mother's face, as she sat in a low chair rolling bandages, with a basket beside her in which were piles of old linen, lint, plaster, and other matters, needed for the dressing of wounds. As he looked, Jack remembered how steadily and tenderly she had stood by him all through the hard times just past, and how carefully she had bathed and dressed his wound each day in spite of the effort it cost her to give him pain or even see him suffer.

"That's a better sort of strength than swinging twenty-pound dumb-bells or running races; I guess I'll try for that kind, too, and not howl or let her see me squirm when the doctor hurts," thought the boy, as he saw that gentle face so pale and tired with much watching and anxiety, yet so patient, serene, and cheerful, that it was like sunshine.

"Lie down and take a good nap, mother dear, I feel first-rate, and Frank can see to me if I want anything. Do, now," he added, with a persuasive nod toward the couch, and a boyish relish in stirring up his lazy brother.

After some urging, Mamma consented to go to her room for forty winks, leaving Jack in the care of Frank, begging him to be as quiet as possible if the dear boy wished to sleep, and to amuse him if he did not.

Being worn out, Mrs. Minot lengthened her forty winks into a three hours nap, and as the "dear boy" scorned repose, Mr. Frank had his hands full while on guard.

"I'll read to you. Here's Watt, Arkwright, Fulton, and a lot of capital fellows, with pictures that will do your heart good. Have a bit, will you?" asked the new nurse, flapping the leaves invitingly for Frank had a passion for such things, and drew steam-engines all over his slate, as Tommy Traddles drew hosts of skeletons when low in his spirits.

"I don't want any of your old boilers and stokers and whirligigs. I'm tired of reading, and want something regularly jolly," answered Jack, who had been chasing white buffaloes with "The Hunters of the West," till he was a trifle tired and fractious.

"Play cribbage, euchre, anything you like;" and Frank obligingly disinterred himself from under the folios, feeling that it was hard for a fellow to lie flat a whole week.

"No fun; just two of us. Wish school was over, so the boys would come in; doctor said I might see them now."

"They'll be along by and by, and I'll hail them. Till then, what shall we do? I'm your man for anything, only put a name to it."

"Just wish I had a telegraph or a telephone, so I could talk to Jill. Wouldn't it be fun to pipe across and get an answer!"

"I'll make either you say;" and Frank looked as if trifles of that sort were to be had for the asking.

"Could you, really?"

"We'll start the telegraph first, then you can send things over if you like," said Frank, prudently proposing the surest experiment.

"Go ahead, then. I'd like that, and so would Jill, for I know she wants to hear from me."

"There's one trouble, though; I shall have to leave you alone for a few minutes while I rig up the ropes;" and Frank looked sober, for he was a faithful boy, and did not want to desert his post.

"Oh, never mind; I won't want anything. If I do, I can pound for Ann."

"And wake mother. I'll fix you a better way than that;" and, full of inventive genius, our young Edison spliced the poker to part of a fishing-rod in a jiffy, making a long-handled hook which reached across the room.

"There's an arm for you; now hook away, and let's see how it works," he said, handing over the instrument to Jack, who proceeded to show its unexpected capabilities by hooking the cloth off the table in attempting to get his handkerchief, catching Frank by the hair when fishing for a book, and breaking a pane of glass in trying to draw down the curtain.

"It's so everlasting long, I can't manage it," laughed Jack, as it finally caught in his bed-hangings, and nearly pulled them, ring and all, down upon his head.

"Let it alone, unless you need something very much, and don't bother about the glass. It's just what we want for the telegraph wire or rope to go through. Keep still, and I'll have the thing running in ten minutes;" and, delighted with the job, Frank hurried away, leaving Jack to compose a message to send as soon as it was possible.

"What in the world is that flying across the Minots' yard,--a brown hen or a boy's kite?" exclaimed old Miss Hopkins, peering out of her window at the singular performances going on in her opposite neighbor's garden.

First, Frank appeared with a hatchet and chopped a clear space in the hedge between his own house and the cottage; next, a clothes line was passed through this aperture and fastened somewhere on the other side; lastly, a small covered basket, slung on this rope, was seen hitching along, drawn either way by a set of strings; then, as if satisfied with his job, Frank retired, whistling "Hail Columbia."

"It's those children at their pranks again. I thought broken bones wouldn't keep them out of mischief long," said the old lady, watching with great interest the mysterious basket travelling up and down the rope from the big house to the cottage.

If she had seen what came and went over the wires of the "Great International Telegraph," she would have laughed till her spectacles flew off her Roman nose. A letter from Jack, with a large orange, went first, explaining the new enterprise:

"Dear Jill-It's too bad you can't come over to see me. I am pretty well, but awful tired of keeping still. I want to see you ever so much. Frank has fixed us a telegraph, so we can write and send things. Won't it be jolly! I can't look out to see him do it; but, when you pull your string, my little bell rings, and I know a message is coming. I send you an orange. Do you like gorver jelly? People send in lots of goodies, and we will go halves. Good-by.

"Jack"

Away went the basket, and in fifteen minutes it came back from the cottage with nothing in it but the orange.

"Hullo! Is she mad?" asked Jack, as Frank brought the despatch for him to examine.

But, at the first touch, the hollow peel opened, and out fell a letter, two gum-drops, and an owl made of a peanut, with round eyes drawn at the end where the stem formed a funny beak. Two bits of straw were the legs, and the face looked so like Dr. Whiting that both boys laughed at the sight.

"That's so like Jill; she'd make fun if she was half dead. Let's see what she says;" and Jack read the little note, which showed a sad neglect of the spelling-book:

"Dear Jacky-I can't stir and it's horrid. The telly graf is very nice and we will have fun with it. I never ate any gorver jelly. The orange was first rate. Send me a book to read. All about bears and ships and crockydiles. The doctor was coming to see you, so I sent him the quickest way. Molly Loo says it is dreadful lonesome at school without us. Yours truly,

"Jill"

Jack immediately despatched the book and a sample of guava jelly, which unfortunately upset on the way, to the great detriment of "The Wild Beasts of Asia and Africa." Jill promptly responded with the loan of a tiny black kitten, who emerged spitting and scratching, to Jack's great delight; and he was cudgeling his brains as to how a fat white rabbit could be transported, when a shrill whistle from without saved Jill from that inconvenient offering.

"It's the fellows; do you want to see them?" asked Frank, gazing down with calm superiority upon the three eager faces which looked up at him.

"Guess I do!" and Jack promptly threw the kitten overboard, scorning to be seen by any manly eye amusing himself with such girlish toys.

Bang! went the front door; tramp, tramp, tramp, came six booted feet up the stairs; and, as Frank threw wide the door, three large beings paused on the threshold to deliver the courteous "Hullo!" which is the established greeting among boys on all social occasions.

"Come along, old fellows; I'm ever so glad to see you!" cried the invalid, with such energetic demonstrations of the arms that he looked as if about to fly or crow, like an excited young cockerel.

"How are you, Major?"

"Does the leg ache much, Jack?"

"Mr. Phipps says you'll have to pay for the new rails."

With these characteristic greetings, the gentlemen cast away their hats and sat down, all grinning cheerfully, and all with eyes irresistibly fixed upon the dainties, which proved too much for the politeness of ever-hungry boys.

"Help yourselves," said Jack, with a hospitable wave. "All the dear old ladies in town have been sending in nice things, and I can't begin to eat them up. Lend a hand and clear away this lot, or we shall have to throw them out of the window. Bring on the doughnuts and the tarts and the shaky stuff in the entry closet, Frank, and let's have a lark."

No sooner said than done. Gus took the tarts, Joe the doughnuts, Ed the jelly, and Frank suggested "spoons all round" for the Italian cream. A few trifles in the way of custard, fruit, and wafer biscuits were not worth mentioning; but every dish was soon emptied, and Jack said, as he surveyed the scene of devastation with great satisfaction,

"Call again tomorrow, gentlemen, and we will have another bout. Free lunches at 5 P.M. till further notice. Now tell me all the news."

For half an hour, five tongues went like mill clappers, and there is no knowing when they would have stopped if the little bell had not suddenly rung with a violence that made them jump.

"That's Jill; see what she wants, Frank;" and while his brother sent off the basket, Jack told about the new invention, and invited his mates to examine and admire.

They did so, and shouted with merriment when the next despatch from Jill arrived. A pasteboard jumping-jack, with one leg done up in cotton-wool to preserve the likeness, and a great lump of molasses candy in a brown paper, with accompanying note:

"Dear Sir-I saw the boys go in, and know you are having a nice time, so I send over the candy Molly Loo and Merry brought mc. Mammy says I can't eat it, and it will all melt away if I keep it. Also a picture of Jack Minot, who will dance on one leg and waggle the other, and make you laugh. I wish I could come, too. Don't you hate gruel? I do. In haste,

"J.P."

"Let's all send her a letter," proposed Jack, and out came pens, ink, paper, and the lamp, and everyone fell to scribbling. A droll collection was the result, for Frank drew a picture of the fatal fall with broken rails flying in every direction, Jack with his head swollen to the size of a balloon, and Jill in two pieces, while the various boys and girls were hit off with a sly skill that gave Gus legs like a stork, Molly Loo hair several yards long, and Boo a series of visible howls coming out of an immense mouth in the shape of o's. The oxen were particularly good, for their horns branched like those of the moose, and Mr. Grant had a patriarchal beard which waved in the breeze as he bore the wounded girl to a sled very like a funeral pyre, the stakes being crowned with big mittens like torches.

"You ought to be an artist. I never saw such a dabster as you are. That's the very moral of Joe, all in a bunch on the fence, with a blot to show how purple his nose was," said Gus, holding up the sketch for general criticism and admiration.

"I'd rather have a red nose than legs like a grasshopper; so you needn't twit, Daddy," growled Joe, quite unconscious that a blot actually did adorn his nose, as he labored over a brief despatch.

The boys enjoyed the joke, and one after the other read out his message to the captive lady:

Dear Jill-Sorry you ain't here. Great fun. Jack pretty lively. Laura and Lot would send love if they knew of the chance. Fly round and get well.

Gus

Dear Gilliflower-Hope you are pretty comfortable in your dungeon cell. Would you like a serenade when the moon comes? Hope you will soon be up again, for we miss you very much. Shall be very happy to help in anyway I can. Love to your mother. Your true friend,

E.D.

Miss Pecq.

Dear Madam-I am happy to tell you that we are all well, and hope you are the same. I gave Jem Cox a licking because he went to your desk. You had better send for your books. You won't have to pay for the sled or the fence. Jack says he will see to it. We have been having a spread over here. First-rate things. I wouldn't mind breaking a leg, if I had such good grub and no chores to do. No more now, from yours, with esteem,

Joseph P. Flint

Joe thought that an elegant epistle, having copied portions of it from the "Letter Writer," and proudly read it off to the boys, who assured him that Jill would be much impressed.

"Now, Jack, hurry up and let us send the lot off, for we must go," said Gus, as Frank put the letters in the basket, and the clatter of tea-things was heard below.

"I'm not going to show mine. It's private and you mustn't look," answered Jack, patting down an envelope with such care that no one had a chance to peep.

But Joe had seen the little note copied, and while the others were at the window working the telegraph he caught up the original, carelessly thrust by Jack under the pillow, and read it aloud before anyone knew what he was about.

My Dear-I wish I could send you some of my good times. As I can't, I send you much love, and I hope you will try and be patient as I am going to, for it was our fault, and we must not make a fuss now. Ain't mothers sweet? Mine is coming over to-morrow to see you and tell me how you are. This round thing is a kiss for good-night.

Your Jack

"Isn't that spoony? You'd better hide your face, I think. He's getting to be a regular mollycoddle, isn't he?" jeered Joe, as the boys laughed, and then grew sober, seeing Jack's head buried in the bedclothes, after sending a pillow at his tormentor.

It nearly hit Mrs. Minot, coming in with her patient's tea on a tray, and at sight of her the guests hurriedly took leave, Joe nearly tumbling downstairs to escape from Frank, who would have followed, if his mother had not said quickly, "Stay, and tell me what is the matter."

"Only teasing Jack a bit. Don't be mad, old boy, Joe didn't mean any harm, and it was rather soft, now wasn't it?" asked Frank, trying to appease the wounded feelings of his brother.

"I charged you not to worry him. Those boys were too much for the poor dear, and I ought not to have left him," said Mamma, as she vainly endeavored to find and caress the yellow head burrowed so far out of sight that nothing but one red ear was visible.

"He liked it, and we got on capitally till Joe roughed him about Jill. Ah, Joe's getting it now! I thought Gus and Ed would do that little job for me," added Frank, running to the window as the sound of stifled cries and laughter reached him.

The red ear heard also, and Jack popped up his head to ask, with interest,

"What are they doing to him?"

"Rolling him in the snow, and he's howling like fun."

"Serves him right," muttered Jack, with a frown. Then, as a wail arose suggestive of an unpleasant mixture of snow in the mouth and thumps on the back, he burst out laughing, and said, good-naturedly, "Go and stop them, Frank; I won't mind, only tell him it was a mean trick. Hurry! Gus is so strong he doesn't know how his pounding hurts."

Off ran Frank, and Jack told his wrongs to his mother. She sympathized heartily, and saw no harm in the affectionate little note, which would please Jill, and help her to bear her trials patiently.

"It isn't silly to be fond of her, is it? She is so nice and funny, and tries to be good, and likes me, and I won't be ashamed of my friends, if folks do laugh," protested Jack, with a rap of his teaspoon.

"No, dear, it is quite kind and proper, and I'd rather have you play with a merry little girl than with rough boys till you are big enough to hold your own," answered Mamma, putting the cup to his lips that the reclining lad might take his broma without spilling.

"Pooh! I don't mean that; I'm strong enough now to take care of myself," cried Jack, stoutly. "I can thrash Joe any day, if I like. Just look at my arm; there's muscle for you!" and up went a sleeve, to the great danger of overturning the tray, as the boy proudly displayed his biceps and expanded his chest, both of which were very fine for a lad of his years. "If I'd been on my legs, he wouldn't have dared to insult me, and it was cowardly to hit a fellow when he was down."

Mrs. Minot wanted to laugh at Jack's indignation, but the bell rang, and she had to go and pull in the basket, much amused at the new game.

Burning to distinguish herself in the eyes of the big boys, Jill had sent over a tall, red flannel night-cap, which she had been making for some proposed Christmas plays, and added the following verse, for she was considered a gifted rhymester at the game parties:

> "When it comes night,
> We put out the light.
> Some blow with a puff,
> Some turn down and snuff;
> But neat folks prefer
> A nice extinguisher.
> So here I send you back
> One to put on Mr. Jack."

"Now, I call that regularly smart; not one of us could do it, and I just wish Joe was here to see it. I want to send once more, something good for tea; she hates gruel so;" and the last despatch which the Great International Telegraph carried that day was a baked apple and a warm muffin, with "J. M.'s best regards."

Lesson 105

1. Read chapter 4 of *Jack and Jill*.
2. Tell someone about the chapter.

Chapter 4. Ward No. 2

"I do believe the child will fret herself into a fever, mem, and I'm clean distraught to know what to do for her. She never used to mind trifles, but now she frets about the oddest things, and I can't change them. This wall-paper is well enough, but she has taken a fancy that the spots on it look like spiders, and it makes her nervous. I've no other warm place to put her, and no money for a new paper. Poor lass! There are hard times before her, I'm fearing."

Mrs. Pecq said this in a low voice to Mrs. Minot, who came in as often as she could, to see what her neighbor needed; for both mothers were anxious, and sympathy drew them to one another. While one woman talked, the other looked about the little room, not wondering in the least that Jill found it hard to be contented there. It was very neat, but so plain that there was not even a picture on the walls, nor an ornament upon the mantel, except the necessary clock, lamp, and match-box. The paper was ugly, being a deep buff with a brown figure that did look very like spiders sprawling over it, and might well make one nervous to look at day after day.

Jill was asleep in the folding chair Dr. Whiting had sent, with a mattress to make it soft. The back could be raised or lowered at will; but only a few inches had been gained as yet, and the thin hair pillow was all she could bear. She looked very pretty as she lay, with dark lashes against the feverish cheeks, lips apart, and a cloud of curly black locks all about the face pillowed on one arm. She seemed like a brilliant little flower in that dull place for the French blood in her veins gave her a color, warmth, and grace which were very charming. Her natural love of beauty showed itself in many ways: a red ribbon had tied up her hair, a gay but faded shawl was thrown over the bed, and the gifts sent her were arranged with care upon the table by her side among her own few toys and treasures. There was something pathetic in this childish attempt to beautify the poor place, and Mrs. Minot's eyes were full as she looked at the tired woman, whose one joy and comfort lay there in such sad plight.

"My dear soul, cheer up, and we will help one another through the hard times," she said, with a soft hand on the rough one, and a look that promised much.

"Please God, we will, mem! With such good friends, I never should complain. I try not to do it, but it breaks my heart to see my little lass spoiled for life, most like;" and Mrs. Pecq pressed the kind hand with a despondent sigh.

"We won't say, or even think, that, yet. Everything is possible to youth and health like Janey's. We must keep her happy, and time will do the rest, I'm sure. Let us begin at once, and have a surprise for her when she wakes."

As she spoke, Mrs. Minot moved quietly about the room, pinning the pages of several illustrated papers against the wall at the foot of the bed, and placing to the best advantage the other comforts she had brought.

"Keep up your heart, neighbor. I have an idea in my head which I think will help us all, if I can carry it out," she said, cheerily, as she went, leaving Mrs. Pecq to sew on Jack's new night-gowns, with swift fingers, and the grateful wish that she might work for these good friends forever.

As if the whispering and rustling had disturbed her, Jill soon began to stir, and slowly opened the eyes which had closed so wearily on the dull December afternoon. The bare wall with its brown spiders no longer confronted her, but the colored print of a little girl dancing to the tune her father was playing on a guitar, while a stately lady, with satin dress, ruff, and powder, stood looking on, well pleased. The quaint figure, in its belaced frock, quilted petticoat, and red-heeled shoes, seemed to come tripping toward her in such a life-like way, that she almost saw the curls blow back, heard the rustle of the rich brocade, and caught the sparkle of the little maid's bright eyes.

"Oh, how pretty! Who sent them?" asked Jill, eagerly, as her eye glanced along the wall, seeing other new and interesting things beyond: an elephant-hunt, a ship in full sail, a horse-race, and a ball-room.

"The good fairy who never comes empty-handed. Look round a bit and you will see more pretties all for you, my dearie;" and her mother pointed to a bunch of purple grapes in a green leaf plate, a knot of bright flowers pinned on the white curtain, and a gay little double gown across the foot of the bed.

Jill clapped her hands, and was enjoying her new pleasures, when in came Merry and Molly Loo, with Boo, of course, trotting after her like a fat and amiable puppy. Then the good times began; the gown was put on, the fruit tasted, and the pictures were studied like famous works of art.

"It's a splendid plan to cover up that hateful wall. I'd stick pictures all round and have a gallery. That reminds me! Up in the garret at our house is a box full of old fashion-books my aunt left. I often look at them on rainy days, and they are very funny. I'll go this minute and get everyone. We can pin them up, or make paper dolls;" and away rushed Molly Loo, with the small brother waddling behind, for, when he lost sight of her, he was desolate indeed.

The girls had fits of laughter over the queer costumes of years gone by, and put up a splendid procession of ladies in full skirts, towering hats, pointed slippers, powdered hair, simpering faces, and impossible waists.

"I do think this bride is perfectly splendid, the long train and vail are so sweet," said Jill, revelling in fine clothes as she turned from one plate to another.

"I like the elephants best, and I'd give anything to go on a hunt like that!" cried Molly Loo, who rode cows, drove any horse she could get, had nine cats, and was not afraid of the biggest dog that ever barked.

"I fancy 'The Dancing Lesson;' it is so sort of splendid, with the great windows, gold chairs, and fine folks. Oh, I would like to live in a castle with a father and mother like that," said Merry, who was romantic, and found the old farmhouse on the hill a sad trial to her high-flown ideas of elegance.

"Now, that ship, setting out for some far-away place, is more to my mind. I weary for home now and then, and mean to see it again some day;" and Mrs. Pecq looked longingly at the English ship, though it was evidently outward bound. Then, as if reproaching herself for discontent, she added: "It looks like those I used to see going off to India with a load of missionaries. I came near going myself once, with a lady bound for Siam; but I went to Canada with her sister, and here I am."

"I'd like to be a missionary and go where folks throw their babies to the crocodiles. I'd watch and fish them out, and have a school, and bring them up, and convert all the people till they knew better," said warm-hearted Molly Loo, who befriended every abused animal and forlorn child she met.

"We needn't go to Africa to be missionaries; they have 'em nearer home and need 'em, too. In all the big cities there are a many, and they have their hands full with the poor, the wicked, and the helpless. One can find that sort of work anywhere, if one has a mind," said Mrs. Pecq.

"I wish we had some to do here. I'd so like to go round with baskets of tea and rice, and give out tracts and talk to people. Wouldn't you, girls?" asked Molly, much taken with the new idea.

"It would be rather nice to have a society all to ourselves, and have meetings and resolutions and things," answered Merry, who was fond of little ceremonies, and always went to the sewing circle with her mother.

"We wouldn't let the boys come in. We'd have it a secret society, as they do their temperance lodge, and we'd have badges and pass-words and grips. It would be fun if we can only get some heathen to work at!" cried Jill, ready for fresh enterprises of every sort.

"I can tell you someone to begin on right away," said her mother, nodding at her. "As wild a little savage as I'd wish to see. Take her in hand, and make a pretty-mannered lady of her. Begin at home, my lass, and you'll find missionary work enough for a while."

"Now, Mammy, you mean me! Well, I will begin; and I'll be so good, folks won't know me. Being sick makes naughty children behave in story-books, I'll see if live ones can't;" and Jill put on such a sanctified face that the girls laughed and asked for their missions also, thinking they would be the same.

"You, Merry, might do a deal at home helping mother, and setting the big brothers a good example. One little girl in a house can do pretty much as she will, especially if she has a mind to make plain things nice and comfortable, and not long for castles before she knows how to do her own tasks well," was the first unexpected reply.

Merry colored, but took the reproof sweetly, resolving to do what she could, and surprised to find how many ways seemed open to her after a few minutes thought.

"Where shall I begin? I'm not afraid of a dozen crocodiles after Miss Bat;" and Molly Loo looked about her with a fierce air, having had practice in battles with the old lady who kept her father's house.

"Well, dear, you haven't far to look for as nice a little heathen as you'd wish;" and Mrs. Pecq glanced at Boo, who sat on the floor staring hard at them, attracted by the dread word "crocodile." He had a cold and no handkerchief, his little hands were red with chilblains, his clothes shabby, he had untidy darns in the knees of his stockings, and a head of tight curls that evidently had not been combed for some time.

"Yes, I know he is, and I try to keep him decent, but I forget, and he hates to be fixed, and Miss Bat doesn't care, and father laughs when I talk about it."

Poor Molly Loo looked much ashamed as she made excuses, trying at the same time to mend matters by seizing Boo and dusting him all over with her handkerchief, giving a pull at his hair as if ringing bells, and then dumping him down again with the despairing exclamation: "Yes, we're a pair of heathens, and there's no one to save us if I don't."

That was true enough; for Molly's father was a busy man, careless of everything but his mills, Miss Bat was old and lazy, and felt as if she might take life easy after serving the motherless children for many years as well as she knew how. Molly was beginning to see how much amiss things were at home, and old enough to feel mortified, though, as yet, she had done nothing to mend the matter except be kind to the little boy.

"You will, my dear," answered Mrs. Pecq, encouragingly, for she knew all about it. "Now you've each got a mission, let us see how well you will get on. Keep it secret, if you like, and report once a week. I'll be a member, and we'll do great things yet."

"We won't begin till after Christmas; there is so much to do, we never shall have time for any more. Don't tell, and we'll start fair at New Year's, if not before," said Jill, taking the lead as usual. Then they went on with the gay ladies, who certainly were heathen enough in dress to be in sad need of conversion to common-sense at least.

"I feel as if I was at a party," said Jill, after a pause occupied in surveying her gallery with great satisfaction, for dress was her delight, and here she had every conceivable style and color.

"Talking of parties, isn't it too bad that we must give up our Christmas fun? Can't get on without you and Jack, so we are not going to do a thing, but just have our presents," said Merry, sadly, as they began to fit different heads and bodies together, to try droll effects.

"I shall be all well in a fortnight, I know; but Jack won't, for it will take more than a month to mend his poor leg. Maybe, they will have a dance in the boys big room, and he can look on," suggested Jill, with a glance at the dancing damsel on the wall, for she dearly loved it, and never guessed how long it would be before her light feet would keep time to music again.

"You'd better give Jack a hint about the party. Send over some smart ladies, and say they have come to his Christmas ball," proposed audacious Molly Loo, always ready for fun.

So they put a preposterous green bonnet, top-heavy with plumes, on a little lady in yellow, who sat in a carriage; the lady beside her, in winter costume of velvet pelisse and ermine boa, was fitted to a bride's head with its orange flowers and veil, and these works of art were sent over to Jack, labelled "Miss Laura and Lotty Burton going to the Minots' Christmas ball"--a piece of naughtiness on Jill's part, for she knew Jack liked the pretty sisters, whose gentle manners made her own wild ways seem all the more blamable.

No answer came for a long time, and the girls had almost forgotten their joke in a game of Letters, when "Tingle, tangle!" went the bell, and the basket came in heavily laden. A roll of colored papers was tied outside, and within was a box that rattled, a green and silver horn, a roll of narrow ribbons, a spool of strong thread, some large needles, and a note from Mrs. Minot:

> Dear Jill-I think of having a Christmas tree so that our invalids can enjoy it, and all your elegant friends are cordially invited. Knowing that you would like to help, I send some

paper for sugar-plum horns and some beads for necklaces. They will brighten the tree and please the girls for themselves or their dolls. Jack sends you a horn for a pattern, and will you make a ladder-necklace to show him how? Let me know if you need anything.

Yours in haste,

Anna Minot

"She knew what the child would like, bless her kind heart," said Mrs. Pecq to herself, and something brighter than the most silvery bead shone on Jack's shirt-sleeve, as she saw the rapture of Jill over the new work and the promised pleasure.

Joyful cries greeted the opening of the box, for bunches of splendid large bugles appeared in all colors, and a lively discussion went on as to the best contrasts. Jill could not refuse to let her friends share the pretty work, and soon three necklaces glittered on three necks, as each admired her own choice.

"I'd be willing to hurt my back dreadfully, if I could lie and do such lovely things all day," said Merry, as she reluctantly put down her needle at last, for home duties waited to be done, and looked more than ever distasteful after this new pleasure.

"So would I! Oh, do you think Mrs. Minot will let you fill the horns when they are done? I'd love to help you then. Be sure you send for me!" cried Molly Loo, arching her neck like a proud pigeon to watch the glitter of her purple and gold necklace on her brown gown.

"I'm afraid you couldn't be trusted, you love sweeties so, and I'm sure Boo couldn't. But I'll see about it," replied Jill, with a responsible air.

The mention of the boy recalled him to their minds, and looking round they found him peacefully absorbed in polishing up the floor with Molly's pocket-handkerchief and oil from the little machine-can. Being torn from this congenial labor, he was carried off shining with grease and roaring lustily.

But Jill did not mind her loneliness now, and sang like a happy canary while she threaded her sparkling beads, or hung the gay horns to dry, ready for their cargoes of sweets. So Mrs. Minot's recipe for sunshine proved successful, and mother-wit made the wintry day a bright and happy one for both the little prisoners.

Lesson 106

1. Read chapter 5 of *Jack and Jill*.
2. Demosthenes was a Greek statesman and a renowned orator (i.e. famous for his speeches).
3. What adjective describes the "hero" George Washington and what does it mean? Look it up if you don't know. What is she saying about Washington? (Answers)

Chapter 5. Secrets

There were a great many clubs in Harmony Village, but as we intend to interest ourselves with the affairs of the young folks only, we need not dwell upon the intellectual amusements of the elders. In summer, the boys devoted themselves to baseball, the girls to boating, and all got rosy, stout, and strong, in these healthful exercises. In winter, the lads had their debating club, the lasses a dramatic ditto. At the former, astonishing bursts of oratory were heard; at the latter, everything was boldly attempted, from Romeo and Juliet to Mother Goose's immortal melodies. The two clubs frequently met and mingled their attractions in a really entertaining manner, for the speakers made good actors, and the young actresses were most appreciative listeners to the eloquence of each budding Demosthenes.

Great plans had been afoot for Christmas or New Year, but when the grand catastrophe put an end to the career of one of the best "spouters," and caused the retirement of the favorite "singing chambermaid," the affair was postponed till February, when Washington's birthday was always celebrated by the patriotic town, where the father of his country once put on his nightcap, or took off his boots, as that ubiquitous hero appears to have done in every part of the United States.

Meantime the boys were studying Revolutionary characters, and the girls rehearsing such dramatic scenes as they thought most appropriate and effective for the 22d. In both of these attempts they were much helped by the sense and spirit of Ralph Evans, a youth of nineteen, who was a great favorite with the young folks, not only because he was a good, industrious fellow, who supported his grandmother, but also full of talent, fun, and ingenuity. It was no wonder everyone who really knew him liked him, for he could turn his hand to anything, and loved to do it. If the girls were in despair about a fire-place when acting "The Cricket on the Hearth," he painted one, and put a gas-log in it that made the kettle really boil, to their great delight. If the boys found the interest of their club flagging, Ralph would convulse them by imitations of the "Member from Cranberry Centre," or fire them with speeches of famous statesmen. Charity fairs could not get on without him, and in the store where he worked he did many an ingenious job, which made him valued for his mechanical skill, as well as for his energy and integrity.

Mrs. Minot liked to have him with her sons, because they also were to paddle their own canoes by and by, and she believed that, rich or poor, boys make better men for learning to use the talents they possess, not merely as ornaments, but tools with which to carve their own fortunes; and the best help toward this end is an example of faithful work, high aims, and honest living. So Ralph came often, and in times of trouble was a real rainy-day friend. Jack grew very fond of him during his imprisonment, for the good youth ran in every evening to get commissions, amuse the boy with droll accounts of the day's adventures, or invent lifts, bed-tables, and foot-rests for the impatient invalid. Frank found him a sure guide through the mechanical mysteries which he loved, and spent many a useful half-hour discussing cylinders, pistons, valves, and balance-wheels. Jill also came in for her share of care and comfort; the poor little back lay all the easier for the air-cushion Ralph got her, and the weary headaches found relief from the spray atomizer, which softly distilled its scented dew on the hot forehead till she fell asleep.

Round the beds of Jack and Jill met and mingled the schoolmates of whom our story treats. Never, probably, did invalids have gayer times than our two, after a week of solitary confinement; for school gossip crept in, games could not be prevented, and Christmas secrets were concocted in those rooms till they were regular conspirators' dens, when they were not little Bedlams.

After the horn and bead labors were over, the stringing of pop-corn on red, and cranberries on white, threads, came next, and Jack and Jill often looked like a new kind of spider in the pretty webs hung about them, till reeled off to bide their time in the Christmas closet. Paper flowers followed, and gay garlands and bouquets blossomed, regardless of the snow and frost without. Then there was a great scribbling of names, verses, and notes to accompany the steadily increasing store of odd parcels which were collected at the Minots', for gifts from everyone were to ornament the tree, and contributions poured in as the day drew near.

But the secret which most excited the young people was the deep mystery of certain proceedings at the Minot house. No one but Frank, Ralph, and Mamma knew what it was, and the two boys nearly drove the others distracted by the tantalizing way in which they hinted at joys to come, talked strangely about birds, went measuring round with foot-rules, and shut themselves up in the Boys' Den, as a certain large room was called. This seemed to be the centre of operations, but beyond the fact of the promised tree no ray of light was permitted to pass the jealously guarded doors. Strange men with paste-pots and ladders went in, furniture was dragged about, and all sorts of boyish lumber was sent up garret and down cellar. Mrs. Minot was seen pondering over heaps of green stuff, hammering was heard, singular bundles were smuggled upstairs, flowering plants betrayed their presence by whiffs of fragrance when the door was opened, and Mrs. Pecq was caught smiling all by herself in a back bedroom, which usually was shut up in winter.

"They are going to have a play, after all, and that green stuff was the curtain," said Molly Loo, as the girls talked it over one day, when they sat with their backs turned to one another, putting last stitches in certain bits of work which had to be concealed from all eyes, though it was found convenient to ask one another's taste as to the color, materials, and sizes of these mysterious articles.

"I think it is going to be a dance. I heard the boys doing their steps when I went in last evening to find out whether Jack liked blue or yellow best, so I could put the bow on his pen-wiper," declared Merry, knitting briskly away at the last of the pair of pretty white bed-socks she was making for Jill right under her inquisitive little nose.

"They wouldn't have a party of that kind without Jack and me. It is only an extra nice tree, you see if it isn't," answered Jill from behind the pillows which made a temporary screen to hide the toilet mats she was preparing for all her friends.

"Everyone of you is wrong, and you'd better rest easy, for you won't find out the best part of it, try as you may." And Mrs. Pecq actually chuckled as she, too, worked away at some bits of muslin, with her back turned to the very unsocial-looking group.

"Well, I don't care, we've got a secret all our own, and won't ever tell, will we?" cried Jill, falling back on the Home Missionary Society, though it was not yet begun.

"Never!" answered the girls, and all took great comfort in the idea that one mystery would not be cleared up, even at Christmas.

Jack gave up guessing, in despair, after he had suggested a new dining-room where he could eat with the family, a private school in which his lessons might go on with a tutor, or a theatre for the production of the farces in which he delighted.

"It is going to be used to keep something in that you are very fond of," said Mamma, taking pity on him at last.

"Ducks?" asked Jack, with a half pleased, half puzzled air, not quite seeing where the water was to come from.

Frank exploded at the idea, and added to the mystification by saying,

"There will be one little duck and one great donkey in it." Then, fearing he had told the secret, he ran off, quacking and braying derisively.

"It is to be used for creatures that I, too, am fond of, and you know neither donkeys nor ducks are favorites of mine," said Mamma, with a demure expression, as she sat turning over old clothes for the bundles that always went to poor neighbors, with a little store of goodies, at this time of the year.

"I know! I know! It is to be a new ward for more sick folks, isn't it, now?" cried Jack, with what he thought a great proof of shrewdness.

"I don't see how I could attend to many more patients till this one is off my hands," answered Mamma, with a queer smile, adding quickly, as if she too was afraid of letting the cat out of the bag: "That reminds me of a Christmas I once spent among the hospitals and poor-houses of a great city with a good lady who, for thirty years, had made it her mission to see that these poor little souls had one merry day. We gave away two hundred dolls, several great boxes of candy and toys, besides gay pictures, and new clothes to orphan children, sick babies, and half-grown innocents. Ah, my boy, that was a day to remember all my life, to make me doubly grateful for my blessings, and very glad to serve the helpless and afflicted, as that dear woman did."

The look and tone with which the last words were uttered effectually turned Jack's thoughts from the great secret, and started another small one, for he fell to planning what he would buy with his pocket-money to surprise the little Pats and Biddies who were to have no Christmas tree.

Lesson 107

1. Read chapter 6 of *Jack and Jill*.
2. A fandango is a Spanish cultural dance marked in part by the use of castanets or clapping.
3. Jack and Jill have a discussion about how it's not easy being good when you are sick. How does each of them react to the frustration of being an invalid? (Answers)
4. How do you respond when you are frustrated?

Vocabulary

1. Match the prefixes to their definitions. Use words you know that begin with these prefixes as clues to their meaning. Write the letters and numbers of the matches on a separate piece of paper. (Answers)

1. ad	A. reversal
2. anti	B. not
3. de	C. increase
4. ex	D. beyond
5. hyper	E. across
6. over	F. opposing
7. trans	G. out
8. un	H. excessive

Chapter 6. Surprises

"Is it pleasant?" was the question Jill asked before she was fairly awake on Christmas morning.

"Yes, dear; as bright as heart could wish. Now eat a bit, and then I'll make you nice for the day's pleasure. I only hope it won't be too much for you," answered Mrs. Pecq, bustling about, happy, yet anxious, for Jill was to be carried over to Mrs. Minot's, and it was her first attempt at going out since the accident.

It seemed as if nine o'clock would never come, and Jill, with wraps all ready, lay waiting in a fever of impatience for the doctor's visit, as he wished to superintend the moving. At last he came, found all promising, and having bundled up his small patient, carried her, with Frank's help, in her chair-bed to the ox-sled, which was drawn to the next door, and Miss Jill landed in the Boys' Den before she had time to get either cold or tired. Mrs. Minot took her things off with a cordial welcome, but Jill never said a word, for, after one exclamation, she lay staring about her, dumb with surprise and delight at what she saw.

The great room was entirely changed; for now it looked like a garden, or one of the fairy scenes children love, where in-doors and out-of-doors are pleasantly combined. The ceiling was pale blue, like the sky; the walls were covered with a paper like a rustic trellis, up which climbed morning-glories so naturally that the many-colored bells seemed dancing in the wind. Birds and butterflies flew among them, and here and there, through arches in the trellis, one seemed to look into a sunny summer world, contrasting curiously with the wintry landscape lying beyond the real windows, festooned with evergreen garlands, and curtained only by stands of living flowers. A green drugget covered the floor like grass, rustic chairs from the garden stood about, and in the middle of the room a handsome hemlock waited for its pretty burden. A Yule-log blazed on the wide hearth, and over the chimney-piece, framed in holly, shone the words that set all hearts to dancing, "Merry Christmas!"

"Do you like it, dear? This is our surprise for you and Jack, and here we mean to have good times together," said Mrs. Minot, who had stood quietly enjoying the effect of her work.

"Oh, it is so lovely I don't know what to say!" and Jill put up both arms, as words failed her, and grateful kisses were all she had to offer.

"Can you suggest anything more to add to the pleasantness?" asked the gentle lady, holding the small hands in her own, and feeling well repaid by the child's delight.

"Only Jack;" and Jill's laugh was good to hear, as she glanced up with merry, yet wistful eyes.

"You are right. We'll have him in at once, or he will come hopping on one leg;" and away hurried his mother, laughing, too, for whistles, shouts, thumps, and violent demonstrations of all kinds had been heard from the room where Jack was raging with impatience, while he waited for his share of the surprise.

Jill could hardly lie still when she heard the roll of another chair-bed coming down the hall, its passage enlivened with cries of "Starboard! Port! Easy now! Pull away!" from Ralph and Frank, as they steered the recumbent Columbus on his first voyage of discovery.

"Well, I call that handsome!" was Jack's exclamation, when the full beauty of the scene burst upon his view. Then he forgot all about it and gave a whoop of pleasure, for there beside the fire was an eager face, two hands beckoning, and Jill's voice crying, joyfully.

"I'm here! I'm here! Oh, do come, quick!" Down the long room rattled the chair, Jack cheering all the way, and brought up beside the other one, as the long-parted friends exclaimed, with one accord,

"Isn't this jolly!"

It certainly did look so, for Ralph and Frank danced a wild sort of fandango round the tree, Dr. Whiting stood and laughed, while the two mothers beamed from the door-way, and the children, not knowing whether to laugh or to cry, compromised the matter by clapping their hands and shouting, "Merry Christmas to everybody!" like a pair of little maniacs.

Then they all sobered down, and the busy ones went off to the various duties of the day, leaving the young invalids to repose and enjoy themselves together.

"How nice you look," said Jill, when they had duly admired the pretty room.

"So do you," gallantly returned Jack, as he surveyed her with unusual interest.

They did look very nice, though happiness was the principal beautifier. Jill wore a red wrapper, with the most brilliant of all the necklaces sparkling at her throat, over a nicely crimped frill her mother had made in honor of the day. All the curly black hair was gathered into a red net, and a pair of smart little moccasins covered the feet that had not stepped for many a weary day. Jack was not so gay, but had made himself as fine as circumstances would permit. A gray dressing-gown, with blue cuffs and collar, was very becoming to the blonde youth; an immaculate shirt, best studs, sleeve-buttons, blue tie, and handkerchief wet with cologne sticking out of the breast-pocket, gave an air of elegance in spite of the afghan spread over the lower portions of his manly form. The yellow hair was brushed till it shone, and being parted in the middle, to hide the black patch, made two engaging little "quiris" on his forehead. The summer tan had faded from his cheeks, but his eyes were as blue as the wintry sky, and nearly every white tooth was visible as he smiled on his partner in misfortune, saying cheerily,

"I'm ever so glad to see you again; guess we are over the worst of it now, and can have good times. Won't it be fun to stay here all the while, and amuse one another?"

"Yes, indeed; but one day is so short! It will be stupider than ever when I go home to-night," answered Jill, looking about her with longing eyes.

"But you are not going home to-night; you are to stay ever so long. Didn't Mamma tell you?"

"No. Oh, how splendid! Am I really? Where will I sleep? What will Mammy do without me?" and Jill almost sat up, she was so delighted with the new surprise.

"That room in there is all fixed for you. I made Frank tell me so much. Mamma said I might tell you, but I didn't think she would be able to hold in if she saw you first. Your mother is coming, too, and we are all going to have larks together till we are well."

The splendor of this arrangement took Jill's breath away, and before she got it again, in came Frank and Ralph with two clothes-baskets of treasures to be hung upon the tree. While they wired on the candles the children asked questions, and found out all they wanted to know about the new plans and pleasures.

'Who fixed all this?"

"Mamma thought of it, and Ralph and I did it. He's the man for this sort of thing, you know. He proposed cutting out the arches and sticking on birds and butterflies just where they looked best. I put those canaries over there, they looked so well against the blue;" and Frank proudly pointed out some queer orange-colored fowls, looking as if they were having fits in the air, but very effective, nevertheless.

"Your mother said you might call this the Bird Room. We caught a scarlet-tanager for you to begin with, didn't we, Jack?" and Ralph threw a hon-hon at Jill, who looked very like a bright little bird in a warm nest.

"Good for you! Yes, and we are going to keep her in this pretty cage till we can both fly off together. I say, Jill, where shall we be in our classes when we do get back?" and Jack's merry face fell at the thought.

"At the foot, if we don't study and keep up. Doctor said I might study sometimes, if I'd lie still as long as he thought best, and Molly brought home my books, and Merry says she will come in every day and tell me where the lessons are. I don't mean to fall behind, if my backbone is cracked," said Jill, with a decided nod that made several black rings fly out of the net to dance on her forehead.

"Frank said he'd pull me along in my Latin, but I've been lazy and haven't done a thing. Let's go at it and start fair for New Year," proposed Jack, who did not love study as the bright girl did, but was ashamed to fall behind her in anything.

"All right. They've been reviewing, so we can keep up when they begin, if we work next week, while the rest have a holiday. Oh, dear, I do miss school dreadfully;" and Jill sighed for the old desk, every blot and notch of which was dear to her.

"There come our things, and pretty nice they look, too," said Jack; and his mother began to dress the tree, hanging up the gay horns, the gilded nuts, red and yellow apples and oranges, and festooning long strings of pop-corn and scarlet cranberries from bough to bough, with the glittering necklaces hung where the light would show their colors best.

"I never saw such a splendid tree before. I'm glad we could help, though we were ill. Is it all done now?" asked Jill, when the last parcel was tied on and everybody stood back to admire the pretty sight.

"One thing more. Hand me that box, Frank, and be very careful that you fasten this up firmly, Ralph," answered Mrs. Minot, as she took from its wrappings the waxen figure of a little child. The rosy limbs were very life-like, so was the smiling face under the locks of shining hair. Both plump arms were outspread as if to scatter blessings over all, and downy wings seemed to flutter from the dimpled shoulders, making an angel of the baby.

"Is it St. Nicholas?" asked Jill, who had never seen that famous personage, and knew but little of Christmas festivities.

"It is the Christ-child, whose birthday we are celebrating. I got the best I could find, for I like the idea better than old Santa Claus; though we may have him, too," said Mamma, holding the little image so that both could see it well.

"It looks like a real baby;" and Jack touched the rosy foot with the tip of his finger, as if expecting a crow from the half-open lips.

"It reminds me of the saints in the chapel of the Sacred Heart in Montreal. One little St. John looked like this, only he had a lamb instead of wings," said Jill, stroking the flaxen hair, and wishing she dared ask for it to play with.

"He is the children's saint to pray to, love, and imitate, for he never forgot them, but blessed and healed and taught them all his life. This is only a poor image of the holiest baby ever born, but I hope it will keep his memory in your minds all day, because this is the day for good resolutions, happy thoughts, and humble prayers, as well as play and gifts and feasting."

While she spoke, Mrs. Minot, touching the little figure as tenderly as if it were alive, had tied a broad white ribbon round it, and, handing it to Ralph, bade him fasten it to the hook above the tree-top, where it seemed to float as if the downy wings supported it.

Jack and Jill lay silently watching, with a sweet sort of soberness in their young faces, and for a moment the room was very still as all eyes looked up at the Blessed Child. The sunshine seemed to grow more golden as it flickered on the little head, the flames glanced about the glittering tree as if trying to climb and kiss the baby feet, and, without, a chime of bells rang sweetly, calling people to hear again the lovely story of the life begun on Christmas Day.

Only a minute, but it did them good, and presently, when the pleasant work was over, and the workers gone, the boys to church, and Mamma to see about lunch for the invalids, Jack said, gravely, to Jill,

"I think we ought to be extra good, everyone is so kind to us, and we are getting well, and going to have such capital times. Don't see how we can do anything else to show we are grateful."

"It isn't easy to be good when one is sick," said Jill, thoughtfully. "I fret dreadfully, I get so tired of being still. I want to scream sometimes, but I don't, because it would scare Mammy, so I cry. Do you cry, Jack?"

"Men never do. I want to tramp round when things bother me; but I can't, so I kick and say, 'Hang it!' and when I get very bad I pitch into Frank, and he lets me. I tell you, Jill, he's a good brother!" and Jack privately resolved then and there to invite Frank to take it out of him in any form he pleased as soon as health would permit.

"I rather think we shall grow good in this pretty place, for I don't see how we can be bad if we want to, it is all so nice and sort of pious here," said Jill, with her eyes on the angel over the tree.

"A fellow can be awfully hungry, I know that. I didn't half eat breakfast, I was in such a hurry to see you, and know all about the secrets. Frank kept saying I couldn't guess, that you had come, and I never would be ready, till finally I got mad and fired an egg at him, and made no end of a mess."

Jack and Jill went off into a gale of laughter at the idea of dignified Frank dodging the egg that smashed on the wall, leaving an indelible mark of Jack's besetting sin, impatience.

Just then Mrs. Minot came in, well pleased to hear such pleasant sounds, and to see two merry faces, where usually one listless one met her anxious eyes.

"The new medicine works well, neighbor," she said to Mrs. Pecq, who followed with the lunch tray.

"Indeed it does, mem. I feel as if I'd taken a sup myself, I'm that easy in my mind."

And she looked so, too, for she seemed to have left all her cares in the little house when she locked the door behind her, and now stood smiling with a clean apron on, so fresh and cheerful, that Jill hardly knew her own mother.

"Things taste better when you have someone to eat with you," observed Jack, as they devoured sandwiches, and drank milk out of little mugs with rosebuds on them.

"Don't eat too much, or you won't be ready for the next surprise," said his mother, when the plates were empty, and the last drop gone down throats dry with much chatter.

"More surprises! Oh, what fun!" cried Jill. And all the rest of the morning, in the intervals of talk and play, they tried to guess what it could be.

At two o'clock they found out, for dinner was served in the Bird Room, and the children revelled in the simple feast prepared for them. The two mothers kept the little bed-tables well supplied, and fed their nurslings like maternal birds, while Frank presided over the feast with great dignity, and ate a dinner which would have astonished Mamma, if she had not been too busy to observe how fast the mince pie vanished.

"The girls said Christmas was spoiled because of us; but I don't think so, and they won't either, when they see this splendid place and know all about our nice plans," said Jill, luxuriously eating the nut-meats Jack picked out for her, as they lay in Eastern style at the festive board.

"I call this broken bones made easy. I never had a better Christmas. Have a raisin? Here's a good fat one." And Jack made a long arm to Jill's mouth, which began to sing "Little Jack Horner" as an appropriate return.

"It would have been a lonesome one to all of us, I'm thinking, but for your mother, boys. My duty and hearty thanks to you, mem," put in grateful Mrs. Pecq, bowing over her coffee-cup as she had seen ladies bow over their wine-glasses at dinner parties in Old England.

"I rise to propose a health, Our Mothers." And Frank stood up with a goblet of water, for not even at Christmas time was wine seen on that table.

"Hip, hip, hurrah!" called Jack, baptizing himself with a good sprinkle, as he waved his glass and drank the toast with a look that made his mother's eyes fill with happy tears.

Jill threw her mother a kiss, feeling very grown up and elegant to be dining out in such style. Then they drank everyone's health with much merriment, till Frank declared that Jack would float off on the deluge of water he splashed about in his enthusiasm, and Mamma proposed a rest after the merry-making.

"Now the best fun is coming, and we have not long to wait," said the boy, when naps and rides about the room had whiled away the brief interval between dinner and dusk, for the evening entertainment was to be an early one, to suit the invalids' bedtime.

"I hope the girls will like their things. I helped to choose them, and each has a nice present. I don't know mine, though, and I'm in a twitter to see it," said Jill, as they lay waiting for the fun to begin.

"I do; I chose it, so I know you will like one of them, anyway."

"Have I got more than one?"

"I guess you'll think so when they are handed down. The bell was going all day yesterday, and the girls kept bringing in bundles for you; I see seven now," and Jack rolled his eyes from one mysterious parcel to another hanging on the laden boughs.

"I know something, too. That square bundle is what you want ever so much. I told Frank, and he got it for his present. It is all red and gold outside, and every sort of color inside; you'll hurrah when you see it. That roundish one is yours too; I made them," cried Jill, pointing to a flat package tied to the stem of the tree, and a neat little roll in which were the blue mittens that she had knit for him.

"I can wait;" but the boy's eyes shone with eagerness, and he could not resist firing two or three pop-corns at it to see whether it was hard or soft.

"That barking dog is for Boo, and the little yellow sled, so Molly can drag him to school, he always tumbles down so when it is slippery," continued Jill, proud of her superior knowledge, as she showed a small spotted animal hanging by its tail, with a red tongue displayed as if about to taste the sweeties in the horn below.

"Don't talk about sleds, for mercy's sake! I never want to see another, and you wouldn't, either, if you had to lie with a flat-iron tied to your ankle, as I do," said Jack, with a kick of the well leg and an ireful glance at the weight attached to the other that it might not contract while healing.

"Well, I think plasters, and liniment, and rubbing, as bad as flat-irons any day. I don't believe you have ached half so much as I have, though it sounds worse to break legs than to sprain your back," protested Jill, eager to prove herself the greater sufferer, as invalids are apt to be.

"I guess you wouldn't think so if you'd been pulled round as I was when they set my leg. Caesar, how it did hurt!" and Jack squirmed at the recollection of it.

"You didn't faint away as I did when the doctor was finding out if my vertebrums were hurt, so now!" cried Jill, bound to carry her point, though not at all clear what vertebrae were.

"Pooh! Girls always faint. Men are braver, and I didn't faint a bit in spite of all that horrid agony."

"You howled; Frank told me so. Doctor said I was a brave girl, so you needn't brag, for you'll have to go on a crutch for a while. I know that."

"You may have to use two of them for years, maybe. I heard the doctor tell my mother so. I shall be up and about long before you will. Now then!"

Both children were getting excited, for the various pleasures of the day had been rather too much for them, and there is no knowing but they would have added the sad surprise of a quarrel to the pleasant ones of the day, if a cheerful whistle had not been heard, as Ralph came in to light the candles and give the last artistic touches to the room.

"Well, young folks, how goes it? Had a merry time so far?" he asked, as he fixed the steps and ran up with a lighted match in his hand.

"Very nice, thank you," answered a prim little voice from the dusk below, for only the glow of the fire filled the room just then.

Jack said nothing, and two red sulky faces were hidden in the dark, watching candle after candle sputter, brighten, and twinkle, till the trembling shadows began to flit away like imps afraid of the light.

"Now he will see my face, and I know it is cross," thought Jill, as Ralph went round the last circle, leaving another line of sparks among the hemlock boughs.

Jack thought the same, and had just got the frown smoothed out of his forehead, when Frank brought a fresh log, and a glorious blaze sprung up, filling every corner of the room, and dancing over the figures in the long chairs till they had to brighten whether they liked it or not. Presently the bell began to ring and gay voices to sound below: then Jill smiled in spite of herself as Molly Loo's usual cry of "Oh, dear, where is that child?" reached her, and Jack could not help keeping time to the march Ed played, while Frank and Gus marshalled the procession.

"Ready!" cried Mrs. Minot, at last, and up came the troop of eager lads and lasses, brave in holiday suits, with faces to match. A unanimous "O, o, o!" burst from twenty tongues, as the full splendor of the tree, the room, and its inmates, dawned upon them; for not only did the pretty Christ-child hover above, but Santa Claus himself stood below, fur-clad, white-bearded, and powdered with snow from the dredging-box.

Ralph was a good actor, and, when the first raptures were over he distributed the presents with such droll speeches, jokes, and gambols, that the room rang with merriment, and passers-by paused to listen, sure that here, at least, Christmas was merry. It would be impossible to tell about all the gifts or the joy of the receivers, but everyone was satisfied, and the king and queen of the revels so overwhelmed with little tokens of good-will, that their beds looked like booths at a fair. Jack beamed over the handsome postage-stamp book which had long been the desire of his heart, and Jill felt like a millionaire, with a silver fruit-knife, a pretty work-basket, and oh!--coals of fire on her head!--a ring from Jack.

A simple little thing enough, with one tiny turquoise forget-me-not, but something like a dew-drop fell on it when no one was looking, and she longed to say, "I'm sorry I was cross; forgive me, Jack." But it could not be done then, so she turned to admire Merry's bed-shoes, the pots of pansies, hyacinths, and geranium which Gus and his sisters sent for her window garden, Molly's queer Christmas pie, and the zither Ed promised to teach her how to play upon.

The tree was soon stripped, and pop-corns strewed the floor as the children stood about picking them off the red threads when candy gave out, with an occasional cranberry by way of relish. Boo insisted on trying the new sled at once, and enlivened the trip by the squeaking of the spotted dog, the toot of a tin trumpet, and shouts of joy at the splendor of the turn-out.

The girls all put on their necklaces, and danced about like fine ladies at a ball. The boys fell to comparing skates, balls, and cuff-buttons on the spot, while the little ones devoted all their energies to eating everything eatable they could lay their hands on.

Games were played till nine o'clock, and then the party broke up, after they had taken hands round the tree and sung a song written by one whom you all know--so faithfully and beautifully does she love and labor for children the world over.

    THE BLESSED DAY

      "What shall little children bring
      On Christmas Day, on Christmas Day?
      What shall little children bring
      On Christmas Day in the morning?
      This shall little children bring
      On Christmas Day, on Christmas Day;
      Love and joy to Christ their king,
      On Christmas Day in the morning!

"What shall little children sing
On Christmas Day, on Christmas Day?
What shall little children sing
On Christmas Day in the morning?
The grand old carols shall they sing
On Christmas Day, on Christmas Day;
With all their hearts, their offerings bring
On Christmas Day in the morning."

Jack was carried off to bed in such haste that he had only time to call out, "Good-night!" before he was rolled away, gaping as he went. Jill soon found herself tucked up in the great white bed she was to share with her mother, and lay looking about the pleasant chamber, while Mrs. Pecq ran home for a minute to see that all was safe there for the night.

After the merry din the house seemed very still, with only a light step now and then, the murmur of voices not far away, or the jingle of sleigh-bells from without, and the little girl rested easily among the pillows, thinking over the pleasures of the day, too wide-awake for sleep. There was no lamp in the chamber, but she could look into the pretty Bird Room, where the fire-light still shone on flowery walls, deserted tree, and Christ-child floating above the green. Jill's eyes wandered there and lingered till they were full of regretful tears, because the sight of the little angel recalled the words spoken when it was hung up, the good resolution she had taken then, and how soon it was broken.

"I said I couldn't be bad in that lovely place, and I was a cross, ungrateful girl after all they've done for Mammy and me. Poor Jack was hurt the worst, and he was brave, though he did scream. I wish I could go and tell him so, and hear him say, 'All right.' Oh, me, I've spoiled the day!"

A great sob choked more words, and Jill was about to have a comfortable cry, when someone entered the other room, and she saw Frank doing something with a long cord and a thing that looked like a tiny drum. Quiet as a bright-eyed mouse, Jill peeped out wondering what it was, and suspecting mischief, for the boy was laughing to himself as he stretched the cord, and now and then bent over the little object in his hand, touching it with great care.

"Maybe it's a torpedo to blow up and scare me; Jack likes to play tricks. Well, I'll scream loud when it goes off, so he will be satisfied that I'm dreadfully frightened," thought Jill, little dreaming what the last surprise of the day was to be.

Presently a voice whispered,

"Are you awake?"

"Yes."

"Anyone there but you?"

"No."

"Catch this, then. Hold it to your ear and see what you'll get."

The little drum came flying in, and, catching it, Jill, with some hesitation, obeyed Frank's order. Judge of her amazement when she caught in broken whispers these touching words:

"Sorry I was cross. Forgive and forget. Start fair to-morrow. All right. Jack."

Jill was so delighted with this handsome apology, that she could not reply for a moment, then steadied her voice, and answered back in her sweetest tone,

"I'm sorry, too. Never, never, will again. Feel much better now. Good-night, you dear old thing."

Satisfied with the success of his telephone, Frank twitched back the drum and vanished, leaving Jill to lay her cheek upon the hand that wore the little ring and fall asleep, saying to herself, with a farewell glance at the children's saint, dimly seen in the soft gloom, "I will not forget. I will be good!"

Lesson 108

1. Read chapter 7 of *Jack and Jill*.
2. Tell someone about this chapter.

Chapter 7. Jill's Mission

The good times began immediately, and very little studying was done that week in spite of the virtuous resolutions made by certain young persons on Christmas Day. But, dear me, how was it possible to settle down to lessons in the delightful Bird Room, with not only its own charms to distract one, but all the new gifts to enjoy, and a dozen calls a day to occupy one's time?

"I guess we'd better wait till the others are at school, and just go in for fun this week," said Jack, who was in great spirits at the prospect of getting up, for the splints were off, and he hoped to be promoted to crutches very soon.

"I shall keep my Speller by me and take a look at it every day, for that is what I'm most backward in. But I intend to devote myself to you, Jack, and be real kind and useful. I've made a plan to do it, and I mean to carry it out, anyway," answered Jill, who had begun to be a missionary, and felt that this was a field of labor where she could distinguish herself.

"Here's a home mission all ready for you, and you can be paying your debts beside doing yourself good," Mrs. Pecq said to her in private, having found plenty to do herself.

Now Jill made one great mistake at the outset--she forgot that she was the one to be converted to good manners and gentleness, and devoted her efforts to looking after Jack, finding it much easier to cure other people's faults than her own. Jack was a most engaging heathen, and needed very little instruction; therefore Jill thought her task would be an easy one. But three or four weeks of petting and play had rather demoralized both children, so Jill's Speller, though tucked under the sofa pillow every day, was seldom looked at, and Jack shirked his Latin shamefully. Both read all the story-books they could get, held daily levees in the Bird Room, and all their spare minutes were spent in teaching Snowdrop, the great Angora cat, to bring the ball when they dropped it in their game. So Saturday came, and both were rather the worse for so much idleness, since daily duties and studies are the wholesome bread which feeds the mind better than the dyspeptic plum-cake of sensational reading, or the unsubstantial bon-bons of frivolous amusement.

It was a stormy day, so they had few callers, and devoted themselves to arranging the album; for these books were all the rage just then, and boys met to compare, discuss, buy, sell, and "swap" stamps with as much interest as men on 'Change gamble in stocks. Jack had a nice little collection, and had been saving up pocket-money to buy a book in which to preserve his treasures. Now, thanks to Jill's timely suggestion, Frank had given him a fine one, and several friends had contributed a number of rare stamps to grace the large, inviting pages. Jill wielded the gum-brush and fitted on the little flaps, as her fingers were skillful at this nice work, and Jack put each stamp in its proper place with great rustling of leaves and comparing of marks. Returning, after a brief absence, Mrs. Minot beheld the countenances of the workers adorned with gay stamps, giving them a very curious appearance.

"My dears! what new play have you got now? Are you wild Indians? or letters that have gone round the world before finding the right address?" she asked, laughing at the ridiculous sight, for both were as sober as judges and deeply absorbed in some doubtful specimen.

"Oh, we just stuck them there to keep them safe; they get lost if we leave them lying round. It's very handy, for I can see in a minute what I want on Jill's face and she on mine, and put our fingers on the right chap at once," answered Jack, adding, with an anxious gaze at his friend's variegated countenance, "Where the dickens is my New Granada? It's rare, and I wouldn't lose it for a dollar."

"Why, there it is on your own nose. Don't you remember you put it there because you said mine was not big enough to hold it?" laughed Jill, tweaking a large orange square off the round nose of her neighbor, causing it to wrinkle up in a droll way, as the gum made the operation slightly painful.

"So I did, and gave you Little Bolivar on yours. Now I'll have Alsace and Lorraine, 1870. There are seven of them, so hold still and see how you like it," returned Jack, picking the large, pale stamps one by one from Jill's forehead, which they crossed like a band.

She bore it without flinching, saying to herself with a secret smile, as she glanced at the hot fire, which scorched her if she kept near enough to Jack to help him, "This really is being like a missionary, with a tattooed savage to look after. I have to suffer a little, as the good folks did who got speared and roasted sometimes; but I won't complain a bit, though my forehead smarts, my arms are tired, and one cheek is as red as fire."

"The Roman States make a handsome page, don't they?" asked Jack, little dreaming of the part he was playing in Jill's mind. "Oh, I say, isn't Corea a beauty? I'm ever so proud of that;" and he gazed fondly on a big blue stamp, the sole ornament of one page.

"I don't see why the Cape of Good Hope has pyramids. They ought to go in Egypt. The Sandwich Islands are all right, with heads of the black kings and queens on them," said Jill, feeling that they were very appropriate to her private play.

"Turkey has crescents, Australia swans, and Spain women's heads, with black bars across them. Frank says it is because they keep women shut up so; but that was only his fun. I'd rather have a good, honest green United States, with Washington on it, or a blue one-center with old Franklin, than all their eagles and lions and kings and queens put together," added the democratic boy, with a disrespectful slap on a crowned head as he settled Heligoland in its place.

"Why does Austria have Mercury on the stamp, I wonder? Do they wear helmets like that?" asked Jill, with the brush-handle in her mouth as she cut a fresh batch of flaps.

"Maybe he was postman to the gods, so he is put on stamps now. The Prussians wear helmets, but they have spikes like the old Roman fellows. I like Prussians ever so much; they fight splendidly, and always beat. Austrians have a handsome uniform, though."

"Talking of Romans reminds me that I have not heard your Latin for two days. Come, lazybones, brace up, and let us have it now. I've done my compo, and shall have just time before I go out for a tramp with Gus," said Frank, putting by a neat page to dry, for he studied every day like a conscientious lad as he was.

"Don't know it. Not going to try till next week. Grind away over your old Greek as much as you like, but don't bother me," answered Jack, frowning at the mere thought of the detested lesson.

But Frank adored his Xenophon, and would not see his old friend, Caesar, neglected without an effort to defend him; so he confiscated the gum-pot, and effectually stopped the stamp business by whisking away at one fell swoop all that lay on Jill's table.

"Now then, young man, you will quit this sort of nonsense and do your lesson, or you won't see these fellows again in a hurry. You asked me to hear you, and I'm going to do it; here's the book."

Frank's tone was the dictatorial one, which Jack hated and always found hard to obey, especially when he knew he ought to do it. Usually, when his patience was tried, he strode about the room, or ran off for a race round the garden, coming back breathless, but good-tempered. Now both these vents for irritation were denied him, and he had fallen into the way of throwing things about in a pet. He longed to send Caesar to perpetual banishment in the fire blazing close by, but resisted the temptation, and answered honestly, though gruffly: "I know I did, but I don't see any use in pouncing on a fellow when he isn't ready. I haven't got my lesson, and don't mean to worry about it; so you may just give me back my things and go about your business."

"I'll give you back a stamp for every perfect lesson you get, and you won't see them on any other terms;" and, thrusting the treasures into his pocket, Frank caught up his rubber boots, and went off swinging them like a pair of clubs, feeling that he would give a trifle to be able to use them on his lazy brother.

At this high-handed proceeding, and the threat which accompanied it, Jack's patience gave out, and catching up Caesar, as he thought, sent him flying after the retreating tyrant with the defiant declaration,

"Keep them, then, and your old book, too! I won't look at it till you give all my stamps back and say you are sorry. So now!"

It was all over before Mamma could interfere, or Jill do more than clutch and cling to the gum-brush. Frank vanished unharmed, but the poor book dashed against the wall to fall half open on the floor, its gay cover loosened, and its smooth leaves crushed by the blow.

"It's the album! O Jack, how could you?" cried Jill, dismayed at sight of the precious book so maltreated by the owner.

"Thought it was the other. Guess it isn't hurt much. Didn't mean to hit him, anyway. He does provoke me so," muttered Jack, very red and shamefaced as his mother picked up the book and laid it silently on the table before him. He did not know what to do with himself, and was thankful for the stamps still left him, finding great relief in making faces as he plucked them one by one from his mortified countenance. Jill looked on, half glad, half sorry that her savage showed such signs of unconverted ferocity, and Mrs. Minot went on writing letters, wearing the grave look her sons found harder to bear than another person's scolding. No one spoke for a moment, and the silence was becoming awkward when Gus appeared in a rubber suit, bringing a book to Jack from Laura and a note to Jill from Lotty.

"Look here, you just trundle me into my den, please, I'm going to have a nap, it's so dull to-day I don't feel like doing much," said Jack, when Gus had done his errands, trying to look as if he knew nothing about the fracas.

Jack folded his arms and departed like a warrior borne from the battle-field, to be chaffed unmercifully for a "pepper-pot," while Gus made him comfortable in his own room.

"I heard once of a boy who threw a fork at his brother and put his eye out. But he didn't mean to, and the brother forgave him, and he never did so any more," observed Jill, in a pensive tone, wishing to show that she felt all the dangers of impatience, but was sorry for the culprit.

"Did the boy ever forgive himself?" asked Mrs. Minot.

"No, 'm; I suppose not. But Jack didn't hit Frank, and feels real sorry, I know."

"He might have, and hurt him very much. Our actions are in our own hands, but the consequences of them are not. Remember that, my dear, and think twice before you do anything."

"Yes, 'm, I will;" and Jill composed herself to consider what missionaries usually did when the natives hurled tomahawks and boomerangs at one another, and defied the rulers of the land.

Mrs. Minot wrote one page of a new letter, then stopped, pushed her papers about, thought a little, and finally got up, saying, as if she found it impossible to resist the yearning of her heart for the naughty boy,

"I am going to see if Jack is covered up, he is so helpless, and liable to take cold. Don't stir till I come back."

"No, 'm, I won't."

Away went the tender parent to find her son studying Caesar for dear life, and all the more amiable for the little gust which had blown away the temporary irritability. The brothers were often called "Thunder and Lightning," because Frank lowered and growled and was a good while clearing up, while Jack's temper came and went like a flash, and the air was all the clearer for the escape of dangerous electricity. Of course Mamma had to stop and deliver a little lecture, illustrated by sad tales of petulant boys, and punctuated with kisses which took off the edge of these afflicting narratives.

Jill meantime meditated morally on the superiority of her own good temper over the hasty one of her dear playmate, and just when she was feeling unusually uplifted and secure, alas! like so many of us, she fell, in the most deplorable manner.

Glancing about the room for something to do, she saw a sheet of paper lying exactly out of reach, where it had fluttered from the table unperceived. At first her eye rested on it as carelessly as it did on the stray stamp Frank had dropped; then, as if one thing suggested the other, she took it into her head that the paper was Frank's composition, or, better still, a note to Annette, for the two corresponded when absence or weather prevented the daily meeting at school.

"Wouldn't it be fun to keep it till he gives back Jack's stamps? It would plague him so if it was a note, and I do believe it is, for compo's don't begin with two words on one side. I'll get it, and Jack and I will plan some way to pay him off, cross thing!"

Forgetting her promise not to stir, also how dishonorable it was to read other people's letters, Jill caught up the long-handled hook, often in use now, and tried to pull the paper nearer. It would not come at once, for a seam in the carpet held it, and Jill feared to tear or crumple it if she was not very careful. The hook was rather heavy and long for her to manage, and Jack usually did the fishing, so she was not very skillful; and just as she was giving a particularly quick jerk, she lost her balance, fell off the sofa, and dropped the pole with a bang.

"Oh, my back!" was all she could think or say as she felt the jar all through her little body, and a corresponding fear in her guilty little mind that someone would come and find out the double mischief she had been at. For a moment she lay quite still to recover from the shock, then as the pain passed she began to wonder how she should get back, and looked about her to see if she could do it alone. She thought she could, as the sofa was near and she had improved so much that she could sit up a little if the doctor would have let her. She was gathering herself together for the effort, when, within arm's reach now, she saw the tempting paper, and seized it with glee, for in spite of her predicament she did want to tease Frank. A glance showed that it was not the composition nor a note, but the beginning of a letter from Mrs. Minot to her sister, and Jill was about to lay it down when her own name caught her eye, and she could not resist reading it. Hard words to write of one so young, doubly hard to read, and impossible to forget.

"Dear Lizzie, Jack continues to do very well, and will soon be up again. But we begin to fear that the little girl is permanently injured in the back. She is here, and we do our best for her; but I never look at her without thinking of Lucinda Snow, who, you remember, was bedridden for twenty years, owing to a fall at fifteen. Poor little Janey does not know yet, and I hope"-- There it ended, and "poor little Janey's" punishment for disobedience began that instant. She thought she was getting well because she did not suffer all the time, and everyone spoke cheerfully about "by and by." Now she knew the truth, and shut her eyes with a shiver as she said, low, to herself,

"Twenty years! I couldn't bear it; oh, I couldn't bear it!"

A very miserable Jill lay on the floor, and for a while did not care who came and found her; then the last words of the letter-- "I hope"--seemed to shine across the blackness of the dreadful "twenty years" and cheer her up a bit, for despair never lives long in young hearts, and Jill was a brave child.

"That is why Mammy sighs so when she dresses me, and everyone is so good to me. Perhaps Mrs. Minot doesn't really know, after all. She was dreadfully scared about Jack, and he is getting well. I'd like to ask Doctor, but he might find out about the letter. Oh, dear, why didn't I keep still and let the horrid thing alone!"

As she thought that, Jill pushed the paper away, pulled herself up, and with much painful effort managed to get back to her sofa, where she laid herself down with a groan, feeling as if the twenty years had already passed over her since she tumbled off.

"I've told a lie, for I said I wouldn't stir. I've hurt my back, I've done a mean thing, and I've got paid for it. A nice missionary I am; I'd better begin at home, as Mammy told me to;" and Jill groaned again, remembering her mother's words. "Now I've got another secret to keep all alone, for I'd be ashamed to tell the girls. I guess I'll turn round and study my spelling; then no one will see my face."

Jill looked the picture of a good, industrious child as she lay with her back to the large table, her book held so that nothing was to be seen but one cheek and a pair of lips moving busily. Fortunately, it is difficult for little sinners to act a part, and, even if the face is hidden, something in the body seems to betray the internal remorse and shame. Usually, Jill lay flat and still; now her back was bent in a peculiar way as she leaned over her book, and one foot wagged nervously, while on the visible cheek was a Spanish stamp with a woman's face looking through the black bars, very suggestively, if she had known it. How long the minutes seemed till someone came, and what a queer little jump her heart gave when Mrs. Minot's voice said, cheerfully, "Jack is all right, and, I declare, so is Jill. I really believe there is a telegraph still working somewhere between you two, and each knows what the other is about without words."

"I didn't have any other book handy, so I thought I'd study awhile," answered Jill, feeling that she deserved no praise for her seeming industry.

She cast a sidelong glance as she spoke, and seeing that Mrs. Minot was looking for the letter, hid her face and lay so still she could hear the rustle of the paper as it was taken from the floor. It was well she did not also see the quick look the lady gave her as she turned the letter and found a red stamp sticking to the under side, for this unlucky little witness told the story.

Mrs. Minot remembered having seen the stamp lying close to the sofa when she left the room, for she had had half a mind to take it to Jack, but did not, thinking Frank's plan had some advantages. She also recollected that a paper flew off the table, but being in haste she had not stopped to see what it was. Now, the stamp and the letter could hardly have come together without hands, for they lay a yard apart, and here, also, on the unwritten portion of the page, was the mark of a small green thumb. Jill had been winding wool for a stripe in her new afghan, and the green ball lay on her sofa. These signs suggested and confirmed what Mrs. Minot did not want to believe; so did the voice, attitude, and air of Jill, all very unlike her usual open, alert ways.

The kind lady could easily forgive the reading of her letter since the girl had found such sad news there, but the dangers of disobedience were serious in her case, and a glance showed that she was suffering either in mind or body--perhaps both.

"I will wait for her to tell me. She is an honest child, and the truth will soon come out," thought Mrs. Minot, as she took a clean sheet, and Jill tried to study.

"Shall I hear your lesson, dear? Jack means to recite his like a good boy, so suppose you follow his example," she said, presently.

"I don't know as I can say it, but I'll try."

Jill did try, and got on bravely till she came to the word "permanent;" there she hesitated, remembering where she saw it last.

"Do you know what that means?" asked her teacher, thinking to help her on by defining the word.

"Always--for a great while--or something like that; doesn't it?" faltered Jill, with a tight feeling in her throat, and the color coming up, as she tried to speak easily, yet felt so shame-stricken she could not.

"Are you in pain, my child? Never mind the lesson; tell me, and I'll do something for you."

The kind words, the soft hand on her hot cheek, and the pity in the eyes that looked at her, were too much for Jill. A sob came first, and then the truth, told with hidden face and tears that washed the blush away, and set free the honest little soul that could not hide its fault from such a friend.

"I knew it all before, and was sure you would tell me, else you would not be the child I love and like to help so well."

Then, while she soothed Jill's trouble, Mrs. Minot told her story and showed the letter, wishing to lessen, if possible, some part of the pain it had given.

"Sly old stamp! To go and tell on me when I meant to own up, and get some credit if I could, after being so mean and bad," said Jill, smiling through her tears when she saw the tell-tale witnesses against her.

"You had better stick it in your book to remind you of the bad consequences of disobedience, then perhaps this lesson will leave a permanent impression on your mind and memory," answered Mrs. Minot, glad to see her natural gayety coming back, and hoping that she had forgotten the contents of the unfortunate letter. But she had not; and presently, when the sad affair had been talked over and forgiven, Jill asked, slowly, as she tried to put on a brave look,

"Please tell me about Lucinda Snow. If I am to be like her, I might as well know how she managed to bear it so long."

"I'm sorry you ever heard of her, and yet perhaps it may help you to bear your trial, dear, which I hope will never be as heavy a one as hers. This Lucinda I knew for years, and though at first I thought her fate the saddest that could be, I came at last to see how happy she was in spite of her affliction, how good and useful and beloved."

"Why, how could she be? What did she do?" cried Jill, forgetting her own troubles to look up with an open, eager face again.

"She was so patient, other people were ashamed to complain of their small worries; so cheerful, that her own great one grew lighter; so industrious, that she made both money and friends by pretty things she worked and sold to her many visitors. And, best of all, so wise and sweet that she seemed to get good out of everything, and make her poor room a sort of chapel where people went for comfort, counsel, and an example of a pious life. So, you see, Lucinda was not so very miserable after all."

"Well, if I could not be as I was, I'd like to be a woman like that. Only, I hope I shall not!" answered Jill, thoughtfully at first, then coming out so decidedly with the last words that it was evident the life of a bedridden saint was not at all to her mind.

"So do I; and I mean to believe that you will not. Meantime, we can try to make the waiting as useful and pleasant as possible. This painful little back will be a sort of conscience to remind you of what you ought to do and leave undone, and so you can be learning obedience. Then, when the body is strong, it will have formed a good habit to make duty easier; and my Lucinda can be a sweet example, even while lying here, if she chooses."

"Can I?" and Jill's eyes were full of softer tears as the comfortable, cheering words sank into her heart, to blossom slowly by and by into her life, for this was to be a long lesson, hard to learn, but very useful in the years to come.

When the boys returned, after the Latin was recited and peace restored, Jack showed her a recovered stamp promptly paid by Frank, who was as just as he was severe, and Jill asked for the old red one, though she did not tell why she wanted it, nor show it put away in the spelling-book, a little seal upon a promise made to be kept.

Lesson 109

1. Read chapter 8 of *Jack and Jill*.
2. Write a one-sentence summary of this chapter.

Chapter 8. Merry and Molly

Farmer Grant was a thrifty, well-to-do man, anxious to give his children greater advantages than he had enjoyed, and to improve the fine place of which he was justly proud. Mrs. Grant was a notable housewife, as ambitious and industrious as her husband, but too busy to spend any time on the elegancies of life, though always ready to help the poor and sick like a good neighbor and Christian woman. The three sons--Tom, Dick, and Harry--were big fellows of seventeen, nineteen, and twenty-one; the first two on the farm, and the elder in a store just setting up for himself. Kind-hearted but rough-mannered youths, who loved Merry very much, but teased her sadly about her "fine lady airs," as they called her dainty ways and love of beauty.

Merry was a thoughtful girl, full of innocent fancies, refined tastes, and romantic dreams, in which no one sympathized at home, though she was the pet of the family. It did seem, to an outsider, as if the delicate little creature had got there by mistake, for she looked very like a tea-rose in a field of clover and dandelions, whose highest aim in life was to feed cows and help make root beer.

When the girls talked over the new society, it pleased Merry very much, and she decided not only to try and love work better, but to convert her family to a liking for pretty things, as she called her own more cultivated tastes.

"I will begin at once, and show them that I don't mean to shirk my duty, though I do want to be nice," thought she, as she sat at supper one night and looked about her, planning her first move.

Not a very cheering prospect for a lover of the beautiful, certainly, for the big kitchen, though as neat as wax, had nothing lovely in it, except a red geranium blooming at the window. Nor were the people all that could be desired, in some respects, as they sat about the table shovelling in pork and beans with their knives, drinking tea from their saucers, and laughing out with a hearty "Haw, haw," when anything amused them. Yet the boys were handsome, strong specimens, the farmer a hale, benevolent-looking man, the housewife a pleasant, sharp-eyed matron, who seemed to find comfort in looking often at the bright face at her elbow, with the broad forehead, clear eyes, sweet mouth, and quiet voice that came like music in among the loud masculine ones, or the quick, nervous tones of a woman always in a hurry.

Merry's face was so thoughtful that evening that her father observed it, for, when at home, he watched her as one watches a kitten, glad to see anything so pretty, young, and happy, at its play.

"Little daughter has got something on her mind, I mistrust. Come and tell father all about it," he said, with a sounding slap on his broad knee as he turned his chair from the table to the ugly stove, where three pairs of wet boots steamed underneath, and a great kettle of cider apple-sauce simmered above.

"When I've helped clear up, I'll come and talk. Now, mother, you sit down and rest; Roxy and I can do everything," answered Merry, patting the old rocking-chair so invitingly that the tired woman could not resist, especially as watching the kettle gave her an excuse for obeying.

"Well, I don't care if I do, for I've been on my feet since five o'clock. Be sure you cover things up, and shut the buttery door, and put the cat down cellar, and sift your meal. I'll see to the buckwheats last thing before I go to bed."

Mrs. Grant subsided with her knitting, for her hands were never idle; Tom tilted his chair back against the wall and picked his teeth with his pen-knife; Dick got out a little pot of grease, to make the boots water-tight; and Harry sat down at the small table to look over his accounts, with an important air--for everyone occupied this room, and the work was done in the out-kitchen behind.

Merry hated clearing up, but dutifully did every distasteful task, and kept her eye on careless Roxy till all was in order; then she gladly went to perch on her father's knee, seeing in all the faces about her the silent welcome they always wore for the "little one."

"Yes, I do want something, but I know you will say it is silly," she began, as her father pinched her blooming cheek, with the wish that his peaches would ever look half as well.

"Shouldn't wonder if it was a doll now;" and Mr. Grant stroked her head with an indulgent smile, as if she was about six instead of fifteen.

"Why, father, you know I don't! I haven't played with dollies for years and years. No; I want to fix up my room pretty, like Jill's. I'll do it all myself, and only want a few things, for I don't expect it to look as nice as hers."

Indignation gave Merry courage to state her wishes boldly, though she knew the boys would laugh. They did, and her mother said in a tone of surprise,

"Why, child, what more can you want? I'm sure your room is always as neat as a new pin, thanks to your bringing up, and I told you to have a fire there whenever you wanted to."

"Let me have some old things out of the garret, and I'll show you what I want. It is neat, but so bare and ugly I hate to be there. I do so love something pretty to look at!" and Merry gave a little shiver of disgust as she turned her eyes away from the large greasy boot Dick was holding up to be sure it was well lubricated all round.

"So do I, and that's a fact. I couldn't get on without my pretty girl here, anyway. Why, she touches up the old place better than a dozen flower-pots in full blow," said the farmer, as his eye went from the scarlet geranium to the bright young face so near his own.

"I wish I had a dozen in the sitting-room window. Mother says they are not tidy, but I'd keep them neat, and I know you'd like it," broke in Merry, glad of the chance to get one of the long-desired wishes of her heart fulfilled.

"I'll fetch you some next time I go over to Ballad's. Tell me what you want, and we'll have a posy bed somewhere round, see if we don't," said her father, dimly understanding what she wanted.

"Now, if mother says I may fix my room, I shall be satisfied, and I'll do my chores without a bit of fuss, to show how grateful I am," said the girl, thanking her father with a kiss, and smiling at her mother so wistfully that the good woman could not refuse.

"You may have anything you like out of the blue chest. There's a lot of things there that the moths got at after Grandma died, and I couldn't bear to throw or give 'em away. Trim up your room as you like, and mind you don't forget your part of the bargain," answered Mrs. Grant, seeing profit in the plan.

"I won't; I'll work all the morning to-morrow, and in the afternoon I'll get ready to show you what I call a nice, pretty room," answered Merry, looking so pleased it seemed as if another flower had blossomed in the large bare kitchen.

She kept her word, and the very stormy afternoon when Jill got into trouble, Merry was working busily at her little bower. In the blue chest she found a variety of treasures, and ignoring the moth holes, used them to the best advantage, trying to imitate the simple comfort with a touch of elegance which prevailed in Mrs. Minot's back bedroom.

Three faded red-moreen curtains went up at the windows over the chilly paper shades, giving a pleasant glow to the bare walls. A red quilt with white stars, rather the worse for many washings, covered the bed, and a gay cloth the table, where a judicious arrangement of books and baskets concealed the spots. The little air-tight stove was banished, and a pair of ancient andirons shone in the fire-light. Grandma's last and largest braided rug lay on the hearth, and her brass candlesticks adorned the bureau, over the mirror of which was festooned a white muslin skirt, tied up with Merry's red sash. This piece of elegance gave the last touch to her room, she thought, and she was very proud of it, setting forth all her small store of trinkets in a large shell, with an empty scent bottle, and a clean tidy over the pincushion. On the walls she hung three old-fashioned pictures, which she ventured to borrow from the garret till better could be found. One a mourning piece, with a very tall lady weeping on an urn in a grove of willows, and two small boys in knee breeches and funny little square tails to their coats, looking like cherubs in large frills. The other was as good as a bonfire, being an eruption of Vesuvius, and very lurid indeed, for the Bay of Naples was boiling like a pot, the red sky raining rocks, and a few distracted people lying flat upon the shore. The third was a really pretty scene of children dancing round a May-pole, for though nearly a hundred years old, the little maids smiled and the boys pranced as gayly as if the flowers they carried were still alive and sweet.

"Now I'll call them all to see, and say that it is pretty. Then I'll enjoy it, and come here when things look dismal and bare everywhere else," said Merry, when at last it was done. She had worked all the afternoon, and only finished at supper time, so the candles had to be lighted that the toilette might look its best, and impress the beholders with an idea of true elegance. Unfortunately, the fire smoked a little, and a window was set ajar to clear the room; an evil disposed gust blew in, wafting the thin drapery within reach of the light, and when Merry threw open the door proudly thinking to display her success, she was horrified to find the room in a blaze, and half her labor all in vain.

The conflagration was over in a minute, however, for the boys tore down the muslin and stamped out the fire with much laughter, while Mrs. Grant bewailed the damage to her carpet, and poor Merry took refuge in her father's arms, refusing to be comforted in spite of his kind commendation of "Grandma's fixins."

The third little missionary had the hardest time of all, and her first efforts were not much more satisfactory nor successful than the others. Her father was away from morning till night, and then had his paper to read, books to keep, or "a man to see down town," so that, after a hasty word at tea, he saw no more of the children till another evening, as they were seldom up at his early breakfast. He thought they were well taken care of, for Miss Bathsheba Dawes was an energetic, middle-aged spinster when she came into the family, and had been there fifteen years, so he did not observe, what a woman would have seen at once, that Miss Bat was getting old and careless, and everything about the house was at sixes and sevens. She took good care of him, and thought she had done her duty if she got three comfortable meals, nursed the children when they were ill, and saw that the house did not burn up. So Maria Louisa and Napoleon Bonaparte got on as they could, without the tender cares of a mother. Molly had been a happy-go-lucky child, contented with her pets, her freedom, and little Boo to love; but now she was just beginning to see that they were not like other children, and to feel ashamed of it.

"Papa is busy, but Miss Bat ought to see to us; she is paid for it, and goodness knows she has an easy time now, for if I ask her to do anything, she groans over her bones, and tells me young folks should wait on themselves. I take all the care of Boo off her hands, but I can't wash my own things, and he hasn't a decent trouser to his blessed little legs. I'd tell papa, but it wouldn't do any good; he'd only say, 'Yes, child, yes, I'll attend to it,' and never do a thing."

This used to be Molly's lament, when some especially trying event occurred, and if the girls were not there to condole with her, she would retire to the shed-chamber, call her nine cats about her, and, sitting in the old bushel basket, pull her hair about her ears, and scold all alone. The cats learned to understand this habit, and nobly did their best to dispel the gloom which now and then obscured the sunshine of their little mistress. Some of them would creep into her lap and purr till the comfortable sound soothed her irritation; the sedate elders sat at her feet blinking with such wise and sympathetic faces, that she felt as if half a dozen Solomons were giving her the sagest advice; while the kittens frisked about, cutting up their drollest capers till she laughed in spite of herself. When the laugh came, the worst of the fit was over, and she soon cheered up, dismissing the consolers with a pat all round, a feast of good things from Miss Bat's larder, and the usual speech:

"Well, dears, it's of no use to worry. I guess we shall get along somehow, if we don't fret."

With which wise resolution, Molly would leave her retreat and freshen up her spirits by a row on the river or a romp with Boo, which always finished the case. Now, however, she was bound to try the new plan and do something toward reforming not only the boy's condition, but the disorder and discomfort of home.

"I'll play it is Siam, and this the house of a native, and I'm come to show the folks how to live nicely. Miss Bat won't know what to make of it, and I can't tell her, so I shall get some fun out of it, anyway," thought Molly, as she surveyed the dining-room the day her mission began.

The prospect was not cheering; and, if the natives of Siam live in such confusion, it is high time they were attended to. The breakfast-table still stood as it was left, with slops of coffee on the cloth; bits of bread, egg-shells, and potato-skins lay about, and one lonely sausage was cast away in the middle of a large platter. The furniture was dusty, stove untidy, and the carpet looked as if crumbs had been scattered to chickens who declined their breakfast. Boo was sitting on the sofa, with his arm through a hole in the cover, hunting for some lost treasure put away there for safe keeping, like a little magpie as he was. Molly fancied she washed and dressed him well enough; but to-day she seemed to see more dearly, and sighed as she thought of the hard job in store for her if she gave him the thorough washing he needed, and combed out that curly mop of hair.

"I'll clear up first and do that by and by. I ought to have a nice little tub and good towels, like Mrs. Minot, and I will, too, if I buy them myself," she said, piling up cups with an energy that threatened destruction to handles.

Miss Bat, who was trailing about the kitchen, with her head pinned up in a little plaid shawl, was so surprised by the demand for a pan of hot water and four clean towels, that she nearly dropped her snuff-box, chief comfort of her lazy soul.

"What new whimsey now? Generally, the dishes stand round till I have time to pick 'em up, and you are off coasting or careering somewhere. Well, this tidy fit won't last long, so I may as well make the most of it," said Miss Bat, as she handed out the required articles, and then pushed her spectacles from the tip of her sharp nose to her sharper black eyes for a good look at the girl who stood primly before her, with a clean apron on and her hair braided up instead of flying wildly about her shoulders.

"Umph!" was all the comment that Miss Bat made on this unusual neatness, and she went on scraping her saucepans, while Molly returned to her work, very well pleased with the effect of her first step, for she felt that the bewilderment of Miss Bat would be a constant inspiration to fresh efforts.

An hour of hard work produced an agreeable change in the abode of the native, for the table was cleared, room swept and dusted, fire brightened, and the holes in the sofa-covering were pinned up till time could be found to mend them. To be sure, rolls of lint lay in corners, smears of ashes were on the stove hearth, and dust still lurked on chair rounds and table legs. But too much must not be expected of a new convert, so the young missionary sat down to rest, well pleased and ready for another attempt as soon as she could decide in what direction it should be made. She quailed before Boo as she looked at the unconscious innocent peacefully playing with the spotted dog, now bereft of his tail, and the lone sausage with which he was attempting to feed the hungry animal, whose red mouth always gaped for more.

"It will be an awful job, and he is so happy I won't plague him yet. Guess I'll go and put my room to rights first, and pick up some clean clothes to put on him, if he is alive after I get through with him," thought Molly, foreseeing a stormy passage for the boy, who hated a bath as much as some people hate a trip across the Atlantic.

Up she went, and finding the fire out felt discouraged, thought she would rest a little more, so retired under the blankets to read one of the Christmas books. The dinner-bell rang while she was still wandering happily in "Nelly's Silver Mine," and she ran down to find that Boo had laid out a railroad all across her neat room, using bits of coal for sleepers and books for rails, over which he was dragging the yellow sled laden with a dismayed kitten, the tailless dog, and the remains of the sausage, evidently on its way to the tomb, for Boo took bites at it now and then, no other lunch being offered him.

"Oh dear! why can't boys play without making such a mess," sighed Molly, picking up the feathers from the duster with which Boo had been trying to make a "cocky-doo" of the hapless dog. "I'll wash him right after dinner, and that will keep him out of mischief for a while," she thought, as the young engineer unsuspiciously proceeded to ornament his already crocky countenance with squash, cranberry sauce, and gravy, till he looked more like a Fiji chief in full war-paint than a Christian boy.

"I want two pails of hot water, please, Miss Bat, and the big tub," said Molly, as the ancient handmaid emptied her fourth cup of tea, for she dined with the family, and enjoyed her own good cooking in its prime.

"What are you going to wash now?"

"Boo--I'm sure he needs it enough;" and Molly could not help laughing as the victim added to his brilliant appearance by smearing the colors all together with a rub of two grimy hands, making a fine Turner, of himself.

"Now, Maria Louisa Bemis, you ain't going to cut up no capers with that child! The idea of a hot bath in the middle of the day, and him full of dinner, and croupy into the bargain! Wet a corner of a towel at the kettle-spout and polish him off if you like, but you won't risk his life in no bath-tubs this cold day."

Miss Bat's word was law in some things, so Molly had to submit, and took Boo away, saying, loftily, as she left the room,

"I shall ask father, and do it to-night, for I will not have my brother look like a pig."

"My patience! how the Siamese do leave their things round," she exclaimed, as she surveyed her room after making up the fire and polishing off Boo. "I'll put things in order, and then mend up my rags, if I can find my thimble. Now, let me see;" and she went to exploring her closet, bureau, and table, finding such disorder everywhere that her courage nearly gave out.

She had clothes enough, but all needed care; even her best dress had two buttons off, and her Sunday hat but one string. Shoes, skirts, books, and toys lay about, and her drawers were a perfect chaos of soiled ruffles, odd gloves, old ribbons, boot lacings, and bits of paper.

"Oh, my heart, what a muddle! Mrs. Minot wouldn't think much of me if she could see that," said Molly, recalling how that lady once said she could judge a good deal of a little girl's character and habits by a peep at her top drawer, and went on, with great success, to guess how each of the school-mates kept her drawer.

"Come, missionary, clear up, and don't let me find such a gloryhole again, or I'll report you to the society," said Molly, tipping the whole drawer-full out upon the bed, and beguiling the tiresome job by keeping up the new play.

Twilight came before it was done, and a great pile of things loomed up on her table, with no visible means of repair--for Molly's work-basket was full of nuts, and her thimble down a hole in the shed-floor, where the cats had dropped it in their play.

"I'll ask Bat for hooks and tape, and papa for some money to buy scissors and things, for I don't know where mine are. Glad I can't do any more now! Being neat is such hard work!" and Molly threw herself down on the rug beside the old wooden cradle in which Boo was blissfully rocking, with a cargo of toys aboard.

She watched her time, and as soon as her father had done supper, she hastened to say, before he got to his desk,

"Please, papa, I want a dollar to get some brass buttons and things to fix Boo's clothes with. He wore a hole in his new trousers coasting down the Kembles' steps. And can't I wash him? He needs it, and Miss Bat won't let me have a tub."

"Certainly, child, certainly; do what you like, only don't keep me. I must be off, or I shall miss Jackson, and he's the man I want;" and, throwing down two dollars instead of one, Mr. Bemis hurried away, with a vague impression that Boo had swallowed a dozen brass buttons, and Miss Bat had been coasting somewhere in a bath-pan; but catching Jackson was important, so he did not stop to investigate.

Armed with the paternal permission, Molly carried her point, and oh, what a dreadful evening poor Boo spent! First, he was decoyed upstairs an hour too soon, then put in a tub by main force and sternly scrubbed, in spite of shrieks that brought Miss Bat to the locked door to condole with the sufferer, scold the scrubber, and depart, darkly prophesying croup before morning.

"He always howls when he is washed; but I shall do it, since you won't, and he must get used to it. I will not have people tell me he's neglected, if I can help it," cried Molly, working away with tears in her eyes--for it was as hard for her as for Boo; but she meant to be thorough for once in her life, no matter what happened.

When the worst was over, she coaxed him with candy and stories till the long task of combing out the curls was safely done; then, in the clean night-gown with a blue button newly sewed on, she laid him in bed, worn out, but sweet as a rose.

"Now, say your prayers, darling, and go to sleep with the nice red blanket all tucked round so you won't get cold," said Molly, rather doubtful of the effect of the wet head.

"No, I won't! Going to sleep now!" and Boo shut his eyes wearily, feeling that his late trials had not left him in a prayerful mood.

"Then you'll be a real little heathen, as Mrs. Pecq called you, and I don't know what I shall do with you," said Molly, longing to cuddle rather than scold the little fellow, whose soul needed looking after as well as his body.

"No, no; I won't be a heevin! I don't want to be frowed to the trockindiles. I will say my prayers! oh, I will!" and, rising in his bed, Boo did so, with the devotion of an infant Samuel, for he remembered the talk when the society was formed.

Molly thought her labors were over for that night, and soon went to bed, tired with her first attempts. But toward morning she was wakened by the hoarse breathing of the boy, and was forced to patter away to Miss Bat's room, humbly asking for the squills, and confessing that the prophecy had come to pass.

"I knew it! Bring the child to me, and don't fret. I'll see to him, and next time you do as I say," was the consoling welcome she received as the old lady popped up a sleepy but anxious face in a large flannel cap, and shook the bottle with the air of a general who had routed the foe before and meant to do it again.

Leaving her little responsibility in Miss Bat's arms, Molly retired to wet her pillow with a few remorseful tears, and to fall asleep, wondering if real missionaries ever killed their pupils in the process of conversion.

So the girls all failed in the beginning; but they did not give up, and succeeded better next time, as we shall see.

Lesson 110

1. Read chapter 9 of *Jack and Jill*.
2. "'My Merry seems to be contented with her brothers so far, but I shouldn't wonder if I had my hands full by and by,' added Mrs. Grant, who already foresaw that her sweet little daughter would be sought after as soon as she should lengthen her skirts and

turn up her bonny brown hair." This sentence is about when a girl went out into "society." They used to have a dance when a girl reached sixteen; I believe it was to show her off to potential husbands. When she started wearing long dresses instead of short (good for playing) and wearing her hair up, she was no longer a girl, but a woman, and men were permitted to ask for her hand.

3. Tell someone about the chapter. What's your opinion on boys and girls going to school together? Just talk about it. You don't need to write anything.

Chapter 9. The Debating Club

"Look here, old man, we ought to have a meeting. Holidays are over, and we must brace up and attend to business," said Frank to Gus, as they strolled out of the schoolyard one afternoon in January, apparently absorbed in conversation, but in reality waiting for a blue cloud and a scarlet feather to appear on the steps.

"All right. When, where, and what?" asked Gus, who was a man of few words.

"To-night, our house, subject, 'Shall girls go to college with us?' Mother said we had better be making up our minds, because everyone is talking about it, and we shall have to be on one side or the other, so we may as well settle it now," answered Frank, for there was an impression among the members that all vexed questions would be much helped by the united eloquence and wisdom of the club.

"Very good; I'll pass the word and be there. Hullo, Neddy! The D. C. meets to-night, at Minot's, seven sharp. Co-ed, &c.," added Gus, losing no time, as a third boy came briskly round the corner, with a little bag in his hand.

"I'll come. Got home an hour earlier to-night, and thought I'd look you up as I went by," responded Ed Devlin, as he took possession of the third post, with a glance toward the schoolhouse to see if a seal-skin cap, with a long, yellow braid depending therefrom, was anywhere in sight.

"Very good of you, I'm sure," said Gus, ironically, not a bit deceived by this polite attention.

"The longest way round is sometimes the shortest way home, hey, Ed?" and Frank gave him a playful poke that nearly sent him off his perch.

Then they all laughed at some joke of their own, and Gus added, "No girls coming to hear us to-night. Don't think it, my son.

"More's the pity," and Ed shook his head regretfully over the downfall of his hopes.

"Can't help it; the other fellows say they spoil the fun, so we have to give in, sometimes, for the sake of peace and quietness. Don't mind having them a bit myself," said Frank, in such a tone of cheerful resignation that they laughed again, for the "Triangle," as the three chums were called, always made merry music.

"We must have a game party next week. The girls like that, and so do I," candidly observed Gus, whose pleasant parlors were the scene of many such frolics.

"And so do your sisters and your cousins and your aunts," hummed Ed, for Gus was often called Admiral because he really did possess three sisters, two cousins, and four aunts, besides mother and grandmother, all living in the big house together.

The boys promptly joined in the popular chorus, and other voices all about the yard took it up, for the "Pinafore" epidemic raged fearfully in Harmony Village that winter.

"How's business?" asked Gus, when the song ended, for Ed had not returned to school in the autumn, but had gone into a store in the city.

"Dull; things will look up toward spring, they say. I get on well enough, but I miss you fellows dreadfully;" and Ed put a hand on the broad shoulder of each friend, as if he longed to be a school-boy again.

"Better give it up and go to college with me next year," said Frank, who was preparing for Boston University, while Gus fitted for Harvard.

"No; I've chosen business, and I mean to stick to it, so don't you unsettle my mind. Have you practised that March?" asked Ed, turning to a gayer subject, for he had his little troubles, but always looked on the bright side of things.

"Skating is so good, I don't get much time. Come early, and we'll have a turn at it."

"I will. Must run home now."

"Pretty cold loafing here."

"Mail is in by this time."

And with these artless excuses the three boys leaped off the posts, as if one spring moved them, as a group of girls came chattering down the path. The blue cloud floated away beside Frank, the scarlet feather marched off with the Admiral, while the fur cap nodded to the gray hat as two happy faces smiled at each other.

The same thing often happened, for twice a-day the streets were full of young couples walking to and from school together, smiled at by the elders, and laughed at by the less susceptible boys and girls, who went alone or trooped along in noisy groups. The prudent mothers had tried to stop this guileless custom, but found it very difficult, as the fathers usually sympathized with their sons, and dismissed the matter with the comfortable phrase, "Never mind; boys will be boys." "Not forever," returned the anxious mammas, seeing the tall lads daily grow more manly, and the pretty daughters fast learning to look demure when certain names were mentioned.

It could not be stopped without great parental sternness and the danger of deceit, for co-education will go on outside of school if not inside, and the safest way is to let sentiment and study go hand in hand, with teachers and parents to direct and explain the great lesson all are the better for learning soon or late. So the elders had to give in, acknowledging that this sudden readiness to go to school was a comfort, that the new sort of gentle emulation worked wonders in lazy girls and boys, and that watching these "primrose friendships" bud, blossom, and die painless deaths, gave a little touch of romance to their own work-a-day lives.

"On the whole I'd rather have my sons walking, playing, and studying with bright, well-mannered girls, than always knocking about with rough boys," said Mrs. Minot at one of the Mothers' Meetings, where the good ladies met to talk over their children, and help one another to do their duty by them.

"I find that Gus is more gentle with his sisters since Juliet took him in hand, for he wants to stand well with her, and they report him if he troubles them. I really see no harm in the little friendship, though I never had any such when I was a girl," said Mrs. Burton, who adored her one boy and was his confidante.

"My Merry seems to be contented with her brothers so far, but I shouldn't wonder if I had my hands full by and by," added Mrs. Grant, who already foresaw that her sweet little daughter would be sought after as soon as she should lengthen her skirts and turn up her bonny brown hair.

Molly Loo had no mother to say a word for her, but she settled matters for herself by holding fast to Merry, and declaring that she would have no escort but faithful Boo.

It is necessary to dwell a moment upon this new amusement, because it was not peculiar to Harmony Village, but appears everywhere as naturally as the game parties and croquet which have taken the place of the husking frolics and apple-bees of olden times, and it is impossible to dodge the subject if one attempts to write of boys and girls as they really are nowadays.

"Here, my hero, see how you like this. If it suits, you will be ready to march as soon as the doctor gives the word," said Ralph, coming into the Bird Room that evening with a neat little crutch under his arm.

"Ha, ha, that looks fine! I'd like to try it right off, but I won't till I get leave. Did you make it yourself, Ral?" asked Jack, handling it with delight, as he sat bolt upright, with his leg on a rest, for he was getting on capitally now.

"Mostly. Rather a neat job, I flatter myself."

"I should say so. What a clever fellow you are! Any new inventions lately?" asked Frank, coming up to examine and admire.

Only an anti-snoring machine and an elbow-pad, answered Ralph, with a twinkle in his eye, as if reminded of something funny.

"Go on, and tell about them. I never heard of an anti-snorer. Jack better have one," said Frank, interested at once.

"Well, a rich old lady kept her family awake with that lively music, so she sent to Shirtman and Codleff for something to stop it. They thought it was a good joke, and told me to see what I could do. I thought it over, and got up the nicest little affair you ever saw. It went over the mouth, and had a tube to fit the ear, so when the lady snored she woke herself up and stopped it. It suited exactly. I think of taking out a patent," concluded Ralph, joining in the boys' laugh at the droll idea.

"What was the pad?" asked Frank, returning to the small model of an engine he was making.

"Oh, that was a mere trifle for a man who had a tender elbow-joint and wanted something to protect it. I made a little pad to fit on, and his crazy-bone was safe."

"I planned to have you make me a new leg if this one was spoilt," said Jack, sure that his friend could invent anything under the sun.

"I'd do my best for you. I made a hand for a fellow once, and that got me my place, you know," answered Ralph, who thought little of such mechanical trifles, and longed to be painting portraits or modelling busts, being an artist as well as an inventor.

Here Gus, Ed, and several other boys came in, and the conversation became general. Grif, Chick, and Brickbat were three young gentlemen whose own respectable names were usually ignored, and they cheerfully answered to these nicknames.

As the clock struck seven, Frank, who ruled the club with a rod of iron when Chairman, took his place behind the study table. Seats stood about it, and a large, shabby book lay before Gus, who was Secretary, and kept the records with a lavish expenditure of ink, to judge by the blots. The members took their seats, and nearly all tilted back their chairs and put their hands in their pockets, to keep them out of mischief; for, as everyone knows, it is impossible for two lads to be near each other and refrain from tickling or pinching. Frank gave three raps with an old croquet-mallet set on a short handle, and with much dignity opened the meeting.

"Gentlemen, the business of the club will be attended to, and then we will discuss the question, 'Shall girls go to our colleges?' The Secretary will now read the report of the last meeting."

Clearing his throat, Gus read the following brief and elegant report:

"Club met, December 18th, at the house of G. Burton, Esq. Subject:

"Is summer or winter best fun?' A lively pow-wow. About evenly divided. J. Flint fined five cents for disrespect to the Chair. A collection of forty cents taken up to pay for breaking a pane of glass during a free fight of the members on the door-step. E. Devlin was chosen Secretary for the coming year, and a new book contributed by the Chairman.

"That's all."

"Is there any other business before the meeting?" asked Frank, as the reader closed the old book with a slam and shoved the new one across the table.

Ed rose, and glancing about him with an appealing look, said, as if sure his proposition would not be well received, "I wish to propose the name of a new member. Bob Walker wants to join, and I think we ought to let him. He is trying to behave well, and I am sure we could help him. Can't we?"

All the boys looked sober, and Joe, otherwise Brickbat, said, bluntly, "I won't. He's a bad lot, and we don't want any such here. Let him go with chaps of his own sort."

"That is just what I want to keep him from! He's a good-hearted boy enough, only no one looks after him; so he gets into scrapes, as we should, if we were in his place, I dare say. He wants to come here, and would be so proud if he was let in, I know he'd behave. Come now, let's give him a chance," and Ed looked at Gus and Frank, sure that if they stood by him he should carry his point.

But Gus shook his head, as if doubtful of the wisdom of the plan, and Frank said gravely: "You know we made the rule that the number should never be over eight, and we cannot break it."

"You needn't. I can't he here half the time, so I will resign and let Bob have my place," began Ed, but he was silenced by shouts of "No, no, you shan't!" "We won't let you off!" "Club would go to smash, if you back out!"

"Let him have my place; I'm the youngest, and you won't miss me," cried Jack, bound to stand by Ed at all costs.

"We might do that," said Frank, who did object to small boys, though willing to admit this particular one.

"Better make a new rule to have ten members, and admit both Bob and Tom Grant," said Ralph, whereat Grif grinned and Joe scowled, for one lad liked Merry's big brother and the other did not.

"That's a good idea! Put it to vote," said Gus, too kind-hearted to shut the door on anyone.

"First I want to ask if all you fellows are ready to stand by Bob, out of the club as well as in, for it won't do much good to be kind to him here and cut him at school and in the street," said Ed, heartily in earnest about the matter.

"I will!" cried Jack, ready to follow where his beloved friend led, and the others nodded, unwilling to be outdone by the youngest member.

"Good! With all of us to lend a hand, we can do a great deal; and I tell you, boys, it is time, if we want to keep poor Bob straight. We all turn our backs on him, so he loafs round the tavern, and goes with fellows we don't care to know. But he isn't bad yet, and we can keep him up, I'm sure, if we just try. I hope to get him into the Lodge, and that will be half the battle, won't it, Frank?" added Ed, sure that this suggestion would have weight with the honorable Chairman.

"Bring him along; I'm with you!" answered Frank, making up his mind at once, for he had joined the Temperance Lodge four years ago, and already six boys had followed his example.

"He is learning to smoke, but we'll make him drop it before it leads to worse. You can help him there, Admiral, if you only will," added Ed, giving a grateful look at one friend, and turning to the other.

"I'm your man;" and Gus looked as if he knew what he promised, for he had given up smoking to oblige his father, and kept his word like a hero.

"You other fellows can do a good deal by just being kind and not twitting him with old scrapes, and I'll do anything I can for you all to pay for this;" and Ed sat down with a beaming smile, feeling that his cause was won.

The vote was taken, and all hands went up, for even surly Joe gave in; so Bob and Tom were duly elected, and proved their gratitude for the honor done them by becoming worthy members of the club. It was only boys' play now, but the kind heart and pure instincts of one lad showed the others how to lend a helping hand to a comrade in danger, and win him away from temptation to the safer pastimes of their more guarded lives.

Well pleased with themselves--for every genuine act or word, no matter how trifling it seems, leaves a sweet and strengthening influence behind--the members settled down to the debate, which was never very long, and often only an excuse for fun of all sorts.

"Ralph, Gus, and Ed are for, and Brickbat, Grif, and Chick against, I suppose?" said Frank, surveying his company like a general preparing for battle.

"No, sir! I believe in co-everything!" cried Chick, a mild youth, who loyally escorted a chosen damsel home from school every day.

A laugh greeted this bold declaration, and Chick sat down, red but firm.

"I'll speak for two since the Chairman can't, and Jack won't go against those who pet him most to death," said Joe, who, not being a favorite with the girls, considered them a nuisance and lost no opportunity of telling them so.

"Fire away, then, since you are up;" commanded Frank.

"Well," began Joe, feeling too late how much he had undertaken, "I don't know a great deal about it, and I don't care, but I do not believe in having girls at college. They don't belong there, nobody wants 'em, and they'd better be at home darning their stockings."

"Yours, too," put in Ralph, who had heard that argument so often he was tired of it.

"Of course; that's what girls are for. I don't mind 'em at school, but I'd just as soon they had a room to themselves. We should get on better."

"You would if Mabel wasn't in your class and always ahead of you," observed Ed, whose friend was a fine scholar, and he very proud of the fact.

"Look here, if you fellows keep interrupting, I won't sit down for half an hour," said Joe, well knowing that eloquence was not his gift, but bound to have his say out.

Deep silence reigned, for that threat quelled the most impatient member, and Joe prosed on, using all the arguments he had ever heard, and paying off several old scores by six hits of a personal nature, as older orators often do.

"It is clear to my mind that boys would get on better without any girls fooling round. As for their being as smart as we are, it is all nonsense, for some of 'em cry over their lessons every day, or go home with headaches, or get mad and scold all recess, because something 'isn't fair.' No, sir; girls ain't meant to know much, and they can't. Wise folks say so and I believe 'em. Haven't got any sisters myself, and I don't want any, for they don't seem to amount to much, according to those who do have 'em."

Groans from Gus and Ed greeted the closing remarks of the ungallant Joe, who sat down, feeling that he had made somebody squirm. Up jumped Grif, the delight of whose life was practical jokes, which amiable weakness made him the terror of the girls, though they had no other fault to find with the merry lad.

"Mr. Chairman, the ground I take is this: girls have not the strength to go to college with us. They couldn't row a race, go on a lark, or take care of themselves, as we do. They are all well enough at home, and I like them at parties, but for real fun and go I wouldn't give a cent for them," began Grif, whose views of a collegiate life were confined to the enjoyments rather than the studies of that festive period. "I have tried them, and they can't stand anything. They scream if you tell them there is a mouse in the room, and run if they see a big dog. I just put a cockroach in Molly's desk one day, and when she opened it she jumped as if she was shot."

So did the gentlemen of the club, for at that moment half-a-dozen fire-crackers exploded under the chair Grif had left, and flew wildly about the room. Order was with difficulty restored, the mischievous party summarily chastised and commanded to hold his tongue, under penalty of ejectment from the room if he spoke again. Firmly grasping that red and unruly member, Grif composed himself to listen, with his nose in the air and his eyes shining like black beads.

Ed was always the peace-maker, and now, when he rose with his engaging smile, his voice fell like oil upon the troubled waters, and his bright face was full of the becoming bashfulness which afflicts youths of seventeen when touching upon such subjects of newly acquired interest as girls and their pleasant but perplexing ways.

"It seems to me we have hardly considered the matter enough to be able to say much. But I think that school would be awfully dry and dismal without--ahem!--any young ladies to make it nice. I wouldn't give a pin to go if there was only a crowd of fellows, though I like a good game as well as any man. I pity any boy who has no sisters," continued Ed, warming up as he thought of his own, who loved him dearly, as well they might, for a better brother never lived. "Home wouldn't be worth having without them to look after a fellow, to keep him out of scrapes, help him with his lessons, and make things jolly for his friends. I tell you we can't do without girls, and I'm not ashamed to say that I think the more we see of them, and try to be like them in many ways, the better men we shall be by and by."

"Hear! hear!" cried Frank, in his deepest tone, for he heartily agreed to that, having talked the matter over with his mother, and received much light upon things which should always be set right in young heads and hearts. And who can do this so wisely and well as mothers, if they only will?

Feeling that his sentiments had been approved, and he need not be ashamed of the honest color in his cheeks, Ed sat down amid the applause of his side, especially of Jack, who pounded so vigorously with his crutch that Mrs. Pecq popped in her head to see if anything was wanted.

"No, thank you, ma'am, we were only cheering Ed," said Gus, now upon his legs, and rather at a loss what to say till Mrs. Pecq's appearance suggested an idea, and he seized upon it.

"My honored friend has spoken so well that I have little to add. I agree with him, and if you want an example of what girls can do, why, look at Jill. She's young, I know, but a first-rate scholar for her age. As for pluck, she is as brave as a boy, and almost as smart at running, rowing, and so on. Of course, she can't play ball--no girl can; their arms are not made right to throw--but she can catch remarkably well. I'll say that for her. Now, if she and Mabel--and-- and--some others I could name, are so clever and strong at the beginning, I don't see why they shouldn't keep up and go along with us all through. I'm willing, and will do what I can to help other fellows' sisters as I'd like to have them help mine. And I'll punch their heads if they don't;" and Gus subsided, assured, by a burst of applause, that his manly way of stating the case met with general approval.

"We shall be happy to hear from our senior member if he will honor us with a few remarks," said Frank, with a bow to Ralph.

No one ever knew whom he would choose to personate, for he never spoke in his own character. Now he rose slowly, put one hand in his bosom, and fixing his eye sternly on Grif, who was doing something suspicious with a pin, gave them a touch of Sergeant Buzfuz, from the Pickwick trial, thinking that the debate was not likely to throw much light on the subject under discussion. In the midst of this appeal to "Me lud and gentlemen of the jury," he suddenly paused, smoothed his hair down upon his forehead, rolled up his eyes, and folding his hands, droned out Mr. Chadband's sermon on Peace, delivered over poor Jo, and ending with the famous lines:

> Oh, running stream of sparkling joy,
> To be a glorious human boy!

Then, setting his hair erect with one comprehensive sweep, he caught up his coat-skirts over his arm, and, assuming a parliamentary attitude, burst into a comical medley, composed of extracts from Jefferson Brick's and Lafayette Kettle's speeches, and Elijah Pogram's Defiance, from "Martin Chuzzlewit." Gazing at Gus, who was convulsed with suppressed merriment, he thundered forth:

"In the name of our common country, sir, in the name of that righteous cause in which we are jined, and in the name of the star-spangled banner, I thank you for your eloquent and categorical remarks. You, sir, are a model of a man fresh from Natur's mould. A true-born child of this free hemisphere; verdant as the mountains of our land; bright and flowin' as our mineral Licks; unspiled by fashion as air our boundless perearers. Rough you may be; so air our Barrs. Wild you may be; so air our Buff alers. But, sir, you air a Child of Freedom, and your proud answer to the Tyrant is, that your bright home is in the Settin' Sun. And, sir, if any man denies this fact, though it be the British Lion himself, I defy him. Let me have him here!"--smiting the table, and causing the inkstand to skip-- "here, upon this sacred altar! Here, upon the ancestral ashes cemented with the glorious blood poured out like water on the plains of Chickabiddy Lick. Alone I dare that Lion, and tell him that Freedom's hand once twisted in his mane, he rolls a corse before me, and the Eagles of the Great Republic scream, Ha, ha!"

By this time the boys were rolling about in fits of laughter; even sober Frank was red and breathless, and Jack lay back, feebly squealing, as he could laugh no more. In a moment Ralph was as meek as a Quaker, and sat looking about him with a mildly astonished air, as if inquiring the cause of such unseemly mirth. A knock at the door produced a lull, and in came a maid with apples.

"Time's up; fall to and make yourselves comfortable," was the summary way in which the club was released from its sterner duties and permitted to unbend its mighty mind for a social half hour, chiefly devoted to whist, with an Indian war-dance as a closing ceremony.

Lesson 111

1. Read chapter 10 of *Jack and Jill*.
2. Write a one-sentence summary of this chapter.

Chapter 10. The Dramatic Club

While Jack was hopping gayly about on his crutches, poor Jill was feeling the effects of her second fall, and instead of sitting up, as she hoped to do after six weeks of rest, she was ordered to lie on a board for two hours each day. Not an easy penance, by any means, for the board was very hard, and she could do nothing while she lay there, as it did not slope enough to permit her to read without great fatigue of both eyes and hands. So the little martyr spent her first hour of trial in sobbing, the second in singing, for just as her mother and Mrs. Minot were deciding in despair that neither she nor they could bear it, Jill suddenly broke out into a merry chorus she used to hear her father sing:

> "Faut jouer le mirliton,
> Faut jouer le mirlitir,
> Faut jouer le mirliter,
> Mir--li--ton."

The sound of the brave little voice was very comforting to the two mothers hovering about her, and Jack said, with a look of mingled pity and admiration, as he brandished his crutch over the imaginary foes,

"That's right! Sing away, and we'll play you are an Indian captive being tormented by your enemies, and too proud to complain. I'll watch the clock, and the minute time is up I'll rush in and rescue you."

Jill laughed, but the fancy pleased her, and she straightened herself out under the gay afghan, while she sang, in a plaintive voice, another little French song her father taught her:

> "J'avais une colombe blanche,
> J'avais un blanc petit pigeon,
> Tous deux volaient, de branche en branche,
> Jusqu'au faîte de mon dongeon:
> Mais comme un coup de vent d'automne,
> S'est abattu là, l'épervier,
> Et ma colombe si mignonne
> Ne revient plus au colombier."

"My poor Jean had a fine voice, and always hoped the child would take after him. It would break his heart to see her lying there trying to cheer her pain with the songs he used to sing her to sleep with," said Mrs. Pecq, sadly.

"She really has a great deal of talent, and when she is able she shall have some lessons, for music is a comfort and a pleasure, sick or well," answered Mrs. Minot, who had often admired the fresh voice, with its pretty accent.

Here Jill began the Canadian boat-song, with great vigor, as if bound to play her part of Indian victim with spirit, and not disgrace herself by any more crying. All knew the air, and joined in, especially Jack, who came out strong on the "Row, brothers, row," but ended in a squeak on a high note, so drolly, that the rest broke down. So the hour that began with tears ended with music and laughter, and a new pleasure to think of for the future.

After that day Jill exerted all her fortitude, for she liked to have the boys call her brave and admire the cheerful way in which she endured two hours of discomfort. She found she could use her zither as it lay upon her breast, and every day the pretty music began at a certain hour, and all in the house soon learned to love and listen for it. Even the old cook set open her kitchen door, saying pitifully, "Poor darlint, hear how purty she's singin', wid the pain, on that crewel boord. It's a little saint, she is. May her bed above be aisy!"

Frank would lift her gently on and off, with a kind word that comforted her immensely, and gentle Ed would come and teach her new bits of music, while the other fellows were frolicking below. Ralph added his share to her amusement, for he asked leave to model her head in clay, and set up his work in a corner, coming to pat, scrape, and mould whenever he had a spare minute, amusing her by his lively chat, and showing her how to shape birds, rabbits, and queer faces in the soft clay, when the songs were all sung and her fingers tired of the zither.

The girls sympathized very heartily with her new trial, and brought all manner of gifts to cheer her captivity. Merry and Molly made a gay screen by pasting pictures on the black cambric which covered the folding frame that stood before her to keep the draughts from her as she lay on her board. Bright birds and flowers, figures and animals, covered one side, and on the other they put mottoes, bits of poetry, anecdotes, and short stories, so that Jill could lie and look or read without the trouble of holding a book. It was not all done at once, but grew slowly, and was a source of instruction as well as amusement to them all, as they read carefully, that they might make good selections.

But the thing that pleased Jill most was something Jack did, for he gave up going to school, and stayed at home nearly a fortnight after he might have gone, all for her sake. The day the doctor said he might try it if he would be very careful, he was in great spirits, and limped about, looking up his books, and planning how he would astonish his mates by the rapidity of his recovery. When he sat down to rest he remembered Jill, who had been lying quietly behind the screen, while he talked with his mother, busy putting fresh covers on the books.

"She is so still, I guess she is asleep," thought Jack, peeping round the corner.

No, not asleep, but lying with her eyes fixed on the sunny window, beyond which the bright winter world sparkled after a fresh snow-fall. The jingle of sleigh-bells could be heard, the laughter of boys and girls on their way to school, all the pleasant stir of a new day of happy work and play for the rest of the world, more lonely, quiet, and wearisome than ever to her since her friend and fellow-prisoner was set free and going to leave her.

Jack understood that patient, wistful look, and, without a word, went back to his seat, staring at the fire so soberly, that his mother presently asked: "What are you thinking of so busily, with that pucker in your forehead?"

"I've about made up my mind that I won't go to school just yet," answered Jack, slowly lifting his head, for it cost him something to give up the long-expected pleasure.

"Why not?" and Mrs. Minot looked much surprised, till Jack pointed to the screen, and, making a sad face to express Jill's anguish, answered in a cheerful tone, "Well, I'm not sure that it is best. Doctor did not want me to go, but said I might because I teased. I shall be sure to come to grief,

71

and then everyone will say, 'I told you so,' and that is so provoking. I'd rather keep still a week longer. Hadn't I better?"

His mother smiled and nodded as she said, sewing away at much-abused old Caesar, as if she loved him, "Do as you think best, dear. I always want you at home, but I don't wonder you are rather tired of it after this long confinement."

"I say, Jill, should I be in your way if I didn't go to school till the first of February?" called Jack, laughing to himself at the absurdity of the question.

"Not much!" answered a glad voice from behind the screen, and he knew the sorrowful eyes were shining with delight, though he could not see them.

"Well, I guess I may as well, and get quite firm on my legs before I start. Another week or so will bring me up if I study hard, so I shall not lose my time. I'll tackle my Latin as soon as it's ready, mother."

Jack got a hearty kiss with the neatly covered book, and Mamma loved him for the little sacrifice more than if he had won a prize at school. He did get a reward, for, in five minutes from the time he decided, Jill was singing like a bobolink, and such a medley of merry music came from behind the screen, that it was a regular morning concert. She did not know then that he stayed for her sake, but she found it out soon after, and when the time came did as much for him, as we shall see.

It proved a wise decision, for the last part of January was so stormy Jack could not have gone half the time. So, while the snow drifted, and bitter winds raged, he sat snugly at home amusing Jill, and getting on bravely with his lessons, for Frank took great pains with him to show his approbation of the little kindness, and, somehow, the memory of it seemed to make even the detested Latin easier.

With February fair weather set in, and Jack marched happily away to school, with Jill's new mittens on his hands, Mamma nodding from the door-step, and Frank ready to give him a lift on the new sled, if the way proved too long or too rough.

"I shall not have time to miss him now, for we are to be very busy getting ready for the Twenty-second. The Dramatic Club meets to-night, and would like to come here, if they may, so I can help?" said Jill, as Mrs. Minot came up, expecting to find her rather low in her mind.

"Certainly; and I have a basket of old finery I looked up for the club when I was rummaging out bits of silk for your blue quilt," answered the good lady, who had set up a new employment to beguile the hours of Jack's absence.

When the girls arrived, that evening, they found Mrs. Chairwoman surrounded by a strew of theatrical properties, enjoying herself very much. All brought such contributions as they could muster, and all were eager about a certain tableau which was to be the gem of the whole, they thought. Jill, of course, was not expected to take any part, but her taste was good, so all consulted her as they showed their old silks, laces, and flowers, asking who should be this, and who that. All wanted to be the "Sleeping Beauty," for that was the chosen scene, with the slumbering court about the princess, and the prince in the act of awakening her. Jack was to be the hero, brave in his mother's velvet cape, red boots, and a real sword, while the other boys were to have parts of more or less splendor.

"Mabel should be the Beauty, because her hair is so lovely," said Juliet, who was quite satisfied with her own part of the Queen.

"No, Merry ought to have it, as she is the prettiest, and has that splendid veil to wear," answered Molly, who was to be the maid of honor, cuffing the little page, Boo.

"I don't care a bit, but my feather would be fine for the Princess, and I don't know as Emma would like to have me lend it to anyone else," said Annette, waving a long white plume over her head, with girlish delight in its grace.

"I should think the white silk dress, the veil, and the feather ought to go together, with the scarlet crape shawl and these pearls. That would be sweet, and just what princesses really wear," advised Jill, who was stringing a quantity of old Roman pearls.

"We all want to wear the nice things, so let us draw lots. Wouldn't that be the fairest way?" asked Merry, looking like a rosy little bride, under a great piece of illusion, which had done duty in many plays.

"The Prince is light, so the Princess must be darkish. We ought to choose the girl who will look best, as it is a picture. I heard Miss Delano say so, when the ladies got up the tableaux, last winter, and everyone wanted to be Cleopatra," said Jill decidedly.

"You choose, and then if we can't agree we will draw lots," proposed Susy, who, being plain, knew there was little hope of her getting a chance in any other way.

So all stood in a row, and Jill, from her sofa, surveyed them critically, feeling that the one Jack would really prefer was not among the number.

"I choose that one, for Juliet wants to be Queen, Molly would make faces, and the others are too big or too light," pronounced Jill, pointing to Merry, who looked pleased, while Mabel's face darkened, and Susy gave a disdainful sniff.

"You'd better draw lots, and then there will be no fuss. Ju and I are out of the fight, but you three can try, and let this settle the matter," said Molly, handing Jill a long strip of paper.

All agreed to let it be so, and when the bits were ready drew in turn. This time fate was evidently on Merry's side, and no one grumbled when she showed the longest paper.

"Go and dress, then come back, and we'll plan how we are to be placed before we call up the boys," commanded Jill, who was manager, since she could be nothing else.

The girls retired to the bedroom and began to "rig up," as they called it; but discontent still lurked among them, and showed itself in sharp words, envious looks, and disobliging acts.

"Am I to have the white silk and the feather?" asked Merry, delighted with the silvery shimmer of the one and the graceful droop of the other, though both were rather shabby.

"You can use your own dress. I don't see why you should have everything," answered Susy, who was at the mirror, putting a wreath of scarlet flowers on her red head, bound to be gay since she could not be pretty.

"I think I'd better keep the plume, as I haven't anything else that is nice, and I'm afraid Emma wouldn't like me to lend it," added Annette, who was disappointed that Mabel was not to be the Beauty.

"1 don't intend to act at all!" declared Mabel, beginning to braid up her hair with a jerk, out of humor with the whole affair.

"1 think you are a set of cross, selfish girls to back out and keep your nice things just because you can't all have the best part. I'm ashamed of you!" scolded Molly, standing by Merry, who was sadly surveying her mother's old purple silk, which looked like brown in the evening.

"I'm going to have Miss Delano's red brocade for the Queen, and I shall ask her for the yellow-satin dress for Merry when I go to get mine, and tell her how mean you are," said Juliet, frowning under her gilt-paper crown as she swept about in a red table-cloth for train till the brocade arrived.

"Perhaps you'd like to have Mabel cut her hair off, so Merry can have that, too?" cried Susy, with whom hair was a tender point.

"Light hair isn't wanted, so Ju will have to give hers, or you'd better borrow Miss Bat's frisette," added Mabel, with a scornful laugh.

"I just wish Miss Bat was here to give you girls a good shaking. Do let someone else have a chance at the glass, you peacock!" exclaimed Molly Loo, pushing Susy aside to arrange her own blue turban, out of which she plucked the pink pompon to give Merry.

"Don't quarrel about me. I shall do well enough, and the scarlet shawl will hide my ugly dress," said Merry, from the corner, where she sat waiting for her turn at the mirror.

As she spoke of the shawl her eye went in search of it, and something that she saw in the other room put her own disappointment out of her head. Jill lay there all alone, rather tired with the lively chatter, and the effort it cost her not to repine at being shut out from the great delight of dressing up and acting.

Her eyes were closed, her net was off, and all the pretty black curls lay about her shoulders as one hand idly pulled them out, while the other rested on the red shawl, as if she loved its glowing color and soft texture. She was humming to herself the little song of the dove and the donjon, and something in the plaintive voice, the solitary figure, went straight to Merry's gentle heart.

"Poor Jilly can't have any of the fun," was the first thought; then came a second, that made Merry start and smile, and in a minute whisper so that all but Jill could hear her, "Girls, I'm not going to be the Princess. But I've thought of a splendid one!"

"Who?" asked the rest, staring at one another, much surprised by this sudden announcement.

"Hush! Speak low, or you will spoil it all. Look in the Bird Room, and tell me if that isn't a prettier Princess than I could make?"

They all looked, but no one spoke, and Merry added, with sweet eagerness, "It is the only thing poor Jill can be, and it would make her so happy; Jack would like it, and it would please everyone, I know. Perhaps she will never walk again, so we ought to be very good to her, poor dear."

The last words, whispered with a little quiver in the voice, settled the matter better than hours of talking, for girls are tenderhearted creatures, and not one of these but would have gladly given all the pretty things she owned to see Jill dancing about well and strong again. Like a ray of sunshine the kind thought touched and brightened every face; envy, impatience, vanity, and discontent flew away like imps at the coming of the good fairy, and with one accord they all cried,

"It will be lovely; let us go and tell her!"

Forgetting their own adornment, out they trooped after Merry, who ran to the sofa, saying, with a smile which was reflected in all the other faces, "Jill, dear, we have chosen another Princess, and I know you'll like her."

"Who is it?" asked Jill, languidly, opening her eyes without the least suspicion of the truth.

"I'll show you;" and taking the cherished veil from her own head, Merry dropped it like a soft cloud over Jill; Annette added the long plume, Susy laid the white silk dress about her, while Juliet and Mabel lifted the scarlet shawl to spread it over the foot of the sofa, and Molly tore the last ornament from her turban, a silver star, to shine on Jill's breast. Then they all took hands and danced round the couch, singing, as they laughed at her astonishment, "There she is! There she is! Princess Jill as fine as you please!"

"Do you really mean it? But can I? Is it fair? How sweet of you! Come here and let me hug you all!" cried Jill, in a rapture at the surprise, and the pretty way in which it was done.

The grand scene on the Twenty-second was very fine, indeed; but the little tableau of that minute was infinitely better, though no one saw it, as Jill tried to gather them all in her arms, for that nosegay of girlish faces was the sweeter, because each one had sacrificed her own little vanity to please a friend, and her joy was reflected in the eyes that sparkled round the happy Princess.

"Oh, you dear, kind things, to think of me and give me all your best clothes! I never shall forget it, and I'll do anything for you. Yes! I'll write and ask Mrs. Piper to lend us her ermine cloak for the king. See if I don't!"

Shrieks of delight hailed this noble offer, for no one had dared to borrow the much-coveted mantle, but all agreed that the old lady would not refuse Jill. It was astonishing how smoothly everything went after this, for each was eager to help, admire, and suggest, in the friendliest way; and when all were dressed, the boys found a party of very gay ladies waiting for them round the couch, where lay the brightest little Princess ever seen.

"Oh, Jack, I'm to act! Wasn't it dear of the girls to choose me? Don't they look lovely? Aren't you glad?" cried Jill, as the lads stared and the lasses blushed and smiled, well pleased at the frank admiration the boyish faces showed.

"I guess I am! You are a set of trumps, and we'll give you a first-class spread after the play to pay for it. Won't we, fellows?" answered Jack, much gratified, and feeling that now he could act his own part capitally.

"We will. It was a handsome thing to do, and we think well of you for it. Hey, Gus?" and Frank nodded approvingly at all, though he looked only at Annette.

"As king of this crowd, I call it to order," said Gus, retiring to the throne, where Juliet sat laughing in her red table-cloth.

"We'll have 'The Fair One with Golden Locks' next time; I promise you that," whispered Ed to Mabel, whose shining hair streamed over her blue dress like a mantle of gold-colored silk.

"Girls are pretty nice things, aren't they? Kind of 'em to take Jill in. Don't Molly look fine, though?" and Grif's black eyes twinkled as he planned to pin her skirts to Merry's at the first opportunity.

"Susy looks as gay as a feather-duster. I like her. She never snubs a fellow," said Joe, much impressed with the splendor of the court ladies.

The boys' costumes were not yet ready, but they posed well, and all had a merry time, ending with a game of blind-man's-buff, in which everyone caught the right person in the most singular way, and all agreed as they went home in the moonlight that it had been an unusually jolly meeting.

So the fairy play woke the sleeping beauty that lies in all of us, and makes us lovely when we rouse it with a kiss of unselfish good-will, for, though the girls did not know it then, they had adorned themselves with pearls more precious than the waxen ones they decked their Princess in.

Lesson 112

1. Read chapter 11 of *Jack and Jill.*
2. Summarize the chapter for someone.

Vocabulary

1. Review your vocabulary from Lesson 68.

Chapter 11. "Down Brakes"

The greatest people have their weak points, and the best-behaved boys now and then yield to temptation and get into trouble, as everybody knows. Frank was considered a remarkably well-bred and proper lad, and rather prided himself on his good reputation, for he never got into scrapes like the other fellows. Well, hardly ever, for we must confess that at rare intervals his besetting sin overcame his prudence, and he proved himself an erring, human boy. Steam-engines had been his idols for years, and they alone could lure him from the path of virtue. Once, in trying to investigate the mechanism of a toy specimen, which had its little boiler and ran about whistling and puffing in the most delightful way, he nearly set the house afire by the sparks that dropped on the straw carpet. Another time, in trying experiments with the kitchen tea-kettle, he blew himself up, and the scars of that explosion he still carried on his hands.

He was long past such childish amusements now, but his favorite haunt was the engine-house of the new railroad, where he observed the habits of his pets with never-failing interest, and cultivated the good-will of stokers and brakemen till they allowed him many liberties, and were rather flattered by the admiration expressed for their iron horses by a young gentleman who liked them better even than his Greek and Latin.

There was not much business doing on this road as yet, and the two cars of the passenger-trains were often nearly empty, though full freight-trains rolled from the factory to the main road, of which this was only a branch. So things went on in a leisurely manner, which gave Frank many opportunities of pursuing his favorite pastime. He soon knew all about No. ii, his pet engine, and had several rides on it with Bill, the engineer, so that he felt at home there, and privately resolved that when he was a rich man he would have a road of his own, and run trains as often as he liked.

Gus took less interest than his friend in the study of steam, but usually accompanied him when he went over after school to disport himself in the engine-house, interview the stoker, or see if there was anything new in the way of brakes.

One afternoon they found No. 11 on the side-track, puffing away as if enjoying a quiet smoke before starting. No cars were attached, and no driver was to be seen, for Bill was off with the other men behind the station-house, helping the expressman, whose horse had backed down a bank and upset the wagon.

"Good chance for a look at the old lady," said Frank, speaking of the engine as Bill did, and jumping aboard with great satisfaction, followed by Gus.

"I'd give ten dollars if I could run her up to the bend and back," he added, fondly touching the bright brass knobs and glancing at the fire with a critical eye.

"You couldn't do it alone," answered Gus, sitting down on the grimy little perch, willing to indulge his mate's amiable weakness.

"Give me leave to try? Steam is up, and I could do it as easy as not;" and Frank put his hand on the throttle-valve, as if daring Gus to give the word.

"Fire up and make her hum!" laughed Gus, quoting Bill's frequent order to his mate, but with no idea of being obeyed.

"All right; I'll just roll her up to the switch and back again. I've often done it with Bill;" and Frank cautiously opened the throttle-valve, threw back the lever, and the great thing moved with a throb and a puff.

"Steady, old fellow, or you'll come to grief. Here, don't open that!" shouted Gus, for just at that moment Joe appeared at the switch, looking ready for mischief.

"Wish he would; no train for twenty minutes, and we could run up to the bend as well as not," said Frank, getting excited with the sense of power, as the monster obeyed his hand so entirely that it was impossible to resist prolonging the delight.

"By George, he has! Stop her! Back her! Hold on, Frank!" cried Gus, as Joe, only catching the words "Open that!" obeyed, without the least idea that they would dare to leave the siding.

77

But they did, for Frank rather lost his head for a minute, and out upon the main track rolled No. 11 as quietly as a well-trained horse taking a familiar road.

"Now you've done it! I'll give you a good thrashing when I get back!" roared Gus, shaking his fist at Joe, who stood staring, half-pleased, half-scared, at what he had done.

"Are you really going to try it?" asked Gus, as they glided on with increasing speed, and he, too, felt the charm of such a novel adventure, though the consequences bid fair to be serious.

"Yes, I am," answered Frank, with the grim look he always wore when his strong will got the upper hand. "Bill will give it to us, anyway, so we may as well have our fun out. If you are afraid, I'll slow down and you can jump off," and his brown eyes sparkled with the double delight of getting his heart's desire and astonishing his friend at the same time by his skill and coolness.

"Go ahead. I'll jump when you do;" and Gus calmly sat down again, bound in honor to stand by his mate till the smash came, though rather dismayed at the audacity of the prank.

"Don't you call this just splendid?" exclaimed Frank, as they rolled along over the crossing, past the bridge, toward the curve, a mile from the station.

"Not bad. They are yelling like mad after us. Better go back, if you can," said Gus, who was anxiously peering out, and, in spite of his efforts to seem at ease, not enjoying the trip a particle.

"Let them yell. I started to go to the curve, and I'll do it if it costs me a hundred dollars. No danger; there's no train under twenty minutes, I tell you," and Frank pulled out his watch. But the sun was in his eyes, and he did not see clearly, or he would have discovered that it was later than he thought.

On they went, and were just rounding the bend when a shrill whistle in front startled both boys, and drove the color out of their cheeks.

"It's the factory train!" cried Gus, in a husky tone, as he sprang to his feet.

"No; it's the five-forty on the other road," answered Frank, with a queer thrill all through him at the thought of what might happen if it was not. Both looked straight ahead as the last tree glided by, and the long track lay before them, with the freight train slowly coming down. For an instant, the boys stood as if paralyzed.

"Jump!" said Gus, looking at the steep bank on one side and the river on the other, undecided which to try.

"Sit still!" commanded Frank, collecting his wits, as he gave a warning whistle to retard the on-coming train, while he reversed the engine and went back faster than he came.

A crowd of angry men was waiting for them, and Bill stood at the open switch in a towering passion as No. 11 returned to her place unharmed, but bearing two pale and frightened boys, who stepped slowly and silently down, without a word to say for themselves, while the freight train rumbled by on the main track.

Frank and Gus never had a very clear idea as to what occurred during the next few minutes, but vaguely remembered being well shaken, sworn at, questioned, threatened with direful penalties, and finally ordered off the premises forever by the wrathful depot-master. Joe was nowhere to be seen, and as the two culprits walked away, trying to go steadily, while their heads spun round, and all the strength seemed to have departed from their legs, Frank said, in an exhausted tone,

"Come down to the boat-house and rest a minute."

Both were glad to get out of sight, and dropped upon the steps red, rumpled, and breathless, after the late exciting scene. Gus generously forebore to speak, though he felt that he was the least to blame; and Frank, after eating a bit of snow to moisten his dry lips, said, handsomely,

"Now, don't you worry, old man. I'll pay the damages, for it was my fault. Joe will dodge, but I won't, so make your mind easy.

"We sha'n't hear the last of this in a hurry," responded Gus, relieved, yet anxious, as he thought of the reprimand his father would give him.

"I hope mother won't hear of it till I tell her quietly myself. She will be so frightened, and think I'm surely smashed up, if she is told in a hurry;" and Frank gave a shiver, as all the danger he had run came over him suddenly.

"I thought we were done for when we saw that train. Guess we should have been if you had not had your wits about you. I always said you were a cool one;" and Gus patted Frank's back with a look of great admiration, for, now that it was all over, he considered it a very remarkable performance.

"Which do you suppose it will be, fine or imprisonment?" asked Frank, after sitting in a despondent attitude for a moment.

"Shouldn't wonder if it was both. Running off with an engine is no joke, you know."

"What did possess me to be such a fool?" groaned Frank, repenting, all too late, of yielding to the temptation which assailed him.

"Bear up, old fellow, I'll stand by you; and if the worst comes, I'll call as often as the rules of the prison allow," said Gus, consolingly, as he gave his afflicted friend an arm, and they walked away, both feeling that they were marked men from that day forth.

Meantime, Joe, as soon as he recovered from the shock of seeing the boys actually go off, ran away, as fast as his legs could carry him, to prepare Mrs. Minot for the loss of her son; for the idea of their coming safely back never occurred to him, his knowledge of engines being limited. A loud ring at the bell brought Mrs. Pecq, who was guarding the house, while Mrs. Minot entertained a parlor full of company.

"Frank's run off with No. 11, and he'll be killed sure. Thought I'd come up and tell you," stammered Joe, all out of breath and looking wild.

He got no further, for Mrs. Pecq clapped one hand over his mouth, caught him by the collar with the other, and hustled him into the ante-room before anyone else could hear the bad news.

"Tell me all about it, and don't shout. What's come to the boy?" she demanded, in a tone that reduced Joe to a whisper at once.

"Go right back and see what has happened to him, then come and tell me quietly. I'll wait for you here. I wouldn't have his mother startled for the world," said the good soul, when she knew all.

"Oh, I dar'sn't! I opened the switch as they told me to, and Bill will half kill me when he knows it!" cried Joe, in a panic, as the awful consequences of his deed rose before him, showing both boys mortally injured and several trains wrecked.

"Then take yourself off home and hold your tongue. I'll watch the door, for I won't have any more ridiculous boys tearing in to disturb my lady."

Mrs. Pecq often called this good neighbor "my lady" when speaking of her, for Mrs. Minot was a true gentlewoman, and much pleasanter to live with than the titled mistress had been.

Joe scudded away as if the constable was after him, and presently Frank was seen slowly approaching with an unusually sober face and a pair of very dirty hands.

"Thank heaven, he's safe!" and, softly opening the door, Mrs. Pecq actually hustled the young master into the ante-room as unceremoniously as she had hustled Joe.

"I beg pardon, but the parlor is full of company, and that fool of a Joe came roaring in with a cock-and-bull story that gave me quite a turn. What is it, Mr. Frank?" she asked eagerly, seeing that something was amiss.

He told her in a few words, and she was much relieved to find that no harm had been done.

"Ah, the danger is to come," said Frank, darkly, as he went away to wash his hands and prepare to relate his misdeeds.

It was a very bad quarter of an hour for the poor fellow, who so seldom had any grave faults to confess; but he did it manfully, and his mother was so grateful for the safety of her boy that she found it difficult to be severe enough, and contented herself with forbidding any more visits to the too charming No. 11.

"What do you suppose will be done to me?" asked Frank, on whom the idea of imprisonment had made a deep impression.

"I don't know, dear, but I shall go over to see Mr. Burton right after tea. He will tell us what to do and what to expect. Gus must not suffer for your fault."

"He'll come off clear enough, but Joe must take his share, for if he hadn't opened that confounded switch, no harm would have been done. But when I saw the way clear, I actually couldn't resist going ahead," said Frank, getting excited again at the memory of that blissful moment when he started the engine.

Here Jack came hurrying in, having heard the news, and refused to believe it from any lips but Frank's. When he could no longer doubt, he was so much impressed with the daring of the deed that he had nothing but admiration for his brother, till a sudden thought made him clap his hands and exclaim exultingly,

"His runaway beats mine all hollow, and now he can't crow over me! Won't that be a comfort? The good boy has got into a scrape. Hooray!"

This was such a droll way of taking it, that they had to laugh; and Frank took his humiliation so meekly that Jack soon fell to comforting him, instead of crowing over him.

Jill thought it a most interesting event; and, when Frank and his mother went over to consult Mr. Burton, she and Jack planned out for the dear culprit a dramatic trial which would have convulsed the soberest of judges. His sentence was ten years' imprisonment, and such heavy fines that the family would have been reduced to beggary but for the sums made by Jill's fancy work and Jack's success as a champion pedestrian.

They found such comfort and amusement in this sensational programme that they were rather disappointed when Frank returned, reporting that a fine would probably be all the penalty exacted, as no harm had been done, and he and Gus were such respectable boys. What would happen to Joe, he could not tell, but he thought a good whipping ought to be added to his share.

Of course, the affair made a stir in the little world of children; and when Frank went to school, feeling that his character for good behavior was forever damaged, he found himself a lion, and was in danger of being spoiled by the admiration of his comrades, who pointed him out with pride as "the fellow who ran off with a steam-engine."

But an interview with Judge Kemble, a fine of twenty-five dollars, and lectures from all the grown people of his acquaintance, prevented him from regarding his escapade as a feat to boast of. He discovered, also, how fickle a thing is public favor, for very soon those who had praised began to tease, and it took all his courage, patience, and pride to carry him through the next week or two. The lads were never tired of alluding to No. 11, giving shrill whistles in his ear, asking if his watch was right, and drawing locomotives on the blackboard whenever they got a chance.

The girls, too, had sly nods and smiles, hints and jokes of a milder sort, which made him color and fume, and once lose his dignity entirely. Molly Loo, who dearly loved to torment the big boys, and dared attack even solemn Frank, left one of Boo's old tin trains on the door-step, directed to "Conductor Minot," who, I regret to say, could not refrain from kicking it into the street, and slamming the door with a bang that shook the house. Shrieks of laughter from wicked Molly and her coadjutor, Grif, greeted this explosion of wrath, which did no good, however, for half an hour later the same cars, all in a heap, were on the steps again, with two headless dolls tumbling out of the cab, and the dilapidated engine labelled, "No. 11 after the collision."

No one ever saw that ruin again, and for days Frank was utterly unconscious of Molly's existence, as propriety forbade his having it out with her as he had with Grif. Then Annette made peace between them, and the approach of the Twenty-second gave the wags something else to think of.

But it was long before Frank forgot that costly prank; for he was a thoughtful boy, who honestly wanted to be good; so he remembered this episode humbly, and whenever he felt the approach of temptation he made the strong will master it, saying to himself "Down brakes!" thus saving the precious freight he carried from many of the accidents which befall us when we try to run our trains without orders, and so often wreck ourselves as well as others.

Lesson 113

1. Read chapter 12 of *Jack and Jill*.

2. Tell someone a summary of this chapter.

Chapter 12. The Twenty-Second of February

Of course, the young ladies and gentlemen had a ball on the evening of that day, but the boys and girls were full of excitement about their "Scenes from the Life of Washington and other brilliant tableaux," as the programme announced. The Bird Room was the theatre, being very large, with four doors conveniently placed. Ralph was in his element, putting up a little stage, drilling boys, arranging groups, and uniting in himself carpenter, scene-painter, manager, and gas man. Mrs. Minot permitted the house to be turned topsy-turvy, and Mrs. Pecq flew about, lending a hand everywhere. Jill was costumer, with help from Miss Delano, who did not care for balls, and kindly took charge of the girls. Jack printed tickets, programmes, and placards of the most imposing sort, and the work went gayly on till all was ready.

When the evening came, the Bird Room presented a fine appearance. One end was curtained off with red drapery; and real footlights, with tin shades, gave a truly theatrical air to the little stage. Rows of chairs, filled with mammas and little people, occupied the rest of the space. The hall and Frank's room were full of amused papas, uncles, and old gentlemen whose patriotism brought them out in spite of rheumatism. There was a great rustling of skirts, fluttering of fans, and much lively chat, till a bell rang and the orchestra struck up.

Yes, there really was an orchestra, for Ed declared that the national airs *must* be played, or the whole thing would be a failure. So he had exerted himself to collect all the musical talent he could find, a horn, a fiddle, and a flute, with drum and fife for the martial scenes. Ed looked more beaming than ever, as he waved his baton and led off with Yankee Doodle as a safe beginning, for every one knew that. It was fun to see little Johnny Cooper bang away on a big drum, and old Mr. Munson, who had been a fifer all his days, blow till he was as red as a lobster, while every one kept time to the music which put them all in good spirits for the opening scene.

Up went the curtain and several trees in tubs appeared, then a stately gentleman in small clothes, cocked hat, gray wig, and an imposing cane, came slowly walking in. It was Gus, who had been unanimously chosen not only for Washington but for the father of the hero also, that the family traits of long legs and a somewhat massive nose might be preserved.

"Ahem! My trees are doing finely," observed Mr. W., senior, strolling along with his hands behind him, casting satisfied glances at the dwarf orange, oleander, abutilon, and little pine that represented his orchard.

Suddenly he starts, pauses, frowns, and, after examining the latter shrub, which displayed several hacks in its stem and a broken limb with six red-velvet cherries hanging on it, he gave a thump with his cane that made the little ones jump, and cried out,

"Can it have been my son?"

He evidently thought it *was*, for he called, in tones of thunder,

"George! George Washington, come hither this moment!"

Great suspense on the part of the audience, then a general burst of laughter as Boo trotted in, a perfect miniature of his honored parent, knee breeches, cocked hat, shoe buckles and all. He was so fat that the little tails of his coat stuck out in the drollest way, his chubby legs could hardly carry the big buckles, and the rosy face displayed, when he took his hat off with a dutiful bow, was so solemn, the real George could not have looked more anxious when he gave the immortal answer.

"Sirrah, did you cut that tree?" demanded the papa, with another rap of the cane, and such a frown that poor Boo looked dismayed, till Molly whispered, "Put your hand up, dear." Then he remembered his part, and, putting one finger in his mouth, looked down at his square-toed shoes, the image of a shame-stricken boy.

"My son, do not deceive me. If you have done this deed I shall chastise you, for it is my duty not to spare the rod, lest I spoil the child. But if you lie about it you disgrace the name of Washington forever."

This appeal seemed to convulse George with inward agony, for he squirmed most effectively as he drew from his pocket a toy hatchet, which would not have cut a straw, then looking straight up into the awe-inspiring countenance of his parent, he bravely lisped,

"Papa, I tannot tell a lie. I did tut it with my little hanchet."

"Noble boy come to my arms! I had rather you spoilt *all* my cherry trees than tell one lie!" cried the delighted gentleman, catching his son in an embrace so close that the fat legs kicked convulsively, and the little coat-tails waved in the breeze, while cane and hatchet fell with a dramatic bang.

The curtain descended on this affecting tableau; but the audience called out both Washingtons, and they came, hand in hand, bowing with the cocked hats pressed to their breasts, the elder smiling blandly, while the younger, still flushed by his exertions, nodded to his friends, asking, with engaging frankness, "Wasn't it nice?"

The next was a marine piece, for a boat was seen, surrounded by tumultuous waves of blue cambric, and rowed by a party of stalwart men in regimentals, who with difficulty kept their seats, for the boat was only a painted board, and they sat on boxes or stools behind it. But few marked the rowers, for in their midst, tall, straight, and steadfast as a mast, stood one figure in a cloak, with folded arms, high boots, and, under the turned-up hat, a noble countenance, stern with indomitable courage. A sword glittered at his side, and a banner waved over him, but his eye was fixed on the distant shore, and he was evidently unconscious of the roaring billows, the blocks of ice, the discouragement of his men, or the danger and death that might await him. Napoleon crossing the Alps was not half so sublime, and with one voice the audience cried, "Washington crossing the Delaware!" while the band burst forth with, "See, the conquering hero comes!" all out of tune, but bound to play it or die in the attempt.

It would have been very successful if, all of a sudden, one of the rowers had not "caught a crab" with disastrous consequences. The oars were not moving, but a veteran, who looked very much like Joe, dropped the one he held, and in trying to turn and pummel the black-eyed warrior behind him, he tumbled off his seat, upsetting two other men, and pulling the painted boat upon them as they lay kicking in the cambric deep. Shouts of laughter greeted this mishap, but George Washington never stirred. Grasping the banner, he stood firm when all else went down in the general wreck, and the icy waves engulfed his gallant crew, leaving him erect amid a chaos of wildly tossing boots, entangled oars, and red-faced victims. Such god-like dignity could not fail to impress the frivolous crowd of laughers, and the curtain fell amid a round of applause for him alone.

"Quite exciting, wasn't it? Didn't know Gus had so much presence of mind," said Mr. Burton, well pleased with his boy.

"If we did not know that Washington died in his bed, December 14, 1799, I should fear that we'd seen the last of him in that shipwreck," laughed an old gentleman, proud of his memory for dates.

Much confusion reigned behind the scenes; Ralph was heard scolding, and Joe set every one off again by explaining, audibly, that Grif tickled him, and he couldn't stand it. A pretty, old-fashioned picture of the "Daughters of Liberty" followed, for the girls were determined to do honor to the brave and patient women who so nobly bore their part in the struggle, yet are usually forgotten when those days are celebrated. The damsels were charming in the big caps, flowered gowns, and high-heeled shoes of their great-grandmothers, as they sat about a spider-legged table talking over the tax, and pledging themselves to drink no more tea till it was taken off. Molly was on her feet proposing, "Liberty forever, and down with all tyrants," to judge from her flashing eyes as she held her egg-shell cup aloft, while the others lifted theirs to drink the toast, and Merry, as hostess, sat with her hand on an antique teapot, labelled "Sage," ready to fill again when the patriotic ladies were ready for a second "dish."

This was much applauded, and the curtain went up again, for the proud parents enjoyed seeing their pretty girls in the faded finery of a hundred years ago. The band played "Auld Lang Syne," as a gentle hint that our fore-mothers should be remembered as well as the fore-fathers.

It was evident that something very martial was to follow, for a great tramping, clashing, and flying about took place behind the scenes while the tea-party was going on. After some delay, "The Surrender of Cornwallis" was presented in the most superb manner, as you can believe when I tell you that the stage was actually lined with a glittering array of Washington and his generals, Lafayette, Kosciusko, Rochambeau and the rest, all in astonishing uniforms, with swords which were evidently the pride of their lives. Fife and drum struck up a march, and in came Cornwallis, much cast down but full of manly resignation, as he surrendered his sword, and stood aside with averted eyes while his army marched past, piling their arms at the hero's feet.

This scene was the delight of the boys, for the rifles of Company F had been secured, and at least a dozen soldiers kept filing in and out in British uniform till Washington's august legs were hidden by the heaps of arms rattled down before him. The martial music, the steady tramp, and the patriotic memories awakened, caused this scene to be enthusiastically encored, and the boys would have gone on marching till midnight if Ralph had not peremptorily ordered down the curtain and cleared the stage for the next tableau.

This had been artfully slipped in between two brilliant ones, to show that the Father of his Country had to pay a high price for his glory. The darkened stage represented what seemed to be a camp in a snow-storm, and a very forlorn camp, too; for on "the cold, cold ground" (a reckless display of cotton batting) lay ragged soldiers, sleeping without blankets, their worn-out boots turned up pathetically, and no sign of food or fire to be seen. A very shabby sentinel, with feet bound in bloody cloths, and his face as pale as chalk could make it, gnawed a dry crust as he kept his watch in the wintry night.

A tent at the back of the stage showed a solitary figure sitting on a log of wood, poring over the map spread upon his knee, by the light of one candle stuck in a bottle. There could be no doubt who this was, for the buff-and-blue coat, the legs, the nose, the attitude, all betrayed the great George laboring to save his country, in spite of privations, discouragements, and dangers which would have daunted any other man.

"Valley Forge," said someone, and the room was very still as old and young looked silently at this little picture of a great and noble struggle in one of its dark hours. The crust, the wounded feet, the rags, the snow, the loneliness, the indomitable courage and endurance of these men touched the hearts of all, for the mimic scene grew real for a moment; and, when a child's voice broke the silence, asking pitifully, "Oh, mamma, was it truly as dreadful as that?" a general outburst answered, as if every one wanted to cheer up the brave fellows and bid them fight on, for victory was surely coming.

In the next scene it did come, and "Washington at Trenton" was prettily done. An arch of flowers crossed the stage, with the motto, "The Defender of the Mothers will be the Preserver of the Daughters;" and, as the hero with his generals advanced on one side, a troop of girls, in old-fashioned muslin frocks, came to scatter flowers before him, singing the song of long ago:

> "Welcome, mighty chief, once more
> Welcome to this grateful shore;
> Now no mercenary foe
> Aims again the fatal blow,
> Aims at thee the fatal blow.

> "Virgins fair and matrons grave,
> Those thy conquering arm did save,
> Build for thee triumphal bowers;
> Strew, ye fair, his way with flowers,
> Strew your hero's way with flowers."

And they did, singing with all their hearts as they flung artificial roses and lilies at the feet of the great men, who bowed with benign grace. Jack, who did Lafayette with a limp, covered himself with glory by picking up one of the bouquets and pressing it to his heart with all the gallantry of a Frenchman; and when Washington lifted the smallest of the maids and kissed her, the audience cheered. Couldn't help it, you know, it was so pretty and inspiring.

The Washington Family, after the famous picture, came next, with Annette as the serene and sensible Martha, in a very becoming cap. The General was in uniform, there being no time to change, but his attitude was quite correct, and the Custis boy and girl displayed the wide sash and ruffled collar with historic fidelity. The band played "Home," and every one agreed that it was "Sweet!"

"Now I don't see what more they can have except the death-bed, and that would be rather out of place in this gay company," said the old gentleman to Mr. Burton, as he mopped his heated face after pounding so heartily he nearly knocked the ferule off his cane.

"No; they gave that up, for my boy wouldn't wear a night-gown in public. I can't tell secrets, but I think they have got a very clever little finale for the first part a pretty compliment to one person and a pleasant surprise to all," answered Mr. Burton, who was in great spirits, being fond of theatricals and very justly proud of his children, for the little girls had been among the Trenton maids, and the mimic General had kissed his own small sister, Nelly, very tenderly.

A great deal of interest was felt as to what this surprise was to be, and a general "Oh!" greeted the "Minute Man," standing motionless upon his pedestal. It was Frank, and Ralph had done his best to have the figure as perfect as possible, for the maker of the original had been a good friend to him; and, while the young sculptor was dancing gayly at the ball, this copy of his work was doing him honor among the children. Frank looked it very well, for his firm-set mouth was full of resolution, his eyes shone keen and courageous under the three-cornered hat, and the muscles stood out upon the bare arm that clutched the old gun. Even the buttons on the gaiters seemed to flash defiance, as the sturdy legs took the first step from the furrow toward the bridge where the young farmer became a hero when he "fired the shot heard 'round the world."

"That *is* splendid!" "As like to the original as flesh can be to bronze." "How still he stands!" "He'll fight when the time comes, and die hard, won't he?" "Hush! You make the statue blush!" These very audible remarks certainly did, for the color rose visibly as the modest lad heard himself praised, though he saw but one face in all the crowd, his mother's, far back, but full of love and pride, as she looked up at her young minute man waiting for the battle which often calls us when we least expect it, and for which she had done her best to make him ready.

If there had been any danger of Frank being puffed up by the success of his statue, it was counteracted by irrepressible Grif, who, just at the most interesting moment, when all were gazing silently, gave a whistle, followed by a "Choo, choo, choo!" and "All aboard!" so naturally that no one could mistake the joke, especially as another laughing voice added, "Now, then, No. 11!" which brought down the house and the curtain too.

Frank was so angry, it was very difficult to keep him on his perch for the last scene of all. He submitted, however, rather than spoil the grand finale, hoping that its beauty would efface that ill-timed pleasantry from the public mind. So, when the agreeable clamor of hands and voices called for a repetition, the Minute Man reappeared, grimmer than before. But not alone, for grouped all about his pedestal were Washington and his generals, the matrons and maids, with a background of troops shouldering arms, Grif and Joe doing such rash things with their muskets, that more than one hero received a poke in his august back. Before the full richness of this picture had been taken in, Ed gave a rap, and all burst out with "Hail Columbia," in such an inspiring style that it was impossible for the audience to refrain from joining, which they did, all standing and all singing with a heartiness that made the walls ring. The fife shrilled, the horn blew sweet and clear, the fiddle was nearly drowned by the energetic boom of the drum, and out into the starry night, through open windows, rolled the song that stirs the coldest heart with patriotic warmth and tunes every voice to music.

"'America!' We must have 'America!' Pipe up, Ed, this is too good to end without one song more," cried Mr. Burton, who had been singing like a trumpet; and, hardly waiting to get their breath, off they all went again with the national hymn, singing as they never had sung it before, for somehow the little scenes they had just acted or beheld seemed to show how much this dear America of ours had cost in more than one revolution, how full of courage, energy, and virtue it was in spite of all its faults, and what a privilege, as well as duty, it was for each to do his part toward its safety and its honor in the present, as did those brave men and women in the past.

So the "Scenes from the Life of Washington" were a great success, and, when the songs were over, people were glad of a brief recess while they had raptures, and refreshed themselves with lemonade.

The girls had kept the secret of who the "Princess" was to be, and, when the curtain rose, a hum of surprise and pleasure greeted the pretty group. Jill lay asleep in all her splendor, the bonny "Prince" just lifting the veil to wake her with a kiss, and all about them the court in its nap of a hundred years. The "King" and "Queen" dozing comfortably on the throne; the maids of honor, like a garland of nodding flowers, about the couch; the little page, unconscious of the blow about to fall, and the fool dreaming, with his mouth wide open.

It was so pretty, people did not tire of looking, till Jack's lame leg began to tremble, and he whispered: "Drop her or I shall pitch." Down went the curtain; but it rose in a moment, and there was the court after the awakening: the "King" and "Queen" looking about them with sleepy dignity, the maids in various attitudes of surprise, the fool grinning from ear to ear, and the "Princess" holding out her hand to the "Prince," as if glad to welcome the right lover when he came at last.

Molly got the laugh this time, for she could not resist giving poor Boo the cuff which had been hanging over him so long. She gave it with unconscious energy, and Boo cried "Ow!" so naturally that all the children were delighted and wanted it repeated. But Boo declined, and the scenes which followed were found quite as much to their taste, having been expressly prepared for the little people.

Mother Goose's Reception was really very funny, for Ralph was the old lady, and had hired a representation of the immortal bird from a real theatre for this occasion. There they stood, the dame in her pointed hat, red petticoat, cap, and cane, with the noble fowl, a good deal larger than life, beside her, and Grif inside, enjoying himself immensely as he flapped the wings, moved the yellow legs, and waved the long neck about, while unearthly quacks issued from the bill. That was a great surprise for the children, and they got up in their seats to gaze their fill, many of them firmly believing that they actually beheld the blessed old woman who wrote the nursery songs they loved so well.

Then in came, one after another, the best of the characters she has made famous, while a voice behind the scenes sang the proper rhyme as each made their manners to the interesting pair. "Mistress Mary," and her "pretty maids all in a row," passed by to their places in the background; "King Cole" and his "fiddlers three" made a goodly show; so did the royal couple, who followed the great pie borne before them, with the "four-and-twenty blackbirds" popping their heads out in the most delightful way. Little "Bo-Peep" led a woolly lamb and wept over its lost tail, for not a sign of one appeared on the poor thing. "Simple Simon" followed the pie-man, gloating over his wares with the drollest antics. The little wife came trundling by in a wheelbarrow and was not upset; neither was the lady with "rings on her fingers and bells on her toes," as she cantered along on a rocking-horse. "Bobby Shafto's" yellow hair shone finely as he led in the maid whom he came back from sea to marry. "Miss Muffet," bowl in hand, ran away from an immense black spider, which waggled its long legs in a way so life-like that some of the children shook in their little shoes. The beggars who came to town were out in full force, "rags, tags, and velvet gowns," quite true to life. "Boy Blue" rubbed his eyes, with hay sticking in his hair, and tooted on a tin horn as if bound to get the cows out of the corn. Molly, with a long-handled frying-pan, made a capital "Queen," in a tucked-up gown, checked apron, and high crown, to good "King Arthur," who, very properly, did not appear after stealing the barley-meal, which might be seen in the pan tied up in a pudding, like a cannon-ball, ready to fry.

But Tobias, Molly's black cat, covered himself with glory by the spirit with which he acted his part in,

> "Sing, sing, what shall I sing?
> The cat's run away with the pudding-bag string."

First he was led across the stage on his hind legs, looking very fierce and indignant, with a long tape trailing behind him; and, being set free at the proper moment, he gave one bound over the four-and-twenty blackbirds who happened to be in the way, and dashed off as if an enraged cook had actually been after him, straight downstairs to the coal-bin, where he sat glaring in the dark, till the fun was over.

When all the characters had filed in and stood in two long rows, music struck up and they danced, "All the way to Boston," a simple but lively affair, which gave each a chance to show his or her costume as they pranced down the middle and up outside.

Such a funny medley as it was, for there went fat "King Cole" with the most ragged of the beggar-maids. "Mistress Mary," in her pretty blue dress, tripped along with "Simple Simon" staring about him like a blockhead. The fine lady left her horse to dance with "Bobby Shafto" till every bell on her slippers tinkled its tongue out. "Bo-Peep" and a jolly fiddler skipped gayly up and down. "Miss Muffet" took the big spider for her partner, and made his many legs fly about in the wildest way. The little wife got out of the wheelbarrow to help "Boy Blue" along, and Molly, with the frying-pan over her shoulder, led off splendidly when it was "Grand right and left."

But the old lady and her goose were the best of all, for the dame's shoe-buckles cut the most astonishing pigeon-wings, and to see that mammoth bird waddle down the middle with its wings half open, its long neck bridling, and its yellow legs in the first position as it curtsied to its partner, was a sight to remember, it was so intensely funny.

The merry old gentleman laughed till he cried; Mr. Burton split his gloves, he applauded so enthusiastically; while the children beat the dust out of the carpet hopping up and down, as they cried: "Do it again!" "We want it all over!" when the curtain went down at last on the flushed and panting party, Mother G bowing, with her hat all awry, and the goose doing a double shuffle as if it did not know how to leave off.

But they could not "do it all over again," for it was growing late, and the people felt that they certainly had received their money's worth that evening.

So it all ended merrily, and when the guests departed the boys cleared the room like magic, and the promised supper to the actors was served in handsome style. Jack and Jill were at one end, Mrs. Goose and her bird at the other, and all between was a comical collection of military heroes, fairy characters, and nursery celebrities. All felt the need of refreshment after their labors, and swept over the table like a flight of locusts, leaving devastation behind. But they had earned their fun: and much innocent jollity prevailed, while a few lingering papas and mammas watched the revel from afar, and had not the heart to order these noble beings home till even the Father of his Country declared "that he'd had a perfectly splendid time, but couldn't keep his eyes open another minute," and very wisely retired to replace the immortal cocked hat with a night-cap.

Lesson 114

1. Read chapter 13 of *Jack and Jill*.
2. Write a one-sentence summary of the chapter.

Chapter 13. Jack Has a Mystery

"What is the matter? Does your head ache?" asked Jill, one evening in March, observing that Jack sat with his head in his hands, an attitude which, with him, meant either pain or perplexity.

"No; but I'm bothered. I want some money, and I don't see how I can earn it," he answered, tumbling his hair about, and frowning darkly at the fire.

"How much?" and Jill's ready hand went to the pocket where her little purse lay, for she felt rich with several presents lately made her.

"Two seventy-five. No, thank you, I won't borrow."

"What is it for?"

"Can't tell."

"Why, I thought you told me everything."

"Sorry, but I can't this time. Don't you worry; I shall think of something."

"Couldn't your mother help?"

"Don't wish to ask her."

"Why! can't she know?"

"Nobody can."

"How queer! Is it a scrape, Jack?" asked Jill, looking as curious as a magpie.

"It is likely to be, if I can't get out of it this week, somehow."

"Well, I don't see how I can help if I'm not to know anything;" and Jill seemed rather hurt.

"You can just stop asking questions, and tell me how a fellow can earn some money. That would help. I've got one dollar, but I must have some more;" and Jack looked worried as he fingered the little gold dollar on his watch-guard.

"Oh, do you mean to use that?"

"Yes, I do; a man must pay his debts if he sells all he has to do it," said Jack sternly.

"Dear me; it must be something very serious." And Jill lay quite still for five minutes, thinking over all the ways in which Jack ever did earn money, for Mrs. Minot liked to have her boys work, and paid them in some way for all they did.

"Is there any wood to saw?" she asked presently, being very anxious to help.

"All done."

"Paths to shovel?"

"No snow."

"Lawn to rake, then?"

"Not time for that yet."

"Catalogue of books?"

"Frank got that job."

"Copy those letters for your mother?"

"Take me too long. Must have my money Friday, if possible."

"I don't see what we can do, then. It is too early or too late for everything, and you won't borrow."

"Not of you. No, nor of anyone else, if I can possibly help it. I've promised to do this myself, and I will;" and Jack wagged his head resolutely.

"Couldn't you do something with the printing-press? Do me some cards, and then, perhaps, the other girls will want some," said Jill, as a forlorn hope.

"Just the thing! What a goose I was not to think of it. I'll rig the old machine up at once." And, starting from his seat, Jack dived into the big closet, dragged out the little press, and fell to oiling, dusting, and putting it in order, like one relieved of a great anxiety.

"Give me the types; I'll sort them and set up my name, so you can begin as soon as you are ready. You know what a help I was when we did the programmes. I'm almost sure the girls will want cards, and I know your mother would like some more tags," said Jill, briskly rattling the letters into the different compartments, while Jack inked the rollers and hunted up his big apron, whistling the while with recovered spirits.

A dozen neat cards were soon printed, and Jill insisted on paying six cents for them, as earning was not borrowing. A few odd tags were found and done for Mamma, who immediately ordered four dozen at six cents a dozen, though she was not told why there was such a pressing call for money.

Jack's monthly half-dollar had been spent the first week,--twenty-five cents for a concert, ten paid a fine for keeping a book too long from the library, ten more to have his knife ground, and five in candy, for he dearly loved sweeties, and was under bonds to Mamma not to spend more than five cents a month on these unwholesome temptations. She never asked the boys what they did with their money, but expected them to keep account in the little books she gave them; and, now and then, they showed the neat pages with pardonable pride, though she often laughed at the queer items.

All that evening Jack & Co. worked busily, for when Frank came in he good-naturedly ordered some pale-pink cards for Annette, and ran to the store to choose the right shade, and buy some packages for the young printer also.

"What do you suppose he is in such a pucker for?" whispered Jill, as she set up the new name, to Frank, who sat close by, with one eye on his book and one on her.

"Oh, some notion. He's a queer chap; but I guess it isn't much of a scrape, or I should know it. He's so good-natured he's always promising to do things for people, and has too much pluck to give up when he finds he can't. Let him alone, and it will all come out soon enough," answered Frank, who laughed at his brother, but loved him none the less for the tender heart that often got the better of his young head.

But for once Frank was mistaken; the mystery did not come out, and Jack worked like a beaver all that week, as orders poured in when Jill and Annette showed their elegant cards; for, as everybody knows, if one girl has a new thing all the rest must, whether it is a bow on the top of her head, a peculiar sort of pencil, or the latest kind of chewing-gum. Little play did the poor fellow get, for every spare minute was spent at the press, and no invitation could tempt him away, so much in earnest was our honest little Franklin about paying his debt. Jill helped all she could, and cheered his labors with her encouragement, remembering how he stayed at home for her.

"It is real good of you to lend a hand, and I'm ever so much obliged," said Jack, as the last order was struck off, and the drawer of the type-box held a pile of shining five and ten cent pieces, with two or three quarters.

"I love to; only it would be nicer if I knew what we were working for," she said demurely, as she scattered type for the last time; and seeing that Jack was both tired and grateful, hoped to get a hint of the secret.

"I want to tell you, dreadfully; but I can't, because I've promised."

"What, never?"

"Never!" and Jack looked as firm as a rock.

"Then I shall find out, for I haven't promised."

"You can't."

91

"See if I don't!"

"You are sharp, but you won't guess this. It's a tremendous secret, and nobody will tell it."

"You'll tell it yourself. You always do."

"I won't tell this. It would be mean."

"Wait and see; I can get anything out of you if I try;" and Jill laughed, knowing her power well, for Jack found it very hard to keep a secret from her.

"Don't try; please don't! It wouldn't be right, and you don't want to make me do a dishonorable thing for your sake, I know."

Jack looked so distressed that Jill promised not to make him tell, though she held herself free to find out in other ways, if she could.

Thus relieved, Jack trudged off to school on Friday with the two dollars and seventy-five cents jingling in his pocket, though the dear gold coin had to be sacrificed to make up the sum. He did his lessons badly that day, was late at recess in the afternoon, and, as soon as school was over, departed in his rubber boots "to take a walk," he said, though the roads were in a bad state with a spring thaw. Nothing was seen of him till after tea-time, when he came limping in, very dirty and tired, but with a reposeful expression, which betrayed that a load was off his mind. Frank was busy about his own affairs and paid little attention to him, but Jill was on tender-hooks to know where he had been, yet dared not ask the question.

"Merry's brother wants some cards. He liked hers so much he wishes to make his lady-love a present. Here's the name;" and Jill held up the order from Harry Grant, who was to be married in the autumn.

"Must wait till next week. I'm too tired to do a thing to-night, and I hate the sight of that old press," answered Jack, laying himself down upon the rug as if every joint ached.

"What made you take such a long walk? You look as tired as if you'd been ten miles," said Jill, hoping to discover the length of the trip.

"Had to. Four or five miles isn't much, only my leg bothered me;" and Jack gave the ailing member a slap, as if he had found it much in his way that day; for, though he had given up the crutches long ago, he rather missed their support sometimes. Then, with a great yawn, he stretched himself out to bask in the blaze, pillowing his head on his arms.

"Dear old thing, he looks all used up; I won't plague him with talking;" and Jill began to sing, as she often did in the twilight.

By the time the first song ended a gentle snore was heard, and Jack lay fast asleep, worn out with the busy week and the walk, which had been longer and harder than anyone guessed. Jill took up her knitting and worked quietly by firelight, still wondering and guessing what the secret could be; for she had not much to amuse her, and little things were very interesting if connected with her friends. Presently Jack rolled over and began to mutter in his sleep, as he often did when too weary for sound slumber. Jill paid no attention till he uttered a name which made her prick up her ears and listen to the broken sentences which followed. Only a few words, but she dropped her work, saying to herself,

"I do believe he is talking about the secret. Now I shall find out, and he will tell me himself, as I said he would."

Much pleased, she leaned and listened, but could make no sense of the confused babble about "heavy boots;" "All right, old fellow;" "Jerry's off;" and "The ink is too thick."

The slam of the front door woke Jack, and he pulled himself up, declaring that he believed he had been having a nap.

"I wish you'd have another," said Jill, greatly disappointed at the loss of the intelligence she seemed to be so near getting.

"Floor is too hard for tired bones. Guess I'll go to bed and get rested up for Monday. I've worked like fury this week, so next I'm going in for fun;" and, little dreaming what hard times were in store for him, Jack went off to enjoy his warm bath and welcome bed, where he was soon sleeping with the serene look of one whose dreams were happy, whose conscience was at rest.

"I have a few words to say to you before you go," said Mr. Acton, pausing with his hand on the bell, Monday afternoon, when the hour came for dismissing school.

The bustle of putting away books and preparing for as rapid a departure as propriety allowed, subsided suddenly, and the boys and girls sat as still as mice, while the hearts of such as had been guilty of any small sins began to beat fast.

"You remember that we had some trouble last winter about keeping the boys away from the saloon, and that a rule was made forbidding any pupil to go to town during recess?" began Mr. Acton, who, being a conscientious man as well as an excellent teacher, felt that he was responsible for the children in school hours, and did his best to aid parents in guarding them from the few temptations which beset them in a country town. A certain attractive little shop, where confectionery, baseballs, stationery, and picture papers were sold, was a favorite loafing place for some of the boys till the rule forbidding it was made, because in the rear of the shop was a beer and billiard saloon. A wise rule, for the picture papers were not always of the best sort; cigars were to be had; idle fellows hung about there, and some of the lads, who wanted to be thought manly, ventured to pass the green baize door "just to look on."

A murmur answered the teacher's question, and he continued, "You all know that the rule was broken several times, and I told you the next offender would be publicly reprimanded, as private punishments had no effect. I am sorry to say that the time has come, and the offender is a boy whom I trusted entirely. It grieves me to do this, but I must keep my promise, and hope the example will have a good effect."

Mr. Acton paused, as if he found it hard to go on, and the boys looked at one another with inquiring eyes, for their teacher seldom punished, and when he did, it was a very solemn thing. Several of these anxious glances fell upon Joe, who was very red and sat whittling a pencil as if he dared not lift his eyes.

"He's the chap. Won't he catch it?" whispered Gus to Frank, for both owed him a grudge.

"The boy who broke the rule last Friday, at afternoon recess, will come to the desk," said Mr. Acton in his most impressive manner.

If a thunderbolt had fallen through the roof it would hardly have caused a greater surprise than the sight of Jack Minot walking slowly down the aisle, with a wrathful flash in the eyes he turned on Joe as he passed him.

"Now, Minot, let us have this over as soon as possible, for I do not like it any better than you do, and I am sure there is some mistake. I'm told you went to the shop on Friday. Is it true?" asked Mr. Acton very gently, for he liked Jack and seldom had to correct him in any way.

"Yes, sir;" and Jack looked up as if proud to show that he was not afraid to tell the truth as far as he could.

"To buy something?"

"No, sir."

"To meet someone?"

"Yes, sir."

"Was it Jerry Shannon?"

No answer, but Jack's fists doubled up of themselves as he shot another fiery glance at Joe, whose face burned as if it scorched him.

"I am told it was; also that you were seen to go into the saloon with him. Did you?" and Mr. Acton looked so sure that it was a mistake that it cost Jack a great effort to say, slowly,

"Yes, sir."

Quite a thrill pervaded the school at this confession, for Jerry was one of the wild fellows the boys all shunned, and to have any dealings with him was considered a very disgraceful thing.

"Did you play?"

"No, sir. I can't."

"Drink beer?"

"I belong to the Lodge;" and Jack stood as erect as any little soldier who ever marched under a temperance banner, and fought for the cause none are too young nor too old to help along.

"I was sure of that. Then what took you there, my boy?"

The question was so kindly put that Jack forgot himself an instant, and blurted out,

"I only went to pay him some money, sir."

"Ah, how much?"

"Two seventy-five," muttered Jack, as red as a cherry at not being able to keep a secret better.

"Too much for a lad like you to owe such a fellow as Jerry. How came it?" And Mr. Acton looked disturbed.

Jack opened his lips to speak, but shut them again, and stood looking down with a little quiver about the mouth that showed how much it cost him to be silent.

"Does anyone beside Jerry know of this?"

"One other fellow," after a pause.

"Yes, I understand;" and Mr. Acton's eye glanced at Joe with a look that seemed to say, "I wish he'd held his tongue."

A queer smile flitted over Jack's face, for Joe was not the "other fellow," and knew very little about it, excepting what he had seen when he was sent on an errand by Mr. Acton on Friday.

"I wish you would explain the matter, John, for I am sure it is better than it seems, and it would be very hard to punish you when you don't deserve it."

"But I do deserve it; I've broken the rule, and I ought to be punished," said Jack, as if a good whipping would be easier to bear than this public cross-examination.

"And you can't explain, or even say you are sorry or ashamed?" asked Mr. Acton, hoping to surprise another fact out of the boy.

"No, sir; I can't; I'm not ashamed; I'm not sorry, and I'd do it again to-morrow if I had to," cried Jack, losing patience, and looking as if he would not bear much more.

A groan from the boys greeted this bare-faced declaration, and Susy quite shivered at the idea of having taken two bites out of the apple of such a hardened desperado.

"Think it over till to-morrow, and perhaps you will change your mind. Remember that this is the last week of the month, and reports are given out next Friday," said Mr. Acton, knowing how much the boy prided himself on always having good ones to show his mother.

Poor Jack turned scarlet and bit his lips to keep them still, for he had forgotten this when he plunged into the affair which was likely to cost him dear. Then the color faded away, the boyish face grew steady, and the honest eyes looked up at his teacher as he said very low, but all heard him, the room was so still,

"It isn't as bad as it looks, sir, but I can't say any more. No one is to blame but me; and I couldn't help breaking the rule, for Jerry was going away, I had only that time, and I'd promised to pay up, so I did."

Mr. Acton believed every word he said, and regretted that they had not been able to have it out privately, but he, too, must keep his promise and punish the offender, whoever he was.

"Very well, you will lose your recess for a week, and this month's report will be the first one in which behavior does not get the highest mark. You may go; and I wish it understood that Master Minot is not to be troubled with questions till he chooses to set this matter right."

Then the bell rang, the children trooped out, Mr. Acton went off without another word, and Jack was left alone to put up his books and hide a few tears that would come because Frank turned his eyes away from the imploring look cast upon him as the culprit came down from the platform, a disgraced boy.

Elder brothers are apt to be a little hard on younger ones, so it is not surprising that Frank, who was an eminently proper boy, was much cut up when Jack publicly confessed to dealings with Jerry, leaving it to be supposed that the worst half of the story remained untold. He felt it his duty, therefore, to collar poor Jack when he came out, and talk to him all the way home, like a judge bent on getting at the truth by main force. A kind word would have been very comforting, but the scolding was too much for Jack's temper, so he turned dogged and would not say a word, though Frank threatened not to speak to him for a week.

At tea-time both boys were very silent, one looking grim, the other excited. Frank stared sternly at his brother across the table, and no amount of marmalade sweetened or softened that reproachful look. Jack defiantly crunched his toast, with occasional slashes at the butter, as if he must vent the pent-up emotions which half distracted him. Of course, their mother saw that something was amiss, but did not allude to it, hoping that the cloud would blow over as so many did if left alone. But this one did not, and when both refused cake, this sure sign of unusual perturbation made her anxious to know the cause. As soon as tea was over, Jack retired with gloomy dignity to his own room, and Frank, casting away the paper he had been pretending to read, burst out with the whole story. Mrs. Minot was as much surprised as he, but not angry, because, like most mothers, she was sure that her sons could not do anything very bad.

"I will speak to him; my boy won't refuse to give me some explanation," she said, when Frank had freed his mind with as much warmth as if Jack had broken all the ten commandments.

"He will. You often call me obstinate, but he is as pig-headed as a mule; Joe only knows what he saw, old tell-tale! and Jerry has left town, or I'd have it out of him. Make Jack own up, whether he can or not. Little donkey!" stormed Frank, who hated rowdies and could not forgive his brother for being seen with one.

"My dear, all boys do foolish things sometimes, even the Wisest and best behaved, so don't be hard on the poor child. He has got into trouble, I've no doubt, but it cannot be very bad, and he earned the money to pay for his prank, whatever it was."

Mrs. Minot left the room as she spoke, and Frank cooled down as if her words had been a shower-bath, for he remembered his own costly escapade, and how kindly both his mother and Jack had stood by him on that trying occasion. So, feeling rather remorseful, he went off to talk it over with Gus, leaving Jill in a fever of curiosity, for Merry and Molly had dropped in on their way home to break the blow to her, and Frank declined to discuss it with her, after mildly stating that Jack was "a ninny," in his opinion.

"Well, I know one thing," said Jill confidentially to Snow-ball, when they were left alone together, "if everyone else is scolding him I won't say a word. It's so mean to crow over people when they are down, and I'm sure he hasn't done anything to be ashamed of, though he won't tell."

Snow-ball seemed to agree to this, for he went and sat down by Jack's slippers waiting for him on the hearth, and Jill thought that a very touching proof of affectionate fidelity to the little master who ruled them both.

When he came, it was evident that he had found it harder to refuse his mother than all the rest. But she trusted him in spite of appearances, and that was such a comfort! For poor Jack's heart was very full, and he longed to tell the whole story, but he would not break his promise, and so kept silence bravely. Jill asked no questions, affecting to be anxious for the games they always played together in the evening, but while they played, though the lips were sealed, the bright eyes said as plainly as words, "I trust you," and Jack was very grateful.

It was well he had something to cheer him up at home, for he got little peace at school. He bore the grave looks of Mr. Acton meekly, took the boys' jokes good-naturedly, and withstood the artful teasing of the girls with patient silence. But it was very hard for the social, affectionate fellow to bear the general distrust, for he had been such a favorite he felt the change keenly.

But the thing that tried him most was the knowledge that his report would not be what it usually was. It was always a happy moment when he showed it to his mother, and saw her eye brighten as it fell on the 99 or 100, for she cared more for good behavior than for perfect lessons. Mr. Acton once said that Frank Minot's moral influence in the school was unusual, and Jack never forgot her pride and delight as she told them what Frank himself had not known till then. It was Jack's ambition to have the same said of him, for he was not much of a scholar, and he had tried hard since he went back to school to get good records in that respect at least. Now here was a dreadful downfall, tardy marks, bad company, broken rules, and something too wrong to tell, apparently.

"Well, I deserve a good report, and that's a comfort, though nobody believes it," he said to himself, trying to keep up his spirits, as the slow week went by, and no word from him had cleared up the mystery.

Lesson 115

1. Read chapter 14 of *Jack and Jill*.
2. Tell someone a summary of this chapter.

Chapter 14. And Jill Finds It Out

Jill worried about it more than he did, for she was a faithful little friend, and it was a great trial to have Jack even suspected of doing anything wrong. School is a child's world while he is there, and its small affairs are very important to him, so Jill felt that the one thing to be done was to clear away the cloud about her dear boy, and restore him to public favor.

"Ed will be here Saturday night and maybe he will find out, for Jack tells him everything. I do hate to have him hectored so, for I know he is, though he's too proud to complain," she said, on Thursday evening, when Frank told her some joke played upon his brother that day.

"I let him alone, but I see that he isn't badgered too much. That's all I can do. If Ed had only come home last Saturday it might have done some good, but now it will be too late; for the reports are given out to-morrow, you know," answered Frank, feeling a little jealous of Ed's influence over Jack, though his own would have been as great if he had been as gentle.

"Has Jerry come back?" asked Jill, who kept all her questions for Frank, because she seldom alluded to the tender subject when with Jack.

"No, he's off for the summer. Got a place somewhere. Hope he'll stay there and let Bob alone."

"Where is Bob now? I don't hear much about him lately," said Jill, who was constantly on the lookout for "the other fellow," since it was not Joe.

"Oh, he went to Captain Skinner's the first of March, chores round, and goes to school up there. Captain is strict, and won't let Bob come to town, except Sundays; but he don't mind it much, for he likes horses, has nice grub, and the Hill fellows are good chaps for him to be with. So he's all right, if he only behaves."

"How far is it to Captain Skinner's?" asked Jill suddenly, having listened, with her sharp eyes on Frank, as he tinkered away at his model, since he was forbidden all other indulgence in his beloved pastime.

"It's four miles to Hill District, but the Captain lives this side of the school-house. About three from here, I should say."

"How long would it take a boy to walk up there?" went on the questioner, with a new idea in her head.

"Depends on how much of a walkist he is."

"Suppose he was lame and it was sloshy, and he made a call and came back. How long would that take?" asked Jill impatiently.

"Well, in that case, I should say two or three hours. But it's impossible to tell exactly, unless you know how lame the fellow was, and how long a call he made," said Frank, who liked to be accurate.

"Jack couldn't do it in less, could he?"

"He used to run up that hilly road for a breather, and think nothing of it. It would be a long job for him now, poor little chap, for his leg often troubles him, though he hates to own it."

Jill lay back and laughed, a happy little laugh, as if she was pleased about something, and Frank looked over his shoulder to ask questions in his turn.

"What are you laughing at?"

"Can't tell."

"Why do you want to know about Hill District? Are you going there?"

"Wish I could! I'd soon have it out of him."

"Who?"

"Never mind. Please push up my table. I must write a letter, and I want you to post it for me to-night, and never say a word till I give you leave.

"Oh, now you are going to have secrets and be mysterious, and get into a mess, are you?" and Frank looked down at her with a suspicious air, though he was intensely curious to know what she was about.

"Go away till I'm done. You will have to see the outside, but you can't know the inside till the answer comes;" and propping herself up, Jill wrote the following note, with some hesitation at the beginning and end, for she did not know the gentleman she was addressing, except by sight, and it was rather awkward:

"Robert Walker"

"Dear Sir, I want to ask if Jack Minot came to see you last Friday afternoon. He got into trouble being seen with Jerry Shannon. He paid him some money. Jack won't tell, and Mr. Acton talked to him about it before all the school. We feel bad, because we think Jack did not do wrong. I don't know as you have anything to do with it, but I thought I'd ask. Please answer quick. Respectfully yours,

"Jane Pecq"

To make sure that her despatch was not tampered with, Jill put a great splash of red sealing-wax on it, which gave it a very official look, and much impressed Bob when he received it.

"There! Go and post it, and don't let anyone see or know about it," she said, handing it over to Frank, who left his work with unusual alacrity to do her errand. When his eye fell on the address, he laughed, and said in a teasing way,

"Are you and Bob such good friends that you correspond? What will Jack say?"

"Don't know, and don't care! Be good, now, and let's have a little secret as well as other folks. I'll tell you all about it when he answers," said Jill in her most coaxing tone.

"Suppose he doesn't?"

"Then I shall send you up to see him. I must know something, and I want to do it myself, if I can."

"Look here; what are you after? I do believe you think----" Frank got no farther, for Jill gave a little scream, and stopped him by crying eagerly, "Don't say it out loud! I really do believe it may be, and I'm going to find out."

"What made you think of him?" and Frank looked thoughtfully at the letter, as if turning carefully over in his mind the idea that Jill's quick wits had jumped at.

"Come here and I'll tell you."

Holding him by one button, she whispered something in his ear that made him exclaim, with a look at the rug,

"No! did he? I declare I shouldn't wonder! It would be just like the dear old blunder-head."

"I never thought of it till you told me where Bob was, and then it all sort of burst upon me in one minute!" cried Jill, waving her arms about to express the intellectual explosion which had thrown light upon the mystery, like sky-rockets in a dark night.

"You are as bright as a button. No time to lose; I'm off;" and off he was, splashing through the mud to post the letter, on the back of which he added, to make the thing sure, "Hurry up. F. M."

Both felt rather guilty next day, but enjoyed themselves very much nevertheless, and kept chuckling over the mine they were making under Jack's unconscious feet. They hardly expected an answer at noon, as the Hill people were not very eager for their mail, but at night Jill was sure of a letter, and to her great delight it came. Jack brought it himself, which added to the fun, and while she eagerly read it he sat calmly poring over the latest number of his own private and particular "Youth's Companion."

Bob was not a "complete letter-writer" by any means, and with great labor and much ink had produced the following brief but highly satisfactory epistle. Not knowing how to address his fair correspondent he let it alone, and went at once to the point in the frankest possible way:

> Jack did come up Friday. Sorry he got into a mess. It was real kind of him, and I shall pay him back soon. Jack paid Jerry for me and I made him promise not to tell. Jerry said he'd come here and make a row if I didn't cash up. I was afraid I'd lose the place if he did, for the Capt. is awful strict. If Jack don't tell now, I will. I ain't mean. Glad you wrote.
>
> R. O. W.

"Hurrah!" cried Jill, waving the letter over her head in great triumph. "Call everybody and read it out," she added, as Frank snatched it, and ran for his mother, seeing at a glance that the news was good. Jill was so afraid she should tell before the others came that she burst out singing "Pretty Bobby Shafto" at the top of her voice, to Jack's great disgust, for he considered the song very personal, as he was rather fond of "combing down his yellow hair," and Jill often plagued him by singing it when he came in with the golden quiris very smooth and nice to hide the scar on his forehead.

In about five minutes the door flew open and in came Mamma, making straight for bewildered Jack, who thought the family had gone crazy when his parent caught him in her arms, saying tenderly,

"My good, generous boy! I knew he was right all the time!" while Frank worked his hand up and down like a pump-handle, exclaiming heartily,

"You're a trump, sir, and I'm proud of you!" Jill meantime calling out, in wild delight,

"I told you so! I told you so! I did find out; ha, ha, I did!"

"Come, I say! What's the matter? I'm all right. Don't squeeze the breath out of me, please," expostulated Jack, looking so startled and innocent, as he struggled feebly, that they all laughed, and this plaintive protest caused him to be released. But the next proceeding did not enlighten him much, for Frank kept waving a very inky paper before him and ordering him to read it, while Mamma made a charge at Jill, as if it was absolutely necessary to hug somebody.

"Hullo!" said Jack, when he got the letter into his own hand and read it. "Now who put Bob up to this? Nobody had any business to interfere--but it's mighty good of him, anyway," he added, as the anxious lines in his round face smoothed themselves away, while a smile of relief told how hard it had been for him to keep his word.

"I did!" cried Jill, clapping her hands, and looking so happy that he could not have scolded her if he had wanted to.

"Who told you he was in the scrape?" demanded Jack, in a hurry to know all about it now the seal was taken off his own lips.

"You did;" and Jill's face twinkled with naughty satisfaction, for this was the best fun of all.

"I didn't! When? Where? It's a joke!"

"You did," cried Jill, pointing to the rug. "You went to sleep there after the long walk, and talked in your sleep about 'Bob' and 'All right, old boy,' and ever so much gibberish. I didn't think about it then, but when I heard that Bob was up there I thought maybe he knew something about it, and last night I wrote and asked him, and that's the answer, and now it is all right, and you are the best boy that ever was, and I'm so glad!"

Here Jill paused, all out of breath, and Frank said, with an approving pat on the head,

"It won't do to have such a sharp young person round if we are going to have secrets. You'd make a good detective, miss."

"Catch me taking naps before people again;" and Jack looked rather crestfallen that his own words had set "Fine Ear" on the track. "Never mind, I didn't mean to tell, though I just ached to do it all the time, so I haven't broken my word. I'm glad you all know, but you needn't let it get out, for Bob is a good fellow, and it might make trouble for him," added Jack, anxious lest his gain should be the other's loss.

"I shall tell Mr. Acton myself, and the Captain, also, for I'm not going to have my son suspected of wrong-doing when he has only tried to help a friend, and borne enough for his sake," said Mamma, much excited by this discovery of generous fidelity in her boy; though when one came to look at it calmly, one saw that it might have been done in a wiser way.

"Now, please, don't make a fuss about it; that would be most as bad as having everyone down on me. I can stand your praising me, but I won't be patted on the head by anybody else;" and Jack assumed a manly air, though his face was full of genuine boyish pleasure at being set right in the eyes of those he loved.

"I'll be discreet, dear, but you owe it to yourself, as well as Bob, to have the truth known. Both have behaved well, and no harm will come to him, I am sure. I'll see to that myself," said Mrs. Minot, in a tone that set Jack's mind at rest on that point.

"Now do tell all about it," cried Jill, who was pining to know the whole story, and felt as if she had earned the right to hear it.

"Oh, it wasn't much. We promised Ed to stand by Bob, so I did as well as I knew how;" and Jack seemed to think that was about all there was to say.

"I never saw such a fellow for keeping a promise! You stick to it through thick and thin, no matter how silly or hard it is. You remember, mother, last summer, how you told him not to go in a boat and he promised, the day we went on the picnic. We rode up, but the horse ran off home, so we had to come back by way of the river, all but Jack, and he walked every step of five miles because he wouldn't go near a boat, though Mr. Burton was there to take care of him. I call that rather overdoing the matter;" and Frank looked as if he thought moderation even in virtue a good thing.

"And I call it a fine sample of entire obedience. He obeyed orders, and that is what we all must do, without always seeing why, or daring to use our own judgment. It is a great safeguard to Jack, and a very great comfort to me; for I know that if he promises he will keep his word, no matter what it costs him," said Mamma warmly, as she tumbled up the quirls with an irrepressible caress, remembering how the boy came wearily in after all the others, without seeming for a moment to think that he could have done anything else.

"Like Casablanca!" cried Jill, much impressed, for obedience was her hardest trial.

"I think he was a fool to burn up," said Frank, bound not to give in.

"I don't. It's a splendid piece, and everyone likes to speak it, and it was true, and it wouldn't be in all the books if he was a fool. Grown people know what is good," declared Jill, who liked heroic actions, and was always hoping for a chance to distinguish herself in that way.

"You admire 'The Charge of the Light Brigade,' and glow all over as you thunder it out. Yet they went gallantly to their death rather than disobey orders. A mistake, perhaps, but it makes us thrill to hear of it; and the same spirit keeps my Jack true as steel when once his word is passed, or he thinks it is his duty. Don't be laughed out of it, my son, for faithfulness in little things fits one for heroism when the great trials come. One's conscience can hardly be too tender when honor and honesty are concerned."

"You are right, mother, and I am wrong. I beg your pardon, Jack, and you sha'n't get ahead of me next time."

Frank made his mother a little bow, gave his brother a shake of the hand, and nodded to Jill, as if anxious to show that he was not too proud to own up when he made a mistake.

"Please tell on, Jack. This is very nice, but I do want to know all about the other," said Jill, after a short pause.

"Let me see. Oh, I saw Bob at church, and he looked rather blue; so, after Sunday School, I asked what the matter was. He said Jerry bothered him for some money he lent him at different times when they were loafing round together, before we took him up. He wouldn't get any wages for some time. The Captain keeps him short on purpose, I guess, and won't let him come down town except on Sundays. He didn't want anyone to know about it, for fear he'd lose his place. So I promised I wouldn't tell. Then I was afraid Jerry would go and make a fuss, and Bob would run off, or do something desperate, being worried, and I said I'd pay it for him, if I could. So he went home pretty jolly, and I scratched 'round for the money. Got it, too, and wasn't I glad?"

Jack paused to rub his hands, and Frank said, with more than usual respect,

"Couldn't you get hold of Jerry in any other place, and out of school time? That did the mischief, thanks to Joe. I thrashed him, Jill--did I mention it?"

"I couldn't get all my money till Friday morning, and I knew Jerry was off at night. I looked for him before school, and at noon, but couldn't find him, so afternoon recess was my last chance. I was bound to do it and I didn't mean to break the rule, but Jerry was just going into the shop, so I pelted after him, and as it was private business we went to the billiard-room. I declare I never was so relieved as when I handed over that money, and made him say it was all right, and he wouldn't go near Bob. He's off, so my mind is easy, and Bob will be so grateful I can keep him steady, perhaps. That will be worth two seventy-five, I think," said Jack heartily.

"You should have come to me," began Frank.

"And got laughed at--no, thank you," interrupted Jack, recollecting several philanthropic little enterprises which were nipped in the bud for want of co-operation.

"To me, then," said his mother. "It would have saved so much trouble."

"I thought of it, but Bob didn't want the big fellows to know for fear they'd be down on him, so I thought he might not like me to tell grown people. I don't mind the fuss now, and Bob is as kind as he can be. Wanted to give me his big knife, but I wouldn't take it. I'd rather have this," and Jack put the letter in his pocket with a slap outside, as if it warmed the cockles of his heart to have it there.

"Well, it seems rather like a tempest in a teapot, now it is all over, but I do admire your pluck, little boy, in holding out so well when everyone was scolding at you, and you in the right all the time," said Frank, glad to praise, now that he honestly could, after his wholesale condemnation.

"That is what pulled me through, I suppose. I used to think if I had done anything wrong, that I couldn't stand the snubbing a day. I should have told right off, and had it over. Now, I guess I'll have a good report if you do tell Mr. Acton," said Jack, looking at his mother so wistfully, that she resolved to slip away that very evening, and make sure that the thing was done.

"That will make you happier than anything else, won't it?" asked Jill, eager to have him rewarded after his trials.

"There's one thing I like better, though I'd be very sorry to lose my report. It's the fun of telling Ed I tried to do as he wanted us to, and seeing how pleased he'll be," added Jack, rather bashfully, for the boys laughed at him sometimes for his love of this friend.

"I know he won't be any happier about it than someone else, who stood by you all through, and set her bright wits to work till the trouble was all cleared away," said Mrs. Minot, looking at Jill's contented face, as she lay smiling on them all.

Jack understood, and, hopping across the room, gave both the thin hands a hearty shake; then, not finding any words quite cordial enough in which to thank this faithful little sister, he stooped down and kissed her gratefully.

Lesson 116

1. Read chapter 15 of *Jack and Jill*.
2. Tell someone what happened in the chapter.

Chapter 15. Saint Lucy

Saturday was a busy and a happy time to Jack, for in the morning Mr. Acton came to see him, having heard the story overnight, and promised to keep Bob's secret while giving Jack an acquittal as public as the reprimand had been. Then he asked for the report which Jack had bravely received the day before and put away without showing to anybody.

"There is one mistake here which we must rectify," said Mr. Acton, as he crossed out the low figures under the word "Behavior," and put the much-desired 100 there.

"But I did break the rule, sir," said Jack, though his face glowed with pleasure, for Mamma was looking on.

"I overlook that as I should your breaking into my house if you saw it was on fire. You ran to save a friend, and I wish I could tell those fellows why you were there. It would do them good. I am not going to praise you, John, but I did believe you in spite of appearances, and I am glad to have for a pupil a boy who loves his neighbor better than himself."

Then, having shaken hands heartily, Mr. Acton went away, and Jack flew off to have rejoicings with Jill, who sat up on her sofa, without knowing it, so eager was she to hear all about the call.

In the afternoon Jack drove his mother to the Captain's, confiding to her on the way what a hard time he had when he went before, and how nothing but the thought of cheering Bob kept him up when he slipped and hurt his knee, and his boot sprung a leak, and the wind came up very cold, and the hill seemed an endless mountain of mud and snow.

Mrs. Minot had such a gentle way of putting things that she would have won over a much harder man than the strict old Captain, who heard the story with interest, and was much pleased with the boys' efforts to keep Bob straight. That young person dodged away into the barn with Jack, and only appeared at the last minute to shove a bag of chestnuts into the chaise. But he got a few kind words that did him good, from Mrs. Minot and the Captain, and from that day felt himself under bonds to behave well if he would keep their confidence.

"I shall give Jill the nuts; and I wish I had something she wanted very, very much, for I do think she ought to be rewarded for getting me out of the mess," said Jack, as they drove happily home again.

"I hope to have something in a day or two that will delight her very much. I will say no more now, but keep my little secret and let it be a surprise to all by and by," answered his mother, looking as if she had not much doubt about the matter.

"That will be jolly. You are welcome to your secret, Mamma. I've had enough of them for one while;" and Jack shrugged his broad shoulders as if a burden had been taken off.

In the evening Ed came, and Jack was quite satisfied when he saw how pleased his friend was at what he had done.

"I never meant you should take so much trouble, only be kind to Bob," said Ed, who did not know how strong his influence was, nor what a sweet example of quiet well-doing his own life was to all his mates.

"I wished to be really useful; not just to talk about it and do nothing. That isn't your way, and I want to be like you," answered Jack, with such affectionate sincerity that Ed could not help believing him, though he modestly declined the compliment by saying, as he began to play softly, "Better than I am, I hope. I don't amount to much."

"Yes, you do! and if anyone says you don't I'll shake him. I can't tell what it is, only you always look so happy and contented--sort of sweet and shiny," said Jack, as he stroked the smooth brown head, rather at a loss to describe the unusually fresh and sunny expression of Ed's face, which was always cheerful, yet had a certain thoughtfulness that made it very attractive to both young and old.

"Soap makes him shiny; I never saw such a fellow to wash and brush," put in Frank, as he came up with one of the pieces of music he and Ed were fond of practising together.

"I don't mean that!" said Jack indignantly. "I wash and brush till you call me a dandy, but I don't have the same look--it seems to come from the inside, somehow, as if he was always jolly and clean and good in his mind, you know."

"Born so," said Frank, rumbling away in the bass with a pair of hands that would have been the better for some of the above-mentioned soap, for he did not love to do much in the washing and brushing line.

"I suppose that's it. Well, I like it, and I shall keep on trying, for being loved by everyone is about the nicest thing in the world. Isn't it, Ed?" asked Jack, with a gentle tweak of the ear as he put a question which he knew would get no answer, for Ed was so modest he could not see wherein he differed from other boys, nor believe that the sunshine he saw in other faces was only the reflection from his own.

Sunday evening Mrs. Minot sat by the fire, planning how she should tell some good news she had been saving up all day. Mrs. Pecq knew it, and seemed so delighted that she went about smiling as if she did not know what trouble meant, and could not do enough for the family. She was downstairs now, seeing that the clothes were properly prepared for the wash, so there was no one in the Bird

Room but Mamma and the children. Frank was reading up all he could find about some Biblical hero mentioned in the day's sermon; Jill lay where she had lain for nearly four long months, and though her face was pale and thin with the confinement, there was an expression on it now sweeter even than health. Jack sat on the rug beside her, looking at a white carnation through the magnifying glass, while she was enjoying the perfume of a red one as she talked to him.

"If you look at the white petals you'll see that they sparkle like marble, and go winding a long way down to the middle of the flower where it grows sort of rosy; and in among the small, curly leaves, like fringed curtains, you can see the little green fairy sitting all alone. Your mother showed me that, and I think it is very pretty. I call it a 'fairy,' but it is really where the seeds are hidden and the sweet smell comes from."

Jill spoke softly lest she should disturb the others, and, as she turned to push up her pillow, she saw Mrs. Minot looking at her with a smile she did not understand.

"Did you speak, 'm?" she asked, smiling back again, without in the least knowing why.

"No, dear. I was listening and thinking what a pretty little story one could make out of your fairy living alone down there, and only known by her perfume."

"Tell it, Mamma. It is time for our story, and that would be a nice one, I guess," said Jack, who was as fond of stories as when he sat in his mother's lap and chuckled over the hero of the beanstalk.

"We don't have fairy tales on Sunday, you know," began Jill regretfully.

"Call it a parable, and have a moral to it, then it will be all right," put in Frank, as he shut his big book, having found what he wanted.

"I like stories about saints, and the good and wonderful things they did," said Jill, who enjoyed the wise and interesting bits Mrs. Minot often found for her in grown-up books, for Jill had thoughtful times, and asked questions which showed that she was growing fast in mind if not in body.

"This is a true story; but I will disguise it a little, and call it 'The Miracle of Saint Lucy,'" began Mrs. Minot, seeing a way to tell her good news and amuse the children likewise.

Frank retired to the easy-chair, that he might sleep if the tale should prove too childish for him. Jill settled herself among her cushions, and Jack lay flat upon the rug, with his feet up, so that he could admire his red slippers and rest his knee, which ached.

"Once upon a time there was a queen who had two princes."

"Wasn't there a princess?" asked Jack, interested at once.

"No; and it was a great sorrow to the queen that she had no little daughter, for the sons were growing up, and she was often very lonely.

"Like Snowdrop's mother," whispered Jill.

"Now, don't keep interrupting, children, or we never shall get on," said Frank, more anxious to hear about the boys that were than the girl that was not.

"One day, when the princes were out--ahem! we'll say hunting--they found a little damsel lying on the snow, half dead with cold, they thought. She was the child of a poor woman who lived in the forest--a wild little thing, always dancing and singing about; as hard to catch as a squirrel, and so fearless she would climb the highest trees, leap broad brooks, or jump off the steep rocks to show her courage. The boys carried her home to the palace, and the queen was glad to have her. She had fallen and hurt herself, so she lay in bed week after week, with her mother to take care of her--"

"That's you," whispered Jack, throwing the white carnation at Jill, and she threw back the red one, with her finger on her lips, for the tale was very interesting now.

"She did not suffer much after a time, but she scolded and cried, and could not be resigned, because she was a prisoner. The queen tried to help her, but she could not do much; the princes were kind, but they had their books and plays, and were away a good deal. Some friends she had came often to see her, but still she beat her wings against the bars, like a wild bird in a cage, and soon her spirits were all gone, and it was sad to see her."

"Where was your Saint Lucy? I thought it was about her," asked Jack, who did not like to have Jill's past troubles dwelt upon, since his were not.

"She is coming. Saints are not born--they are made after many trials and tribulations," answered his mother, looking at the fire as if it helped her to spin her little story. "Well, the poor child used to sing sometimes to while away the long hours--sad songs mostly, and one among them which the queen taught her was 'Sweet Patience, Come.'

"This she used to sing a great deal after a while, never dreaming that Patience was an angel who could hear and obey. But it was so; and one night, when the girl had lulled herself to sleep with that song, the angel came. Nobody saw the lovely spirit with tender eyes, and a voice that was like balm. No one heard the rustle of wings as she hovered over the little bed and touched the lips, the eyes, the hands of the sleeper, and then flew away, leaving three gifts behind. The girl did not know why, but after that night the songs grew gayer, there seemed to be more sunshine everywhere her eyes looked, and her hands were never tired of helping others in various pretty, useful, or pleasant ways. Slowly the wild bird ceased to beat against the bars, but sat in its cage and made music for all in the palace, till the queen could not do without it, the poor mother cheered up, and the princes called the girl their nightingale."

"Was that the miracle?" asked Jack, forgetting all about his slippers, as he watched Jill's eyes brighten and the color come up in her white cheeks.

"That was the miracle, and Patience can work far greater ones if you will let her."

"And the girl's name was Lucy?"

"Yes; they did not call her a saint then, but she was trying to be as cheerful as a certain good woman she had heard of, and so the queen had that name for her, though she did not let her know it for a long time."

"That's not bad for a Sunday story, but there might have been more about the princes, seems to me," was Frank's criticism, as Jill lay very still, trying to hide her face behind the carnation, for she had no words to tell how touched and pleased she was to find that her little efforts to be good had been seen, remembered, and now rewarded in this way.

There is more.

"Then the story isn't done?" cried Jack.

"Oh dear, no; the most interesting things are to come, if you can wait for them."

"Yes, I see, this is the moral part. Now keep still, and let us have the rest," commanded Frank, while the others composed themselves for the sequel, suspecting that it was rather nice, because Mamma's sober face changed, and her eyes laughed as they looked at the fire.

"The elder prince was very fond of driving dragons, for the people of that country used these fiery monsters as horses."

"And got run away with, didn't he?" laughed Jack, adding, with great interest, "What did the other fellow do?"

"He went about fighting other people's battles, helping the poor, and trying to do good. But he lacked judgment, so he often got into trouble, and was in such a hurry that he did not always stop to find out the wisest way. As when he gave away his best coat to a beggar boy, instead of the old one which he intended to give."

"I say, that isn't fair, mother! Neither of them was new, and the boy needed the best more than I did, and I wore the old one all winter, didn't I?" asked Jack, who had rather exulted over Frank, and was now taken down himself.

"Yes, you did, my dear; and it was not an easy thing for my dandiprat to do. Now listen, and I'll tell you how they both learned to be wiser. The elder prince soon found that the big dragons were too much for him, and set about training his own little one, who now and then ran away with him. Its name was Will, a good servant, but a bad master; so he learned to control it, and in time this gave him great power over himself, and fitted him to be a king over others."

"Thank you, mother; I'll remember my part of the moral. Now give Jack his," said Frank, who liked the dragon episode, as he had been wrestling with his own of late, and found it hard to manage.

"He had a fine example before him in a friend, and he followed it more reasonably till he grew able to use wisely one of the best and noblest gifts of God--benevolence."

"Now tell about the girl. Was there more to that part of the story?" asked Jack, well pleased with his moral, as it took Ed in likewise.

"That is the best of all, but it seems as if I never should get to it. After Patience made Lucy sweet and cheerful, she began to have a curious power over those about her, and to work little miracles herself, though she did not know it. The queen learned to love her so dearly she could not let her go; she cheered up all her friends when they came with their small troubles; the princes found bright eyes, willing hands, and a kind heart always at their service, and felt, without quite knowing why, that it was good for them to have a gentle little creature to care for; so they softened their rough manners, loud voices, and careless ways, for her sake, and when it was proposed to take her away to her own home they could not give her up, but said she must stay longer, didn't they?"

"I'd like to see them saying anything else," said Frank, while Jack sat up to demand fiercely,

"Who talks about taking Jill away?"

"Lucy's mother thought she ought to go, and said so, but the queen told her how much good it did them all to have her there, and begged the dear woman to let her little cottage and come and be housekeeper in the palace, for the queen was getting lazy, and liked to sit and read, and talk and sew with Lucy, better than to look after things."

"And she said she would?" cried Jill, clasping her hands in her anxiety, for she had learned to love her cage now.

"Yes." Mrs. Minot had no time to say more, for one of the red slippers flew up in the air, and Jack had to clap both hands over his mouth to suppress the "hurrah!" that nearly escaped. Frank said, "That's good!" and nodded with his most cordial smile at Jill who pulled herself up with cheeks now as rosy as the red carnation, and a little catch in her breath as she said to herself,

"It's too lovely to be true."

"That's a first-rate end to a very good story," began Jack, with grave decision, as he put on his slipper and sat up to pat Jill's hand, wishing it was not quite so like a little claw.

"That's not the end;" and Mamma's eyes laughed more than ever as three astonished faces turned to her, and three voices cried out,

"Still more?"

"The very best of all. You must know that, while Lucy was busy for others, she was not forgotten, and when she was expecting to lie on her bed through the summer, plans were being made for all sorts of pleasant changes. First of all, she was to have a nice little brace to support the back which was growing better every day; then, as the warm weather came on, she was to go out, or lie on the piazza; and by and by, when school was done, she was to go with the queen and the princes for a month or two down to the sea-side, where fresh air and salt water were to build her up in the most delightful way. There, now! isn't that the best ending of all?" and Mamma paused to read her answer in the bright faces of two of the listeners, for Jill hid hers in the pillow, and lay quite still, as if it was too much for her.

"That will be regularly splendid! I'll row you all about--boating is so much easier than riding, and I like it on salt water," said Frank, going to sit on the arm of the sofa, quite excited by the charms of the new plan.

"And I'll teach you to swim, and roll you over the beach, and get sea-weed and shells, and no end of nice things, and we'll all come home as strong as lions," added Jack, scrambling up as if about to set off at once.

"The doctor says you have been doing finely of late, and the brace will come to-morrow, and the first really mild day you are to have a breath of fresh air. Won't that be good?" asked Mrs. Minot, hoping her story had not been too interesting.

"Is she crying?" said Jack, much concerned as he patted the pillow in his most soothing way, while Frank lifted one curl after another to see what was hidden underneath.

Not tears, for two eyes sparkled behind the fingers, then the hands came down like clouds from before the sun, and Jill's face shone out so bright and happy it did one's heart good to see it.

"I'm not crying," she said with a laugh which was fuller of blithe music than any song she sung. "But it was so splendid, it sort of took my breath away for a minute. I thought I wasn't any better, and never should be, and I made up my mind I wouldn't ask, it would be so hard for anyone to tell me so. Now I see why the doctor made me stand up, and told me to get my baskets ready to go a-Maying. I thought he was in fun; did he really mean I could go?" asked Jill, expecting too much, for a word of encouragement made her as hopeful as she had been despondent before.

"No, dear, not so soon as that. It will be months, probably, before you can walk and run, as you used to; but they will soon pass. You needn't mind about May-day; it is always too cold for flowers, and you will find more here among your own plants, than on the hills, to fill your baskets," answered Mrs. Minot, hastening to suggest something pleasant to beguile the time of probation.

"I can wait. Months are not years, and if I'm truly getting well, everything will seem beautiful and easy to me," said Jill, laying herself down again, with the patient look she had learned to wear, and gathering up the scattered carnations to enjoy their spicy breath, as if the fairies hidden there had taught her some of their sweet secrets.

"Dear little girl, it has been a long, hard trial for you, but it is coming to an end, and I think you will find that it has not been time wasted, I don't want you to be a saint quite yet, but I am sure a gentler Jill will rise up from that sofa than the one who lay down there in December."

"How could I help growing better, when you were so good to me?" cried Jill, putting up both arms, as Mrs. Minot went to take Frank's place, and he retired to the fire, there to stand surveying the scene with calm approval.

"You have done quite as much for us; so we are even. I proved that to your mother, and she is going to let the little house and take care of the big one for me, while I borrow you to keep me happy and make the boys gentle and kind. That is the bargain, and we get the best of it," said Mrs. Minot, looking well pleased, while Jack added, "That's so!" and Frank observed with an air of conviction, "We couldn't get on without Jill, possibly."

"Can I do all that? I didn't know I was of any use. I only tried to be good and grateful, for there didn't seem to be anything else I could do," said Jill, wondering why they were all so fond of her.

"No real trying is ever in vain. It is like the spring rain, and flowers are sure to follow in good time. The three gifts Patience gave Saint Lucy were courage, cheerfulness, and love, and with these one can work the sweetest miracles in the world, as you see," and Mrs. Minot pointed to the pretty room and its happy inmates.

"Am I really the least bit like that good Lucinda? I tried to be, but I didn't think I was," asked Jill softly.

"You are very like her in all ways but one. She did not get well, and you will."

A short answer, but it satisfied Jill to her heart's core, and that night, when she lay in bed, she thought to herself: "How curious it is that I've been a sort of missionary without knowing it! They all love and thank me, and won't let me go, so I suppose I must have done something, but I don't know what, except trying to be good and pleasant."

That was the secret, and Jill found it out just when it was most grateful as a reward for past efforts, most helpful as an encouragement toward the constant well-doing which can make even a little girl a joy and comfort to all who know and love her.

Lesson 117

1. Read chapter 16 of *Jack and Jill.*
2. Write a single-sentence summary of this chapter.

Chapter 16. Up at Merry's

"Now fly round, child, and get your sweeping done up smart and early."

"Yes, mother."

"I shall want you to help me about the baking, by and by."

"Yes, mother."

"Roxy is cleaning the cellar-closets, so you'll have to get the vegetables ready for dinner. Father wants a boiled dish, and I shall be so busy I can't see to it."

"Yes, mother."

A cheerful voice gave the three answers, but it cost Merry an effort to keep it so, for she had certain little plans of her own which made the work before her unusually distasteful. Saturday always was a trying day, for, though she liked to see rooms in order, she hated to sweep, as no speck escaped Mrs. Grant's eye, and only the good old-fashioned broom, wielded by a pair of strong arms, was allowed. Baking was another trial: she loved good bread and delicate pastry, but did not enjoy burning her face over a hot stove, daubing her hands with dough, or spending hours rolling out cookies for the boys; while a "boiled dinner" was her especial horror, as it was not elegant, and the washing of vegetables was a job she always shirked when she could.

However, having made up her mind to do her work without complaint, she ran upstairs to put on her dust-cap, trying to look as if sweeping was the joy of her life.

"It is such a lovely day, I did want to rake my garden, and have a walk with Molly, and finish my book so I can get another," she said with a sigh, as she leaned out of the open window for a breath of the unusually mild air.

Down in the ten-acre lot the boys were carting and spreading loam; out in the barn her father was getting his plows ready; over the hill rose the smoke of the distant factory, and the river that turned the wheels was gliding through the meadows, where soon the blackbirds would be singing. Old Bess pawed the ground, eager to be off; the gray hens were scratching busily all about the yard; even the green things in the garden were pushing through the brown earth, softened by April rains, and there was a shimmer of sunshine over the wide landscape that made every familiar object beautiful with hints of spring, and the activity it brings.

Something made the old nursery hymn come into Merry's head, and humming to herself,

> In works of labor or of skill
> I would be busy too,

she tied on her cap, shouldered her broom, and fell to work so energetically that she soon swept her way through the chambers, down the front stairs to the parlor door, leaving freshness and order behind her as she went.

She always groaned when she entered that apartment, and got out of it again as soon as possible, for it was, like most country parlors, a prim and chilly place, with little beauty and no comfort. Black horse-hair furniture, very slippery and hard, stood against the wall; the table had its gift books, albums, worsted mat and ugly lamp; the mantel-piece its china vases, pink shells, and clock that never went; the gay carpet was kept distressingly bright by closed shutters six days out of the seven, and a general air of go-to-meeting solemnity pervaded the room. Merry longed to make it pretty and pleasant, but her mother would allow of no change there, so the girl gave up her dreams of rugs and hangings, fine pictures and tasteful ornaments, and dutifully aired, dusted, and shut up this awful apartment once a week, privately resolving that, if she ever had a parlor of her own, it should not be as dismal as a tomb.

The dining-room was a very different place, for here Merry had been allowed to do as she liked, yet so gradual had been the change, that she would have found it difficult to tell how it came about. It seemed to begin with the flowers, for her father kept his word about the "posy pots," and got enough to make quite a little conservatory in the bay-window, which was sufficiently large for three rows all round, and hanging-baskets overhead. Being discouraged by her first failure, Merry gave up trying to have things nice everywhere, and contented herself with making that one nook so pretty that the boys called it her "bower." Even busy Mrs. Grant owned that plants were not so messy as she expected, and the farmer was never tired of watching "little daughter" as she sat at work there, with her low chair and table full of books.

The lamp helped, also, for Merry set up her own, and kept it so well trimmed that it burned clear and bright, shining on the green arch of ivy overhead, and on the nasturtium vines framing the old glass, and peeping at their gay little faces, and at the pretty young girl, so pleasantly that first her father came to read his paper by it, then her mother slipped in to rest on the lounge in the corner, and finally the boys hovered about the door as if the "settin'-room" had grown more attractive than the kitchen.

But the open fire did more than anything else to win and hold them all, as it seldom fails to do when the black demon of an airtight stove is banished from the hearth. After the room was cleaned till it shone, Merry begged to have the brass andirons put in, and offered to keep them as bright as gold if her mother would consent. So the great logs were kindled, and the flames went dancing up the chimney as if glad to be set free from their prison. It changed the whole room like magic, and no one could resist the desire to enjoy its cheery comfort. The farmer's three-cornered leathern chair soon stood on one side, and mother's rocker on the other, as they toasted their feet and dozed or chatted in the pleasant warmth.

The boys' slippers were always ready on the hearth; and when the big boots were once off, they naturally settled down about the table, where the tall lamp, with its pretty shade of pressed autumn leaves, burned brightly, and the books and papers lay ready to their hands instead of being tucked out of sight in the closet. They were beginning to see that "Merry's notions" had some sense in them, since they were made comfortable, and good-naturedly took some pains to please her in various ways. Tom brushed his hair and washed his hands nicely before he came to table. Dick tried to lower his boisterous laughter, and Harry never smoked in the sitting-room. Even Roxy expressed her pleasure in seeing "things kind of spruced up," and Merry's gentle treatment of the hard-working drudge won her heart entirely.

The girl was thinking of these changes as she watered her flowers, dusted the furniture, and laid the fire ready for kindling; and, when all was done, she stood a minute to enjoy the pleasant room, full of spring sunshine, fresh air, and exquisite order. It seemed to give her heart for more distasteful labors, and she fell to work at the pies as cheerfully as if she liked it.

Mrs. Grant was flying about the kitchen, getting the loaves of brown and white bread ready for the big oven. Roxy's voice came up from the cellar singing "Bounding Billows," with a swashing and scrubbing accompaniment which suggested that she was actually enjoying a "life on the ocean wave." Merry, in her neat cap and apron, stood smiling over her work as she deftly rolled and clipped, filled and covered, finding a certain sort of pleasure in doing it well, and adding interest to it by crimping the crust, making pretty devices with strips of paste and star-shaped prickings of the fork.

"Good-will giveth skill," says the proverb, and even particular Mrs. Grant was satisfied when she paused to examine the pastry with her experienced eye.

"You are a handy child and a credit to your bringing up, though I do say it. Those are as pretty pies as I'd wish to eat, if they bake well, and there's no reason why they shouldn't."

"May I make some tarts or rabbits of these bits? The boys like them, and I enjoy modelling this sort of thing," said Merry, who was trying to mould a bird, as she had seen Ralph do with clay to amuse Jill while the bust was going on.

"No, dear; there's no time for knick-knacks to-day. The beets ought to be on this minute. Run and get 'em, and be sure you scrape the carrots well."

Poor Merry put away the delicate task she was just beginning to like, and taking a pan went down cellar, wishing vegetables could be grown without earth, for she hated to put her hands in dirty water. A word of praise to Roxy made that grateful scrubber leave her work to poke about in the root-cellar, choosing "sech as was pretty much of a muchness, else they wouldn't bile even;" so Merry was spared that part of the job, and went up to scrape and wash without complaint, since it was for father. She was repaid at noon by the relish with which he enjoyed his dinner, for Merry tried to make even a boiled dish pretty by arranging the beets, carrots, turnips, and potatoes in contrasting colors, with the beef hidden under the cabbage leaves.

"Now, I'll rest and read for an hour, then I'll rake my garden, or run down town to see Molly and get some seeds," she thought to herself, as she put away the spoons and glasses, which she liked to wash, that they might always be clear and bright.

"If you've done all your own mending, there's a heap of socks to be looked over. Then I'll show you about darning the tablecloths. I do hate to have a stitch of work left over till Monday," said Mrs. Grant, who never took naps, and prided herself on sitting down to her needle at 3 P.M. every day.

"Yes, mother;" and Merry went slowly upstairs, feeling that a part of Saturday ought to be a holiday after books and work all the week. As she braided up her hair, her eye fell upon the reflection of her own face in the glass. Not a happy nor a pretty one just then, and Merry was so unaccustomed to seeing any other, that involuntarily the frown smoothed itself out, the eyes lost their weary look, the drooping lips curved into a smile, and, leaning her elbows on the bureau, she shook her head at herself, saying, half aloud, as she glanced at Ivanhoe lying near,

"You needn't look so cross and ugly just because you can't have what you want. Sweeping, baking, and darning are not so bad as being plagued with lovers and carried off and burnt at the stake, so I won't envy poor Rebecca her jewels and curls and romantic times, but make the best of my own."

Then she laughed, and the bright face came back into the mirror, looking like an old friend, and Merry went on dressing with care, for she took pleasure in her own little charms, and felt a sense of comfort in knowing that she could always have one pretty thing to look at if she kept her own face serene and sweet. It certainly looked so as it bent over the pile of big socks half an hour later, and brightened with each that was laid aside. Her mother saw it, and, guessing why such wistful glances went from clock to window, kindly shortened the task of table-cloth darning by doing a good bit herself, before putting it into Merry's hands.

She was a good and loving mother in spite of her strict ways, and knew that it was better for her romantic daughter to be learning all the housewifery lessons she could teach her, than to be reading novels, writing verses, or philandering about with her head full of girlish fancies, quite innocent in themselves, but not the stuff to live on. So she wisely taught the hands that preferred to pick flowers, trim up rooms and mould birds, to work well with needle, broom, and rolling-pin; put a receipt-book before the eyes that loved to laugh and weep over tender tales, and kept the young head and heart safe and happy with wholesome duties, useful studies, and such harmless pleasures as girls should love, instead of letting them waste their freshness in vague longings, idle dreams, and frivolous pastimes.

But it was often hard to thwart the docile child, and lately she had seemed to be growing up so fast that her mother began to feel a new sort of tenderness for this sweet daughter, who was almost ready to take upon herself the cares, as well as triumphs and delights, of maidenhood. Something in the droop of the brown head, and the quick motion of the busy hand with a little burn on it, made it difficult for Mrs. Grant to keep Merry at work that day, and her eye watched the clock almost as impatiently as the girl's, for she liked to see the young face brighten when the hour of release came.

"What next?" asked Merry, as the last stitch was set, and she stifled a sigh on hearing the clock strike four, for the sun was getting low, and the lovely afternoon going fast,

"One more job, if you are not too tired for it. I want the receipt for diet drink Miss Dawes promised me; would you like to run down and get it for me, dear?"

"Yes, mother!" and that answer was as blithe as a robin's chirp, for that was just where Merry wanted to go.

Away went thimble and scissors, and in five minutes away went Merry, skipping down the hill without a care in the world, for a happy heart sat singing within, and everything seemed full of beauty.

She had a capital time with Molly, called on Jill, did her shopping in the village, and had just turned to walk up the hill, when Ralph Evans came tramping along behind her, looking so pleased and proud about something that she could not help asking what it was, for they were great friends, and Merry thought that to be an artist was the most glorious career a man could choose.

"I know you've got some good news," she said, looking up at him as he touched his hat and fell into step with her, seeming more contented than before.

"I have, and was just coming up to tell you, for I was sure you would be glad. It is only a hope, a chance, but it is so splendid I feel as if I must shout and dance, or fly over a fence or two, to let off steam."

"Do tell me, quick; have you got an order?" asked Merry, full of interest at once, for artistic vicissitudes were very romantic, and she liked to hear about them.

"I may go abroad in the autumn."

"Oh, how lovely!"

"Isn't it? David German is going to spend a year in Rome, to finish a statue, and wants me to go along. Grandma is willing, as cousin Maria wants her for a long visit, so everything looks promising and I really think I may go."

"Won't it cost a great deal?" asked Merry, who, in spite of her little elegancies, had a good deal of her thrifty mother's common sense.

"Yes; and I've got to earn it. But I can--I know I can, for I've saved some, and I shall work like ten beavers all summer. I won't borrow if I can help it, but I know someone who would lend me five hundred if I wanted it;" and Ralph looked as eager and secure as if the earning of twice that sum was a mere trifle when all the longing of his life was put into his daily tasks.

"I wish I had it to give you. It must be so splendid to feel that you can do great things if you only have the chance. And to travel, and see all the lovely pictures and statues, and people and places in Italy. How happy you must be!" and Merry's eyes had the wistful look they always wore when she dreamed dreams of the world she loved to live in.

"I am--so happy that I'm afraid it never will happen. If I do go, I'll write and tell you all about the fine sights, and how I get on. Would you like me to?" asked Ralph, beginning enthusiastically and ending rather bashfully, for he admired Merry very much, and was not quite sure how this proposal would be received.

"Indeed I should! I'd feel so grand to have letters from Paris and Rome, and you'd have so much to tell it would be almost as good as going myself," she said, looking off into the daffodil sky, as they paused a minute on the hill-top to get breath, for both had walked as fast as they talked.

"And will you answer the letters?" asked Ralph, watching the innocent face, which looked unusually kind and beautiful to him in that soft light.

'Why, yes; I'd love to, only I shall not have anything interesting to say. What can I write about?" and Merry smiled as she thought how dull her letters would sound after the exciting details his would doubtless give.

"Write about yourself, and all the rest of the people I know. Grandma will be gone, and I shall want to hear how you get on." Ralph looked very anxious indeed to hear, and Merry promised she would tell all about the other people, adding, as she turned from the evening peace and loveliness to the house, whence came the clatter of milk-pans and the smell of cooking,

"I never should have anything very nice to tell about myself, for I don't do interesting things as you do, and you wouldn't care to hear about school, and sewing, and messing round at home."

Merry gave a disdainful little sniff at the savory perfume of ham which saluted them, and paused with her hand on the gate, as if she found it pleasanter out there than in the house. Ralph seemed to agree with her, for, leaning on the gate, he lingered to say, with real sympathy in his tone and something else in his face, "Yes, I should; so you write and tell me all about it. I didn't know you had any worries, for you always seemed like one of the happiest people in the world, with so many to pet and care for you, and plenty of money, and nothing very hard or hateful to do. You'd think you were well off if you knew as much about poverty and work and never getting what you want, as I do."

"You bear your worries so well that nobody knows you have them. I ought not to complain, and I won't, for I do have all I need. I'm so glad you are going to get what you want at last;" and Merry held out her hand to say good-night, with so much pleasure in her face that Ralph could not make up his mind to go just yet.

"I shall have to scratch round in a lively way before I do get it, for David says a fellow can't live on less than four or five hundred a year, even living as poor artists have to, in garrets and on crusts. I don't mind as long as Grandma is all right. She is away to-night, or I should not be here," he added, as if some excuse was necessary. Merry needed no hint, for her tender heart was touched by the vision of her friend in a garret, and she suddenly rejoiced that there was ham and eggs for supper, so that he might be well fed once, at least, before he went away to feed on artistic crusts.

"Being here, come in and spend the evening. The boys will like to hear the news, and so will father. Do, now."

It was impossible to refuse the invitation he had been longing for, and in they went to the great delight of Roxy, who instantly retired to the pantry, smiling significantly, and brought out the most elaborate pie in honor of the occasion. Merry touched up the table, and put a little vase of flowers in the middle to redeem the vulgarity of doughnuts. Of course the boys upset it, but as there was company nothing was said, and Ralph devoured his supper with the appetite of a hungry boy, while watching Merry eat bread and cream out of an old-fashioned silver porringer, and thinking it the sweetest sight he ever beheld.

Then the young people gathered about the table, full of the new plans, and the elders listened as they rested after the week's work. A pleasant evening, for they all liked Ralph, but as the parents watched Merry sitting among the great lads like a little queen among her subjects, half unconscious as yet of the power in her hands, they nodded to one another, and then shook their heads as if they said,

"I'm afraid the time is coming, mother."

"No danger as long as she don't know it, father."

At nine the boys went off to the barn, the farmer to wind up the eight-day clock, and the housewife to see how the baked beans and Indian pudding for to-morrow were getting on in the oven. Ralph took up his hat to go, saying as he looked at the shade on the tall student lamp,

"What a good light that gives! I can see it as I go home every night, and it burns up here like a beacon. I always look for it, and it hardly ever fails to be burning. Sort of cheers up the way, you know, when I'm tired or low in my mind."

"Then I'm very glad I got it. I liked the shape, but the boys laughed at it as they did at my bulrushes in a ginger-jar over there. I'd been reading about 'household art,' and I thought I'd try a little," answered Merry, laughing at her own whims.

"You've got a better sort of household art, I think, for you make people happy and places pretty, without fussing over it. This room is ever so much improved every time I come, though I hardly see what it is except the flowers," said Ralph, looking from the girl to the tall calla that bent its white cup above her as if to pour its dew upon her head.

"Isn't that lovely? I tried to draw it--the shape was so graceful I wanted to keep it. But I couldn't. Isn't it a pity such beautiful things won't last forever?" and Merry looked regretfully at the half-faded one that grew beside the fresh blossom.

"I can keep it for you. It would look well in plaster. May I?" asked Ralph.

"Thank you, I should like that very much. Take the real one as a model--please do; there are more coming, and this will brighten up your room for a day or two."

As she spoke, Merry cut the stem, and, adding two or three of the great green leaves, put the handsome flower in his hand with so much good-will that he felt as if he had received a very precious gift. Then he said good-night so gratefully that Merry's hand quite tingled with the grasp of his, and went away, often looking backward through the darkness to where the light burned brightly on the hill-top--the beacon kindled by an unconscious Hero for a young Leander swimming gallantly against wind and tide toward the goal of his ambition.

Lesson 118

1. Read chapter 17 of *Jack and Jill*.

2. Tell someone what happened in this chapter in one sentence and then answer their questions. Then try to restate your one-sentence summary adding in the information they had felt missing.

Chapter 17. Down at Molly's

"Now, my dears, I've something very curious to tell you, so listen quietly and then I'll give you your dinners," said Molly, addressing the nine cats who came trooping after her as she went into the shed-chamber with a bowl of milk and a plate of scraps in her hands. She had taught them to behave well at meals, so, though their eyes glared and their tails quivered with impatience, they obeyed; and when she put the food on a high shelf and retired to the big basket, the four old cats sat demurely down before her, while the five kits scrambled after her and tumbled into her lap, as if hoping to hasten the desired feast by their innocent gambols.

Granny, Tobias, Mortification, and Molasses were the elders. Granny, a gray old puss, was the mother and grandmother of all the rest. Tobias was her eldest son, and Mortification his brother, so named because he had lost his tail, which affliction depressed his spirits and cast a blight over his young life. Molasses was a yellow cat, the mamma of four of the kits, the fifth being Granny's latest darling. Toddlekins, the little aunt, was the image of her mother, and very sedate even at that early age; Miss Muffet, so called from her dread of spiders, was a timid black and white kit; Beauty, a pretty Maltese, with a serene little face and pink nose; Ragbag, a funny thing, every color that a cat could be; and Scamp, who well deserved his name, for he was the plague of Miss Bat's life, and Molly's especial pet.

He was now perched on her shoulder, and, as she talked, kept peeping into her face or biting her ear in the most impertinent way, while the others sprawled in her lap or promenaded round the basket rim.

"My friends, something very remarkable has happened: Miss Bat is cleaning house!" and, having made this announcement, Molly leaned back to see how the cats received it, for she insisted that they understood all she said to them.

Tobias stared, Mortification lay down as if it was too much for him, Molasses beat her tail on the floor as if whipping a dusty carpet, and Granny began to purr approvingly. The giddy kits paid no attention, as they did not know what house-cleaning meant, happy little dears!

"I thought you'd like it, Granny, for you are a decent cat, and know what is proper," continued Molly, leaning down to stroke the old puss, who blinked affectionately at her. "I can't imagine what put it into Miss Bat's head. I never said a word, and gave up groaning over the clutter, as I couldn't mend it. I just took care of Boo and myself, and left her to be as untidy as she pleased, and she is a regular old----"

Here Scamp put his paw on her lips because he saw them moving, but it seemed as if it was to check the disrespectful word just coming out.

"Well, I won't call names; but what shall I do when I see everything in confusion, and she won't let me clear up?" asked Molly, looking round at Scamp, who promptly put the little paw on her eyelid, as if the roll of the blue ball underneath amused him.

"Shut my eyes to it, you mean? I do all I can, but it is hard, when I wish to be nice, and do try; don't I?" asked Molly. But Scamp was ready for her, and began to comb her hair with both paws as he stood on his hind legs to work so busily that Molly laughed and pulled him down, saying, as she cuddled the sly kit.

"You sharp little thing! I know my hair is not neat now, for I've been chasing Boo round the garden to wash him for school. Then Miss Bat threw the parlor carpet out of the window, and I was so surprised I had to run and tell you. Now, what had we better do about it?"

The cats all winked at her, but no one had any advice to offer, except Tobias, who walked to the shelf, and, looking up, uttered a deep, suggestive yowl, which said as plainly as words, "Dinner first and discussion afterward."

"Very well, don't scramble," said Molly, getting up to feed her pets. First the kits, who rushed at the bowl and thrust their heads in, lapping as if for a wager; then the cats, who each went to one of the four piles of scraps laid round at intervals and placidly ate their meat; while Molly retired to the basket, to ponder over the phenomena taking place in the house.

She could not imagine what had started the old lady. It was not the example of her neighbors, who had beaten carpets and scrubbed paint every spring for years without exciting her to any greater exertion than cleaning a few windows and having a man to clear away the rubbish displayed when the snow melted. Molly never guessed that her own efforts were at the bottom of the change, or knew that a few words not meant for her ear had shamed Miss Bat into action. Coming home from prayer-meeting one dark night, she trotted along behind two old ladies who were gossiping in loud voices, as one was rather deaf, and Miss Bat was both pleased and troubled to hear herself unduly praised.

"I always said Sister Dawes meant well; but she's getting into years, and the care of two children is a good deal for her, with her cooking and her rheumatiz. I don't deny she did neglect 'em for a spell, but she does well by 'em now, and I wouldn't wish to see better-appearing children."

"You've no idee how improved Molly is. She came in to see my girls, and brought her sewing-work, shirts for the boy, and done it as neat and capable as you'd wish to see. She always was a smart child, but dreadful careless," said the other old lady, evidently much impressed by the change in harum-scarum Molly Loo.

"Being over to Mis Minot's so much has been good for her, and up to Mis Grant's. Girls catch neat ways as quick as they do untidy ones, and them wild little tykes often turn out smart women."

"Sister Dawes has done well by them children, and I hope Mr. Bemis sees it. He ought to give her something comfortable to live on when she can't do for him any longer. He can well afford it."

"I haven't a doubt he will. He's a lavish man when he starts to do a thing, but dreadful unobserving, else he'd have seen to matters long ago. Them children was town-talk last fall, and I used to feel as if it was my bounden duty to speak to Miss Dawes. But I never did, fearing I might speak too plain, and hurt her feelings."

"You've spoken plain enough now, and I'm beholden to you, though you'll never know it," said Miss Bat to herself, as she slipped into her own gate, while the gossips trudged on quite unconscious of the listener behind them.

Miss Bat was a worthy old soul in the main, only, like so many of us, she needed rousing up to her duty. She had got the rousing now, and it did her good, for she could not bear to be praised when she had not deserved it. She had watched Molly's efforts with lazy interest, and when the girl gave up meddling with her affairs, as she called the housekeeping, Miss Bat ceased to oppose her, and let her scrub Boo, mend clothes, and brush her hair as much as she liked. So Molly had worked along without any help from her, running in to Mrs. Pecq for advice, to Merry for comfort, or Mrs. Minot for the higher kind of help one often needs so much. Now Miss Bat found that she was getting the credit and the praise belonging to other people, and it stirred her up to try and deserve a part at least.

"Molly don't want any help about her work or the boy: it's too late for that; but if this house don't get a spring cleaning that will make it shine, my name ain't Bathsheba Dawes," said the old lady, as she put away her bonnet that night, and laid energetic plans for a grand revolution, inspired thereto not only by shame, but by the hint that "Mr. Bemis was a lavish man," as no one knew better than she.

Molly's amazement next day at seeing carpets fly out of window, ancient cobwebs come down, and long-undisturbed closets routed out to the great dismay of moths and mice, has been already confided to the cats, and as she sat there watching them lap and gnaw, she said to herself,

"I don't understand it, but as she never says much to me about my affairs, I won't take any notice till she gets through, then I'll admire everything all I can. It is so pleasant to be praised after you've been trying hard."

She might well say that, for she got very little herself, and her trials had been many, her efforts not always successful, and her reward seemed a long way off. Poor Boo could have sympathized with her, for he had suffered much persecution from his small schoolmates when he appeared with large gray patches on the little brown trousers, where he had worn them out coasting down those too fascinating steps. As he could not see the patches himself, he fancied them invisible, and came home much afflicted by the jeers of his friends. Then Molly tried to make him a new pair out of a sack of her own; but she cut both sides for the same leg, so one was wrong side out. Fondly hoping no one would observe it, she sewed bright buttons wherever they could be put, and sent confiding Boo away in a pair of blue trousers, which were absurdly hunchy behind and buttony before. He came home heart-broken and muddy, having been accidentally tipped into a mud-puddle by two bad boys who felt that such tailoring was an insult to mankind. That roused Molly's spirit, and she begged her father to take the boy and have him properly fitted out, as he was old enough now to be well-dressed, and she wouldn't have him tormented. His attention being called to the trousers, Mr. Bemis had a good laugh over them, and then got Boo a suit which caused him to be the admired of all observers, and to feel as proud as a little peacock.

Cheered by this success, Molly undertook a set of small shirts, and stitched away bravely, though her own summer clothes were in a sad state, and for the first time in her life she cared about what she should wear.

"I must ask Merry, and maybe father will let me go with her and her mother when they do their shopping, instead of leaving it to Miss Bat, who dresses me like an old woman. Merry knows what is pretty and becoming: I don't," thought Molly, meditating in the bushel basket, with her eyes on her snuff-colored gown and the dark purple bow at the end of the long braid Muffet had been playing with.

Molly was beginning to see that even so small a matter as the choice of colors made a difference in one's appearance, and to wonder why Merry always took such pains to have a blue tie for the gray dress, a rosy one for the brown, and gloves that matched her bonnet ribbons. Merry never wore a locket outside her sack, a gay bow in her hair and soiled cuffs, a smart hat and the braid worn off her skirts. She was exquisitely neat and simple, yet always looked well-dressed and pretty; for her love of beauty taught her what all girls should learn as soon as they begin to care for appearances--that neatness and simplicity are their best ornaments, that good habits are better than fine clothes, and the most elegant manners are the kindest.

All these thoughts were dancing through Molly's head, and when she left her cats, after a general romp in which even decorous Granny allowed her family to play leap-frog over her respectable back, she had made up her mind not to have yellow ribbons on her summer hat if she got a pink muslin as she had planned, but to finish off Boo's last shirt before she went shopping with Merry.

It rained that evening, and Mr. Bemis had a headache, so he threw himself down upon the lounge after tea for a nap, with his silk handkerchief spread over his face. He did get a nap, and when he waked he lay for a time drowsily listening to the patter of the rain, and another sound which was even more soothing. Putting back a corner of the handkerchief to learn what it was, he saw Molly sitting by the fire with Boo in her lap, rocking and humming as she warmed his little bare feet, having learned to guard against croup by attending to the damp shoes and socks before going to bed. Boo lay with his round face turned up to hers, stroking her cheek while the sleepy blue eyes blinked lovingly at her as she sang her lullaby with a motherly patience sweet to see. They made a pretty little picture, and Mr. Bemis looked at it with pleasure, having a leisure moment in which to discover, as all parents do sooner or later, that his children were growing up.

"Molly is getting to be quite a woman, and very like her mother," thought papa, wiping the eye that peeped, for he had been fond of the pretty wife who died when Boo was born. "Sad loss to them, poor things! But Miss Bat seems to have done well by them. Molly is much improved, and the boy looks finely. She's a good soul, after all;" and Mr. Bemis began to think he had been hasty when he half made up his mind to get a new housekeeper, feeling that burnt steak, weak coffee, and ragged wristbands were sure signs that Miss Bat's days of usefulness were over.

Molly was singing the lullaby her mother used to sing to her, and her father listened to it silently till Boo was carried away too sleepy for anything but bed. When she came back she sat down to her work, fancying her father still asleep. She had a crimson bow at her throat and one on the newly braided hair, her cuffs were clean, and a white apron hid the shabbiness of the old dress. She looked like a thrifty little housewife as she sat with her basket beside her full of neat white rolls, her spools set forth, and a new pair of scissors shining on the table. There was a sort of charm in watching the busy needle flash to and fro, the anxious pucker of the forehead as she looked to see if the stitches were even, and the expression of intense relief upon her face as she surveyed the finished button-hole with girlish satisfaction. Her father was wide awake and looking at her, thinking, as he did so,

"Really the old lady has worked well to change my tomboy into that nice little girl: I wonder how she did it." Then he gave a yawn, pulled off the handkerchief, and said aloud, "What are you making, Molly?" for it struck him that sewing was a new amusement.

"Shirts for Boo, sir. Four, and this is the last," she answered, with pardonable pride, as she held it up and nodded toward the pile in her basket.

"Isn't that a new notion? I thought Miss Bat did the sewing," said Mr. Bemis, as he smiled at the funny little garment, it looked so like Boo himself.

"No, sir; only yours. I do mine and Boo's. At least, I'm learning how, and Mrs. Pecq says I get on nicely," answered Molly, threading her needle and making a knot in her most capable way.

"I suppose it is time you did learn, for you are getting to be a great girl, and all women should know how to make and mend. You must take a stitch for me now and then: Miss Bat's eyes are not what they were, I find;" and Mr. Bemis looked at his frayed wristband, as if he particularly felt the need of a stitch just then.

"I'd love to, and I guess I could. I can mend gloves; Merry taught me, so I'd better begin on them, if you have any," said Molly, much pleased at being able to do anything for her father, and still more so at being asked.

"There's something to start with;" and he threw her a pair, with nearly every finger ripped.

Molly shook her head over them, but got out her gray silk and fell to work, glad to show how well she could sew.

"What are you smiling about?" asked her father, after a little pause, for his head felt better, and it amused him to question Molly.

"I was thinking about my summer clothes. I must get them before long, and I'd like to go with Mrs. Grant and learn how to shop, if you are willing."

"I thought Miss Bat did that for you."

"She always has, but she gets ugly, cheap things that I don't like. I think I am old enough to choose myself, if there is someone to tell me about prices and the goodness of the stuff. Merry does; and she is only a few months older than I am."

"How old are you, child?" asked her father, feeling as if he had lost his reckoning.

"Fifteen in August;" and Molly looked very proud of the fact.

"So you are! Bless my heart, how the time goes! Well, get what you please; if I'm to have a young lady here, I'd like to have her prettily dressed. It won't offend Miss Bat, will it?"

Molly's eyes sparkled, but she gave a little shrug as she answered, "She won't care. She never troubles herself about me if I let her alone."

"Hey? what? Not trouble herself? If she doesn't, who does?" and Mr. Bemis sat up as if this discovery was more surprising than the other.

"I take care of myself and Boo, and she looks after you. The house goes any way."

"I should think so! I nearly broke my neck over the parlor sofa in the hall to-night. What is it there for?"

Molly laughed. "That's the joke, sir, Miss Bat is cleaning house, and I'm sure it needs cleaning, for it is years since it was properly done. I thought you might have told her to."

"I've said nothing. Don't like house-cleaning well enough to suggest it. I did think the hall was rather dirty when I dropped my coat and took it up covered with lint. Is she going to upset the whole place?" asked Mr. Bemis, looking alarmed at the prospect.

"I hope so, for I really am ashamed when people come, to have them see the dust and cobwebs, and old carpets and dirty windows," said Molly, with a sigh, though she never had cared a bit till lately.

"Why don't you dust round a little, then? No time to spare from the books and play?"

"I tried, father, but Miss Bat didn't like it, and it was too hard for me alone. If things were once in nice order, I think I could keep them so; for I do want to be neat, and I'm learning as fast as I can."

"It is high time someone took hold, if matters are left as you say. I've just been thinking what a clever woman Miss Bat was, to make such a tidy little girl out of what I used to hear called the greatest tomboy in town, and wondering what I could give the old lady. Now I find you are the one to be thanked, and it is a very pleasant surprise to me."

"Give her the present, please; I'm satisfied, if you like what I've done. It isn't much, and I didn't know as you would ever observe any difference. But I did try, and now I guess I'm really getting on," said Molly, sewing away with a bright color in her cheeks, for she, too, found it a pleasant surprise to be praised after many failures and few successes.

"You certainly are, my dear. I'll wait till the house-cleaning is over, and then, if we are all alive, I'll see about Miss Bat's reward. Meantime, you go with Mrs. Grant and get whatever you and the boy need, and send the bills to me;" and Mr. Bemis lighted a cigar, as if that matter was settled.

"Oh, thank you, sir! That will be splendid. Merry always has pretty things, and I know you will like me when I get fixed," said Molly, smoothing down her apron, with a little air.

"Seems to me you look very well as you are. Isn't that a pretty enough frock?" asked Mr. Bemis, quite unconscious that his own unusual interest in his daughter's affairs made her look so bright and winsome.

"This? Why, father, I've worn it all winter, and it's frightfully ugly, and almost in rags. I asked you for a new one a month ago, and you said you'd 'see about it'; but you didn't, so I patched this up as well as I could;" and Molly showed her elbows, feeling that such masculine blindness as this deserved a mild reproof.

"Too bad! Well, go and get half a dozen pretty muslin and gingham things, and be as gay as a butterfly, to make up for it," laughed her father, really touched by the patches and Molly's resignation to the unreliable "I'll see about it," which he recognized as a household word.

Molly clapped her hands, old gloves and all, exclaiming, with girlish delight, "How nice it will seem to have a plenty of new, neat dresses all at once, and be like other girls! Miss Bat always talks about economy, and has no more taste than a--caterpillar." Molly meant to say "cat," but remembering her pets, spared them the insult.

"I think I can afford to dress my girl as well as Grant does his. Get a new hat and coat, child, and any little notions you fancy. Miss Bat's economy isn't the sort I like;" and Mr. Bemis looked at his wristbands again, as if he could sympathize with Molly's elbows.

"At this rate, I shall have more clothes than I know what to do with, after being a rag-bag," thought the girl, in great glee, as she bravely stitched away at the worst glove, while her father smoked silently for a while, feeling that several little matters had escaped his eye which he really ought to "see about."

Presently he went to his desk, but not to bury himself in business papers, as usual, for, after rummaging in several drawers, he took out a small bunch of keys, and sat looking at them with an expression only seen on his face when he looked up at the portrait of a dark-eyed woman hanging in his room. He was a very busy man, but he had a tender place in his heart for his children; and when a look, a few words, a moment's reflection, called his attention to the fact that his little girl was growing up, he found both pride and pleasure in the thought that this young daughter was trying to fill her mother's place, and be a comfort to him, if he would let her.

"Molly, my dear, here is something for you," he said; and when she stood beside him, added, as he put the keys into her hand, keeping both in his own for a minute,

"Those are the keys to your mother's things. I always meant you to have them, when you were old enough to use or care for them. I think you'll fancy this better than any other present, for you are a good child, and very like her."

Something seemed to get into his throat there, and Molly put her arm round his neck, saying, with a little choke in her own voice, "Thank you, father, I'd rather have this than anything else in the world, and I'll try to be more like her every day, for your sake."

He kissed her, then said, as he began to stir his papers about, "I must write some letters. Run off to bed, child. Good-night, my dear, good-night."

Seeing that he wanted to be alone, Molly slipped away, feeling that she had received a very precious gift; for she remembered the dear, dead mother, and had often longed to possess the relics laid away in the one room where order reigned and Miss Bat had no power to meddle. As she slowly undressed, she was not thinking of the pretty new gowns in which she was to be "as gay as a butterfly," but of the half-worn garments waiting for her hands to unfold with a tender touch; and when she fell asleep, with the keys under her pillow and her arms round Boo, a few happy tears on her cheeks seemed to show that, in trying to do the duty which lay nearest her, she had earned a very sweet reward.

So the little missionaries succeeded better in their second attempt than in their first; for, though still very far from being perfect girls, each was slowly learning, in her own way, one of the three lessons all are the better for knowing--that cheerfulness can change misfortune into love and friends; that in ordering one's self aright one helps others to do the same; and that the power of finding beauty in the humblest things makes home happy and life lovely.

Lesson 119

1. Read chapter 18 of *Jack and Jill*.
2. Tell someone what happened in this chapter in one sentence and then answer their questions. Then try and restate your one-sentence summary adding in the information they had felt missing.

Chapter 18. May Baskets

Spring was late that year, but to Jill it seemed the loveliest she had ever known, for hope was growing green and strong in her own little heart, and all the world looked beautiful. With the help of the brace she could sit up for a short time every day, and when the air was mild enough she was warmly wrapped and allowed to look out at the open window into the garden, where the gold and purple crocuses were coming bravely up, and the snowdrops nodded their delicate heads as if calling to her,

"Good day, little sister, come out and play with us, for winter is over and spring is here."

"I wish I could!" thought Jill, as the soft wind kissed a tinge of color into her pale cheeks. "Never mind, they have been shut up in a darker place than I for months, and had no fun at all; I won't fret, but think about July and the seashore while I work."

The job now in hand was May baskets, for it was the custom of the children to hang them on the doors of their friends the night before May-day; and the girls had agreed to supply baskets if the boys would hunt for flowers, much the harder task of the two. Jill had more leisure as well as taste and skill than the other girls, so she amused herself with making a goodly store of pretty baskets of all shapes, sizes, and colors, quite confident that they would be filled, though not a flower had shown its head except a few hardy dandelions, and here and there a small cluster of saxifrage.

The violets would not open their blue eyes till the sunshine was warmer, the columbines refused to dance with the boisterous east wind, the ferns kept themselves rolled up in their brown flannel jackets, and little Hepatica, with many another spring beauty, hid away in the woods, afraid to venture out, in spite of the eager welcome awaiting them. But the birds had come, punctual as ever, and the bluejays were screaming in the orchard, robins were perking up their heads and tails as they went house-hunting, purple finches in their little red hoods were feasting on the spruce buds, and the faithful chip birds chirped gayly on the grapevine trellis where they had lived all winter, warming their little gray breasts against the southern side of the house when the sun shone, and hiding under the evergreen boughs when the snow fell.

"That tree is a sort of bird's hotel," said Jill, looking out at the tall spruce before her window, every spray now tipped with a soft green. "They all go there to sleep and eat, and it has room for everyone, It is green when other trees die, the wind can't break it, and the snow only makes it look prettier. It sings to me, and nods as if it knew I loved it."

"We might call it 'The Holly Tree Inn,' as some of the cheap eating-houses for poor people are called in the city, as my holly bush grows at its foot for a sign. You can be the landlady, and feed your feathery customers every day, till the hard times are over," said Mrs. Minot, glad to see the child's enjoyment of the outer world from which she had been shut so long.

Jill liked the fancy, and gladly strewed crumbs on the window ledge for the chippies, who came confidingly to eat almost from her hand. She threw out grain for the handsome jays, the jaunty robins, and the neighbors' doves, who came with soft flight to trip about on their pink feet, arching their shining necks as they cooed and pecked. Carrots and cabbage-leaves also flew out of the window for the marauding gray rabbit, last of all Jack's half-dozen, who led him a weary life of it because they would not stay in the Bunny-house, but undermined the garden with their burrows, ate the neighbors' plants, and refused to be caught till all but one ran away, to Jack's great relief. This old fellow camped out for the winter, and seemed to get on very well among the cats and the hens, who shared their stores with him, and he might be seen at all hours of the day and night scampering about the place, or kicking up his heels by moonlight, for he was a desperate poacher.

Jill took great delight in her pretty pensioners, who soon learned to love "The Holly Tree Inn," and to feel that the Bird Room held a caged comrade; for, when it was too cold or wet to open the windows, the doves came and tapped at the pane, the chippies sat on the ledge in plump little bunches as if she were their sunshine, the jays called her in their shrill voices to ring the dinner-bell, and the robins tilted on the spruce boughs where lunch was always to be had.

The first of May came on Sunday, so all the celebrating must be done on Saturday, which happily proved fair, though too chilly for muslin gowns, paper garlands, and picnics on damp grass. Being a holiday, the boys decided to devote the morning to ball and the afternoon to the flower hunt, while the girls finished the baskets; and in the evening our particular seven were to meet at the Minots to fill them, ready for the closing frolic of hanging on door-handles, ringing bells, and running away.

"Now I must do my Maying, for there will be no more sunshine, and I want to pick my flowers before it is dark. Come, Mammy, you go too," said Jill, as the last sunbeams shone in at the western window where her hyacinths stood that no fostering ray might be lost.

It was rather pathetic to see the once merry girl who used to be the life of the wood-parties now carefully lifting herself from the couch, and, leaning on her mother's strong arm, slowly take the half-dozen steps that made up her little expedition. But she was happy, and stood smiling out at old Bun skipping down the walk, the gold-edged clouds that drew apart so that a sunbeam might give her a good-night kiss as she gathered her long-cherished daisies, primroses, and hyacinths to fill the pretty basket in her hand.

"Who is it for, my dear?" asked her mother, standing behind her as a prop, while the thin fingers did their work so willingly that not a flower was left.

"For My Lady, of course. Who else would I give my posies to, when I love them so well?" answered Jill, who thought no name too fine for their best friend.

"I fancied it would be for Master Jack," said her mother, wishing the excursion to be a cheerful one.

"I've another for him, but she must have the prettiest. He is going to hang it for me, and ring and run away, and she won't know who it's from till she sees this. She will remember it, for I've been turning and tending it ever so long, to make it bloom to-day. Isn't it a beauty?" and Jill held up her finest hyacinth, which seemed to ring its pale pink bells as if glad to carry its sweet message from a grateful little heart.

"Indeed it is; and you are right to give your best to her. Come away now, you must not stand any longer. Come and rest while I fetch a dish to put the flowers in till you want them;" and Mrs. Pecq turned her round with her small Maying safely done.

"I didn't think I'd ever be able to do even so much, and here I am walking and sitting up, and going to drive some day. Isn't it nice that I'm not to be a poor Lucinda after all?" and Jill drew a long sigh of relief that six months instead of twenty years would probably be the end of her captivity.

"Yes, thank Heaven! I don't think I could have borne that;" and the mother took Jill in her arms as if she were a baby, holding her close for a minute, and laying her down with a tender kiss that made the arms cling about her neck as her little girl returned it heartily, for all sorts of new, sweet feelings seemed to be budding in both, born of great joy and thankfulness.

Then Mrs. Pecq hurried away to see about tea for the hungry boys, and Jill watched the pleasant twilight deepen as she lay singing to herself one of the songs her friend taught her because it fitted her so well.

> A little bird I am,
> Shut from the fields of air,
> And in my cage I sit and sing
> To Him who placed me there:
> Well pleased a prisoner to be,
> Because, my God, it pleases Thee!

> Naught have I else to do;
> I sing the whole day long;
> And He whom most I love to please
> Doth listen to my song,
> He caught and bound my wandering wing,
> But still He bends to hear me sing.

"Now we are ready for you, so bring on your flowers," said Molly to the boys, as she and Merry added their store of baskets to the gay show Jill had set forth on the long table ready for the evening's work.

"They wouldn't let me see one, but I guess they have had good luck, they look so jolly," answered Jill, looking at Gus, Frank, and Jack, who stood laughing, each with a large basket in his hands.

"Fair to middling. Just look in and see;" with which cheerful remark Gus tipped up his basket and displayed a few bits of green at the bottom.

"I did better. Now, don't all scream at once over these beauties;" and Frank shook out some evergreen sprigs, half a dozen saxifrages, and two or three forlorn violets with hardly any stems.

"I don't brag, but here's the best of all the three," chuckled Jack, producing a bunch of feathery carrot-tops, with a few half-shut dandelions trying to look brave and gay.

"Oh, boys, is that all?"

"What shall we do?"

"We've only a few house-flowers, and all those baskets to fill," cried the girls, in despair; for Merry's contribution had been small, and Molly had only a handful of artificial flowers "to fill up," she said.

"It isn't our fault: it is the late spring. We can't make flowers, can we?" asked Frank, in a tone of calm resignation.

"Couldn't you buy some, then?" said Molly, smoothing her crumpled morning-glories, with a sigh.

'Who ever heard of a fellow having any money left the last day of the month?" demanded Gus, severely.

"Or girls either. I spent all mine in ribbon and paper for my baskets, and now they are of no use. It's a shame!" lamented Jill, while Merry began to thin out her full baskets to fill the empty ones.

"Hold on!" cried Frank, relenting. "Now, Jack, make their minds easy before they begin to weep and wail."

"Left the box outside. You tell while I go for it;" and Jack bolted, as if afraid the young ladies might be too demonstrative when the tale was told.

"Tell away," said Frank, modestly passing the story along to Gus, who made short work of it.

"We rampaged all over the country, and got only that small mess of greens. Knew you'd be disgusted, and sat down to see what we could do. Then Jack piped up, and said he'd show us a place where we could get a plenty. 'Come on,' said we, and after leading us a nice tramp, he brought us out at Morse's greenhouse.

So we got a few on tick, as we had but four cents among us, and there you are. Pretty clever of the little chap, wasn't it?"

A chorus of delight greeted Jack as he popped his head in, was promptly seized by his elders and walked up to the table, where the box was opened, displaying gay posies enough to fill most of the baskets if distributed with great economy and much green.

"You are the dearest boy that ever was!" began Jill, with her nose luxuriously buried in the box, though the flowers were more remarkable for color than perfume.

"No, I'm not; there's a much dearer one coming upstairs now, and he's got something that will make you howl for joy," said Jack, ignoring his own prowess as Ed came in with a bigger box, looking as if he had done nothing but go a Maying all his days.

"Don't believe it!" cried Jill, hugging her own treasure jealously. "It's only another joke. I won't look," said Molly, still struggling to make her cambric roses bloom again.

"I know what it is! Oh, how sweet!" added Merry, sniffing, as Ed set the box before her, saying pleasantly,

"You shall see first, because you had faith."

Up went the cover, and a whiff of the freshest fragrance regaled the seven eager noses bent to inhale it, as a general murmur of pleasure greeted the nest of great, rosy mayflowers that lay before them.

"The dear things, how lovely they are!" and Merry looked as if greeting her cousins, so blooming and sweet was her own face.

Molly pushed her dingy garlands away, ashamed of such poor attempts beside these perfect works of nature, and Jill stretched out her hand involuntarily, as she said, forgetting her exotics, "Give me just one to smell of, it is so woodsy and delicious."

"Here you are, plenty for all. Real Pilgrim Fathers, right from Plymouth. One of our fellows lives there, and I told him to bring me a good lot; so he did, and you can do what you like with them," explained Ed, passing round bunches and shaking the rest in a mossy pile upon the table.

"Ed always gets ahead of us in doing the right thing at the right time. Hope you've got some first-class baskets ready for him," said Gus, refreshing the Washingtonian nose with a pink blossom or two.

"Not much danger of his being forgotten," answered Molly; and everyone laughed, for Ed was much beloved by all the girls, and his door-steps always bloomed like a flower-bed on May eve.

"Now we must fly round and fill up. Come, boys, sort out the green and hand us the flowers as we want them. Then we must direct them, and, by the time that is done, you can go and leave them," said Jill, setting all to work.

"Ed must choose his baskets first. These are ours; but any of those you can have;" and Molly pointed to a detachment of gay baskets, set apart from those already partly filled.

Ed chose a blue one, and Merry filled it with the rosiest may-flowers, knowing that it was to hang on Mabel's door-handle.

The others did the same, and the pretty work went on, with much fun, till all were filled, and ready for the names or notes.

"Let us have poetry, as we can't get wild flowers. That will be rather fine," proposed Jill, who liked jingles.

All had had some practice at the game parties, and pencils went briskly for a few minutes, while silence reigned, as the poets racked their brains for rhymes, and stared at the blooming array before them for inspiration.

"Oh, dear! I can't find a word to rhyme to 'geranium,'" sighed Molly, pulling her braid, as if to pump the well of her fancy dry.

"Cranium," said Frank, who was getting on bravely with "Annette" and "violet."

"That is elegant!" and Molly scribbled away in great glee, for her poems were always funny ones.

"How do you spell anemoly--the wild flower, I mean?" asked Jill, who was trying to compose a very appropriate piece for her best basket, and found it easier to feel love and gratitude than to put them into verse.

"Anemone; do spell it properly, or you'll get laughed at," answered Gus, wildly struggling to make his lines express great ardor, without being "too spoony," as he expressed it.

"No, I shouldn't. This person never laughs at other persons' mistakes, as some persons do," replied Jill, with dignity.

Jack was desperately chewing his pencil, for he could not get on at all; but Ed had evidently prepared his poem, for his paper was half full already, and Merry was smiling as she wrote a friendly line or two for Ralph's basket, as she feared he would be forgotten, and knew he loved kindness even more than he did beauty.

"Now let's read them," proposed Molly, who loved to laugh even at herself.

The boys politely declined, and scrambled their notes into the chosen baskets in great haste; but the girls were less bashful. Jill was invited to begin, and gave her little piece, with the pink hyacinth basket before her, to illustrate her poem.

> TO MY LADY
>
> There are no flowers in the fields,
> No green leaves on the tree,
> No columbines, no violets,
> No sweet anemone.
> So I have gathered from my pots
> All that I have to fill
> The basket that I hang to-night,
> With heaps of love from Jill.

"That's perfectly sweet! Mine isn't; but I meant it to be funny," said Molly, as if there could be any doubt about the following ditty:

> Dear Grif,
> Here is a whiff

Of beautiful spring flowers;
The big red rose
Is for your nose,
As toward the sky it towers.

Oh, do not frown
Upon this crown
Of green pinks and blue geranium
But think of me
When this you see,
And put it on your cranium.

"O Molly, you will never hear the last of that if Grif gets it," said Jill, as the applause subsided, for the boys pronounced it "tip-top."

"Don't care, he gets the worst of it anyway, for there is a pin in that rose, and if he goes to smell the mayflowers underneath he will find a thorn to pay for the tack he put in my rubber boot. I know he will play me some joke to-night, and I mean to be first if I can," answered Molly, settling the artificial wreath round the orange-colored canoe which held her effusion.

"Now, Merry, read yours: you always have sweet poems;" and Jill folded her hands to listen with pleasure to something sentimental.

"I can't read the poems in some of mine, because they are for you; but this little verse you can hear, if you like: I'm going to give that basket to Ralph. He said he should hang one for his grandmother, and I thought that was so nice of him, I'd love to surprise him with one all to himself. He's always so good to us;" and Merry looked so innocently earnest that no one smiled at her kind thought or the unconscious paraphrase she had made of a famous stanza in her own "little verse."

To one who teaches me
The sweetness and the beauty
Of doing faithfully
And cheerfully my duty.

"He will like that, and know who sent it, for none of us have pretty pink paper but you, or write such an elegant hand," said Molly, admiring the delicate white basket shaped like a lily, with the flowers inside and the note hidden among them, all daintily tied up with the palest blush-colored ribbon.

"Well, that's no harm. He likes pretty things as much as I do, and I made my basket like a flower because I gave him one of my callas, he admired the shape so much;" and Merry smiled as she remembered how pleased Ralph looked as he went away carrying the lovely thing.

"I think it would be a good plan to hang some baskets on the doors of other people who don't expect or often have any. I'll do it if you can spare some of these, we have so many. Give me only one, and let the others go to old Mrs. Tucker, and the little Irish girl who has been sick so long, and lame

Neddy, and Daddy Munson. It would please and surprise them so. Will we?" asked Ed, in that persuasive voice of his.

All agreed at once, and several people were made very happy by a bit of spring left at their doors by the May elves who haunted the town that night playing all sorts of pranks. Such a twanging of bells and rapping of knockers; such a scampering of feet in the dark; such droll collisions as boys came racing round corners, or girls ran into one another's arms as they crept up and down steps on the sly; such laughing, whistling, flying about of flowers and friendly feeling--it was almost a pity that May-day did not come oftener.

Molly got home late, and found that Grif had been before her, after all; for she stumbled over a market-basket at her door, and on taking it in found a mammoth nosegay of purple and white cabbages, her favorite vegetable. Even Miss Bat laughed at the funny sight, and Molly resolved to get Ralph to carve her a bouquet out of carrots, beets, and turnips for next time, as Grif would never think of that.

Merry ran up the garden-walk alone, for Frank left her at the gate, and was fumbling for the latch when she felt something hanging there. Opening the door carefully, she found it gay with offerings from her mates; and among them was one long quiver-shaped basket of birch bark, with something heavy under the green leaves that lay at the top. Lifting these, a slender bas-relief of a calla lily in plaster appeared, with this couplet slipped into the blue cord by which it was to hang:

> That mercy you to others show
> That Mercy Grant to me.

"How lovely! and this one will never fade, but always be a pleasure hanging there. Now, I really have something beautiful all my own," said Merry to herself as she ran up to hang the pretty thing on the dark wainscot of her room, where the graceful curve of its pointed leaves and the depth of its white cup would be a joy to her eyes as long as they lasted.

"I wonder what that means," and Merry read over the lines again, while a soft color came into her cheeks and a little smile of girlish pleasure began to dimple round her lips; for she was so romantic, this touch of sentiment showed her that her friendship was more valued than she dreamed. But she only said, "How glad I am I remembered him, and how surprised he will be to see mayflowers in return for the lily."

He was, and worked away more happily and bravely for the thought of the little friend whose eyes would daily fall on the white flower which always reminded him of her.

Lesson 120

1. Read chapter 19 of *Jack and Jill*.
2. Write a one-sentence summary of the chapter.

Chapter 19. Good Templars

"Hi there! Bell's rung! Get up, lazy-bones!" called Frank from his room as the clock struck six one bright morning, and a great creaking and stamping proclaimed that he was astir.

"All right, I'm coming," responded a drowsy voice, and Jack turned over as if to obey; but there the effort ended, and he was off again, for growing lads are hard to rouse, as many a mother knows to her sorrow.

Frank made a beginning on his own toilet, and then took a look at his brother, for the stillness was suspicious.

"I thought so! He told me to wake him, and I guess this will do it;" and, filling his great sponge with water, Frank stalked into the next room and stood over the unconscious victim like a stern executioner, glad to unite business with pleasure in this agreeable manner.

A woman would have relented and tried some milder means, for when his broad shoulders and stout limbs were hidden, Jack looked very young and innocent in his sleep. Even Frank paused a moment to look at the round, rosy face, the curly eyelashes, half-open mouth, and the peaceful expression of a dreaming baby. "I must do it, or he won't be ready for breakfast," said the Spartan brother, and down came the sponge, cold, wet, and choky, as it was briskly rubbed to and fro regardless of every obstacle.

"Come, I say! That's not fair! Leave me alone!" sputtered Jack, hitting out so vigorously that the sponge flew across the room, and Frank fell back to laugh at the indignant sufferer.

"I promised to wake you, and you believe in keeping promises, so I'm doing my best to get you up."

"Well, you needn't pour a quart of water down a fellow's neck, and rub his nose off, need you? I'm awake, so take your old sponge and go along," growled Jack, with one eye open and a mighty gape.

"See that you keep so, then, or I'll come and give you another sort of a rouser," said Frank, retiring well-pleased with his success.

"I shall have one good stretch, if I like. It is strengthening to the muscles, and I'm as stiff as a board with all that football yesterday," murmured Jack, lying down for one delicious moment. He shut the open eye to enjoy it thoroughly, and forgot the stretch altogether, for the bed was warm, the pillow soft, and a half-finished dream still hung about his drowsy brain. Who does not know the fatal charm of that stolen moment--for once yield to it, and one is lost.

Jack was miles away "in the twinkling of a bedpost," and the pleasing dream seemed about to return, when a ruthless hand tore off the clothes, swept him out of bed, and he really did awake to find himself standing in the middle of his bath-pan with both windows open, and Frank about to pour a pail of water over him.

"Hold on! Yah, how cold the water is! Why, I thought I was up;" and, hopping out, Jack rubbed his eyes and looked about with such a genuine surprise that Frank put down the pail, feeling that the deluge would not be needed this time.

"You are now, and I'll see that you keep so," he said, as he stripped the bed and carried off the pillows.

"I don't care. What a jolly day!" and Jack took a little promenade to finish the rousing process.

"You'd better hurry up, or you won't get your chores done before breakfast. No time for a go as you please now," said Frank; and both boys laughed, for it was an old joke of theirs, and rather funny.

Going up to bed one night expecting to find Jack asleep, Frank discovered him tramping round and round the room airily attired in a towel, and so dizzy with his brisk revolutions that as his brother looked he tumbled over and lay panting like a fallen gladiator.

"What on earth are you about?"

"Playing Rowell. Walking for the belt, and I've got it too," laughed Jack, pointing to an old gilt chandelier chain hanging on the bedpost.

"You little noodle, you'd better revolve into bed before you lose your head entirely. I never saw such a fellow for taking himself off his legs."

"Well, if I didn't exercise, do you suppose I should be able to do that--or that?" cried Jack, turning a somersault and striking a fine attitude as he came up, flattering himself that he was the model of a youthful athlete.

"You look more like a clothes-pin than a Hercules," was the crushing reply of this unsympathetic brother, and Jack meekly retired with a bad headache.

"I don't do such silly things now: I'm as broad across the shoulders as you are, and twice as strong on my pins, thanks to my gymnastics. Bet you a cent I'll be dressed first, though you have got the start," said Jack, knowing that Frank always had a protracted wrestle with his collar-buttons, which gave his adversary a great advantage over him.

"Done!" answered Frank, and at it they went. A wild scramble was heard in Jack's room, and a steady tramp in the other as Frank worked away at the stiff collar and the unaccommodating button till every finger ached. A clashing of boots followed, while Jack whistled "Polly Hopkins," and Frank declaimed in his deepest voice,

"Arma virumque cano, Trojae qui primus ab oris Italiam, fato profugus, Laviniaque venit litora."

Hair-brushes came next, and here Frank got ahead, for Jack's thick crop would stand straight up on the crown, and only a good wetting and a steady brush would make it lie down.

"Play away, No. 2," called out Frank as he put on his vest, while Jack was still at it with a pair of the stiffest brushes procurable for money.

"Hold hard, No. 11, and don't forget your teeth," answered Jack, who had done his.

Frank took a hasty rub and whisked on his coat, while Jack was picking up the various treasures which had flown out of his pockets as he caught up his roundabout.

"Ready! I'll trouble you for a cent, sonny;" and Frank held out his hand as he appeared equipped for the day.

"You haven't hung up your night-gown, nor aired the bed, nor opened the windows. That's part of the dressing; mother said so. I've got you there, for you did all that for me, except this," and Jack threw his gown over a chair with a triumphant flourish as Frank turned back to leave his room in the order which they had been taught was one of the signs of a good bringing-up in boys as well as girls.

"Ready! I'll trouble you for a cent, old man;" and Jack held out his hand, with a chuckle.

He got the money and a good clap beside; then they retired to the shed to black their boots, after which Frank filled the woodboxes and Jack split kindlings, till the daily allowance was ready. Both went at their lessons for half an hour, Jack scowling over his algebra in the sofa corner, while Frank, with his elbows on and his legs round the little stand which held his books, seemed to be having a wrestling-match with Herodotus.

When the bell rang they were glad to drop the lessons and fall upon their breakfast with the appetite of wolves, especially Jack, who sequestered oatmeal and milk with such rapidity that one would have thought he had a leathern bag hidden somewhere to slip it into, like his famous namesake when he breakfasted with the giant.

"I declare I don't see what he does with it! He really ought not to 'gobble' so, mother," said Frank, who was eating with great deliberation and propriety.

"Never you mind, old quiddle. I'm so hungry I could tuck away a bushel," answered Jack, emptying a glass of milk and holding out his plate for more mush, regardless of his white moustache.

"Temperance in all things is wise, in speech as well as eating and drinking--remember that, boys," said Mamma from behind the urn.

"That reminds me! We promised to do the 'Observer' this week, and here it is Tuesday and I haven't done a thing: have you?" asked Frank.

"Never thought of it. We must look up some bits at noon instead of playing. Dare say Jill has got some: she always saves all she finds for me."

"I have one or two good items, and can do any copying there may be. But I think if you undertake the paper you should give some time and labor to make it good," said Mamma, who was used to this state of affairs, and often edited the little sheet read every week at the Lodge. The boys seldom missed going, but the busy lady was often unable to be there, so helped with the paper as her share of the labor.

"Yes, we ought, but somehow we don't seem to get up much steam about it lately. If more people belonged, and we could have a grand time now and then, it would be jolly;" and Jack sighed at the lack of interest felt by outsiders in the loyal little Lodge which went on year after year kept up by the faithful few.

"I remember when in this very town we used to have a Cold Water Army, and in the summer turn out with processions, banners, and bands of music to march about, and end with a picnic, songs, and speeches in some grove or hall. Nearly all the children belonged to it, and the parents also, and we had fine times here twenty-five or thirty years ago."

"It didn't do much good, seems to me, for people still drink, and we haven't a decent hotel in the place," said Frank, as his mother sat looking out of the window as if she saw again the pleasant sight of old and young working together against the great enemy of home peace and safety.

"Oh yes, it did, my dear; for to this day many of those children are true to their pledge. One little girl was, I am sure, and now has two big boys to fight for the reform she has upheld all her life. The town is better than it was in those days, and if we each do our part faithfully, it will improve yet more. Every boy and girl who joins is one gained, perhaps, and your example is the best temperance lecture you can give. Hold fast, and don't mind if it isn't 'jolly': it is right, and that should be enough for us."

Mamma spoke warmly, for she heartily believed in young people's guarding against this dangerous vice before it became a temptation, and hoped her boys would never break the pledge they had taken; for, young as they were, they were old enough to see its worth, feel its wisdom, and pride themselves on the promise which was fast growing into a principle. Jack's face brightened as he listened, and Frank said, with the steady look which made his face manly,

"It shall be. Now I'll tell you what I was going to keep as a surprise till to-night, for I wanted to have my secret as well as other folks. Ed and I went up to see Bob, Sunday, and he said he'd join the Lodge, if they'd have him. I'm going to propose him to-night."

"Good! good!" cried Jack, joyfully, and Mrs. Minot clapped her hands, for every new member was rejoiced over by the good people, who were not discouraged by ridicule, indifference, or opposition.

"We've got him now, for no one will object, and it is just the thing for him. He wants to belong somewhere, he says, and he'll enjoy the fun, and the good things will help him, and we will look after him, The Captain was so pleased, and you ought to have seen Ed's face when Bob said, 'I'm ready, if you'll have me.'"

Frank's own face was beaming, and Jack forgot to "gobble," he was so interested in the new convert, while Mamma said, as she threw down her napkin and took up the newspaper,

"We must not forget our 'Observer,' but have a good one tonight in honor of the occasion. There may be something here. Come home early at noon, and I'll help you get your paper ready."

"I'll be here, but if you want Frank, you'd better tell him not to dawdle over Annette's gate half an hour," began Jack, who could not resist teasing his dignified brother about one of the few foolish things he was fond of doing.

"Do you want your nose pulled?" demanded Frank, who never would stand joking on that tender point from his brother.

"No, I don't; and if I did, you couldn't do it;" with which taunt he was off and Frank after him, having made a futile dive at the impertinent little nose which was turned up at him and his sweetheart.

"Boys, boys, not through the parlor!" implored Mamma, resigned to skirmishes, but trembling for her piano legs as the four stout boots pranced about the table and then went thundering down the hall, through the kitchen where the fat cook cheered them on, and Mary, the maid, tried to head off Frank as Jack rushed out into the garden. But the pursuer ducked under her arm and gave chase with all speed. Then there was a glorious race all over the place; for both were good runners, and, being as full of spring vigor as frisky calves, they did astonishing things in the way of leaping fences, dodging round corners, and making good time down the wide walks.

But Jack's leg was not quite strong yet, and he felt that his round nose was in danger of a vengeful tweak as his breath began to give out and Frank's long arms drew nearer and nearer to the threatened feature. Just when he was about to give up and meet his fate like a man, old Bunny, who had been much excited by the race, came scampering across the path with such a droll skip into the air and shake of the hind legs that Frank had to dodge to avoid stepping on him, and to laugh in spite of himself. This momentary check gave Jack a chance to bolt up the back stairs and take refuge in the Bird Room, from the window of which Jill had been watching the race with great interest.

No romping was allowed there, so a truce was made by locking little fingers, and both sat down to get their breath.

"I am to go on the piazza, for an hour, by and by, Doctor said. Would you mind carrying me down before you go to school, you do it so nicely, I'm not a bit afraid," said Jill, as eager for the little change as if it had been a long and varied journey.

"Yes, indeed! Come on, Princess," answered Jack, glad to see her so well and happy.

The boys made an arm-chair, and away she went, for a pleasant day downstairs. She thanked Frank with a posy for his buttonhole, well knowing that it would soon pass into other hands, and he departed to join Annette. Having told Jill about Bob, and set her to work on the "Observer," Jack kissed his mother, and went whistling down the street, a gay little bachelor, with a nod and smile for all he met, and no turned-up hat or jaunty turban bobbing along beside him to delay his steps or trouble his peace of mind.

At noon they worked on their paper, which was a collection of items, cut from other papers, concerning temperance, a few anecdotes, a bit of poetry, a story, and, if possible, an original article by the editor. Many hands make light work, and nothing remained but a little copying, which Jill promised to do before night. So the boys had time for a game of football after school in the afternoon, which they much enjoyed. As they sat resting on the posts, Gus said,

"Uncle Fred says he will give us a hay-cart ride to-night, as it is moony, and after it you are all to come to our house and have games."

"Can't do it," answered Frank, sadly.

"Lodge," groaned Jack, for both considered a drive in the cart, where they all sat in a merry bunch among the hay, one of the joys of life, and much regretted that a prior engagement would prevent their sharing in it.

"That's a pity! I forgot it was Tuesday, and can't put it off, as I've asked all the rest. Give up your old Lodge and come along," said Gus, who had not joined yet.

"We might for once, perhaps, but I don't like to"--began Jack, hesitating.

"I won't. Who's to propose Bob if we don't? I want to go awfully; but I wouldn't disappoint Bob for a good deal, now he is willing to come." And Frank sprang off his post as if anxious to flee temptation, for it was very pleasant to go singing, up hill and down dale, in the spring moonlight, with--well, the fellows of his set.

"Nor Ed, I forgot that. No, we can't go. We want to be Good Templars, and we mustn't shirk," added Jack, following his brother.

"Better come. Can't put it off. Lots of fun," called Gus, disappointed at losing two of his favorite mates.

But the boys did not turn back, and as they went steadily away they felt that they were doing their little part in the good work, and making their small sacrifices, like faithful members.

They got their reward, however, for at home they found Mr. Chauncey, a good and great man, from England, who had known their grandfather, and was an honored friend of the family. The boys loved to hear him talk, and all tea-time listened with interest to the conversation, for Mr. Chauncey was a reformer as well as a famous clergyman, and it was like inspiring music to hear him tell about the world's work, and the brave men and women who were carrying it on. Eager to show that they had, at least, begun, the boys told him about their Lodge, and were immensely pleased when their guest took from his pocket-book a worn paper, proving that he too was a Good Templar, and belonged to the same army as they did. Nor was that all, for when they reluctantly excused themselves, Mr. Chauncey gave each a hearty "grip," and said, holding their hands in his, as he smiled at the young faces looking up at him with so much love and honor in them,

"Tell the brothers and sisters that if I can serve them in anyway while here, to command me. I will give them a lecture at their Lodge or in public, whichever they like; and I wish you God-speed, dear boys."

Two prouder lads never walked the streets than Frank and Jack as they hurried away, nearly forgetting the poor little paper in their haste to tell the good news; for it was seldom that such an offer was made the Lodge, and they felt the honor done them as bearers of it.

As the secrets of the association cannot be divulged to the uninitiated, we can only say that there was great rejoicing over the new member, for Bob was unanimously welcomed, and much gratitude both felt and expressed for Mr. Chauncey's interest in this small division of the grand army; for these good folk met with little sympathy from the great people of the town, and it was very cheering to have a well-known and much-beloved man say a word for them. All agreed that the lecture should be public, that others might share the pleasure with them, and perhaps be converted by a higher eloquence than any they possessed.

So the services that night were unusually full of spirit and good cheer; for all felt the influence of a friendly word, the beauty of a fine example. The paper was much applauded, the songs were very hearty, and when Frank, whose turn it was to be chaplain, read the closing prayer, everyone felt that they had much to give thanks for, since one more had joined them, and the work was slowly getting on with unexpected helpers sent to lend a hand. The lights shone out from the little hall across the street, the music reached the ears of passers-by, and the busy hum of voices up there told how faithfully some, at least, of the villagers tried to make the town a safer place for their boys to grow up in, though the tavern still had its private bar and the saloon-door stood open to invite them in.

There are many such quiet lodges, and in them many young people learning as these lads were learning something of the duty they owed their neighbors as well as themselves, and being fitted to become good men and sober citizens by practising and preaching the law and gospel of temperance.

The next night Mr. Chauncey lectured, and the town turned out to hear the distinguished man, who not only told them of the crime and misery produced by this terrible vice which afflicted both England and America, but of the great crusade against it going on everywhere, and the need of courage, patience, hard work, and much faith, that in time it might be overcome. Strong and cheerful words that all liked to hear and many heartily believed, especially the young Templars, whose boyish fancies were won by the idea of fighting as knights of old did in the famous crusades they read about in their splendid new young folks' edition of Froissart.

"We can't pitch into people as the Red Cross fellows did, but we can smash rum-jugs when we get the chance, and stand by our flag as our men did in the war," said Frank, with sparkling eyes, as they went home in the moonlight arm in arm, keeping step behind Mr. Chauncey, who led the way with their mother on his arm, a martial figure though a minister, and a good captain to follow, as the boys felt after hearing his stirring words.

"Let's try and get up a company of boys like those mother told us about, and show people that we mean what we say. I'll be color-bearer, and you may drill us as much as you like. A real Cold Water Army, with flags flying, and drums, and all sorts of larks," said Jack, much excited, and taking a dramatic view of the matter.

"We'll see about it. Something ought to be done, and perhaps we shall be the men to do it when the time comes," answered Frank, feeling ready to shoulder a musket or be a minute-man in good earnest.

Boyish talk and enthusiasm, but it was of the right sort; and when time and training had fitted them to bear arms, these young knights would be worthy to put on the red cross and ride away to help right the wrongs and slay the dragons that afflict the world.

Lesson 121

1. Read chapter 20 of *Jack and Jill.*
2. Write a one–sentence summary of the chapter.

Chapter 20. A Sweet Memory

Now the lovely June days had come, everything began to look really summer-like; school would soon be over, and the young people were joyfully preparing for the long vacation.

"We are all going up to Bethlehem. We take the seashore one year and the mountains the next. Better come along," said Gus, as the boys lay on the grass after beating the Lincolns at one of the first matches of the season.

"Can't; we are off to Pebbly Beach the second week in July. Our invalids need sea air. That one looks delicate, doesn't he?" asked Frank, giving Jack a slight rap with his bat as that young gentleman lay in his usual attitude admiring the blue hose and russet shoes which adorned his sturdy limbs.

"Stop that, Captain! You needn't talk about invalids, when you know mother says you are not to look at a book for a month because you have studied yourself thin and headachy. I'm all right;" and Jack gave himself a sounding slap on the chest, where shone the white star of the H. B. B. C.

"Hear the little cockerel crow! you just wait till you get into the college class, and see if you don't have to study like fun," said Gus, with unruffled composure, for he was going to Harvard next year, and felt himself already a Senior.

"Never shall; I don't want any of your old colleges. I'm going into business as soon as I can. Ed says I may be his book-keeper, if I am ready when he starts for himself. That is much jollier than grinding away for four years, and then having to grind ever so many more at a profession," said Jack, examining with interest the various knocks and bruises with which much ball-playing had adorned his hands.

"Much you know about it. Just as well you don't mean to try, for it would take a mighty long pull and strong pull to get you in. Business would suit you better, and you and Ed would make a capital partnership. Devlin, Minot, & Co. sounds well, hey, Gus?"

"Very, but they are such good-natured chaps, they'd never get rich. By the way, Ed came home at noon today sick. I met him, and he looked regularly knocked up," answered Gus, in a sober tone.

"I told him he'd better not go down Monday, for he wasn't well Saturday, and couldn't come to sing Sunday evening, you remember. I must go right round and see what the matter is;" and Jack jumped up, with an anxious face.

"Let him alone till to-morrow. He won't want anyone fussing over him now. We are going for a pull; come along and steer," said Frank, for the sunset promised to be fine, and the boys liked a brisk row in their newly painted boat, the "Rhodora."

"Go ahead and get ready, I'll just cut round and ask at the door. It will seem kind, and I must know how Ed is. Won't be long;" and Jack was off at his best pace.

The others were waiting impatiently when he came back with slower steps and a more anxious face.

"How is the old fellow?" called Frank from the boat, while Gus stood leaning on an oar in a nautical attitude.

"Pretty sick. Had the doctor. May have a fever. I didn't go in, but Ed sent his love, and wanted to know who beat," answered Jack, stepping to his place, glad to rest and cool himself.

"Guess he'll be all right in a day or two;" and Gus pushed off, leaving all care behind.

"Hope he won't have typhoid--that's no joke, I tell you," said Frank, who knew all about it, and did not care to repeat the experience.

"He's worked too hard. He's so faithful he does more than his share, and gets tired out. Mother asked him to come down and see us when he has his vacation; we are going to have high old times fishing and boating. Up or down?" asked Jack, as they glided out into the river.

Gus looked both ways, and seeing another boat with a glimpse of red in it just going round the bend, answered, with decision, "Up, of course. Don't we always pull to the bridge?"

"Not when the girls are going down," laughed Jack, who had recognized Juliet's scarlet boating-suit as he glanced over his shoulder.

"Mind what you are about, and don't gabble," commanded Captain Frank, as the crew bent to their oars and the slender boat cut through the water leaving a long furrow trembling behind.

"Oh, ah! I see! There is a blue jacket as well as a red one, so it's all right.

> Lady Queen Anne, she sits in the sun,
> As white as a lily, as brown as a bun,

sung Jack, recovering his spirits, and wishing Jill was there too.

"Do you want a ducking?" sternly demanded Gus, anxious to preserve discipline.

"Shouldn't mind, it's so warm."

But Jack said no more, and soon the "Rhodora" was alongside the "Water Witch," exchanging greetings in the most amiable manner.

"Pity this boat won't hold four. We'd put Jack in yours, and take you girls a nice spin up to the Hemlocks," said Frank, whose idea of bliss was floating down the river with Annette as coxswain.

"You'd better come in here, this will hold four, and we are tired of rowing," returned the "Water Witch," so invitingly that Gus could not resist.

"I don't think it is safe to put four in there. You'd better change places with Annette, Gus, and then we shall be ship-shape," said Frank, answering a telegram from the eyes that matched the blue jacket.

"Wouldn't it be more ship-shape still if you put me ashore at Grif's landing? I can take his boat, or wait till you come back. Don't care what I do," said Jack, feeling himself sadly in the way.

The good-natured offer being accepted with thanks, the changes were made, and, leaving him behind, the two boats went gayly up the river. He really did not care what he did, so sat in Grif's boat awhile watching the red sky, the shining stream, and the low green meadows, where the blackbirds were singing as if they too had met their little sweethearts and were happy.

Jack remembered that quiet half-hour long afterward, because what followed seemed to impress it on his memory. As he sat enjoying the scene, he very naturally thought about Ed; for the face of the sister whom he saw was very anxious, and the word "fever" recalled the hard times when Frank was ill, particularly the night it was thought the boy would not live till dawn, and Jack cried himself to sleep, wondering how he ever could get on without his brother. Ed was almost as dear to him, and the thought that he was suffering destroyed Jack's pleasure for a little while. But, fortunately, young people do not know how to be anxious very long, so our boy soon cheered up, thinking about the late match between the Stars and the Lincolns, and after a good rest went whistling home, with a handful of mint for Mrs. Pecq, and played games with Jill as merrily as if there was no such thing as care in the world.

Next day Ed was worse, and for a week the answer was the same, when Jack crept to the back door with his eager question.

Others came also, for the dear boy lying upstairs had friends everywhere, and older neighbors thought of him even more anxiously and tenderly than his mates. It was not fever, but some swifter trouble, for when Saturday night came, Ed had gone home to a longer and more peaceful Sabbath than any he had ever known in this world.

Jack had been there in the afternoon, and a kind message had come down to him that his friend was not suffering so much, and he had gone away, hoping, in his boyish ignorance, that all danger was over. An hour later he was reading in the parlor, having no heart for play, when Frank came in with a look upon his face which would have prepared Jack for the news if he had seen it. But he did not look up, and Frank found it so hard to speak, that he lingered a moment at the piano, as he often did when he came home. It stood open, and on the rack was the "Jolly Brothers' Galop," which he had been learning to play with Ed. Big boy as he was, the sudden thought that never again would they sit shoulder to shoulder, thundering the marches or singing the songs both liked so well, made his eyes fill as he laid away the music, and shut the instrument, feeling as if he never wanted to touch it again. Then he went and sat down beside Jack with an arm round his neck, trying to steady his voice by a natural question before he told the heavy news.

"What are you reading, Jacky?"

The unusual caress, the very gentle tone, made Jack look up, and the minute he saw Frank's face he knew the truth.

"Is Ed----?" he could not say the hard word, and Frank could only answer by a nod as he winked fast, for the tears would come. Jack said no more, but as the book dropped from his knee he hid his face in the sofa-pillow and lay quite still, not crying, but trying to make it seem true that his dear Ed had gone away for ever. He could not do it, and presently turned his head a little to say, in a despairing tone, "I don't see what I shall do without him!"

"I know it's hard for you. It is for all of us."

"You've got Gus, but now I haven't anybody. Ed was always so good to me!" and with the name so many tender recollections came, that poor Jack broke down in spite of his manful attempts to smother the sobs in the red pillow.

There was an unconscious reproach in the words, Frank thought; for he was not as gentle as Ed, and he did not wonder that Jack loved and mourned for the lost friend like a brother.

"You've got me. I'll be good to you; cry if you want to, I don't mind."

There was such a sympathetic choke in Frank's voice that Jack felt comforted at once, and when he had had his cry out, which was very soon, he let Frank pull him up with a bear-like but affectionate hug, and sat leaning on him as they talked about their loss, both feeling that there might have been a greater one, and resolving to love one another very much hereafter.

Mrs. Minot often called Frank the "father-boy," because he was now the head of the house, and a sober, reliable fellow for his years. Usually he did not show much affection except to her, for, as he once said, "I shall never be too old to kiss my mother," and she often wished that he had a little sister, to bring out the softer side of his character. He domineered over Jack and laughed at his affectionate little ways, but now when trouble came, he was as kind and patient as a girl; and when Mamma came in, having heard the news, she found her "father-boy" comforting his brother so well that she slipped away without a word, leaving them to learn one of the sweet lessons sorrow teaches--to lean on one another, and let each trial bring them closer together.

It is often said that there should be no death or grief in children's stories. It is not wise to dwell on the dark and sad side of these things; but they have also a bright and lovely side, and since even the youngest, dearest, and most guarded child cannot escape some knowledge of the great mystery, is it not well to teach them in simple, cheerful ways that affection sweetens sorrow, and a lovely life can make death beautiful? I think so, therefore try to tell the last scene in the history of a boy who really lived and really left behind him a memory so precious that it will not be soon forgotten by those who knew and loved him. For the influence of this short life was felt by many, and even this brief record of it may do for other children what the reality did for those who still lay flowers on his grave, and try to be "as good as Eddy."

Few would have thought that the death of a quiet lad of seventeen would have been so widely felt, so sincerely mourned; but virtue, like sunshine, works its own sweet miracles, and when it was known that never again would the bright face be seen in the village streets, the cheery voice heard, the loving heart felt in any of the little acts which so endeared Ed Devlin to those about him, it seemed as if young and old grieved alike for so much promise cut off in its spring-time. This was proved at the funeral, for, though it took place at the busy hour of a busy day, men left their affairs, women their households, young people their studies and their play, and gave an hour to show their affection, respect, and sympathy for those who had lost so much.

The girls had trimmed the church with all the sweetest flowers they could find, and garlands of lilies of the valley robbed the casket of its mournful look. The boys had brought fresh boughs to make the grave a green bed for their comrade's last sleep. Now they were all gathered together, and it was a touching sight to see the rows of young faces sobered and saddened by their first look at sorrow. The girls sobbed, and the boys set their lips tightly as their glances fell upon the lilies under which the familiar face lay full of solemn peace. Tears dimmed older eyes when the hymn the dead boy loved was sung, and the pastor told with how much pride and pleasure he had watched the gracious growth of this young parishioner since he first met the lad of twelve and was attracted by the shining face, the pleasant manners. Dutiful and loving; ready to help; patient to bear and forbear; eager to excel; faithful to the smallest task, yet full of high ambitions; and, better still, possessing the childlike piety that can trust and believe, wait and hope. Good and happy--the two things we all long for and so few of us truly are. This he was, and this single fact was the best eulogy his pastor could pronounce over the beloved youth gone to a nobler manhood whose promise left so sweet a memory behind.

As the young people looked, listened, and took in the scene, they felt as if some mysterious power had changed their playmate from a creature like themselves into a sort of saint or hero for them to look up to, and imitate if they could. "What has he done, to be so loved, praised, and mourned?" they thought, with a tender sort of wonder; and the answer seemed to come to them as never before, for never had they been brought so near the solemn truth of life and death. "It was not what he did but what he was that made him so beloved. All that was sweet and noble in him still lives; for goodness is the only thing we can take with us when we die, the only thing that can comfort those we leave behind, and help us to meet again hereafter."

This feeling was in many hearts when they went away to lay him, with prayer and music, under the budding oak that leaned over his grave, a fit emblem of the young life just beginning its new spring. As the children did their part, the beauty of the summer day soothed their sorrow, and something of the soft brightness of the June sunshine seemed to gild their thoughts, as it gilded the flower-strewn mound they left behind. The true and touching words spoken cheered as well as impressed them, and made them feel that their friend was not lost but gone on into a higher class of the great school whose Master is eternal love and wisdom. So the tears soon dried, and the young faces looked up like flowers after rain. But the heaven-sent shower sank into the earth, and they were the stronger, sweeter for it, more eager to make life brave and beautiful, because death had gently shown them what it should be.

When the boys came home they found their mother already returned, and Jill upon the parlor sofa listening to her account of the funeral with the same quiet, hopeful look which their own faces wore; for somehow the sadness seemed to have gone, and a sort of Sunday peace remained.

"I'm glad it was all so sweet and pleasant. Come and rest, you look so tired;" and Jill held out her hands to greet them--a crumpled handkerchief in one and a little bunch of fading lilies in the other.

Jack sat down in the low chair beside her and leaned his head against the arm of the sofa, for he was tired. But Frank walked slowly up and down the long rooms with a serious yet serene look on his face, for he felt as if he had learned something that day, and would always be the better for it. Presently he said, stopping before his mother, who leaned in the easy-chair looking up at the picture of her boys' father,

"I should like to have just such things said about me when I die."

"So should I, if I deserved them as Ed did!" cried Jack, earnestly.

"You may if you try. I should be proud to hear them, and if they were true, they would comfort me more than anything else. I am glad you see the lovely side of sorrow, and are learning the lesson such losses teach us," answered their mother, who believed in teaching young people to face trouble bravely, and find the silver lining in the clouds that come to all of us.

"I never thought much about it before, but now dying doesn't seem dreadful at all--only solemn and beautiful. Somehow everybody seems to love everybody else more for it, and try to be kind and good and pious. I can't say what I mean, but you know, mother;" and Frank went pacing on again with the bright look his eyes always wore when he listened to music or read of some noble action.

"That's what Merry said when she and Molly came in on their way home. But Molly felt dreadfully, and so did Mabel. She brought me these flowers to press, for we are all going to keep some to remember dear Ed by," said Jill, carefully smoothing out the little bells as she laid the lilies in her hymn-book, for she too had had a thoughtful hour while she lay alone, imagining all that went on in the church, and shedding a few tender tears over the friend who was always so kind to her.

"I don't want anything to remember him by. I was so fond of him, I couldn't forget if I tried. I know I ought not to say it, but I don't see why God let him die," said Jack, with a quiver in his voice, for his loving heart could not help aching still.

"No, dear, we cannot see or know many things that grieve us very much, but we can trust that it is right, and try to believe that all is meant for our good. That is what faith means, and without it we are miserable. When you were little, you were afraid of the dark, but if I spoke or touched you, then you were sure all was well, and fell asleep holding my hand. God is wiser and stronger than any father or mother, so hold fast to Him, and you will have no doubt or fear, however dark it seems."

"As you do," said Jack, going to sit on the arm of Mamma's chair, with his cheek to hers, willing to trust as she bade him, but glad to hold fast the living hand that had led and comforted him all his life.

"Ed used to say to me when I fretted about getting well, and thought nobody cared for me, which was very naughty, 'Don't be troubled, God won't forget you; and if you must be lame, He will make you able to bear it,'" said Jill, softly, her quick little mind all alive with new thoughts and feelings.

"He believed it, and that's why he liked that hymn so much. I'm glad they sung it to-day," said Frank, bringing his heavy dictionary to lay on the book where the flowers were pressing.

"Oh, thank you! Could you play that tune for me? I didn't hear it, and I'd love to, if you are willing," asked Jill.

"I didn't think I ever should want to play again, but I do. Will you sing it for her, mother? I'm afraid I shall break down if I try alone."

"We will all sing, music is good for us now," said Mamma; and in rather broken voices they did sing Ed's favorite words:

> Not a sparrow falleth but its God doth know,
> Just as when his mandate lays a monarch low;
> Not a leaflet moveth, but its God doth see,
> Think not, then, O mortal, God forgetteth thee.
> Far more precious surely than the birds that fly
> Is a Father's image to a Father's eye.
> E'en thy hairs are numbered; trust Him full and free,
> Cast thy cares before Him, He will comfort thee;
> For the God that planted in thy breast a soul,
> On his sacred tables doth thy name enroll.
> Cheer thine heart, then, mortal, never faithless be,
> He that marks the sparrows will remember thee.

Lesson 122

1. Read chapter 21 of *Jack and Jill.*
2. Tell someone about the chapter.

Chapter 21. Pebbly Beach

"Now, Mr. Jack, it is a moral impossibility to get all those things into one trunk, and you mustn't ask it of me," said Mrs. Pecq, in a tone of despair, as she surveyed the heap of treasures she was expected to pack for the boys.

"Never mind the clothes, we only want a boating-suit apiece. Mamma can put a few collars in her trunk for us; but these necessary things must go," answered Jack, adding his target and air-pistol to the pile of bats, fishing-tackle, games, and a choice collection of shabby balls.

"Those are the necessaries and clothes the luxuries, are they? Why don't you add a velocipede, wheelbarrow, and printing-press, my dear?" asked Mrs. Pecq, while Jill turned up her nose at "boys' rubbish."

"Wish I could. Dare say we shall want them. Women don't know what fellows need, and always must put in a lot of stiff shirts and clean handkerchiefs and clothes-brushes and pots of cold cream. We are going to rough it, and don't want any fuss and feathers," said Jack, beginning to pack the precious balls in his rubber boots, and strap them up with the umbrellas, rods, and bats, seeing that there was no hope of a place in the trunk.

Here Frank came in with two big books, saying calmly, "Just slip these in somewhere, we shall need them."

"But you are not to study at all, so you won't want those great dictionaries," cried Jill, busily packing her new travelling-basket with all sorts of little rolls, bags, and boxes.

"They are not dics, but my Encyclopedia. We shall want to know heaps of things, and this tells about everything. With those books, and a microscope and a telescope, you could travel round the world, and learn all you wanted to. Can't possibly get on without them," said Frank, fondly patting his favorite work.

"My patience! What queer cattle boys are!" exclaimed Mrs. Pecq, while they all laughed. "It can't be done, Mr. Frank; all the boxes are brim full, and you'll have to leave those fat books behind, for there's no place anywhere."

"Then I'll carry them myself;" and Frank tucked one under each arm, with a determined air, which settled the matter.

"I suppose you'll study cockleology instead of boating, and read up on polywogs while we play tennis, or go poking round with your old spy-glass instead of having a jolly good time," said Jack, hauling away on the strap till all was taut and ship-shape with the bundle.

"Tadpoles don't live in salt water, my son, and if you mean conchology, you'd better say so. I shall play as much as I wish, and when I want to know about any new or curious thing, I shall consult my Cyclo, instead of bothering other people with questions, or giving it up like a dunce;" with which crushing reply Frank departed, leaving Jill to pack and unpack her treasures a dozen times, and Jack to dance jigs on the lids of the trunks till they would shut.

A very happy party set off the next day, leaving Mrs. Pecq waving her apron on the steps. Mrs. Minot carried the lunch, Jack his precious bundle with trifles dropping out by the way, and Jill felt very elegant bearing her new basket with red worsted cherries bobbing on the outside. Frank actually did take the Encyclopedia, done up in the roll of shawls, and whenever the others wondered about anything--tides, lighthouses, towns, or natural productions--he brought forth one of the books and triumphantly read therefrom, to the great merriment, if not edification, of his party.

A very short trip by rail and the rest of the journey by boat, to Jill's great contentment, for she hated to be shut up; and while the lads roved here and there she sat under the awning, too happy to talk. But Mrs. Minot watched with real satisfaction how the fresh wind blew the color back into the pale cheeks, how the eyes shone and the heart filled with delight at seeing the lovely world again, and being able to take a share in its active pleasures.

The Willows was a long, low house close to the beach, and as full as a beehive of pleasant people, all intent on having a good time. A great many children were swarming about, and Jill found it impossible to sleep after her journey, there was such a lively clatter of tongues on the piazzas, and so many feet going to and fro in the halls. She lay down obediently while Mrs. Minot settled matters in the two airy rooms and gave her some dinner, but she kept popping up her head to look out of the window to see what she could see. Just opposite stood an artist's cottage and studio, with all manner of charming galleries, towers, steps, and even a sort of drawbridge to pull up when the painter wished to be left in peace. He was absent now, and the visitors took possession of this fine play-place. Children were racing up and down the galleries, ladies sitting in the tower, boys disporting themselves on the roof, and young gentlemen preparing for theatricals in the large studio.

"What fun I'll have over there," thought Jill, watching the merry scene with intense interest, and wondering if the little girls she saw were as nice as Molly and Merry.

Then there were glimpses of the sea beyond the green bank where a path wound along to the beach, whence came the cool dash of waves, and now and then the glimmer of a passing sail.

"Oh, when can I go out? It looks so lovely, I can't wait long," she said, looking as eager as a little gull shut up in a cage and pining for its home on the wide ocean.

"As soon as it is a little cooler, dear, I'm getting ready for our trip, but we must be careful and not do too much at once. 'Slow and sure' is our motto," answered Mrs. Minot, busily collecting the camp-stools, the shawls, the air-cushions, and the big parasols.

"I'll be good, only do let me have my sailor-hat to wear, and my new suit. I'm not a bit tired, and I do want to be like other folks right off," said Jill, who had been improving rapidly of late, and felt much elated at being able to drive out nearly every day, to walk a little, and sit up some hours without any pain or fatigue.

To gratify her, the blue flannel suit with its white trimming was put on, and Mamma was just buttoning the stout boots when Jack thundered at the door, and burst in with all sorts of glorious news.

"Do come out, mother, it's perfectly splendid on the beach! I've found a nice place for Jill to sit, and it's only a step. Lots of capital fellows here; one has a bicycle, and is going to teach us to ride. No end of fun up at the hotel, and everyone seems glad to see us. Two ladies asked about Jill, and one of the girls has got some shells all ready for her, Gerty Somebody, and her mother is so pretty and jolly, I like her ever so much. They sit at our table, and Wally is the boy, younger than I am, but very pleasant. Bacon is the fellow in knickerbockers; just wish you could see what stout legs he's got! Cox is the chap for me, though: we are going fishing to-morrow. He's got a sweet-looking mother, and a sister for you, Jill. Now, then, do come on, I'll take the traps."

Off they went, and Jill thought that very short walk to the shore the most delightful she ever took; for people smiled at the little invalid as she went slowly by leaning on Mrs. Minot's arm, while Jack pranced in front, doing the honors, as if he owned the whole Atlantic. A new world opened to her eyes as they came out upon the pebbly beach full of people enjoying their afternoon promenade. Jill save one rapturous "Oh!" and then sat on her stool, forgetting everything but the beautiful blue ocean rolling away to meet the sky, with nothing to break the wide expanse but a sail here and there, a point of rocks on one hand, the little pier on the other, and white gulls skimming by on their wide wings.

While she sat enjoying herself, Jack showed his mother the place he had found, and a very nice one it was. Just under the green bank lay an old boat propped up with some big stones. A willow drooped over it, the tide rippled up within a few yards of it, and a fine view of the waves could be seen as they dashed over the rocks at the point.

"Isn't it a good cubby-house? Ben Cox and I fixed it for Jill, and she can have it for hers. Put her cushions and things there on the sand the children have thrown in--that will make it soft; then these seats will do for tables; and up in the bow I'm going to have that old rusty tin boiler full of salt-water, so she can put seaweed and crabs and all sorts of chaps in it for an aquarium, you know," explained Jack, greatly interested in establishing his family comfortably before he left them.

"There couldn't be a nicer place, and it is very kind of you to get it ready. Spread the shawls and settle Jill, then you needn't think of us any more, but go and scramble with Frank. I see him over there with his spy-glass and some pleasant-looking boys," said Mamma, bustling about in great spirits.

So the red cushions were placed, the plaids laid, and the little work-basket set upon the seat, all ready for Jill, who was charmed with her nest, and cuddled down under the big parasol, declaring she would keep house there every day.

Even the old boiler pleased her, and Jack raced over the beach to begin his search for inhabitants for the new aquarium, leaving Jill to make friends with some pretty babies digging in the sand, while Mamma sat on the camp-stool and talked with a friend from Harmony Village.

It seemed as if there could not be anything more delightful than to lie there lulled by the sound of the sea, watching the sunset and listening to the pleasant babble of little voices close by. But when they went to tea in the great hall, with six tables full of merry people, and half a dozen maids flying about, Jill thought that was even better, because it was so new to her. Gerty and Wally nodded to her, and their pretty mamma was so kind and so gay, that Jill could not feel bashful after the first few minutes, and soon looked about her, sure of seeing friendly faces everywhere. Frank and Jack ate as if the salt air had already improved their appetites, arid talked about Bacon and Cox as if they had been bosom friends for years. Mamma was as happy as they for her friend, Mrs. Hammond, sat close by; and this rosy lady, who had been a physician, cheered her up by predicting that Jill would soon be running about as well as ever.

But the best of all was in the evening, when the elder people gathered in the parlors and played Twenty Questions, while the children looked on for an hour before going to bed, much amused at the sight of grown people laughing, squabbling, dodging, and joking as if they had all become young again; for, as everyone knows, it is impossible to help lively skirmishes when that game is played. Jill lay in the sofa corner enjoying it all immensely; for she never saw anything so droll, and found it capital fun to help guess the thing, or try to puzzle the opposite side. Her quick wits and bright face attracted people, and in the pauses of the sport she held quite a levee, for everybody was interested in the little invalid. The girls shyly made friends in their own way, the mammas told thrilling tales of the accidents their darlings had survived, several gentlemen kindly offered their boats, and the boys, with the best intentions in life, suggested strolls of two or three miles to Rafe's Chasm and Norman's Woe, or invited her to tennis and archery, as if violent exercise was the cure for all human ills. She was very grateful, and reluctantly went away to bed, declaring, when she got upstairs, that these new friends were the dearest people she ever met, and the Willows the most delightful place in the whole world.

Next day a new life began for the young folks--a very healthy, happy life; and all threw themselves into it so heartily, that it was impossible to help getting great good from it, for these summer weeks, if well spent, work miracles in tired bodies and souls. Frank took a fancy to the bicycle boy, and, being able to hire one of the breakneck articles, soon learned to ride it; and the two might be seen wildly working their long legs on certain smooth stretches of road, or getting up their muscle rowing about the bay till they were almost as brown and nautical in appearance and language as the fishermen who lived in nooks and corners along the shore.

Jack struck up a great friendship with the sturdy Bacon and the agreeable Cox: the latter, being about his own age, was his especial favorite; and they soon were called Box and Cox by the other fellows, which did not annoy them a bit, as both had played parts in that immortal farce. They had capital times fishing, scrambling over the rocks, playing ball and tennis, and rainy days they took possession of the studio opposite, drew up the portcullis, and gallantly defended the castle, which some of the others besieged with old umbrellas for shields, bats for battering-rams, and bunches of burrs for cannon-balls. Great larks went on over there, while the girls applauded from the piazza or chamber-windows, and made a gay flag for the victors to display from the tower when the fight was over.

But Jill had the best time of all, for each day brought increasing strength and spirits, and she improved so fast it was hard to believe that she was the same girl who lay so long almost helpless in the Bird Room at home. Such lively letters as she sent her mother, all about her new friends, her fine sails, drives, and little walks; the good times she had in the evening, the lovely things people gave her, and she was learning to make with shells and sea-weed, and what splendid fun it was to keep house in a boat.

This last amusement soon grew quite absorbing, and her "cubby," as she called it, rapidly became a pretty grotto, where she lived like a little mermaid, daily loving more and more the beauty of the wonderful sea, Finding the boat too sunny at times, the boys cut long willow boughs and arched them over the seats, laying hemlock branches across till a green roof made it cool and shady inside. There Jill sat or lay among her cushions reading, trying to sketch, sorting shells, drying gay sea-weeds, or watching her crabs, jelly-fish, and anemones in the old boiler, now buried in sand and edged about with moss from the woods.

Nobody disturbed her treasures, but kindly added to them, and often when she went to her nest she found fruit or flowers, books or bon-bons, laid ready for her. Everyone pitied and liked the bright little girl who could not run and frisk with the rest, who was so patient and cheerful after her long confinement, ready to help others, and so grateful for any small favor. She found now that the weary months had not been wasted, and was very happy to discover in herself a new sort of strength and sweetness that was not only a comfort to her, but made those about her love and trust her. The songs she had learned attracted the babies, who would leave their play to peep at her and listen when she sung over her work. Passers-by paused to hear the blithe voice of the bird in the green cage, and other invalids, strolling on the beach, would take heart when they saw the child so happy in spite of her great trial.

The boys kept all their marine curiosities for her, and were always ready to take her a row or a sail, as the bay was safe and that sort of travelling suited her better than driving. But the girls had capital times together, and it did Jill good to see another sort from those she knew at home. She had been so much petted of late, that she was getting rather vain of her small accomplishments, and being with strangers richer, better bred and educated than herself, made her more humble in some things, while it showed her the worth of such virtues as she could honestly claim. Mamie Cox took her to drive in the fine carriage of her mamma, and Jill was much impressed by the fact that Mamie was not a bit proud about it, and did not put on any airs, though she had a maid to take care of her. Gerty wore pretty costumes, and came down with pink and blue ribbons in her hair that Jill envied very much; yet Gerty liked her curls, and longed to have some, while her mother, "the lady from Philadelphia," as they called her, was so kind and gay that Jill quite adored her, and always felt as if sunshine had come into the room when she entered. Two little sisters were very interesting to her, and made her long for one of her own when she saw them going about together and heard them talk of their pleasant home, where the great silk factories were. But they invited her to come and see the wonderful cocoons, and taught her to knot pretty gray fringe on a cushion, which delighted her, being so new and easy. There were several other nice little lasses, and they all gathered about Jill with the sweet sympathy children are so quick to show toward those in pain or misfortune. She thought they would not care for a poor little girl like herself, yet here she was the queen of the troupe, and this discovery touched and pleased her very much.

In the morning they camped round the boat on the stones with books, gay work, and merry chatter, till bathing-time. Then the beach was full of life and fun, for everyone looked so droll in the flannel suits, it was hard to believe that the neat ladies and respectable gentlemen who went into the little houses could be the same persons as the queer, short-skirted women with old hats tied down, and bareheaded, barefooted men in old suits, who came skipping over the sand to disport themselves in the sea in the most undignified ways. The boys raced about, looking like circus-tumblers, and the babies were regular little cupids, running away from the waves that tried to kiss their flying feet.

Some of the young ladies and girls were famous swimmers, and looked very pretty in their bright red and blue costumes, with loose hair and gay stockings, as they danced into the water and floated away as fearlessly as real mermaids. Jill had her quiet dip and good rubbing each fine day, and then lay upon the warm sand watching the pranks of the others, and longing to run and dive and shout and tumble with the rest. Now that she was among the well and active, it seemed harder to be patient than when shut up and unable to stir. She felt so much better, and had so little pain to remind her of past troubles, it was almost impossible to help forgetting the poor back and letting her recovered spirits run away with her. If Mrs. Minot had not kept good watch, she would have been off more than once, so eager was she to be "like other girls" again, so difficult was it to keep the restless feet quietly folded among the red cushions.

One day she did yield to temptation, and took a little voyage which might have been her last, owing to the carelessness of those whom she trusted. It was a good lesson, and made her as meek as a lamb during the rest of her stay. Mrs. Minot drove to Gloucester one afternoon, leaving Jill safely established after her nap in the boat, with Gerty and Mamie making lace beside her.

"Don't try to walk or run about, my dear. Sit on the piazza if you get tired of this, and amuse yourself quietly till I come back. I'll not forget the worsted and the canvas," said Mamma, peeping over the bank for a last word as she waited for the omnibus to come along.

"Oh, don't forget the Gibraltars!" cried Jill, popping her head out of the green roof.

"Nor the bananas, please!" added Gerty, looking round one end.

"Nor the pink and blue ribbon to tie our shell-baskets," called Mamie, nearly tumbling into the aquarium at the other end.

Mrs. Minot laughed, and promised, and rumbled away, leaving Jill to an experience which she never forgot.

For half an hour the little girls worked busily, then the boys came for Gerty and Mamie to go to the Chasm with a party of friends who were to leave next day. Off they went, and Jill felt very lonely as the gay voices died away. Everyone had gone somewhere, and only little Harry Hammond and his maid were on the beach. Two or three sand-pipers ran about among the pebbles, and Jill envied them their nimble legs so much, that she could not resist getting up to take a few steps. She longed to run straight away over the firm, smooth sand, and feel again the delight of swift motion; but she dared not try it, and stood leaning on her tall parasol with her book in her hand, when Frank, Jack, and the bicycle boy came rowing lazily along and hailed her.

"Come for a sail, Jill? Take you anywhere you like," called Jack, touched by the lonely figure on the beach.

"I'd love to go, if you will row. Mamma made me promise not to go sailing without a man to take care of me. Would it spoil your fun to have me?" answered Jill, eagerly.

"Not a bit; come out on the big stones and we'll take you aboard," said Frank, as they steered to the place where she could embark the easiest.

"All the rest are gone to the Chasm. I wanted to go, because I've never seen it; but, of course, I had to give it up, as I do most of the fun;" and Jill sat down with an impatient sigh.

"We'll row you round there. Can't land, but you can see the place and shout to the others, if that will be any comfort to you," proposed Frank, as they pulled away round the pier.

"Oh, yes, that would be lovely!" and Jill smiled at Jack, who was steering, for she found it impossible to be dismal now with the fresh wind blowing in her face, the blue waves slapping against the boat, and three good-natured lads ready to gratify her wishes.

Away they went, laughing and talking gayly till they came to Goodwin's Rocks, where an unusual number of people were to be seen though the tide was going out, and no white spray was dashing high into the air to make a sight worth seeing.

"What do you suppose they are about? Never saw such a lot of folks at this time. Shouldn't wonder if something had happened. I say, put me ashore, and I'll cut up and see," said the bicycle boy, who was of an inquiring turn.

"I'll go with you," said Frank; "it won't take but a minute, and I'd like to discover what it is. Maybe something we ought to know about."

So the boys pulled round into a quiet nook, and the two elder ones scrambled up the rocks, to disappear in the crowd. Five, ten, fifteen minutes passed, and they did not return. Jack grew impatient, so did Jill, and bade him run up and bring them back. Glad to know what kept them, Jack departed, to be swallowed up in his turn, for not a sign of a boy did she see after that; and, having vainly strained her eyes to discover the attraction which held them, she gave it up, lay down on their jackets, and began to read.

Then the treacherous tide, as it ebbed lower and lower down the beach, began to lure the boat away; for it was not fastened, and when lightened of its load was an easy prize to the hungry sea, always ready to steal all it can. Jill knew nothing of this, for her story was dull, the gentle motion proved soothing, and before she knew it she was asleep. Little by little the runaway boat slid farther from the shore, and presently was floating out to sea with its drowsy freight, while the careless boys, unconscious of the time they were wasting, lingered to see group after group photographed by the enterprising man who had trundled his camera to the rocks.

In the midst of a dream about home, Jill was roused by a loud shout, and, starting up so suddenly that the sun-umbrella went overboard, she found herself sailing off alone, while the distracted lads roared and beckoned vainly from the cove. The oars lay at their feet, where they left them; and the poor child was quite helpless, for she could not manage the sail, and even the parasol, with which she might have paddled a little, had gone down with all sail set. For a minute, Jill was so frightened that she could only look about her with a scared face, and wonder if drowning was a very disagreeable thing. Then the sight of the bicycle boy struggling with Jack, who seemed inclined to swim after her, and Frank shouting wildly, "Hold on! Come back!" made her laugh in spite of her fear, it was so comical, and their distress so much greater than hers, since it was their own carelessness which caused the trouble.

"I can't come back! There's nothing to hold on to! You didn't fasten me, and now I don't know where I'm going!" cried Jill, looking from the shore to the treacherous sea that was gently carrying her away.

"Keep cool! We'll get a boat and come after you!" roared Frank, before he followed Jack, who had collected his wits and was tearing up the rocks like a chamois hunter.

The bicycle boy calmly sat down to keep his eye on the runaway, calling out from time to time such cheering remarks as "All aboard for Liverpool! Give my love to Victoria! Luff and bear away when you come to Halifax! If you are hard up for provisions, you'll find an apple and some bait in my coat-pocket," and other directions for a comfortable voyage, till his voice was lost in the distance as a stronger current bore her swiftly away and the big waves began to tumble and splash.

At first Jill had laughed at his efforts to keep up her spirits, but when the boat floated round a point of rock that shut in the cove, she felt all alone, and sat quite still, wondering what would become of her. She turned her back to the sea and looked at the dear, safe land, which never had seemed so green and beautiful before. Up on the hill rustled the wood through which the happy party were wandering to the Chasm. On the rocks she still saw the crowd all busy with their own affairs, unconscious of her danger. Here and there artists were sketching in picturesque spots, and in one place an old gentleman sat fishing peacefully. Jill called and waved her handkerchief, but he never looked up, and an ugly little dog barked at her in what seemed to her a most cruel way.

"Nobody sees or hears or cares, and those horrid boys will never catch up!" she cried in despair, as the boat began to rock more and more, and the loud swash of water dashing in and out of the Chasm drew nearer and nearer. Holding on now with both hands she turned and looked straight before her, pale and shivering, while her eyes tried to see some sign of hope among the steep cliffs that rose up on the left. No one was there, though usually at this hour they were full of visitors, and it was time for the walkers to have arrived.

"I wonder if Gerty and Mamie will be sorry if I'm drowned," thought Jill, remembering the poor girl who had been lost in the Chasm not long ago. Her lively fancy pictured the grief of her friends at her loss; but that did not help or comfort her now, and as her anxious gaze wandered along the shore, she said aloud, in a pensive tone.

"Perhaps I shall be wrecked on Norman's Woe, and somebody will make poetry about me. It would be pretty to read, but I don't want to die that way. Oh, why did I come! Why didn't I stay safe and comfortable in my own boat?"

At the thought a sob rose, and poor Jill laid her head down on her lap to cry with all her heart, feeling very helpless, small, and forsaken alone there on the great sea. In the midst of her tears came the thought, "When people are in danger, they ask God to save them;" and, slipping down upon her knees, she said her prayer as she had never said it before, for when human help seems gone we turn to Him as naturally as lost children cry to their father, and feel sure that he will hear and answer them.

After that she felt better, and wiped away the drops that blinded her, to look out again like a shipwrecked mariner watching for a sail. And there it was! Close by, coming swiftly on with a man behind it, a sturdy brown fisher, busy with his lobster-pots, and quite unconscious how like an angel he looked to the helpless little girl in the rudderless boat.

"Hi! hi! Oh, please do stop and get me! I'm lost, no oars, nobody to fix the sail! Oh, oh! please come!" screamed Jill, waving her hat frantically as the other boat skimmed by and the man stared at her as if she really was a mermaid with a fishy tail.

"Keep still! I'll come about and fetch you!" he called out; and Jill obeyed, sitting like a little image of faith, till with a good deal of shifting and flapping of the sail, the other boat came alongside and took her in tow.

A few words told the story, and in five minutes she was sitting snugly tucked up watching an unpleasant mass of lobsters flap about dangerously near her toes, while the boat bounded over the waves with a delightful motion, and every instant brought her nearer borne. She did not say much, but felt a good deal; and when they met two boats coming to meet her, manned by very anxious crews of men and boys, she was so pale and quiet that Jack was quite bowed down with remorse, and Frank nearly pitched the bicycle boy overboard because he gayly asked Jill how she left her friends in England. There was great rejoicing over her, for the people on the rocks had heard of her loss, and ran about like ants when their hill is disturbed. Of course half a dozen amiable souls posted off to the Willows to tell the family that the little girl was drowned, so that when the rescuers appeared quite a crowd was assembled on the beach to welcome her. But Jill felt so used up with her own share of the excitement that she was glad to be carried to the house by Frank and Jack, and laid upon her bed, where Mrs. Hammond soon restored her with sugar-coated pills, and words even sweeter and more soothing.

Other people, busied with their own pleasures, forgot all about it by the next day; but Jill remembered that hour long afterward, both awake and asleep, for her dreams were troubled, and she often started up imploring someone to save her. Then she would recall the moment when, feeling most helpless, she had asked for help, and it had come as quickly as if that tearful little cry had been heard and answered, though her voice had been drowned by the dash of the waves that seemed ready to devour her. This made a deep impression on her, and a sense of childlike faith in the Father of all began to grow up within her; for in that lonely voyage, short as it was, she had found a very precious treasure to keep for ever, to lean on, and to love during the longer voyage which all must take before we reach our home.

Lesson 123

1. Read chapter 22 of *Jack and Jill*.
2. Tell someone what happened in this chapter.

Chapter 22. A Happy Day

"Oh dear! Only a week more, and then we must go back. Don't you hate the thoughts of it?" said Jack, as he was giving Jill her early walk on the beach one August morning.

"Yes, it will be dreadful to leave Gerty and Mamie and all the nice people. But I'm so much better I won't have to be shut up again, even if I don't go to school. How I long to see Merry and Molly. Dear things, if it wasn't for them I should hate going home more than you do," answered Jill, stepping along quite briskly, and finding it very hard to resist breaking into a skip or a run, she felt so well and gay.

"Wish they could be here to-day to see the fun," said Jack, for it was the anniversary of the founding of the place, and the people celebrated it by all sorts of festivity.

"I did want to ask Molly, but your mother is so good to me I couldn't find courage to do it. Mammy told me not to ask for a thing, and I'm sure I don't get a chance. I feel just as if I was your truly born sister, Jack."

"That's all right, I'm glad you do," answered Jack, comfortably, though his mind seemed a little absent and his eyes twinkled when she spoke of Molly. "Now, you sit in the cubby-house, and keep quiet till the boat comes in. Then the fun will begin, and you must be fresh and ready to enjoy it. Don't run off, now, I shall want to know where to find you by and by."

"No more running off, thank you. I'll stay here till you come, and finish this box for Molly; she has a birthday this week, and I've written to ask what day, so I can send it right up and surprise her."

Jack's eyes twinkled more than ever as he helped Jill settle herself in the boat, and then with a whoop he tore over the beach, as if practising for the race which was to come off in the afternoon.

Jill was so busy with her work that time went quickly, and the early boat came in just as the last pink shell was stuck in its place. Putting the box in the sun to dry, she leaned out of her nook to watch the gay parties land, and go streaming up the pier along the road that went behind the bank that sheltered her. Flocks of children were running about on the sand, and presently strangers appeared, eager to see and enjoy all the delights of this gala-day.

"There's a fat little boy who looks ever so much like Boo," said Jill to herself, watching the people and hoping they would not come and find her, since she had promised to stay till Jack returned.

The fat little boy was staring about him in a blissful sort of maze, holding a wooden shovel in one hand and the skirts of a young girl with the other. Her back was turned to Jill, but something in the long brown braid with a fly-away blue bow hanging down her back looked very familiar to Jill. So did the gray suit and the Japanese umbrella; but the hat was strange, and while she was thinking how natural the boots looked, the girl turned round.

"Why, how much she looks like Molly! It can't be--yes, it might, I do believe it is!" cried Jill, starting up and hardly daring to trust her own eyes.

As she came out of her nest and showed herself, there could be no doubt about the other girl, for she gave one shout and came racing over the beach with both arms out, while her hat blew off unheeded, and the gay umbrella flew away, to the great delight of all the little people except Boo, who was upset by his sister's impetuous rush, and lay upon his back howling. Molly did not do all the running, though, and Jill got her wish, for, never stopping to think of herself, she was off at once, and met her friend half-way with an answering cry. It was a pretty sight to see them run into

155

one another's arms and hug and kiss and talk and skip in such a state of girlish joy they never cared who saw or laughed at their innocent raptures.

"You darling dear! where did you come from?" cried Jill, holding Molly by both shoulders, and shaking her a little to be sure she was real.

"Mrs. Minot sent for us to spend a week. You look so well, I can't believe my eyes!" answered Molly, patting Jill's cheeks and kissing them over and over, as if to make sure the bright color would not come off.

"A week? How splendid! Oh, I've such heaps to tell and show you; come right over to my cubby and see how lovely it is," said Jill, forgetting everybody else in her delight at getting Molly.

"I must get poor Boo, and my hat and umbrella, I left them all behind me when I saw you," laughed Molly, looking back.

But Mrs. Minot and Jack had consoled Boo and collected the scattered property, so the girls went on arm in arm, and had a fine time before anyone had the heart to disturb them. Molly was charmed with the boat, and Jill very glad the box was done in season. Both had so much to tell and hear and plan, that they would have sat there for ever if bathing-time had not come, and the beach suddenly looked like a bed of red and yellow tulips, for everyone took a dip, and the strangers added much to the fun.

Molly could swim like a duck, and quite covered herself with glory by diving off the pier. Jack undertook to teach Boo, who was a promising pupil, being so plump that he could not sink if he tried. Jill was soon through, and lay on the sand enjoying the antics of the bathers till she was so faint with laughter she was glad to hear the dinner-horn and do the honors of the Willows to Molly, whose room was next hers.

Boat-races came first in the afternoon, and the girls watched them, sitting luxuriously in the nest, with the ladies and children close by. The sailing-matches were very pretty to see; but Molly and Jill were more interested in the rowing, for Frank and the bicycle boy pulled one boat, and the friends felt that this one must win. It did, though the race was not very exciting nor the prize of great worth; but the boys and girls were satisfied, and Jack was much exalted, for he always told Frank he could do great things if he would only drop books and "go in on his muscle."

Foot-races followed, and, burning to distinguish himself also, Jack insisted on trying, though his mother warned him that the weak leg might be harmed, and he had his own doubts about it, as he was all out of practice. However, he took his place with a handkerchief tied round his head, red shirt and stockings, and his sleeves rolled up as if he meant business. Jill and Molly could not sit still during this race, and stood on the bank quite trembling with excitement as the half-dozen runners stood in a line at the starting-post waiting for the word "Go!"

Off they went at last over the smooth beach to the pole with the flag at the further end, and everyone watched them with mingled interest and merriment, for they were a droll set, and the running not at all scientific with most of them. One young fisherman with big boots over his trousers started off at a great pace, pounding along in the most dogged way, while a little chap in a tight bathing-suit with very thin legs skimmed by him, looking so like a sand-piper it was impossible to help laughing at both. Jack's former training stood him in good stead now; for he went to work in professional style, and kept a steady trot till the flagpole had been passed, then he put on his speed and shot ahead of all the rest, several of whom broke down and gave up. But Cox and Bacon held on gallantly; and soon it was evident that the sturdy legs in the knickerbockers were gaining fast, for Jack gave his ankle an ugly wrench on a round pebble, and the weak knee began to fail. He did his best, however, and quite a breeze of enthusiasm stirred the spectators as the three boys came down the course like mettlesome horses, panting, pale, or purple, but each bound to win at any cost.

"Now, Bacon!" "Go it, Minot!" "Hit him up, Cox!" "Jack's ahead!" "No, he isn't!" "Here they come!" "Bacon's done it!" shouted the other boys, and they were right; Bacon had won, for the gray legs came in just half a yard ahead of the red ones, and Minot tumbled into his brother's arms with hardly breath enough left to gasp out, good-humoredly, "All right, I'm glad he beat!"

Then the victor was congratulated and borne off by his friends to refresh himself, while the lookers-on scattered to see a game of tennis and the shooting of the Archery Club up at the hotel. Jack was soon rested, and, making light of his defeat, insisted on taking the girls to see the fun. So they drove up in the old omnibus, and enjoyed the pretty sight very much; for the young ladies were in uniform, and the broad green ribbons over the white dresses, the gay quivers, long bows, and big targets, made a lively scene. The shooting was good; a handsome damsel got the prize of a dozen arrows, and everyone clapped in the most enthusiastic manner.

Molly and Jill did not care about tennis, so they went home to rest and dress for the evening, because to their minds the dancing, the illumination, and the fireworks were the best fun of all. Jill's white bunting with cherry ribbons was very becoming, and the lively feet in the new slippers patted the floor impatiently as the sound of dance music came down to the Willows after tea, and the other girls waltzed on the wide piazza because they could not keep still.

"No dancing for me, but Molly must have a good time. You'll see that she does, won't you, boys?" said Jill, who knew that her share of the fun would be lying on a settee and watching the rest enjoy her favorite pastime.

Frank and Jack promised, and kept their word handsomely; for there was plenty of room in the great dancing-hall at the hotel, and the band in the pavilion played such inspiring music that, as the bicycle boy said, "Everyone who had a leg couldn't help shaking it." Molly was twirled about to her heart's content, and flew hither and thither like a blue butterfly; for all the lads liked her, and she kept running up to tell Jill the funny things they said and did.

As night darkened from all the houses in the valley, on the cliffs and along the shore lights shone and sparkled; for everyone decorated with gay lanterns, and several yachts in the bay strung colored lamps about the little vessels, making a pretty picture on the quiet sea. Jill thought she had never seen anything so like fairy-land, and felt very like one in a dream as she drove slowly up and down with Mamie, Gerty, Molly, and Mrs. Cox in the carriage, so that she might see it all without too much fatigue. It was very lovely; and when rockets began to whizz, filling the air with golden rain, a shower of colored stars, fiery dragons, or glittering wheels, the girls could only shriek with delight, and beg to stay a little longer each time the prudent lady proposed going home.

It had to be at last; but Molly and Jill comforted themselves by a long talk in bed, for it was impossible to sleep with glares of light coming every few minutes, flocks of people talking and tramping by in the road, and bursts of music floating down to them as the older but not wiser revellers kept up the merriment till a late hour. They dropped off at last; but Jill had the nightmare, and Molly was waked up by a violent jerking of her braid as Jill tried to tow her along, dreaming she was a boat.

They were too sleepy to laugh much then, but next morning they made merry over it, and went to breakfast with such happy faces that all the young folks pronounced Jill's friend a most delightful girl. What a good time Molly did have that week! Other people were going to leave also, and therefore much picnicking, boating, and driving was crowded into the last days. Clambakes on the shore, charades in the studio, sewing-parties at the boat, evening frolics in the big dining-room, farewell calls, gifts, and invitations, all sorts of plans for next summer, and vows of eternal friendship exchanged between people who would soon forget each other. It was very pleasant, till poor Boo innocently added to the excitement by poisoning a few of his neighbors with a bad lobster.

The ambitious little soul pined to catch one of these mysterious but lovely red creatures, and spent days fishing on the beach, investigating holes and corners, and tagging after the old man who supplied the house. One day after a high wind he found several "lobs" washed up on the beach, and, though disappointed at their color, he picked out a big one, and set off to show his prize to Molly. Half-way home he met the old man on his way with a basket of fish, and being tired of lugging his contribution laid it with the others, meaning to explain later. No one saw him do it, as the old man was busy with his pipe; and Boo ran back to get more dear lobs, leaving his treasure to go into the kettle and appear at supper, by which time he had forgotten all about it.

Fortunately none of the children ate any, but several older people were made ill, and quite a panic prevailed that night as one after the other called up the doctor, who was boarding close by; and good Mrs. Grey, the hostess, ran about with hot flannels, bottles of medicine, and distracted messages from room to room. All were comfortable by morning, but the friends of the sufferers lay in wait for the old fisherman, and gave him a good scolding for his carelessness. The poor man was protesting his innocence when Boo, who was passing by, looked into the basket, and asked what had become of his lob. A few questions brought the truth to light, and a general laugh put everyone in good humor, when poor Boo mildly said, by way of explanation,

"I fought I was helpin' Mrs. Dray, and I did want to see the dreen lob come out all red when she boiled him. But I fordot, and I don't fink I'll ever find such a nice big one any more."

"For our sakes, I hope you won't, my dear," said Mrs. Hammond, who had been nursing one of the sufferers.

"It's lucky we are going home to-morrow, or that child would be the death of himself and everybody else. He is perfectly crazy about fish, and I've pulled him out of that old lobster-pot on the beach a dozen times," groaned Molly, much afflicted by the mishaps of her young charge.

There was a great breaking up next day, and the old omnibus went off to the station with Bacon hanging on behind, the bicycle boy and his iron whirligig atop, and heads popping out of all the windows for last good-byes. Our party and the Hammonds were going by boat, and were all ready to start for the pier when Boo and little Harry were missing. Molly, the maid, and both boys ran different ways to find them; and all sorts of dreadful suggestions were being made when shouts of laughter were heard from the beach, and the truants appeared, proudly dragging in Harry's little wagon a dead devil-fish, as the natives call that ugly thing which looks like a magnified tadpole-- all head and no body.

"We've dot him!" called the innocents, tugging up their prize with such solemn satisfaction it was impossible to help laughing.

"I always wanted to tatch a whale, and this is a baby one, I fink. A boy said, when they wanted to die they comed on the sand and did it, and we saw this one go dead just now. Ain't lie pretty?" asked Boo, displaying the immense mouth with fond pride, while his friend flapped the tail.

"What are you going to do with him?" said Mrs. Hammond, regarding her infant as if she often asked herself the same question about her boy.

"Wap him up in a paper and tate him home to pay wid," answered Harry, with such confidence in his big blue eyes that it was very hard to disappoint his hopes and tell him the treasure must be left behind.

Wails of despair burst from both children as the hard-hearted boys tipped out the little whale, and hustled the indignant fishermen on board the boat, which had been whistling for them impatiently. Boo recovered his spirits first, and gulping down a sob that nearly shook his hat off, consoled his companion in affliction and convulsed his friends by taking from his pocket several little crabs, the remains of a jelly-fish, and such a collection of pebbles that Frank understood why he found the fat boy such a burden when he shouldered him, kicking and howling, in the late run to the boat. These delicate toys healed the wounds of Boo and Harry, and they were soon happily walking the little "trabs" about inside a stone wall of their own building, while the others rested after their exertions, and laid plans for coming to the Willows another year, as people usually did who had once tasted the wholesome delights and cordial hospitality of this charming place.

Lesson 124

1. Read chapter 23 of *Jack and Jill.*
2. Write a one-sentence summary of the chapter.

Chapter 23. Cattle Show

The children were not the only ones who had learned something at Pebbly Beach. Mrs. Minot had talked a good deal with some very superior persons, and received light upon various subjects which had much interested or perplexed her. While the ladies worked or walked together, they naturally spoke oftenest and most earnestly about their children, and each contributed her experience. Mrs. Hammond, who had been a physician for many years, was wise in the care of healthy little bodies, and the cure of sick ones. Mrs. Channing, who had read, travelled, and observed much in the cause of education, had many useful hints about the training of young minds and hearts. Several teachers reported their trials, and all the mothers were eager to know how to bring up their boys and girls to be healthy, happy, useful men and women.

As young people do not care for such discussions, we will not describe them, but as the impression they made upon one of the mammas affected our hero and heroine, we must mention the changes which took place in their life when they all got home again.

"School begins tomorrow. Oh, dear!" sighed Jack, as he looked up his books in the Bird Room, a day or two after their return.

"Don't you want to go? I long to, but don't believe I shall. I saw our mothers talking to the doctor last night, but I haven't dared to ask what they decided," said Jill, affectionately eying the long-unused books in her little library.

"I've had such a jolly good time, that I hate to be shut up all day worse than ever. Don't you, Frank?" asked Jack, with a vengeful slap at the arithmetic which was the torment of his life.

"Well, I confess I don't hanker for school as much as I expected. I'd rather take a spin on the old bicycle. Our roads are so good, it is a great temptation to hire a machine, and astonish the natives. That's what comes of idleness. So brace up, my boy, and go to work, for vacation is over," answered Frank, gravely regarding the tall pile of books before him, as if trying to welcome his old friends, or tyrants, rather, for they ruled him with a rod of iron when he once gave himself up to them.

"Ah, but vacation is not over, my dears," said Mrs. Minot, hearing the last words as she came in prepared to surprise her family.

"Glad of it. How much longer is it to be?" asked Jack, hoping for a week at least.

"Two or three years for some of you."

"What?" cried all three, in utter astonishment, as they stared at Mamma, who could not help smiling, though she was very much in earnest.

"For the next two or three years I intend to cultivate my boys' bodies, and let their minds rest a good deal, from books at least. There is plenty to learn outside of school-houses, and I don't mean to shut you up just when you most need all the air and exercise you can get. Good health, good principles, and a good education are the three blessings I ask for you, and I am going to make sure of the first, as a firm foundation for the other two."

"But, mother, what becomes of college?" asked Frank, rather disturbed at this change of base.

"Put it off for a year, and see if you are not better fitted for it then than now."

"But I am already fitted: I've worked like a tiger all this year, and I'm sure I shall pass."

"Ready in one way, but not in another. That hard work is no preparation for four years of still harder study. It has cost you these round shoulders, many a headache, and consumed hours when you had far better have been on the river or in the fields. I cannot have you break down, as so many boys do, or pull through at the cost of ill-health afterward. Eighteen is young enough to begin the steady grind, if you have a strong constitution to keep pace with the eager mind. Sixteen is too young to send even my good boy out into the world, just when he most needs his mother's care to help him be the man she hopes to see him."

Mrs. Minot laid her hand on his shoulder as she spoke, looking so fond and proud that it was impossible to rebel, though some of his most cherished plans were spoilt.

"Other fellows go at my age, and I was rather pleased to be ready at sixteen," he began. But she added, quickly,

"They go, but how do they come out? Many lose health of body, and many what is more precious still, moral strength, because too young and ignorant to withstand temptations of all sorts. The best part of education does not come from books, and the good principles I value more than either of the other things are to be carefully watched over till firmly fixed; then you may face the world, and come to no real harm. Trust me, dear, I do it for your sake; so bear the disappointment bravely, and in the end I think you will say I'm right."

"I'll do my best; but I don't see what is to become of us if we don't go to school. You will get tired of it first," said Frank, trying to set a good example to the others, who were looking much impressed and interested.

"No danger of that, for I never sent my children to school to get rid of them, and now that they are old enough to be companions, I want them at home more than ever. There are to be some lessons, however, for busy minds must be fed, but not crammed; so you boys will go and recite at certain hours such things as seem most important. But there is to be no studying at night, no shutting up all the best hours of the day, no hurry and fret of getting on fast, or skimming over the surface of many studies without learning any thoroughly."

"So I say!" cried Jack, pleased with the new idea, for he never did love books. "I do hate to be driven so I don't half understand, because there is no time to have things explained. School is good fun as far as play goes; but I don't see the sense of making a fellow learn eighty questions in geography one day, and forget them the next."

"What is to become of me, please?" asked Jill, meekly.

"You and Molly are to have lessons here. I was a teacher when I was young, you know, and liked it, so I shall be school-ma'am, and leave my house-keeping in better hands than mine. I always thought that mothers should teach their girls during these years, and vary their studies to suit the growing creatures as only mothers can."

"That will be splendid! Will Molly's father let her come?" cried Jill, feeling quite reconciled to staying at home, if her friend was to be with her.

"He likes the plan very much, for Molly is growing fast, and needs a sort of care that Miss Dawes cannot give her. I am not a hard mistress, and I hope you will find my school a pleasant one."

"I know I shall; and I'm not disappointed, because I was pretty sure I couldn't go to the old school again, when I heard the doctor say I must be very careful for a long time. I thought he meant months; but if it must be years, I can bear it, for I've been happy this last one though I was sick," said Jill, glad to show that it had not been wasted time by being cheerful and patient now.

"That's my good girl!" and Mrs. Minot stroked the curly black head as if it was her own little daughter's. "You have done so well, I want you to go on improving, for care now will save you pain and disappointment by and by. You all have got a capital start during these six weeks, so it is a good time to begin my experiment. If it does not work well, we will go back to school and college next spring."

"Hurrah for Mamma and the long vacation!" cried Jack, catching up two big books and whirling them round like clubs, as if to get his muscles in order at once.

"Now I shall have time to go to the Gymnasium and straighten out my back," said Frank, who was growing so tall he needed more breadth to make his height symmetrical.

"And to ride horseback. I am going to hire old Jane and get out the little phaeton, so we can all enjoy the fine weather while it lasts. Molly and I can drive Jill, and you can take turns in the saddle when you are tired of ball and boating. Exercise of all sorts is one of the lessons we are to learn," said Mrs. Minot, suggesting all the pleasant things she could to sweeten the pill for her pupils, two of whom did love their books, not being old enough to know that even an excellent thing may be overdone.

"Won't that be gay? I'll get down the saddle to-day, so we can begin right off. Lem rides, and we can go together. Hope old Jane will like it as well as I shall," said Jack, who had found a new friend in a pleasant lad lately come to town.

"You must see that she does, for you boys are to take care of her. We will put the barn in order, and you can decide which shall be hostler and which gardener, for I don't intend to hire labor on the place any more. Our estate is not a large one, and it will be excellent work for you, my men."

"All right! I'll see to Jane. I love horses," said Jack, well pleased with the prospect.

"My horse won't need much care. I prefer a bicycle to a beast, so I'll get in the squashes, pick the apples, and cover the strawberry bed when it is time," added Frank, who had enjoyed the free life at Pebbly Beach so much that he was willing to prolong it.

"You may put me in a hen-coop, and keep me there a year, if you like. I won't fret, for I'm sure you know what is best for me," said Jill, gayly, as she looked up at the good friend who had done so much for her.

"I'm not sure that I won't put you in a pretty cage and send you to Cattle Show, as a sample of what we can do in the way of taming a wild bird till it is nearly as meek as a dove," answered Mrs. Minot, much gratified at the amiability of her flock.

"I don't see why there should not be an exhibition of children, and prizes for the good and pretty ones, as well as for fat pigs, fine horses, or handsome fruit and flowers--I don't mean a baby show, but boys and girls, so people can see what the prospect is of a good crop for the next generation," said Frank, glancing toward the tower of the building where the yearly Agricultural Fair was soon to be held.

"Years ago, there was a pretty custom here of collecting all the schools together in the spring, and having a festival at the Town Hall. Each school showed its best pupils, and the parents looked on at the blooming flower show. It was a pity it was ever given up, for the schools have never been so good as then, nor the interest in them so great;" and Mrs. Minot wondered, as many people do, why farmers seem to care more for their cattle and crops than for their children, willingly spending large sums on big barns and costly experiments, while the school-houses are shabby and inconvenient, and the cheapest teachers preferred.

"Ralph is going to send my bust. He asked if he might, and mother said Yes. Mr. German thinks it very good, and I hope other people will," said Jill, nodding toward the little plaster head that smiled down from its bracket with her own merry look.

"I could send my model; it is nearly done. Ralph told me it was a clever piece of work, and he knows," added Frank, quite taken with the idea of exhibiting his skill in mechanics.

"And I could send my star bed quilt! They always have things of that kind at Cattle Show;" and Jill began to rummage in the closet for the pride of her heart, burning to display it to an admiring world.

"I haven't got anything. Can't sew rags together; or make baby engines, and I have no live-stock-- yes, I have too! There's old Bun. I'll send him, for the fun of it; he really is a curiosity, for he is the biggest one I ever saw, and hopping into the lime has made his fur such a queer color, he looks like a new sort of rabbit. I'll catch and shut him up before he gets wild again;" and off rushed Jack to lure unsuspecting old Bun, who had grown tame during their absence, into the cage which he detested.

They all laughed at his ardor, but the fancy pleased them; and as Mamma saw no reason why their little works of art should not be sent, Frank fell to work on his model, and Jill resolved to finish her quilt at once, while Mrs. Minot went off to see Mr. Acton about the hours and studies for the boys.

In a week or two, the young people were almost resigned to the loss of school, for they found themselves delightfully fresh for the few lessons they did have, and not weary of play, since it took many useful forms. Old Jane not only carried them all to ride, but gave Jack plenty of work keeping her premises in nice order. Frank mourned privately over the delay of college, but found a solace in his whirligig and the Gymnasium, where he set himself to developing a chest to match the big head above, which head no longer ached with eight or ten hours of study. Harvesting beans and raking up leaves seemed to have a soothing effect upon his nerves, for now he fell asleep at once instead of thumping his pillow with vexation because his brain would go on working at difficult problems and passages when he wanted it to stop.

Jill and Molly drove away in the little phaeton every fair morning over the sunny hills and through the changing woods, filling their hands with asters and golden-rod, their lungs with the pure, invigorating air, and their heads with all manner of sweet and happy fancies and feelings born of the wholesome influences about them, People shook their heads, and said it was wasting time; but the rosy-faced girls were content to trust those wiser than themselves, and found their new school very pleasant. They read aloud a good deal, rapidly acquiring one of the rarest and most beautiful accomplishments; for they could stop and ask questions as they went along, so that they understood what they read, which is half the secret. A thousand things came up as they sewed together in the afternoon, and the eager minds received much general information in an easy and well-ordered way. Physiology was one of the favorite studies, and Mrs. Hammond often came in to give them a little lecture, teaching them to understand the wonders of their own systems, and how to keep them in order--a lesson of far more importance just then than Greek or Latin, for girls are the future mothers, nurses, teachers, of the race, and should feel how much depends on them. Merry could not resist the attractions of the friendly circle, and soon persuaded her mother to let her do as they did; so she got more exercise and less study, which was just what the delicate girl needed.

The first of the new ideas seemed to prosper, and the second, though suggested in joke, was carried out in earnest, for the other young people were seized with a strong desire to send something to the Fair. In fact, all sorts of queer articles were proposed, and much fun prevailed, especially among the boys, who ransacked their gardens for mammoth vegetables, sighed for five-legged calves, blue roses, or any other natural curiosity by means of which they might distinguish themselves. Ralph was the only one who had anything really worth sending; for though Frank's model seemed quite perfect, it obstinately refused to go, and at the last moment blew up with a report like a pop-gun. So it was laid away for repairs, and its disappointed maker devoted his energies to helping Jack keep Bun in order; for that indomitable animal got out of every prison they put him in, and led Jack a dreadful life during that last week. At all hours of the day and night that distracted boy would start up, crying, "There he is again!" and dart out to give chase and capture the villain now grown too fat to run as he once did.

The very night before the Fair, Frank was wakened by a chilly draught, and, getting up to see where it came from, found Jack's door open and bed empty, while the vision of a white ghost flitting about the garden suggested a midnight rush after old Bun. Frank watched laughingly, till poor Jack came toward the house with the gentleman in gray kicking lustily in his arms, and then whispered in a sepulchral tone,

"Put him in the old refrigerator, he can't get out of that,"

Blessing him for the suggestion, the exhausted hunter shut up his victim in the new cell, and found it a safe one, for Bun could not burrow through a sheet of zinc, or climb up the smooth walls.

Jill's quilt was a very elaborate piece of work, being bright blue with little white stars all over it; this she finished nicely, and felt sure no patient old lady could outdo it. Merry decided to send butter, for she had been helping her mother in the dairy that summer, and rather liked the light part of the labor. She knew it would please her very much if she chose that instead of wild flowers, so she practised moulding the yellow pats into pretty shapes, that it might please both eye and taste.

Molly declared she would have a little pen, and put Boo in it, as the prize fat boy--a threat which so alarmed the innocent that he ran away, and was only two or three miles from home, asleep under the wall, with two seed-cakes and a pair of socks done up in a bundle. Being with difficulty convinced that it was a joke, he consented to return to his family, but was evidently suspicious, till Molly decided to send her cats, and set about preparing them for exhibition. The Minots' deserted Bunny-house was rather large; but as cats cannot be packed as closely as much-enduring sheep, Molly borrowed this desirable family mansion, and put her darlings into it, where they soon settled down, and appeared to enjoy their new residence. It had been scrubbed up and painted red, cushions and plates put in, and two American flags adorned the roof. Being barred all round, a fine view of the Happy Family could be had, now twelve in number, as Molasses had lately added three white kits to the varied collection.

The girls thought this would be the most interesting spectacle of all, and Grif proposed to give some of the cats extra tails, to increase their charms, especially poor Mortification, who would appreciate the honor of two, after having none for so long. But Molly declined, and Grif looked about him for some attractive animal to exhibit, so that he too might go in free and come to honor, perhaps.

A young lady in the town owned a donkey, a small, gray beast, who insisted on tripping along the sidewalks and bumping her rider against the walls as she paused to browse at her own sweet will, regardless of blows or cries, till ready to move on. Expressing great admiration for this rare animal, Grif obtained leave to display the charms of Graciosa at the Fair. Little did she guess the dark designs entertained against her dignity, and happily she was not as sensitive to ridicule as a less humble-minded animal, so she went willingly with her new friend, and enjoyed the combing and trimming up which she received at his hands, while he prepared for the great occasion.

When the morning of September 28th arrived, the town was all astir, and the Fair ground a lively scene. The air was full of the lowing of cattle, the tramp of horses, squealing of indignant pigs, and clatter of tongues, as people and animals streamed in at the great gate and found their proper places. Our young folks were in a high state of excitement, as they rumbled away with their treasures in a hay-cart. The Bunny-house might have been a cage of tigers, so rampant were the cats at this new move. Old Bun, in a small box, brooded over the insult of the refrigerator, and looked as fierce as a rabbit could. Gus had a coop of rare fowls, who clucked wildly all the way, while Ralph, with the bust in his arms, stood up in front, and Jill and Molly bore the precious bed quilt, as they sat behind.

These objects of interest were soon arranged, and the girls went to admire Merry's golden butter cups among the green leaves, under which lay the ice that kept the pretty flowers fresh. The boys were down below, where the cackling was very loud, but not loud enough to drown the sonorous bray which suddenly startled them as much as it did the horses outside. A shout of laughter followed, and away went the lads, to see what the fun was, while the girls ran out on the balcony, as someone said, "It's that rogue of a Grif with some new joke."

It certainly was, and, to judge from the peals of merriment, the joke was a good one. In at the gate came a two-headed donkey, ridden by Grif, in great spirits at his success, for the gate-keeper laughed so he never thought to ask for toll. A train of boys followed him across the ground, lost in admiration of the animal and the cleverness of her rider. Among the stage properties of the Dramatic Club was the old ass's head once used in some tableaux from "Midsummer Night's Dream." This Grif had mended up, and fastened by means of straps and a collar to poor Graciosa's neck, hiding ~ work with a red cloth over her back. One eye was gone, but the other still opened and shut, and the long ears wagged by means of strings, which he slyly managed with the bridle, so the artificial head looked almost as natural as the real one. The funniest thing of all was the innocent air of Graciosa, and the mildly inquiring expression with which she now and then turned to look at or to smell of the new ornament as if she recognized a friend's face, yet was perplexed by its want of animation. She vented her feelings in a bray, which Grif imitated, convulsing all hearers by the sound as well as by the wink the one eye gave, and the droll waggle of one erect ear, while the other pointed straight forward.

The girls laughed so at the ridiculous sight that they nearly fell over the railing, and the boys were in ecstasies, especially when Grif, emboldened by his success, trotted briskly round the race-course, followed by the cheers of the crowd. Excited by the noise, Graciosa did her best, till the false head, loosened by the rapid motion, slipped round under her nose, causing her to stop so suddenly that Grif flew off, alighting on his own head with a violence which would have killed any other boy. Sobered by his downfall, he declined to mount again, but led his steed to repose in a shed, while he rejoined his friends, who were waiting impatiently to congratulate him on his latest and best prank.

The Committee went their rounds soon after, and, when the doors were again opened, everyone hurried to see if their articles had received a premium. A card lay on the butter cups, and Mrs. Grant was full of pride because her butter always took a prize, and this proved that Merry was walking in her mother's steps, in this direction at least. Another card swung from the blue quilt, for the kindly judges knew who made it, and were glad to please the little girl, though several others as curious but not so pretty hung near by. The cats were admired, but, as they were not among the animals usually exhibited, there was no prize awarded. Gus hoped his hens would get one; hut somebody else outdid him, to the great indignation of Laura and Lotty, who had fed the white biddies faithfully for months. Jack was sure his rabbit was the biggest there, and went eagerly to look for his premium. But neither card nor Bun were to be seen, for the old rascal had escaped for the last time, and was never seen again; which was a great comfort to Jack, who was heartily tired of him.

Ralph's bust was the best of all, for not only did it get a prize, and was much admired, but a lady, who found Jill and Merry rejoicing over it, was so pleased with the truth and grace of the little head, that she asked about the artist, and whether he would do one of her own child, who was so delicate she feared he might not live long.

Merry gladly told the story of her ambitious friend, and went to find him, that he might secure the order. While she was gone, Jill took up the tale, gratefully telling how kind he had been to her, how patiently he worked and waited, and how much he longed to go abroad. Fortunately the lady was rich and generous, as well as fond of art, and being pleased with the bust, and interested in the young sculptor, gave him the order where he came, and filled his soul with joy by adding, that, if it suited her when done, it should be put into marble. She lived in the city, and Ralph soon arranged his work so that he could give up his noon hour, and go to model the child; for every penny he could earn or save now was very precious, as he still hoped to go abroad.

The girls were so delighted with this good fortune, that they did not stay for the races, but went home to tell the happy news, leaving the boys to care for the cats, and enjoy the various matches to come off that day.

"I'm so glad I tried to look pleasant when I was lying on the board while Ralph did my head, for the pleasantness got into the clay face, and that made the lady like it," said Jill, as she lay resting on the sofa.

"I always thought it was a dear, bright little face, but now I love and admire it more than ever," cried Merry, kissing it gratefully, as she remembered the help and pleasure it had given Ralph.

Lesson 125

1. Read chapter 24 of *Jack and Jill*.
2. Tell someone about how the book ends.

Chapter 24. Down the River

A fortnight later, the boys were picking apples one golden October afternoon, and the girls were hurrying to finish their work, that they might go and help the harvesters. It was six weeks now since the new school began, and they had learned to like it very much, though they found that it was not all play, by any means. But lessons, exercise, and various sorts of housework made an agreeable change, and they felt that they were learning things which would be useful to them all their lives. They had been making underclothes for themselves, and each had several neatly finished garments cut, fitted, and sewed by herself, and trimmed with the pretty tatting Jill made in such quantities while she lay on her sofa.

Now they were completing new dressing sacks, and had enjoyed this job very much, as each chose her own material, and suited her own taste in the making. Jill's was white, with tiny scarlet leaves all over it, trimmed with red braid and buttons so like checkerberries she was tempted to eat them. Molly's was gay, with bouquets of every sort of flower, scalloped all round, and adorned with six buttons, each of a different color, which she thought the last touch of elegance. Merry's, though the simplest, was the daintiest of the three, being pale blue, trimmed with delicate edging, and beautifully made.

Mrs. Minot had been reading from Miss Strickland's "Queens of England" while the girls worked, and an illustrated Shakespeare lay open on the table, as well as several fine photographs of historical places for them to look at as they went along. The hour was over now, the teacher gone, and the pupils setting the last stitches as they talked over the lesson, which had interested them exceedingly.

"I really believe I have got Henry's six wives into my head right at last. Two Annes, three Katherines, and one Jane. Now I've seen where they lived and heard their stories, I quite feel as if I knew them," said Merry, shaking the threads off her work before she folded it up to carry home.

> King Henry the Eighth to six spouses was wedded,
> One died, one survived, two divorced, two beheaded,

was all I knew about them before. Poor things, what a bad time they did have," added Jill, patting down the red braid, which would pucker a bit at the corners.

"Katherine Parr had the best of it, because she outlived the old tyrant and so kept her head on," said Molly, winding the thread round her last button, as if bound to fasten it on so firmly that nothing should decapitate that.

"I used to think I'd like to be a queen or a great lady, and wear velvet and jewels, and live in a palace, but now I don't care much for that sort of splendor. I like to make things pretty at home, and know that they all depend on me, and love me very much. Queens are not happy, and I am," said Merry, pausing to look at Anne Hathaway's cottage as she put up the picture, and to wonder if it was very pleasant to have a famous man for one's husband.

"I guess your missionarying has done you good; mine has, and I'm getting to have things my own way more and more every day. Miss Bat is so amiable, I hardly know her, and father tells her to ask Miss Molly when she goes to him for orders. Isn't that fun?" laughed Molly, in high glee, at the agreeable change. "I like it ever so much, but I don't want to stay so all my days. I mean to travel, and just as soon as I can I shall take Boo and go all round the world, and see everything," she added, waving her gay sack, as if it were the flag she was about to nail to the masthead of her ship.

"Well, I should like to be famous in some way, and have people admire me very much. I'd like to act, or dance, or sing, or be what I heard the ladies at Pebbly Beach call a 'queen of society.' But I don't expect to be anything, and I'm not going to worry I shall not be a Lucinda, so I ought to be contented and happy all my life," said Jill, who was very ambitious in spite of the newly acquired meekness, which was all the more becoming because her natural liveliness often broke out like sunshine through a veil of light clouds.

If the three girls could have looked forward ten years they would have been surprised to see how different a fate was theirs from the one each had chosen, and how happy each was in the place she was called to fill. Merry was not making the old farmhouse pretty, but living in Italy, with a young sculptor for her husband, and beauty such as she never dreamed of all about her. Molly was not travelling round the world, but contentedly keeping house for her father and still watching over Boo, who was becoming her pride and joy as well as care. Neither was Jill a famous woman, but a very happy and useful one, with the two mothers leaning on her as they grew old, the young men better for her influence over them, many friends to love and honor her, and a charming home, where she was queen by right of her cheery spirit, grateful heart, and unfailing devotion to those who had made her what she was.

If any curious reader, not content with this peep into futurity, asks, "Did Molly and Jill ever marry?" we must reply, for the sake of peace--Molly remained a merry spinster all her days, one of the independent, brave, and busy creatures of whom there is such need in the world to help take care of other peoples' wives and children, and do the many useful jobs that the married folk have no time for. Jill certainly did wear a white veil on the day she was twenty-five and called her husband Jack. Further than that we cannot go, except to say that this leap did not end in a catastrophe, like the first one they took together.

That day, however, they never dreamed of what was in store for them, but chattered away as they cleared up the room, and then ran off ready for play, feeling that they had earned it by work well done. They found the lads just finishing, with Boo to help by picking up the windfalls for the cider-heap, after he had amused himself by putting about a bushel down the various holes old Bun had left behind him. Jack was risking his neck climbing in the most dangerous places, while Frank, with a long-handled apple-picker, nipped off the finest fruit with care, both enjoying the pleasant task and feeling proud of the handsome red and yellow piles all about the little orchard. Merry and Molly caught up baskets and fell to work with all their might, leaving Jill to sit upon a stool and sort the early apples ready to use at once, looking up now and then to nod and smile at her mother who watched her from the window, rejoicing to see her lass so well and happy.

It was such a lovely day, they all felt its cheerful influence; for the sun shone bright and warm, the air was full of an invigorating freshness which soon made the girls' faces look like rosy apples, and their spirits as gay as if they had been stealing sips of new cider through a straw. Jack whistled like a blackbird as he swung and bumped about, Frank orated and joked, Merry and Molly ran races to see who would fill and empty fastest, and Jill sung to Boo, who reposed in a barrel, exhausted with his labors.

"These are the last of the pleasant days, and we ought to make the most of them. Let's have one more picnic before the frost spoils the leaves," said Merry, resting a minute at the gate to look down the street, which was a glorified sort of avenue, with brilliant maples lining the way and carpeting the ground with crimson and gold.

"Oh, yes! Go down the river once more and have supper on the Island. I couldn't go to some of your picnics, and I do long for a last good time before winter shuts me up again," cried Jill, eager to harvest all the sunshine she could, for she was not yet quite her old self again.

"I'm your man, if the other fellows agree. We can't barrel these up for a while, so to-morrow will be a holiday for us. Better make sure of the day while you can, this weather can't last long;" and Frank shook his head like one on intimate terms with Old Prob.

"Don't worry about those high ones, Jack. Give a shake and come down and plan about the party," called Molly, throwing up a big Baldwin with what seemed a remarkably good aim, for a shower of apples followed, and a boy came tumbling earthward to catch on the lowest bough and swing down like a caterpillar, exclaiming, as he landed,

"I'm glad that job is done! I've rasped every knuckle I've got and worn out the knees of my pants. Nice little crop though, isn't it?"

"It will be nicer if this young man does not bite every apple he touches. Hi there! Stop it, Boo," commanded Frank, as he caught his young assistant putting his small teeth into the best ones, to see if they were sweet or sour.

Molly set the barrel up on end, and that took the boy out of the reach of mischief, so he retired from view and peeped through a crack as he ate his fifth pearmain, regardless of consequences.

"Gus will be at home tomorrow. He always comes up early on Saturday, you know. We can't get on without him," said Frank, who missed his mate very much, for Gus had entered college, and so far did not like it as much as he had expected.

"Or Ralph; he is very busy every spare minute on the little boy's bust, which is getting on nicely, he says; but he will be able to come home in time for supper, I think," added Merry, remembering the absent, as usual.

"I'll ask the girls on my way home, and all meet at two o'clock for a good row while it's warm. What shall I bring?" asked Molly, wondering if Miss Bat's amiability would extend to making goodies in the midst of her usual Saturday's baking.

"You bring coffee and the big pot and some buttered crackers. I'll see to the pie and cake, and the other girls can have anything else they like," answered Merry, glad and proud that she could provide the party with her own inviting handiwork.

"I'll take my zither, so we can have music as we sail, and Grif will bring his violin, and Ralph can imitate a banjo so that you'd be sure he had one. I do hope it will be fine, it is so splendid to go round like other folks and enjoy myself," cried Jill, with a little bounce of satisfaction at the prospect of a row and ramble.

"Come along, then, and make sure of the girls," said Merry, catching up her roll of work, for the harvesting was done.

Molly put her sack on as the easiest way of carrying it, and, extricating Boo, they went off, accompanied by the boys, "to make sure of the fellows" also, leaving Jill to sit among the apples, singing and sorting like a thrifty little housewife.

Next day eleven young people met at the appointed place, basket in hand. Ralph could not come till later, for he was working now as he never worked before. They were a merry flock, for the mellow autumn day was even brighter and clearer than yesterday, and the river looked its loveliest, winding away under the sombre hemlocks, or through the fairyland the gay woods made on either side. Two large boats and two small ones held them all, and away they went, first up through the three bridges and round the bend, then, turning, they floated down to the green island, where a grove of oaks rustled their sere leaves and the squirrels were still gathering acorns. Here they often met to keep their summer revels, and here they now spread their feast on the flat rock which needed no cloth beside its own gray lichens. The girls trimmed each dish with bright leaves, and made the supper look like a banquet for the elves, while the boys built a fire in the nook where ashes and blackened stones told of many a rustic meal. The big tin coffee-pot was not so romantic, but more successful than a kettle slung on three sticks, gypsy fashion; so they did not risk a downfall, but set the water boiling, and soon filled the air with the agreeable perfume associated in their minds with picnics, as most of them never tasted the fascinating stuff at any other time, being the worst children can drink.

Frank was cook, Gus helped cut bread and cake, Jack and Grif brought wood, while Bob Walker took Joe's place and made himself generally useful, as the other gentleman never did, and so was quite out of favor lately.

All was ready at last, and they were just deciding to sit down without Ralph, when a shout told them he was coming, and down the river skimmed a wherry at such a rate the boys wondered whom he had been racing with.

"Something has happened, and he is coming to tell us," said Jill, who sat where she could see his eager face.

"Nothing bad, or he wouldn't smile so. He is glad of a good row and a little fun after working so hard all the week;" and Merry shook a red napkin as a welcoming signal.

Something certainly had happened, and a very happy something it must be, they all thought, as Ralph came on with flashing oars, and leaping out as the boat touched the shore, ran up the slope, waving his hat, and calling in a glad voice, sure of sympathy in his delight,

"Good news! good news! Hurrah for Rome, next month!"

The young folks forgot their supper for a moment, to congratulate him on his happy prospect, and hear all about it, while the leaves rustled as if echoing the kind words, and the squirrels sat up aloft, wondering what all the pleasant clamor was about.

Yes, I'm really going in November. German asked me to go with him to-day, and if there is any little hitch in my getting off, he'll lend a hand, and I--I'll black his boots, wet his clay, and run his errands the rest of my life to pay for this!" cried Ralph, in a burst of gratitude; for, independent as he was, the kindness of this successful friend to a deserving comrade touched and won his heart.

"I call that a handsome thing to do!" said Frank, warmly, for noble actions always pleased him. "I heard my mother say that making good or useful men was the best sort of sculpture, so I think David German may be proud of this piece of work, whether the big statue succeeds or not."

"I'm very glad, old fellow. When I run over for my trip four years from now. I'll look you up, and see how you are getting on," said Gus, with a hearty shake of the hand; and the younger lads grinned cheerfully, even while they wondered where the fun was in shaping clay and chipping marble.

"Shall you stay four years?" asked Merry's soft voice, while a wistful look came into her happy eyes.

"Ten, if I can," answered Ralph, decidedly, feeling as if a long lifetime would be all too short for the immortal work he meant to do. "I've got so much to learn, that I shall do whatever David thinks best for me at first, and when I can go alone, I shall just shut myself up and forget that there is any world outside my den."

"Do write and tell us how you get on now and then; I like to hear about other people's good times while I'm waiting for my own," said Molly, too much interested to observe that Grif was sticking burrs up and down her braids.

"Of course I shall write to some of you, but you mustn't expect any great things for years yet. People don't grow famous in a hurry, and it takes a deal of hard work even to earn your bread and butter, as you'll find if you ever try it," answered Ralph, sobering down a little as he remembered the long and steady effort it had taken to get even so far.

"Speaking of bread and butter reminds me that we'd better eat ours before the coffee gets quite cold," said Annette, for Merry seemed to have forgotten that she had been chosen to play matron, as she was the oldest.

The boys seconded the motion, and for a few minutes supper was the all-absorbing topic, as the cups went round and the goodies vanished rapidly, accompanied by the usual mishaps which make picnic meals such fun. Ralph's health was drunk with all sorts of good wishes; and such splendid prophecies were made, that he would have far surpassed Michael Angelo, if they could have come true. Grif gave him an order on the spot for a full-length statue of himself, and stood up to show the imposing attitude in which he wished to be taken, but unfortunately slipped and fell forward with one hand in the custard pie, the other clutching wildly at the coffee-pot, which inhospitably burnt his fingers.

"I think I grasp the idea, and will be sure to remember not to make your hair blow one way and the tails of your coat another, as a certain sculptor made those of a famous man," laughed Ralph, as the fallen hero scrambled up, amidst general merriment.

"Will the little bust be done before you go?" asked Jill, anxiously, feeling a personal interest in the success of that order.

"Yes: I've been hard at it every spare minute I could get, and have a fortnight more. It suits Mrs. Lennox, and she will pay well for it, so I shall have something to start with, though I haven't been able to save much. I'm to thank you for that, and I shall send you the first pretty thing I get hold of," answered Ralph, looking gratefully at the bright face, which grew still brighter as Jill exclaimed,

"I do feel so proud to know a real artist, and have my bust done by him. I only wish I could pay for it as Mrs. Lennox does; but I haven't any money, and you don't need the sort of things I can make," she added, shaking her head, as she thought over knit slippers, wall-pockets, and crochet in all its forms, as offerings to her departing friend.

"You can write often, and tell me all about everybody, for I shall want to know, and people will soon forget me when I'm gone," said Ralph, looking at Merry, who was making a garland of yellow leaves for Juliet's black hair.

Jill promised, and kept her word; but the longest letters went from the farm-house on the hill, though no one knew the fact till long afterward. Merry said nothing now, but she smiled, with a pretty color in her cheeks, and was very much absorbed in her work, while the talk went on.

"I wish I was twenty, and going to seek my fortune, as you are," said Jack; and the other boys agreed with him, for something in Ralph's new plans and purposes roused the manly spirit in all of them, reminding them that playtime would soon be over, and the great world before them, where to choose.

"It is easy enough to say what you'd like; but the trouble is, you have to take what you can get, and make the best of it," said Gus, whose own views were rather vague as yet.

"No you don't, always; you can make things go as you want them, if you only try hard enough, and walk right over whatever stands in the way. I don't mean to give up my plans for any man; but, if I live, I'll carry them out--you see if I don't;" and Frank gave the rock where he lay a blow with his fist, that sent the acorns flying all about.

One of them hit Jack, and he said, sorrowfully, as he held it in his hand so carefully it was evident he had some association with it,

"Ed used to say that, and he had some splendid plans, but they didn't come to anything."

"Perhaps they did; who can tell? Do your best while you live, and I don't believe anything good is lost, whether we have it a long or a short time," said Ralph, who knew what a help and comfort high hopes were, and how they led to better things, if worthily cherished.

"A great many acorns are wasted, I suppose; but some of them sprout and grow, and make splendid trees," added Merry, feeling more than she knew how to express, as she looked up at the oaks overhead.

Only seven of the party were sitting on the knoll now, for the rest had gone to wash the dishes and pack the baskets down by the boats. Jack and Jill, with the three elder boys, were in a little group, and as Merry spoke, Gus said to Frank,

"Did you plant yours?"

"Yes, on the lawn, and I mean it shall come up if I can make it," answered Frank, gravely.

"I put mine where I can see it from the window, and not forget to water and take care of it," added Jack, still turning the pretty brown acorn to and fro as if he loved it.

"What do they mean?" whispered Merry to Jill, who was leaning against her knee to rest.

"The boys were walking in the Cemetery last Sunday, as they often do, and when they came to Ed's grave, the place was all covered with little acorns from the tree that grows on the bank. They each took up some as they stood talking, and Jack said he should plant his, for he loved Ed very much, you know. The others said they would, too; and I hope the trees will grow, though we don't need anything to remember him by," answered Jill, in a low tone, thinking of the pressed flowers the girls kept for his sake.

The boys heard her, but no one spoke for a moment as they sat looking across the river toward the hill where the pines whispered their lullabies and pointed heavenward, steadfast and green, all the year round. None of them could express the thought that was in their minds as Jill told the little story; but the act and the feeling that prompted it were perhaps as beautiful an assurance as could have been given that the dear dead boy's example had not been wasted, for the planting of the acorns was a symbol of the desire budding in those young hearts to be what he might have been, and to make their lives nobler for the knowledge and the love of him.

"It seems as if a great deal had happened this year," said Merry, in a pensive tone, for this quiet talk just suited her mood.

"So I say, for there's been a Declaration of Independence and a Revolution in our house, and I'm commander-in-chief now; and don't I like it!" cried Molly, complacently surveying the neat new uniform she wore of her own choosing.

"I feel as if I never learned so much in my life as I have since last December, and yet I never did so little," added Jill, wondering why the months of weariness and pain did not seem more dreadful to her.

"Well, pitching on my head seems to have given me a good shaking up, somehow, and I mean to do great things next year in better ways than breaking my bones coasting," said Jack, with a manly air.

"I feel like a Siamese twin without his mate now you are gone, but I'm under orders for a while, and mean to do my best. Guess it won't be lost time;" and Frank nodded at Gus, who nodded back with the slightly superior expression all Freshmen wear.

"Hope you won't find it so. My work is all cut out for me, and I intend to go in and win, though it is more of a grind than you fellows know."

"I'm sure I have everything to be grateful for. It won't be plain sailing--I don't expect it; but, if I live, I'll do something to be proud of," said Ralph, squaring his shoulders as if to meet and conquer all obstacles as he looked into the glowing west, was not fairer than his ambitious dreams.

Here we will say good-by to these girls and boys of ours as they sit together in the sunshine talking over a year that was to be for ever memorable to them, not because of any very remarkable events, but because they were just beginning to look about them as they stepped out of childhood into youth, and some of the experiences of the past months had set them to thinking, taught them to see the use and beauty of the small duties, joys, and sorrows which make up our lives, and inspired them to resolve that the coming year should be braver and brighter than the last.

There are many such boys and girls, full of high hopes, lovely possibilities, and earnest plans, pausing a moment before they push their little boats from the safe shore. Let those who launch them see to it that they have good health to man the oars, good education for ballast, and good principles as pilots to guide them as they voyage down an ever-widening river to the sea.

Lesson 126

1. Write a review of *Jack and Jill.* Write an introductory sentence and then tell about the book: characters, setting, plot. Tell what you liked and didn't like about the book. Would you recommend it to others? Why?

Lesson 127

1. The story you are going to read today was the story that first made Mark Twain famous (the man who wrote about Tom Sawyer and Huckleberry Finn.)
2. Read it out loud. What makes it funny? What do you think makes him a good story teller?
3. Read "The Celebrated Jumping Frog of Calaveras Country."

In compliance with the request of a friend of mine, who wrote me from the East, I called on good-natured, garrulous old Simon Wheeler, and inquired after my friend's friend, Leonidas W. Smiley, as requested to do, and I hereunto append the result. I have a lurking suspicion that Leonidas W. Smiley is a myth; that my friend never knew such a personage; and that he only conjectured that, if I asked old Wheeler about him, it would remind him of his infamous Jim Smiley, and he would go to work and bore me nearly to death with some infernal reminiscence of him as long and tedious as it should be useless to me. If that was the design, it certainly succeeded.

I found Simon Wheeler dozing comfortably by the bar-room stove of the old, dilapidated tavern in the ancient mining camp of Angel's, and I noticed that he was fat and bald-headed, and had an expression of winning gentleness and simplicity upon his tranquil countenance. He roused up and gave me good-day. I told him a friend of mine had commissioned me to make some inquiries about a cherished companion of his boyhood named *Leonidas W.* Smiley--*Rev. Leonidas W.* Smiley--a young minister of the Gospel, who he had heard was at one time a resident of Angel's Camp. I added that, if Mr. Wheeler could tell me any thing about this Rev. Leonidas W. Smiley, I would feel under many obligations to him.

Simon Wheeler backed me into a corner and blockaded me there with his chair, and then sat me down and reeled off the monotonous narrative which follows this paragraph. He never smiled, he never frowned, he never changed his voice from the gentle-flowing key to which he tuned the initial sentence, he never betrayed the slightest suspicion of enthusiasm; but all through the interminable narrative there ran a vein of impressive earnestness and sincerity, which showed me plainly that, so far from his imagining that there was any thing ridiculous or funny about his story, he regarded it as a really important matter, and admired its two heroes as men of transcendent genius in finesse. To me, the spectacle of a man drifting serenely along through such a queer yarn without ever smiling, was exquisitely absurd. As I said before, I asked him to tell me what he knew of Rev. Leonidas W. Smiley, and he replied as follows. I let him go on in his own way, and never interrupted him once:

There was a feller here once by the name of Jim Smiley, in the winter of '49 or may be it was the spring of '50 I don't recollect exactly, somehow, though what makes me think it was one or the other is because I remember the big flume wasn't finished when he first came to the camp; but any way, he was the curiosest man about always betting on any thing that turned up you ever see, if he could get any body to bet on the other side; and if he couldn't, he'd change sides. Any way that suited the other man would suit him any way just so's he got a bet, he was satisfied. But still he was lucky, uncommon lucky; he most always come out winner. He was always ready and laying for a chance; there couldn't be no solittry thing mentioned but that feller'd offer to bet on it, and take any side you please, as I was just telling you. If there was a horse-race, you'd find him flush, or you'd find him busted at the end of it; if there was a dog-fight, he'd bet on it; if there was a cat-fight, he'd bet on it; if there was a chicken-fight, he'd bet on it; why, if there was two birds setting on a fence, he would bet you which one would fly first; or if there was a camp-meeting, he would be there reg'lar, to bet on Parson Walker, which he judged to be the best exhorter about here, and so he was, too, and a good man. If he even seen a straddle-bug start to go anywheres, he would bet you how long it would take him to get wherever he was going to, and if you took him up, he would foller that straddle-bug to Mexico but what he would find out where he was bound for and how long he was on the road. Lots of the boys here has seen that Smiley, and can tell you about him. Why, it never made no difference to him he would bet on any thing the dangdest feller. Parson Walker's wife laid very sick once, for a good while, and it seemed as if they warn's going to save her; but one morning he come in, and Smiley asked how she was, and he said she was considerable better thank the Lord for his inftnit mercy and coming on so smart that, with the blessing of Providence, she'd get well yet; and Smiley, before he thought, says, "Well, I'll risk two-and-a-half that she don't, any way."

Thish-yer Smiley had a mare--the boys called her the fifteen-minute nag, but that was only in fun, you know, because, of course, she was faster than that--and he used to win money on that horse, for all she was so slow and always had the asthma, or the distemper, or the consumption, or something of that kind. They used to give her two or three hundred yards start, and then pass her under way; but always at the fag-end of the race she'd get excited and desperate-like, and come cavorting and straddling up, and scattering her legs around limber, sometimes in the air, and sometimes out to one side amongst the fences, and kicking up m-o-r-e dust, and raising m-o-r-e racket with her coughing and sneezing and blowing her nose and always fetch up at the stand just about a neck ahead, as near as you could cipher it down.

And he had a little small bull pup, that to look at him you'd think he wan's worth a cent, but to set around and look ornery, and lay for a chance to steal something. But as soon as money was up on him, he was a different dog; his underjaw'd begin to stick out like the fo'castle of a steamboat, and his teeth would uncover, and shine savage like the furnaces. And a dog might tackle him, and bully-rag him, and bite him, and throw him over his shoulder two or three times, and Andrew Jackson which was the name of the pup--Andrew Jackson would never let on but what he was satisfied, and hadn't expected nothing else and the bets being doubled and doubled on the other side all the time, till the money was all up; and then all of a sudden he would grab that other dog jest by the j'int of his hind leg and freeze on it not chew, you understand, but only jest grip and hang on till they thronged up the sponge, if it was a year. Smiley always come out winner on that pup, till he harnessed a dog once that didn't have no hind legs, because they'd been sawed off by a circular saw, and when the thing had gone along far enough, and the money was all up, and he come to make a snatch for his pet bolt, he saw in a minute how he'd been imposed on, and how the other dog had him in the door, so to speak, and he 'peered sur-prised, and then he looked sorter discouraged-like, and didn't try no more to win the fight, and so he got shucked out bad. He give Smiley a look, as much as to say his heart was broke, and it was his fault, for putting up a dog that hadn't no hind legs for him to take bolt of, which was his main dependence in a fight, and then he limped off a piece and laid down and died. It was a good pup, was that Andrew Jackson, and would have made a name for hisself if he'd lived, for the stuff was in him, and he had genius I know it, because he hadn't had no opportunities to speak of, and it don't stand to reason that a dog could make such a fight as he could under them circumstances, if he hadn't no talent. It always makes me feel sorry when I think of that last fight of his'n, and the way it turned out.

Well, thish-yer Smiley had rat-tarriers, and chicken cocks, and tom-cats, and all of them kind of things, till you couldn't rest, and you couldn't fetch nothing for him to bet on but he'd match you. He ketched a frog one day, and took him home, and said he cal'klated to edercate him; and so he never done nothing for three months but set in his back yard and learn that frog to jump. And you bet you he did learn him, too. He'd give him a little punch behind, and the next minute you'd see that frog whirling in the air like a doughnut see him turn one summerset, or may be a couple, if he got a good start, and come down flat-footed and all right, like a cat. He got him up so in the matter of catching flies, and kept him in practice so constant, that he'd nail a fly every time as far as he could see him. Smiley said all a frog wanted was education, and he could do most any thing and I believe him. Why, I've seen him set Dan'l Webster down here on this floor--Dan'l Webster was the name of the frog--and sing out, "Flies, Dan'l, flies!" and quicker'n you could wink, he'd spring straight up, and snake a fly off'n the counter there, and flop down on the floor again as solid as a gob of mud, and fall to scratching the side of his head with his hind foot as indifferent as if he hadn't no idea he'd been doin' any more'n any frog might do. You never see a frog so modest and straightforward as he was, for all he was so gifted. And when it come to fair and square jumping on a dead level, he could get over more ground at one straddle than any animal of his breed you ever see. Jumping on a dead level was his strong suit, you understand; and when it come to that, Smiley would ante up money on him as long as he had a red. Smiley was monstrous proud of his frog, and well he might be, for fellers that had traveled and been everywheres, all said he laid over any frog that ever they see.

Well, Smiley kept the beast in a little lattice box, and he used to fetch him down town sometimes and lay for a bet. One day a feller a stranger in the camp, he was come across him with his box, and says:

"What might it be that you've got in the box?"

And Smiley says, sorter indifferent like, "It might be a parrot, or it might be a canary, may be, but it an't--it's only just a frog."

And the feller took it, and looked at it careful, and turned it round this way and that, and says, "H'm so 'tis. Well, what's he good for?"

"Well," Smiley says, easy and careless, "He's good enough for one thing, I should judge he can outjump any frog in Calaveras county."

The feller took the box again, and took another long, particular look, and give it back to Smiley, and says, very deliberate, "Well, I don't see no p'ints about that frog that's any better'n any other frog."

"May be you don't," Smiley says. "May be you understand frogs, and may be you don't understand 'em; may be you've had experience, and may be you an't only a amature, as it were. Anyways, I've got my opinion, and I'll risk forty dollars that he can outjump any frog in Calaveras county."

And the feller studied a minute, and then says, kinder sad like, "Well, I'm only a stranger here, and I an't got no frog; but if I had a frog, I'd bet you."

And then Smiley says, "That's all right--that's all right--if you'll hold my box a minute, I'll go and get you a frog." And so the feller took the box, and put up his forty dollars along with Smiley's, and set down to wait.

So he set there a good while thinking and thinking to hisself, and then he got the frog out and prized his mouth open and took a tea-spoon and filled him full of quail shot filled him pretty near up to his chin and set him on the floor. Smiley he went to the swamp and slopped around in the mud for a long time, and finally he ketched a frog, and fetched him in, and give him to this feller, and says:

"Now, if you're ready, set him alongside of Dan'l, with his fore-paws just even with Dan'l, and I'll give the word." Then he says, "One-two-three-jump!" and him and the feller touched up the frogs from behind, and the new frog hopped off, but Dan'l give a heave, and hysted up his shoulders so--like a Frenchman, but it wan's no use--he couldn't budge; he was planted as solid as an anvil, and he couldn't no more stir than if he was anchored out. Smiley was a good deal surprised, and he was disgusted too, but he didn't have no idea what the matter was, of course.

The feller took the money and started away; and when he was going out at the door, he sorter jerked his thumb over his shoulders--this way--at Dan'l, and says again, very deliberate, "Well, I don't see no p'ints about that frog that's any better'n any other frog."

Smiley he stood scratching his head and looking down at Dan'l a long time, and at last he says, "I do wonder what in the nation that frog throw'd off for--I wonder if there an't something the matter with him--he 'pears to look mighty baggy, somehow." And he ketched Dan'l by the nap of the neck, and lifted him up and says, "Why, blame my cats, if he don't weigh five pound!" and turned him upside down, and he belched out a double handful of shot. And then he see how it was, and he was the maddest man--he set the frog down and took out after that feller, but he never ketchd him. And-

[Here Simon Wheeler heard his name called from the front yard, and got up to see what was wanted.] And turning to me as he moved away, he said: "Just set where you are, stranger, and rest easy--I an't going to be gone a second."

But, by your leave, I did not think that a continuation of the history of the enterprising vagabond Jim Smiley would be likely to afford me much information concerning the *Rev. Leonidas W.* Smiley, and so I started away.

At the door I met the sociable Wheeler returning, and he button-holed me and recommenced:

"Well, thish-yer Smiley had a yeller one-eyed cow that didn't have no tail, only jest a short stump like a bannanner, and--"

"Oh! hang Smiley and his afflicted cow!" I muttered, good-naturedly, and bidding the old gentleman good-day, I departed.

Lesson 128

1. Read the first part of "The Send-and-Fotch Book" by Esther Greenacre Hall.

TWILIGHT was weaving dusky blue threads through the warp of the tree branches as Nancy Davis stepped from the back door of the log cabin that squatted like a gray toad on the bank of Dog-leg Creek. For a moment she paused, feeling herself a part of the pattern of the Kentucky forest. Only a whippoorwill's soft call and the murmur of the water broke the stillness.

"Hit's that still you could nigh hear the roots of growing things a-pushing through the ground," she murmured to herself. "'Pears like a pretty spring night like this oughter quiet my spirits and keep 'em from festerin' fer want of a new dress. But la me! Hit's sech a sweety dress—leastways the picter in the book makes hit seem so. Gin I had that dress I could hold up my head to be above even that proudful Mary Perkins."

With a shake of her tousled brown head as though to brush aside troublesome thoughts, Nancy tilted up her pointed chin and in a high sing-song called out, "Here pig-wee, pig-wee, pig-wee. Here piggy, piggy, pig." Her call trailed away over the narrow valley. She paused. Then in a loud, guttural tone added, "Ugh-ugh-ugh."

There was a rustle at the edge of the clearing and an elephantine hog lumbered into the open. From the gourd in the crook of her arm, Nancy threw out table scraps.

"Hit's a pure pity you hain't got any appetite, George Washington," she chuckled. "Any sence we found you half starved last winter you been eating more of our vittles than us young-uns put together."

"Nancy, oh, Nannie," called a small girl from the door.

"Won't you leave us study on the send-and-fotch book now? We'll both be mighty keerful of it—honest."

"Shore 'nough. I'll get hit fer you," answered Nancy. "Bye, Washington. Come on into the house, children."

Inside the one-room cabin a fire flamed on the stone hearth, casting vagrant shadows on the log walls and lighting up the faces of the small boy and girl and old man as they sat before it. From the mantel Nancy took down the brilliantly colored mail-order catalogue and dropped down on a hickory stool close to the fire.

"Lemme hold hit," cried Tom, making a grab at the book.

But Nancy hugged it close in her arms. "Fer shame on you, Tom Davis. We got to gentle this book. Never have we had sech a pretty thing afore and hit's untelling when we'll e'er ag'in possess one. You and Lucy stand beside me and look on whilst I turn the pages. La, Gran'pappy," she added, smiling up at the old man, "I shore wish you could pleasure in this book, too."

Gran'pappy blinked his faded eyes. "I shore do crave to look, too, gal. Gin my eyes could see right I'd read off as smart as you, fer I reckon I'm the onliest old body on Dog-leg Creek as can read."

The girl nodded. "You're the knowingest man here-abouts. Any body knows hit's your eyes 'n' not your skull-piece that don't work to do no good."

"Haste, Nannie. Show us the play pretties." Tom nudged his big sister impatiently. Intently the three scrutinized the toys.

"There's one o'them engine buggies like teacher narrates about." Tom pointed to a toy automobile.

"And there's a store least-un. Hain't hit sweety-looking," cried Lucy indicating a doll pictured on one of the pages.

The toys entirely inspected, Lucy asked to turn to the clothes. "I plumb hate to look at wearing things," Nancy said hesitantly. "Hit hurts my feelings to see clothes we need so turrible bad and can't buy."

Lucy's face was wistful as she eyed the models in the dress section. "Them dresses is too pretty to wear," she sighed. "I allow folks jest buys them to gladden their hearts by looking on them any day. They don't never wear them, do they?"

"Silly-wit," scoffed her brother. "Course folks wear them. Hurry up and leave me see the overalls. They're what I want."

But Lucy hovered over the dresses. "That blue one's the dress I hungers atter," she said. "And Nannie wants that red one. Don't you, Nannie?"

Nancy said nothing but stared at her favorite. It was a large colored style plate—red and white print with perky ruffles. "That's jest the kind of dress I been acraving all my days—only I didn't know it," she thought. "Gin Mary Perkins could see me in sech a fine frock—"

She bent close to the page and read below the picture: "One of the loveliest dresses $1.35 ever bought. Study its lines a moment! The graceful drooping bow—the graceful ripple of the new flounced cuffs, of the fashionable peplum ruffle in front, of the all-around flared skirt, the easy curve of the fitted waist! Picture the gay red background with white figures. Remember that the fabric is guaranteed washable. Sizes fourteen to twenty years—$1.35."

Some of the words Nancy did not understand. But they sounded grand, like poetry the teacher read in school. She shut the catalogue abruptly.

"Oh, Nannie, I hain't finished looking!"

"Lemme see the overalls."

But Nancy was firm. "Gin we look on hit much longer we'll get to craving things so bad we won't pleasure in ary thing we have or do."

Gran'pappy looked at her understandingly. "Nancy's right," he quavered. "Hit's a pure pity to think too much on what we hain't got."

Nancy stood up and put the catalogue back on the mantel.

"Shuck off your clothes, young-uns, and go to bed," she said.

When the rest were asleep Nancy crawled out of bed and wrapped a quilt around her shoulders. "I'm weak, pure weak," she thought as she took down the catalogue and crouched beside the hearth. By the light of the dying embers she stared at the red and white dress, reading again and again, "One of the loveliest dresses $1.35 ever bought."

May slipped slowly into June. Every day from sun-up to sun-setting the Davis children hoed corn in the steep patch that lay high on the hillside above the cabin. The children's legs ached. Their backs ached. The sun was a great hot hand pressing mercilessly down upon their heads. Nancy hoed with slow, even strokes. Several rows above her, Tom and Lucy lifted their hoes jerkily, stopping often to rest.

"Psst, Nannie. Thar comes Mary Perkins," warned Lucy.

Nancy pushed back her straw hat. Sure enough. Picking her way up the slope was a girl in a crisp black and white calico. Mary's father was the biggest moonshiner on Dog-leg. It was no wonder that Mary always had pretty dresses and even wore shoes in summer time. Nancy disliked Mary because of her superior manner, while Mary bore a grudge against the other girl for beating her in a spell-down before school closed. Their manner bespoke their mutual dislike.

"Howdy," said Mary, not too warmly, yet affably enough.

"Howdy," Nancy gruffly returned the greeting. She was acutely aware of the tear in her skimpy skirt and of dust on her legs and face.

"I jest been down to the store sending off an order fer some new clothes," volunteered the visitor. "I figgered I'd need a new dress fer the anniversary celebration."

Tom and Lucy edged down the hill. "What cel'bration?" asked Tom.

"Why, ain't you heern tell? Thar's going to be great goings-on in Windsor-town fireworks 'n' a merry-go- round 'n' speeches 'n' the governor hisself will be thar."

"Really!"

"The governor!"

"Yes. I allow folks from ary holler fer miles around will be thar. Hit's too bad you got young-uns and an old grandsir' to keer fer, Nancy. I don't reckon you'll be going. Will you?"

"Likely not," Nancy answered.

Lesson 129

1. Read the second part of "The Send-and-Fotch Book" by Hall.

Tom and Lucy raced down to the cabin to tell their grandparent the news, and Nancy followed as soon as Mary had left.

"To think that the governor of this great Kaintucky-land will be thar!" exclaimed the old man when he heard the news. "I'm too trimblish to go the twenty mile to Windsor-town, e'en gin we had a mule to ride. But you young-uns can go. There's no need for you to stay home with me."

Tom and Lucy set up whoops of glee, but Nancy's face was sober. "I don't feel to go without you, Gran'pappy," she said. "I'd ruther bide at home."

"Shame on you, Nancy Davis," scolded Gran'pappy. "Would you keep the younguns from paying honor to our grandsir's that made this Kaintucky-land free from the English rule? I'm nigh the end of the trail. But you young-uns are jest putting foot to life. You need to see great folk like a governor so's you'll everly grow big in your deeds and thoughts."

"What'll we wear?" cried Lucy.

Nancy frowned. "Fer massy sake, I don't see how we can go to Windsor-town! Tom's trousers are nigh worn through the seat. And Lucy's calico has more holes than our picket fence. This dress of mine is so short I'm ashamed to have even the chickens see me in hit."

Gran'pappy blinked in distress. "I hain't never put countenance to vanity," he said. "But I'd ruther you stayed home than to be unseemly clad in the presence of the governor."

"Aw shucks! We can't go then. We'll never get money fer clothes," grumbled Tom.

"'Pears like we never do have ary frolicking," choked Lucy.

"Waal, mayhaps we can contrive clothes some way," said Nancy, but in her heart she was doubtful.

One noon several days later as Nancy was putting cornpone to bake on the hot hearthstones, Tom burst in the door crying, "Nat Hill and Sam Perkins are quarreling at each other over George Washington. They both claims him."

Nancy flew outside, Gran'pappy hobbling after her. The two men down at the picket fence took no notice of the children as they eyed the hog which was rooting around the porch.

"That thar's my hog," shrilled Nat Hill. "Hit run wild last summer with my other shotes but hit never come home in the fall. Hit's my own hog I tell you, Sam Perkins."

"That's jest how come me to lose my hog," declared Perkins. "See that long scar on that creetur's left shoulder? Waal, my brute had a scar jest like that. He laid down on my scythe and cut hisself."

"Shucks, ary hog is likely to get cut up in the brush. That ain't nary proof. That's my hog and gin you doubt hit look at hits left hind leg. See? Hit's shorter than tothers."

"Hit is that," reluctantly agreed Perkins.

"Yes, and hogs can't shorten their legs theirselves. Their legs are born right or not right. Now my hog was born with three right legs and one short-like. That's my hog fer sartain 'n' I'll jest take him long home."

"Neither of you is toting that hog away," cried Nancy.

The men turned to her in surprise. "How come you by that hog, gal?" drawled Perkins.

"He come here nigh starved last winter," answered Nancy. "We fed him like a leastun fer months. Being's how you hain't sartain you ever even seen him afore, I'll keep him." Her eyes flashed and her voice was determined.

"Dad-burned, but I craves that shote," grumbled Perkins.

Nancy's eyes narrowed. "Fer-why don't you buy hit offen me?" The men shuffled their feet in the dust.

"Waal, I don't—" began Hill.

But Perkins smiled in a superior manner. "I'll give a dollar."

Hill's mouth dropped in surprise but Nancy turned and walked away. "A dollar!" she said scornfully over her shoulder.

"Hey, gal, I'll part with two dollar," called Hill.

"Four," shouted Perkins.

"Four-fifty." The men glared at each other.

"Five dollar," boomed Perkins.

Nancy hastened back to the fence. "He's yourn. Gin you got the money you can tote him home now."

In awed silence the others watched Perkins open a worn leather pouch and extract five crumpled dollar bills. Who but a moonshiner could possess that much money at one time! Nancy stretched out her hand. Her fingers trembled slightly as they gripped the bills. "Run fetch a rope fer Washington," she told Tom in a voice husky with suppressed excitement.

"Waal, five dollar's a right smart bit of money," said Hill as he started off to follow Perkins and the hog down the trail. "That money'd buy enough store vittles to last our folks all winter. I'm right proud I didn't squander any cash. Besides the shote hain't as fine looking as I jedged it was at first."

As soon as the men were out of sight, the Davises hugged one another excitedly. "Now we can buy some clothes," squealed Lucy.

"We'll go to Windsor-town."

"You can see the governor," beamed Gran'pappy.

All afternoon the family pored over the catalogue, Gran'pappy hovering around the children giving advice and trying unsuccessfully to distinguish the objects on the pages. At last the list was completed and Nancy read aloud: "Shirt fer Gran'pappy, seventy cents; overalls fer Gran'pappy, seventy-nine cents; shirt fer Tom, fifty cents; over-alls fer Tom, seventy-nine cents; dress fer Lucy, seventy-nine cents; dress fer me, one dollar and thirty-five cents."

She paused. "Hit ain't seemly fer me to get a costlier frock than Lucy. I—"

"Shucks, gal, you need that red dress fer your sperrit's good," said her grandfather.

"Now you tote that order right down to the store and have Lucas Wiley back the letter fer you 'n' help you fill out the order paper proper."

As Nancy stood up, the catalogue slid off her lap to the floor. She stooped to pick it up. It was open at a page of queer-looking articles. Beneath the largest one pictured there she read: "For those who can't see to read, this magnifying glass is a blessing. Guaranteed to make letters three times their normal size. Even the weakest eyes can see when this is used. It sells for only $1.20."

Nancy stared at it. Was there really something that could help Gran'pappy read?

"Hain't you never coming?" called Tom.

"Walk on," answered Nancy. "I'll foller."

With her stubby pencil she crossed out on the paper, "Red and white dress." And in its place she wrote, "Reading glass, $1.20."

"'Bye, Gran'pappy," she said huskily.

Her feet, usually so swift and sure, acted strangely as she hurried down the creek trail. They slipped on wet stones in the branch bed and stumbled. A blackberry bush stretched a teasing bramble across the path. But Nancy neither heard the rip of her dress as she passed it nor felt the ugly scratch it left on her cheek. The red dress was gone. She'd never see its gladsome color, never touch its ruffles that were crisp and white.

There was great excitement in the Davis cabin three weeks later when a neighbor stopped by to leave the mailorder package. Nancy opened the box herself.

"I see some blue. Hit's my dress," shrieked Lucy.

"You're the awkwardest gal. Get out of my way," ordered Tom. "Thar's my overalls."

Nancy handed a package to old John Davis. "Here's a surprise fer you, Gran'pappy," she said.

With trembling fingers he unwrapped it. "Why, what be this? Hit's glass."

Lesson 130

1. Finish reading "The Send-and-Fotch Book" by Hall.

Vocabulary

1. Review your vocabulary from Lesson 8.

Nancy picked up the catalogue. "Hold the glass over some writing," she said eagerly. "I think that's how you use hit. Thar, now look through the glass."

The children crowded close. There was a breathless silence. The old man bent low and squinted through the oval. His voice came slow and wondering.

"Praise be to the Lord! I can read. I can see them words like my eyes was young ag'in. Hit's magic, pure magic. How come this charm to me, Nancy gal?"

Briefly she explained how she'd noticed the glass in the send-and-fotch book.

"Ne'er did I think sech happiness would reach me," marveled Gran'pappy. "I'm plumb wore out with happiness." And he sank down on a chair.

When the excitement had subsided Lucy suddenly cried, "Whar's Nancy's frock?"

"Why, hain't it here?" asked the old man anxiously.

Nancy picked up papers busily. "I changed my mind. It was too noisysome a color."

The children looked at her, perplexed. "But you wanted hit!" Lucy puzzled.

Gran'pappy looked at Nancy searchingly. "I allow with my glass you must 'a' spent all the money. Didn't you, gal?" he asked.

"Nigh all."

"I reckoned so. You're the unselfishest gal ever I knowed, Nancy."

Nancy sent him a quick smile but her lips trembled.

Early in the morning a week later the Davis children started on their journey to Windsor-town. By taking two days for the twenty miles, they could get there easily.

"Now don't mourn e'en a little grain 'cause I can't go," Gran'pappy told them in farewell. "With my reading glass I'm so gladsome that I don't care 'bout seeing ten governors. Jes' go on and have a good time."

Tom and Lucy were in the gayest of spirits, and Nancy had to remind them constantly not to go too fast and get worn out on the first part of the trip. All three wore their old clothes. The new apparel was wrapped in a gunny sack and slung across Nancy's back. Never before had the Davises been away from their valley, and every twist of the trail was alluring. Although Nancy tried her best to think only of the frolicking ahead, her thoughts persisted in turning to the red dress. How happy she would be if it were tucked in the roll on her back. Instead she had with her the linsey dress. It was her winter frock. She had woven it from wool that she had dyed in walnut bark. It was a coarse, heavy dress. How uncomfortable she'd look and feel in it on a hot day.

It was very early in the morning when the children entered Windsor-town on the day of the celebration. But already the town was full of people.

"Lookit the big houses," said Tom, pointing to a small two-story building.

"Lawsy, I never knowed there was so many folks in all Kaintucky," gasped Nancy.

Up and down the street the three went, halting at each tiny store window to inspect the displays with wondering eyes. By nine o'clock the dusty street was milling with people. Soon the crowd began to move toward a vacant lot where stood a great tent. Walking in the midst of the throng, Nancy and the children found themselves pushed into the tent. Grabbing Tom and Lucy, Nancy propelled them up an aisle to a bench directly in front of the platform.

"My, we shore got fine places," she panted.

"What comes now?" whispered Lucy.

"I heered somebody say the governor talks in here," said her sister.

Nancy glanced at the women around her. Most of them wore bright-colored calicoes and ginghams. A few even had cheap silks.

"Howdy, Nancy," said a patronizingly sweet voice.

Directly behind Nancy sat Mary Perkins in a red silk dress with a yellow straw hat atop her yellow curls. Nancy caught her breath at the sight of such finery. She managed a smile. Then she sank down as low as she could so the old winter's dress wouldn't show any more than necessary. The dress was terribly hot and Nancy's face felt red.

Mary leaned forward to say, "I was proud pappy could holp you out by buying that hog. He says hit really wa'n't worth the money but he aimed to give you a little extry money seeing you hain't got ary pappy."

Nancy flushed crimson and opened her lips to answer. But a piano began to bang out the national anthem. There followed speeches by Windsor officials, speeches by politicians from outside towns and more singing. Nancy scarcely heard them all. Why did Mary Perkins have to sit right behind her all dressed up in red silk while she wore her brown winter linsey?

"Ladies and gentlemen, it is my great pleasure and privilege to present the Honorable George Henderson Williams, governor of the state of Kentucky."

With a start Nancy realized where she was. She looked up at the tall, handsome man with white hair and kindly face. In a strong, compelling voice he spoke.

"No people in the United States have more right to be proud of their ancestry than have you mountain folk of Kentucky. It was your great-grandparents and their parents who first hewed their way through the forests from the Atlantic seaboard.

"The early Kentucky men were brave and courageous. But to me the women were the greatest to be admired. They left security and comfort. They came into the wilderness to fight beside their men, to bear children in deprivation, to care for their families undaunted and tireless. They made their own soap. They ground their own corn. They even spun their own clothes and—"

The voice broke off and Nancy, who had been sitting erect with glowing, uplifted face, felt the governor's glance meet hers. He stepped to the edge of the platform. He leaned forward. "Would the little girl with the brown hair and brown dress mind standing up just a moment?"

Nancy looked about her.

"You. I mean you. The little lady in the second row between the two children," said the governor.

Someone touched Nancy's shoulder. "He means you," people said. "Stand up, gal."

Bewildered, Nancy found herself half lifted to her feet by her neighbors.

"That's a lovely dress you have on, little girl," said the speaker. "Isn't it a handwoven linsey?" She nodded dumbly.

"I thought so. My grandmother had one. And who wove it?"

"I—I did."

"Really! Would you come up here?"

As in a dream Nancy walked up the platform steps. The governor took her hand and turned her to the audience. "I singled this girl out while I was talking, for her dress is a linsey like one my grandmother had. I am glad that the customs of our ancestors are not forgotten. I am glad that our mountain women do not all wear store dresses and that by the light of the open fire one Kentucky girl still weaves her gowns.

"I have visited many cities and seen fine ladies in silks and satins, but to me no dress I saw was as lovely as this homespun brown linsey." Turning, he clasped Nancy's hand.

There was tumultuous applause. People stood up as Nancy went down to her seat.

They craned their necks to see the girl who had been honored by the governor. Lucy and Tom gripped her arms tightly, their faces shining. Even Tom was speechless. The governor continued his address, but Nancy's head was so awhirl that she didn't hear his words. Toward the end of the program Nancy could not resist looking over her shoulder at Mary Perkins. Mary's smile was ingratiating and honey sweet. "It's a lovely dress," her lips formed the words.

Nancy smiled a wise little smile of triumph to herself. She smoothed the brown linsey over her knees. It was a pretty weave after all. It must be getting cooler all of a sudden, for she now felt very comfortable in the winter dress. It was lucky she hadn't worn a flimsy store dress like the others.

Lucy plucked at her sleeve. "Hain't you proud you wore your old frock?" she said.

Nancy nodded. "The red dress was right smart looking," she whispered back. "But hit was too noisysome a color. A body wouldn't feel to live with hit long."

Lesson 131

1. We're going to start reading something really different. You are going to be reading a non-fiction book. That means it is factual. I want you to pay attention to how she gives the information.
2. Today read the first part of chapter 1 of *The Fairy Land of Science* by Arabella B. Buckley.
3. Choose a topic from your reading. Write or tell a topic sentence, or main idea sentence, for that topic.

LECTURE I – Part 1

HOW TO ENTER IT; HOW TO USE IT; AND HOW TO ENJOY IT

I HAVE promised to introduce you today to the fairy-land of science – a somewhat bold promise, seeing that most of you probably look upon science as a bundle of dry facts, while fairy-land is all that is beautiful, and full of poetry and imagination. But I thoroughly believe myself, and hope to prove to you, that science is full of beautiful pictures, of real poetry, and of wonder-working fairies; and what is more, I promise you they shall be true fairies, whom you will love just as much when you are old and greyheaded as when you are young; for you will be able to call them up wherever you wander by land or by sea, through meadow or through wood, through water or through air; and though they themselves will always remain invisible, yet you will see their wonderful poet at work everywhere around you.

Let us first see for a moment what kind of tales science has to tell, and how far they are equal to the old fairy tales we all know so well. Who does not remember the tale of the "Sleeping Beauty in the Wood," and how under the spell of the angry fairy the maiden pricked herself with the spindle and slept a hundred years? How the horses in the stall, the dogs in the court-yard, the doves on the roof, the cook who was boxing the scullery boy's ears in the kitchen, and the king and queen with all their courtiers in the hall remained spell-bound, while a thick hedge grew up all round the castle and all within was still as death. But when the hundred years had passed the valiant prince came, the thorny hedge opened before him bearing beautiful flowers; and he, entering the castle, reached the room where the princess lay, and with one sweet kiss raised her and all around her to life again.

Can science bring any tale to match this?

Tell me, is there anything in this world more busy and active than water, as it rushes along in the swift brook, or dashes over the stones, or spouts up in the fountain, or trickles down from the roof, or shakes itself into ripples on the surface of the pond as the wind blows over it? But have you never seen this water spell-bound and motionless? Look out of the window some cold frosty morning in winter, at the little brook which yesterday was flowing gently past the house, and see how still it lies, with the stones over which it was dashing now held tightly in its icy grasp. Notice the wind-ripples on the pond; they have become fixed and motionless. Look up at the roof of the house. There, instead of living doves merely charmed to sleep, we have running water caught in the very act of falling and turned into transparent icicles, decorating the eaves with a beautiful crystal fringe. On every tree and bush you will catch the water-drops napping, in the form of tiny crystals; while the fountain looks like a tree of glass with long down-hanging pointed leaves. Even the damp of your own breath lies rigid and still on the window-pane frozen into delicate patterns like fern-leaves of ice.

All this water was yesterday flowing busily, or falling drop by drop, or floating invisibly in the air; now it is all caught and spell-bound – by whom? By the enchantments of the frost-giant who holds it fast in his grip and will not let it go.

But wait awhile, the deliverer is coming. In a few weeks or days, or it may be in a few hours, the brave sun will shine down; the dull-grey, leaden sky will melt before his, as the hedge gave way before the prince in the fairy tale, and when the sunbeam gently kisses the frozen water it will be set free. Then the brook will flow rippling on again; the frost-drops will be shaken down from the trees, the icicles fall from the roof, the moisture trickle down the window-pane, and in the bright, warm sunshine all will be alive again.

Is not this a fairy tale of nature? and such as these it is which science tells.

Again, who has not heard of Catskin, who came out of a hollow tree, bringing a walnut containing three beautiful dresses – the first glowing as the sun, the second pale and beautiful as the moon, the third spangled like the star-lit sky, and each so fine and delicate that all three could be packed into a walnut shell; and each one of these tiny structures is not the mere dress but the home of a living animal. It is a tiny, tiny shell-palace made of the most delicate lacework, each pattern being more beautiful than the last; and what is more, the minute creature that lives in it has built it out of the foam of the sea, though he himself is nothing more than a drop of jelly.

Lastly, anyone who has read the 'Wonderful Travellers' must recollect the man whose sight was so keen that he could hit the eye of a fly sitting on a tree two miles away. But tell me, can you see gas before it is lighted, even when it is coming out of the gas-jet close to your eyes? Yet, if you learn to use that wonderful instrument the spectroscope, it will enable you to tell one kind of gas from another, even when they are both ninety-one millions of miles away on the face of the sun; nay more, it will read for you the nature of the different gases in the far distant stars, billions of miles away, and actually tell you whether you could find there any of the same metals which we have on the earth.

We might find hundreds of such fairy tales in the domain of science, but these three will serve as examples, and we much pass on to make the acquaintance of the science-fairies themselves, and see if they are as real as our old friends.

Tell me, why do you love fairy-land? what is its charm? Is it not that things happen so suddenly, so mysteriously, and without man having anything to do with it? In fairy-land, flowers blow, houses spring up like Aladdin's palace in a single night, and people are carried hundreds of miles in an instant by the touch of a fairy wand.

And then this land is not some distant country to which we can never hope to travel. It is here in the midst of us, only our eyes must be opened or we cannot see it. Ariel and Puck did not live in some unknown region. On the contrary, Ariel's song is

> Where the bee sucks, there suck I;
> In a cowslip's bell I lie;
> There I couch when owls do cry.
> On the bat's back I do fly,
> After summer, merrily.

The peasant falls asleep some evening in a wood and his eyes are opened by a fairy wand, so that he sees the little goblins and imps dancing around him on the green sward, sitting on mushrooms, or in the heads of the flowers, drinking out of acorn-cups, fighting with blades of grass, and riding on grasshoppers.

So, too, the gallant knight, riding to save some poor oppressed maiden, dashes across the foaming torrent; and just in the middle, as he is being swept away, his eyes are opened, and he sees fairy water-nymphs soothing his terrified horse and guiding him gently to the opposite shore. They are close at hand, these sprites, to the simple peasant or the gallant knight, or to anyone who has the gift of the fairies and can see them. but the man who scoffs at them, and does not believe in them or care for them, he never sees them. Only now and then they play him an ugly trick, leading him into some treacherous bog and leaving him to get out as he may.

Now, exactly all this which is true of the fairies of our childhood is true too of the fairies of science. There are forces around us, and among us, which I shall ask you to allow me to call fairies, and these are ten thousand times more wonderful, more magical, and more beautiful in their work, than those of the old fairy tales. They, too, are invisible, and many people live and die without ever seeing them or caring to see them. These people go about with their eyes shut, either because they will not open them, or because no one has taught them how to see. They fret and worry over their own little work and their own petty troubles, and do not know how to rest and refresh themselves, by letting the fairies open their eyes and show them the calm sweet picture of nature. They are like Peter Bell of whom Wordsworth wrote:

> A primrose by a river's brim
> A yellow primrose was to him,
> And it was nothing more.

But we will not be like these, we will open our eyes and ask, "What are these forces or fairies, and how can we see them?"

Just go out into the country, and sit down quietly and watch nature at work. Listen to the wind as it blows, look at the clouds rolling overhead, and waves rippling on the pond at your feet. Hearken to the brook as it flows by, watch the flower-buds opening one by one, and then ask yourself, "How all this is done?" Go out in the evening and see the dew gather drop by drop upon the grass, or trace the delicate hoar-frost crystals which bespangle every blade on a winter's morning. Look at the vivid flashes of lightening in a storm, and listen to the pealing thunder: and then tell me, by what machinery is all this wonderful work done? Man does none of it, neither could he stop it if he were to try; for it is all the work of those invisible forces or fairies whose acquaintance I wish you to make. Day and night, summer and winter, storm or calm, these fairies are at work, and we may hear them and know them, and make friends of them if we will.

There is only one gift we must have before we can learn to know them – we must have imagination. I do not mean mere fancy, which creates unreal images and impossible monsters, but imagination, the power of making pictures or images in our mind, of that which is, though it is invisible to us. Most children have this glorious gift, and love to picture to themselves all that is told them, and to hear the same tale over and over again till they see every bit of it as if it were real. This is why they are sure to love science it its tales are told them aright; and I, for one, hope the day may never come when we may lose that childish clearness of vision, which enables us through the temporal things which are seen, to realize those eternal truths which are unseen.

If you have this gift of imagination come with me, and in these lectures we will look for the invisible fairies of nature.

Watch a shower of rain. Where do the drops come from? and why are they round, or rather slightly oval? In our fourth lecture we shall see that the little particles of water of which the raindrops are made, were held apart and invisible in the air by heat, one of the most wonderful of our forces* or fairies, till the cold wind passed by and chilled the air. Then, when there was no longer so much heat, another invisible force, cohesion, which is always ready and waiting, seized on the tiny particles at once, and locked them together in a drop, the closest form in which they could lie. Then as the drops became larger and larger they fell into the grasp of another invisible force, gravitation, which dragged them down to the earth, drop by drop, till they made a shower of rain. Pause for a moment and think. You have surely heard of gravitation, by which the sun holds the earth and the planets, and keeps them moving round him in regular order? Well, it is this same gravitation which is at work also whenever a shower of rain falls to the earth. Who can say that he is not a great invisible giant, always silently and invisibly toiling in great things and small whether we wake or sleep?

*(I am quite aware of the danger incurred by using this word "force", especially in the plural; and how even the most modest little book may suffer at the hands of scientific purists by employing it rashly. As, however, the better term "energy" would not serve here, I hope I may be forgiven for retaining the much- abused term, especially as I sin in very good company.)

Lesson 132

1. Today read the next section of *The Fairy Land of Science*.
2. Choose a topic from your reading. Write or tell a topic sentence, or main idea sentence, for that topic.

Lecture I. How to Enter It; How to Use It; And How to Enjoy It. Continued...

Now the shower is over, the sun comes out and the ground is soon as dry as though no rain had fallen. Tell me; what has become of the rain-drops? Part no doubt have sunk into the ground, and as for the rest, why you will say the sun has dried them up. Yes, but how? The sun is more than ninety-one millions of miles away; how has he touched the rain-drops? Have you ever heard that invisible waves are travelling every second over the space between the sun and us? We shall see in the next lecture how these waves are the sun's messengers to the earth, and how they tear asunder the rain-drops on the ground, scattering them in tiny particles too small for us to see, and bearing them away to the clouds. Here are more invisible fairies working every moment around you, and you cannot even look out of the window without seeing the work they are doing.

If, however, the day is cold and frosty, the water does not fall in a shower of rain; it comes down in the shape of noiseless snow. Go out after such a snow-shower, on a calm day, and look at some of the flakes which have fallen; you will see, if you choose good specimens, that they are not mere masses of frozen water, but that each one is a beautiful six-pointed crystal star. How have these crystals been built up?

What power has been at work arranging their delicate forms? In the fourth lecture we shall see that up in the clouds another of our invisible fairies, which, for want of a better name, we call the "force of crystallization," has caught hold of the tiny particles of water before "cohesion" had made them into round drops, and there silently but rapidly, has moulded them into those delicate crystal starts know as "snowflakes".

And now, suppose that this snow-shower has fallen early in February; turn aside for a moment from examining the flakes, and clear the newly-fallen snow from off the flower-bed on the lawn. What is this little green tip peeping up out of the ground under the snowy covering? It is a young snowdrop plant. Can you tell me why it grows? where it finds its food? what makes it spread out its leaves and add to its stalk day by day? What fairies are at work here?

First there is the hidden fairy "life," and of her even our wisest men know but little. But they know something of her way of working, and in Lecture VII we shall learn how the invisible fairy sunbeams have been buy here also; how last year's snowdrop plant caught them and stored them up in it's bulb, and how now in the spring, as soon as warmth and moisture creep down into the earth, these little imprisoned sun-waves begin to be active, stirring up the matter in the bulb, and making it swell and burst upwards till it sends out a little shoot through the surface of the soil. Then the sun-waves above-ground take up the work, and form green granules in the tiny leaves, helping them to take food out of the air, while the little rootlets below are drinking water out of the ground. The invisible life and invisible sunbeams are busy here, setting actively to work another fairy, the force of "chemical attraction," and so the little snowdrop plant grows and blossoms, without any help from you or me.

One picture more, and then I hope you will believe in my fairies. From the cold garden, you run into the house, and find the fire laid indeed in the grate, but the wood dead and the coals black, waiting to be lighted. You strike a match, and soon there is a blazing fire. Where does the heat come from? Why do the coals burn and give out a glowing light? Have you not read of gnomes buried down deep in the earth, in mines, and held fast there till some fairy wand has released them, and allowed them to come to earth again? Well, thousands and millions of years ago, those coals were plants; and like the snowdrop in the garden of to-day, they caught the sunbeams and worked them into their leaves. Then the plants died and were buried deep in the earth and the sunbeams with them; and like the gnomes they lay imprisoned till the coals were dug out by the miners, and brought to your grate; and just now you yourself took hold of the fairy wand which was to release them. You struck a match, and its atoms clashing with atoms of oxygen in the air, set the invisible fairies "heat" and "chemical attraction" to work, and they were soon busy within the wood and the coals causing their atoms too to clash; and the sunbeams, so long imprisoned, leapt into flame. Then you spread out your hands and cried, "Oh, how nice and warm!" and little thought that you were warming yourself with the sunbeams of ages and ages ago.

This is no fancy tale; it is literally true, as we shall see in Lecture VIII, that the warmth of a coal fire could not exist if the plants of long ago had not used the sunbeams to make their leaves, holding them ready to give up their warmth again whenever those crushed leaves are consumed.

Now, do you believe in, and care for, my fairy-land? Can you see in your imagination fairy 'Cohesion' ever ready to lock atoms together when they draw very near to each other: or fairy 'Gravitation' dragging rain-drops down to the earth: or the fairy of 'Crystallization' building up the snow-flakes in the clouds? Can you picture tiny sunbeam-waves of light and heat travelling from the sun to the earth? Do you care to know how another strange fairy, 'Electricity,' flings the lightning across the sky and causes the rumbling thunder? Would you like to learn how the sun makes pictures of the world on which he shines, so that we can carry about with us photographs or sun-pictures of all the beautiful scenery of the earth? And have you any curiosity about 'Chemical action,' which works such wonders in air, and land, and sea? If you have any wish to know and make friends of these invisible forces, the next question is

How are you to enter the fairy-land of science?

There is but one way. Like the knight or peasant in the fairy tales, you must open you eyes. There is no lack of objects, everything around you will tell some history if touched with the fairy wand of imagination. I have often thought, when seeing some sickly child drawn along the street, lying on its back while other children romp and play, how much happiness might be given to sick children at home or in hospitals, if only they were told the stories which lie hidden in the things around them. They need not even move from their beds, for sunbeams can fall on them there, and in a sunbeam there are stories enough to occupy a month. The fire in the grate, the lamp by the bedside, the water in the tumbler, the fly on the ceiling above, the flower in the vase on the table, anything, everything, has its history, and can reveal to us nature's invisible fairies.

Only you must wish to see them. If you go through the world looking upon everything only as so much to eat, to drink, and to use, you will never see the fairies of science. But if you ask yourself why things happen, and how the great God above us has made and governs this world of ours; If you listen to the wind, and care to learn why it blows; if you ask the little flower why it opens in the sunshine and closes in the storm; and if when you find questions you cannot answer, you will take the trouble to hunt out in books, or make experiments to solve your own questions, then you will learn to know and love those fairies.

Mind, I do not advise you to be constantly asking questions of other people; for often a question quickly answered is quickly forgotten, but a difficulty really hunted down is a triumph for ever. For example, if you ask why the rain dries up from the ground, most likely you will be answered, "that the sun dries it," and you will rest satisfied with the sound of the words. But if you hold a wet handkerchief before the fire and see the damp rising out of it, then you have some real idea how moisture may be drawn up by heat from the earth.

A little foreign niece of mine, only four years old, who could scarcely speak English plainly, was standing one morning near the bedroom window and she noticed the damp trickling down the window-pane. "Auntie," she said, "what for it rain inside?" It was quite useless to explain to her in words, how our breath had condensed into drops of water upon the cold glass; but I wiped the pane clear, and breathed on it several times. When new drops were formed, I said, "Cissy and auntie have done like this all night in the room." She nodded her little head and amused herself for a long time breathing on the window-pane and watching the tiny drops; and about a month later, when we were travelling back to Italy, I saw her following the drops on the carriage window with her little finger, and heard her say quietly to herself, "Cissy and auntie made you." Had not even this little child some real picture in her mind of invisible water coming from her mouth, and making drops upon the window-pane?

Then again, you must learn something of the language of science. If you travel in a country with no knowledge of its language, you can learn very little about it: and in the same way if you are to go to books to find answers to your questions, you must know something of the language they speak. You need not learn hard scientific names, for the best books have the fewest of these, but you must really understand what is meant by ordinary words.

For example, how few people can really explain the difference between a solid, such as the wood of the table; a liquid, as water; and a gas, such as I can let off from this gas-jet by turning the tap. And yet any child can make a picture of this in his mind if only it has been properly put before him.

All matter in the world is made up of minute parts or particles; in a solid these particles are locked together so tightly that you must tear them forcibly apart if you with to alter the shape of the solid piece. If I break or bend this wood I have to force the particles to move round each other, and I have great difficulty doing it. But in a liquid, though the particles are still held together, they do not cling so tightly, but are able to roll or glide round each other, so that when you pour water out of a cup on to a table, it loses its cuplike shape and spreads itself out flat. Lastly, in a gas the particles are no longer held together at all, but they try to fly away from each other; and unless you shut a gas in tightly and safely, it will soon have spread all over the room.

A solid, therefore, will retain the same bulk and shape unless you forcibly alter it; a liquid will retain the same bulk, but not the same shape if it be left free; a gas will not retain either the same bulk or the same shape, but will spread over as large a space as it can find wherever it can penetrate. Such simple things as these you must learn from books and by experiment.

Then you must understand what is meant by chemical attraction; and though I can explain this roughly here, you will have to make many interesting experiments before you will really learn to know this wonderful fairy power. If I dissolve sugar in water, though it disappears it still remains sugar, and does not join itself to the water. I have only to let the cup stand till the water dries, and the sugar will remain at the bottom. There has been no chemical attraction here.

But now I will put something else in water which will call up the fairy power. Here is a little piece of the metal potassium, one of the simple substances of the earth; that is to say, we cannot split it up into other substances, wherever we find it, it is always the same. Now if I put this piece of potassium on the water it does not disappear quietly like the sugar. See how it rolls round and round, fizzing violently with a blue flame burning round it, and at last goes off with a pop.

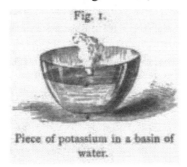

Fig. 1.

Piece of potassium in a basin of water.

Lesson 133

1. Today read the rest of chapter 1 of *The Fairy Land of Science.*
2. Choose a topic from your reading. Write or tell a topic sentence, or main idea sentence, for that topic.

Lecture I. How to Enter It; How to Use It; And How to Enjoy It. Continued…

You must first know that water is made of two substances, hydrogen and oxygen, and these are not merely held together, but are joined to completely that they have lost themselves and have become water; and each atom of water is made of two atoms of hydrogen and one of oxygen.

Now the metal potassium is devotedly fond of oxygen, and the moment I threw it on the water it called the fairy "chemical attraction" to help it, and dragged the atoms of oxygen out of the water and joined them to itself. In doing this it also caught part of the hydrogen, but only half, and so the rest was left out in the cold. No, not in the cold! for the potassium and oxygen made such a great heat in clashing together that the rest of the hydrogen became very hot indeed, and sprang into the air to find some other companion to make up for what it had lost. Here it found some free oxygen floating about, and it seized upon it so violently, that they made a burning flame, while the potassium with its newly found oxygen and hydrogen sank down quietly into the water as potash. And so you see we have got quite a new substance potash in the basin; made with a great deal of fuss by chemical attraction drawing different atoms together.

When you can really picture this power to yourself it will help you very much to understand what you read and observe about nature.

Next, as plants grow around you on every side, and are of so much importance in the world, you must also learn something of the names of the different parts of a flower, so that you may understand those books which explain how a plant grows and lives and forms its seeds. You must also know the common names of the parts of an animal, and of your own body, so that you may be interested in understanding the use of the different organs; how you breathe, and how your blood flows; how one animal walks, another flies, and another swims. Then you must learn something of the various parts of the world, so that you may know what is meant by a river, a plain, a valley, or a delta. All these things are not difficult, you can learn them pleasantly from simple books on physics, chemistry, botany, physiology, and physical geography; and when you understand a few plain scientific terms, then all by yourself, if you will open your eyes and ears, you may wander happily in the fairy-land of science. Then wherever you go you will find

> Tongues in trees, books in the running brooks
> Sermons in stones, and good in everything.

And now we come to the last part of our subject. When you have reached and entered the gates of science, how are you to use and enjoy this new and beautiful land?

This is a very important question for you may make a twofold use of it. If you are only ambitious to shine in the world, you may use it chiefly to get prizes, to be at the top of your class, or to pass in examinations; but if you also enjoy discovering its secrets, and desire to learn more and more of nature and to revel in dreams of its beauty, then you will study science for its own sake as well. Now it is a good thing to win prizes and be at the top of your class, for it shows that you are industrious; it is a good thing to pass well in examinations, for it show that you are accurate; but if you study science for this reason only, do not complain if you find it full, and dry, and hard to master. You may learn a great deal that is useful, and nature will answer you truthfully if you ask you questions accurately, but she will give you dry facts, just such as you ask for. If you do not love her for herself she will never take you to her heart.

This is the reason why so many complain that science is dry and uninteresting. They forget that though it is necessary to learn accurately, for so only we can arrive at truth, it is equally necessary to love knowledge and make it lovely to those who learn, and to do this we must get at the spirit which lies under the facts. What child which loves its mother's face is content to know only that she has brown eyes, a straight nose, a small mouth, and hair arranged in such and such a manner? No, it knows that its mother has the sweetest smile of any woman living; that her eyes are loving, her kiss is sweet, and that when she looks grave, then something is wrong which must be put right. And it is in this way that those who wish to enjoy the fairy-land of science must love nature.

It is well to know that when a piece of potassium is thrown on water the change which takes place is expressed by the formula K + H2O = KHO + H. But it is better still to have a mental picture of the tiny atoms clasping each other, and mingling so as to make a new substance, and to feel how wonderful are the many changing forms of nature. It is useful to be able to classify a flower and to know that the buttercup belongs to the Family Ranunculaceae, with petals free and definite, stamens hypogynous and indefinite, pistil apocarpous. But it is far sweeter to learn about the life of the little plant, to understand why its peculiar flower is useful to it, and how it feeds itself, and makes its seed. No one can love dry facts; we must clothe them with real meaning and love the truths they tell, if we wish to enjoy science.

Piece of white coral.

Let us take an example to show this. I have here a branch of white coral, a beautiful, delicate piece of nature's work. We will begin by copying a description of it from one of those class-books which suppose children to learn words like parrots, and to repeat them with just as little understanding.

"Coral is formed by an animal belonging to the kingdom of Radiates, sub-kingdom Polypes. The soft body of the animal is attached to a support, the mouth opening upwards in a row of tentacles. The coral is secreted in the body of the polyp out of the carbonate of lime in the sea. Thus the coral animalcule rears its polypidom or rocky structure in warm latitudes, and constructs reefs or barriers round islands. It is limited in rage of depth from 25 to 30 fathoms. Chemically considered, coral is carbonate of like; physiologically, it is the skeleton of an animal; geographically, it is characteristic of warm latitudes, especially of the Pacific Ocean." This description is correct, and even fairly complete, if you know enough of the subject to understand it. But tell me, does it lead you to love my piece of coral? Have you any picture in your mind of the coral animal, its home, or its manner of working?

But now, instead of trying to master this dry, hard passage, take Mr. Huxley's penny lecture on 'Coral and Coral Reefs,' and with the piece of coral in your hand try really to learn its history. You will then be able to picture to yourself the coral animal as a kind of sea-anemone, something like those which you have often seen, like red, blue, or green flowers, putting out feelers in sea-water on our coasts, and drawing in the tiny sea-animals to digest them in that bag of fluid which serves

196

the sea-anemone as a stomach. You will learn how this curious jelly animal can split itself in two, and so form two polyps, or send a bud out of its side and so grow up into a kind of "tree or bush of polyps," or how it can hatch little eggs inside it and throw out young ones from its mouth, provided with little hairs, by means of which they swim to new resting-places. You will learn the difference between the animal which builds up the red coral as its skeleton, and the group of animals which build up the white; and you will look with new interest on our piece of white coral, as you read that each of those little sups on its stem with delicate divisions like the spokes of a wheel has been the home of a separate polyp, and that from the sea-water each little jelly animal has drunk in carbonate of lime as you drink in sugar dissolved in water, and then has used it grain by grain to build that delicate cup and add to the coral tree.

We cannot stop to examine all about coral now, we are only learning how to learn, but surely our specimen is already beginning to grow interesting; and when you have followed it out into the great Pacific Ocean, where the wild waves dash restlessly against the coral trees, and have seen these tiny drops of jelly conquering the sea and building huge walls of stone against the rough breakers, you will hardly rest till you know all their history. Look at that curious circular island in the picture, covered with palm trees; it has a large smooth lake in the middle, and the bottom of this lake is covered with blue, red, and green jelly animals, spreading out their feelers in the water and looking like beautiful flowers, and all round the outside of the island similar animals are to be seen washed by the sea waves. Such islands as this have been build entirely by the coral animals, and the history of the way in which the reefs have sunk gradually down, as the tiny creatures added to them inch by inch, is as fascinating as the story of the building of any fairy palace in the days of old. Read all this, and then if you have no coral of your own to examine, go to the British Museum and see the beautiful specimens in the glass cases there, and think that they have been built up under the rolling surf by the tiny jelly animals; and then coral will become a real living thing to you, and you will love the thoughts it awakens.

Coral Island in the Pacific.

But people often ask, what is the use of learning all this? If you do not feel by this time how delightful it is to fill your mind with beautiful pictures of nature, perhaps it would be useless to say more. But in this age of ours, when restlessness and love of excitement pervade so many lives, is it nothing to be taken out of ourselves and made to look at the wonders of nature going on around us? Do you never feel tired and "out of sorts," and want to creep away from your companions, because they are merry and you are not? Then is the time to read about the starts, and how quietly they keep their course from age to age; or to visit some little flower, and ask what story it has to tell; or to watch the clouds, and try to imagine how the winds drive them across the sky. No person is so independent as he who can find interest in a bare rock, a drop of water, the foam of the sea, the spider on the wall, the flower underfoot or the starts overhead. And these interests are open to everyone who enters the fairy-land of science.

Moreover, we learn from this study to see that there is a law and purpose in everything in the Universe, and it makes us patient when we recognize the quiet noiseless working of nature all around us. Study light, and learn how all colour, beauty, and life depend on the sun's rays; note the winds and currents of the air, regular even in their apparent irregularity, as they carry heat and moisture all over the world. Watch the water flowing in deep quiet streams, or forming the vast ocean; and then reflect that every drop is guided by invisible forces working according to fixed laws. See plants springing up under the sunlight, learn the secrets of plant life, and how their scents and colours attract the insects. Read how insects cannot live without plants, nor plants without the flitting butterfly or the busy bee. Realize that all this is worked by fixed laws, and that out of it (even if sometimes in suffering and pain) springs the wonderful universe around us. And then say, can you fear for your own little life, even though it may have its troubles? Can you help feeling a part of this guided and governed nature? or doubt that the power which fixed the laws of the stars and of the tiniest drop of water – that made the plant draw power from the sun, the tine coral animal its food from the dashing waves; that adapted the flower to the insect and the insect to the flower – is also moulding your life as part of the great machinery of the universe, so that you have only to work, and to wait, and to love?

We are all groping dimly for the Unseen Power, but no one who loves nature and studies it can ever feel alone or unloved in the world. Facts, as mere facts, are dry and barren, but nature is full of life and love, and her calm unswerving rule is tending to some great though hidden purpose. You may call this Unseen Power what you will – may lean on it in loving, trusting faith, or bend in reverent and silent awe; but even the little child who lives with nature and gazes on her with open eye, must rise in some sense or other through nature to nature's God.

Lesson 134

1. Today read the first part of chapter 2 of *The Fairy Land of Science*.
2. Choose a topic from your reading. Write or tell a topic sentence, or main idea sentence, for that topic.

Lecture II. Sunbeams and the Work They Do.

Who does not love the sunbeams, and feel brighter and merrier as he watches them playing on the wall, sparkling like diamonds on the ripples of the sea, or making bows of coloured light on the waterfall? Is not the sunbeam so dear to us that it has become a household word for all that is merry and gay? and when we want to describe the dearest, busiest little sprite amongst us, who wakes a smile on all faces wherever she goes, do we not call her the "sunbeam of the house"?

And yet how little even the wisest among us know about the nature and work of these bright messengers of the sun as they dart across space!

Did you ever wake quite early in the morning, when it was pitch- dark and you could see nothing, not even your own hand; and then lie watching as time went on till the light came gradually creeping in at the window? If you have done this you will have noticed that you can at first only just distinguish the dim outline of the furniture; then you can tell the difference between the white cloth on the table and the dark wardrobe beside it; then by degrees all the smaller details, the handles of the drawer, the pattern on the wall, and the different colours of all the objects in the room become clearer and clearer till at last you see all distinctly in broad daylight.

What has been happening here? and why have the things in the room become visible by such slow degrees? We say that the sun is rising, but we know very well that it is not the sun which moves, but that our earth has been turning slowly round, and bringing the little spot on which we live face to face with the great fiery ball, so that his beams can fall upon us.

Take a small globe, and stick a piece of black plaster over England, then let a lighted lamp represent the sun, and turn the globe slowly, so that the spot creeps round from the dark side away from the lamp, until it catches, first the rays which pass along the side of the globe, then the more direct rays, and at last stands fully in the blaze of the light. Just this was happening to our spot of the world as you lay in bed and saw the light appear, and we have to learn today what those beams are which fall upon us and what they do for us.

First we must learn something about the sun itself, since it is the starting-place of all the sunbeams. If the sun were a dark mass instead of a fiery one we should have none of these bright cheering messengers, and though we were turned face to face with him every day we should remain in one cold eternal night. Now you will remember we mentioned in the last lecture that it is heat which shakes apart the little atoms of water and makes them gloat up in the air to fall again as rain; and that if the day is cold they fall as snow, and all the water is turned into ice. But if the sun were altogether dark, think how bitterly cold it would be; far colder than the most wintry weather ever known, because in the bitterest night some warmth comes out of the earth, where it has been stored from the sunlight which fell during the day. But if we never received any warmth at all, no water would ever rise up into the sky, no rain ever fall, no rivers flow, and consequently no plants could grow and no animals live. All water would be in the form of snow and ice, and the earth would be one great frozen mass with nothing moving upon it.

So you see it becomes very interesting for us to learn what the sun is, and how he sends us his beams. How far away from us do you think he is? On a fine summer's day when we can see him clearly, it looks as if we had only to get into a balloon and reach him as he sits in the sky, and yet we know roughly that he is more than ninety-one millions of miles distant from our earth.

These figures are so enormous that you cannot really grasp them. But imagine yourself in an express train, travelling at the tremendous rate of sixty miles an hour and never stopping. At that rate, if you wished to arrive at the sun today you would have been obliged to start 171 years ago. That is, you must have set off in the early part of the reign of Queen Anne, and you must have gone on, never, never resting, through the reigns of George I, George II, and the long reign of George III, then through those of George IV, William IV, and Victoria, whirling on day and night at express speed, and at last, today, you would have reached the sun!

And when you arrived there, how large do you think you would find him to be? Anaxagoras, a learned Greek, was laughed at by all his fellow Greeks because he said that the sun was as large as the Peloponne-sus, that is about the size of Middlesex. How astonished they would have been if they could have known that not only is he bigger than the whole of Greece, but more than a million times bigger than the whole world!

Our world itself is a very large place, so large that our own country looks only like a tiny speck upon it, and an express train would take nearly a month to travel round it. Yet even our whole globe is nothing in size compared to the sun, for it only measures 8000 miles across, while the sun measures more the 852,000.

Imagine for a moment that you could cut the sun and the earth each in half as you would cut an apple; then if you were to lay the flat side of the half-earth on the flat side of the half sun it would take 106 such earths to stretch across the face of the sun. One of these 106 round spots on the diagram represents the size which our earth would look if placed on the sun;

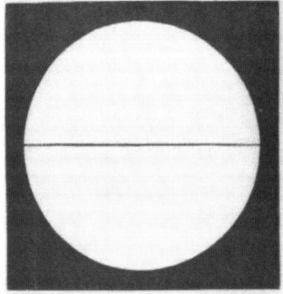

106 earths laid across the face of the sun. Each one of these dots represents roughly the size of the earth as compared to the size of the sun represented by the large circle.

and they are so tiny compared to him that they look only like a string stretched across his face. Only think, then, how many of these minute dots would be required to fill the whole of the inside, if it were a globe.

One of the best ways to form an idea of the whole size of the sun is to imagine it to be hollow, like an air-ball, and then see how many earths it would take to fill it. You would hardly believe that it would take one million, three hundred and thirty-one thousand globes the size of our world squeezed together. Just think, if a huge giant could travel all over the universe and gather worlds, all as big as ours, and were to make first a heap of merely ten such worlds, how huge it would be! Then he must have a hundred such heaps of ten to make a thousand world; and then he must collect again a thousand times that thousand to make a million, and when he had stuffed them all into the sun-ball he would still have only filled three-quarters of it!

After hearing this you will not be astonished that such a monster should give out an enormous quantity of light and heat; so enormous that it is almost impossible to form any idea of it. Sir John Herschel has, indeed, tried to picture it for us. He found that a ball of lime with a flame of oxygen and hydrogen playing round it (such as we use in magic lanterns and call oxy-hydrogen light) becomes so violently hot that it gives the most brilliant artificial light we can get – such that you cannot put your eye near it without injury. Yet if you wanted to have a light as strong as that of our sun, it would not be enough to make such a lime-ball as big as the sun is. No, you must make it as big as 146 suns, or more than 146,000,000 times as big as our earth, in order to get the right amount of light. Then you would have a tolerably good artificial sun; for we know that the body of the sun gives out an intense white light, just as the lime-ball does, and that, like it, it has an atmosphere of glowing gases round it.

But perhaps we get the best idea of the mighty heat and light of the sun by remembering how few of the rays which dart out on all sides from this fiery ball can reach our tiny globe, and yet how powerful they are. Look at the globe of a lamp in the middle of the room, and see how its light pours out on all sides and into every corner; then take a grain of mustard-seed, which will very well represent the comparative size of our earth, and hold it up at a distance from the lamp. How very few of all those rays which are filling the room fall on the little mustard-seed, and just so few does our earth catch of the rays which dart out from the sun. And yet this small quantity (1/2000-millionth part of the whole) does nearly all the work of our world. (These and the preceding numerical statements will be found worked out in Sir J. Herschel's 'Familiar Lectures on Scientific Subjects,' 1868, from which many of the facts in the first part of the lecture are taken.)

In order to see how powerful the sun's rays are, you have only to take a magnifying glass and gather them to a point on a piece of brown paper, for they will set the paper alight. Sir John Herschel tells us that at the Cape of Good Hope the heat was even so great that he cooked a beefsteak and roasted some eggs by merely putting them in the sun, in a box with a glass lid! Indeed, just as we should all be frozen to death if the sun were cold, so we should all be burnt up with intolerable heat if his fierce rays fell with all their might upon us. But we have an invisible veil protecting us, made – of what do you think? Of those tiny particles of water which the sunbeams draw up and scatter in the air, and which, as we shall see in Lecture IV, cut off part of the intense heat and make the air cool and pleasant for us.

We have now learnt something of the distance, the size, the light, and the heat of the sun – the great source of the sunbeams. But we are as yet no nearer the answer to the question, What is a sunbeam? how does the sun touch our earth?

Now suppose I with to touch you from this platform where I stand, I can do it in two ways. Firstly, I can throw something at you and hit you – in this case a thing will have passed across the space from me to you. Or, secondly, if I could make a violent movement so as to shake the floor of the room, you would feel a quivering motion; and so I should touch you across the whole distance of the room. But in this case no thing would have passed from me to you but a movement or wave, which passed along the boards of the floor. Again, if I speak to you, how does the sound reach you ear? Not by anything being thrown from my mouth to your ear, but by the motion of the air. When I speak I agitate the air near my mouth, and that makes a wave in the air beyond, and that one, another, and another (as we shall see more fully in Lecture VI) till the last wave hits the drum of your ear.

Thus we see there are two ways of touching anything at a distance; 1st, by throwing some thing at it and hitting it; 2nd, by sending a movement of wave across to it, as in the case of the quivering boards and the air.

Now the great natural philosopher Newton thought that the sun touched us in the first of these ways, and that sunbeams were made of very minute atoms of matter thrown out by the sun, and making a perpetual cannonade on our eyes. It is easy to understand that this would make us see light and feel heat, just as a blow in the eye makes us see starts, or on the body makes it feel hot: and for a long time this explanation was supposed to be the true one. But we know now that there are many facts which cannot be explained on this theory, though we cannot go into them here. What we will do, is to try and understand what now seems to be the true explanation of the sunbeam.

About the same time that Newton wrote, a Dutchman, named Huyghens, suggested that light comes from the sun in tiny waves, travelling across space much in the same way as ripples travel across a pond. The only difficulty was to explain in what substance these waves could be travelling: not through water, for we know that there is no water in space – nor through air, for the air stops at a comparatively short distance from our earth. There must then be something filling all space between us and the sun, finer than either water or air.

And now I must ask you to use all you imagination, for I want you to picture to yourselves something quite as invisible as the Emperor's new clothes in Andersen's fairy-tale, only with this difference, that our invisible something is very active; and though we can neither see it nor touch it we know it by its effects. You must imagine a fine substance filling all space between us and the sun and the starts. A substance so very delicate and subtle, that not only is it invisible, but it can pass through solid bodies such as glass, ice, or even wood or brick walls. This substance we call "ether." I cannot give you here the reasons why we must assume that it is throughout all space; you must take this on the word of such men as Sir John Herschel or Professor Clerk-Maxwell, until you can study the question for yourselves.

Now if you can imagine this ether filling every corner of space, so that it is everywhere and passes through everything, ask yourselves, what must happen when a great commotion is going on in one of the large bodies which float in it? When the atoms of the gases round the sun are clashing violently together to make all its light and heat, do you not think they must shake this ether all around them? And then, since the ether stretches on all sides from the sun to our earth and all other planets, must not this quivering travel to us, just as the quivering of the boards would from me to you? Take a basin of water to represent the ether, and take a piece of potassium like that which we used in our last lecture, and hold it with a pair of nippers in the middle of the water. You will see that as the potassium hisses and the flame burns round it, they will make waves which will travel all over the water to the edge of the basin,, and you can imagine how in the same way waves travel over the ether from the sun to us.

Lesson 135

1. Today read the next part of chapter 2 of *The Fairy Land of Science*.
2. Choose a topic from your reading. Write or tell a topic sentence, or main idea sentence, for that topic.

Lecture II. Sunbeams and the Work They Do. Continued…

Straight away from the sun on all sides, never stopping, never resting, but chasing after each other with marvellous quickness, these tiny waves travel out into space by night and by day. When our spot of the earth where England lies is turned away from them and they cannot touch us, then it is night for us, but directly England is turned so as to face the sun, then they strike on the land, and the water, and warm it; or upon our eyes, making the nerves quiver so that we see light. Look up at the sun and picture to yourself that instead of one great blow from a fist causing you to see stars for a moment, millions of tiny blows from these sun-waves are striking every instant on you eye; then you will easily understand that his would cause you to see a constant blaze of light.

But when the sun is away, if the night is clear we have light from the stars. Do these then too make waves all across the enormous distance between them and us? Certainly they do, for they too are suns like our own, only they are so far off that the waves they send are more feeble, and so we only notice them when the sun's stronger waves are away.

But perhaps you will ask, if no one has ever seen these waves not the ether in which they are made, what right have we to say they are there? Strange as it may seem, though we cannot see them we have measured them and know how large they are, and how many can go into an inch of space. For as these tiny waves are running on straight forward through the room, if we put something in their way, they will have to run round it; and if you let in a very narrow ray of light through a shutter and put an upright wire in the sunbeam, you actually make the waves run round the wire just as water runs round a post in a river; and they meet behind the wire, just as the water meets in a V shape behind the post. Now when they meet, they run up against each other, and here it is we catch them. For if they meet comfortably, both rising up in a good wave, they run on together and make a bright line of light; but if they meet higgledy-piggledy, one up and the other down, all in confusion, they stop each other, and then there is no light but a line of darkness.

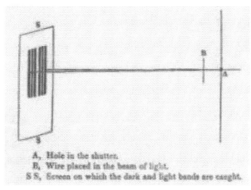

A, Hole in the shutter.
B, Wire placed in the beam of light.
S S, Screen on which the dark and light bands are caught.

And so behind your piece of wire you can catch the waves on a piece of paper, and you will find they make dark and light lines one side by side with the other, and by means of these bands it is possible to find out how large the waves must be. This question is too difficult for us to work it out here, but you can see that large waves will make broader light and dark bands than small ones will, and that in this way the size of the waves may be measured.

And now how large do you think they turn out to be? so very, very tiny that about fifty thousand waves are contained in a single inch of space! I have drawn on the board the length of an inch, and now I will measure the same space in the air between my finger and thumb. Within this space at this moment there are fifty thousand tiny waves moving up and down. I promised you we would find in science things as wonderful as in fairy tales. Are not these tiny invisible messengers coming incessantly from the sun as wonderful as any fairies? and still more so when, as we shall see presently, they are doing nearly all the work of our world.

We must next try to realize how fast these waves travel. You will remember that an express train would take 171 years to reach us from the sun; and even a cannon-ball would take from ten to thirteen years to come that distance. Well, these tiny waves take only seven minutes and a half to come the whole 91 millions of miles. The waves which are hitting your eye at this moment are caused by a movement which began at the sun only 7 1/2 minutes ago. And remember, this movement is going on incessantly, and these waves are always following one after the other so rapidly that they keep up a perpetual cannonade upon the pupil of your eye. So fast do they come that about 608 billion waves enter your eye in one single second.* I do not ask you to remember these figures; I only ask you to try and picture to yourselves these infinitely tiny and active invisible messengers from the sun, and to acknowledge that light is a fairy thing. (*Light travels at the rate of 190,000 miles, or 12,165,120,000 inches in a second. Taking the average number of wave-lengths in an inch at 50,000, then 12,165,120,000 X 50,000 = 608,256,000,000,000.)

But we do not yet know all about our sunbeams. See, I have here a piece of glass with three sides, called a prism.

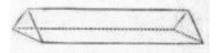

If I put it in the sunlight which is streaming through the window, what happens? Look! on the table there is a line of beautiful colours. I can make it long or short, as I turn the prism, but the colours always remain arranged in the same way. Here at my left hand is the red, beyond it orange, then yellow, green, blue, indigo or deep blue, and violet, shading one into the other all along the line.

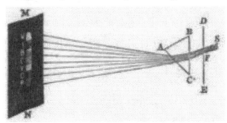

We have all seen these colours dancing on the wall when the sun has been shining brightly on the cut-glass pendants of the chandelier, and you may see them still more distinctly if you let a ray of light into a darkened room, and pass it through the prism as in the diagram. What are these colours? Do they come from the glass? No; for you will remember to have seen them in the rainbow, and in the soap-bubble, and even in a drop of dew or the scum on the top of a pond. This beautiful coloured line is only our sunbeam again, which has been split up into many colours by passing through the glass, as it is in the rain-drops of the rainbow and the bubbles of the scum of the pond.

Till now we have talked of the sunbeam as if it were made of only one set of waves of different sizes, all travelling along together from the sun. These various waves have been measured, and we know that the waves which make up red light are larger and more lazy than those which make violet light, so that there are only thirty-nine thousand red waves in an inch, while there are fifty-seven thousand violet waves in the same space.

How is it then, that if all these different waves making different colours, hit on our eye, they do not always make us see coloured light? Because, unless they are interfered with, they all travel along together, and you know that all colours, mixed together in proper proportion, make white.

I have here a round piece of cardboard, painted with the seven colours in succession several times over. When it is still you can distinguish them all apart, but when I whirl it quickly round – see! – the cardboard looks quite white, because we see them all so instantaneously that they are mingled together. In the same way light looks white to you, because all the different coloured waves strike on your eye at once. You can easily make on of these card for yourselves only the white will always look dirty, because you cannot get the colours pure.

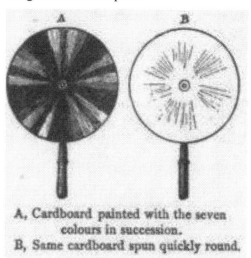

A, Cardboard painted with the seven
colours in succession.
B, Same cardboard spun quickly round.

Now, when the light passes through the three-sided glass or prism, the waves are spread out, and the slow, heavy, red waves lag behind and remain at the lower end R of the coloured line on the wall, while the rapid little violet waves are bent more out of their road and run to V at the farther end of the line; and the orange, yellow, green, blue, and indigo arrange themselves between, according to the size of their waves.

Lesson 136

1. Today read the rest of chapter 2 of *The Fairy Land of Science*.
2. Choose a topic from your reading. Write or tell a topic sentence, or main idea sentence, for that topic.

Lecture II. Sunbeams and the Work They Do. Continued...

And now you are very likely eager to ask why the quick waves should make us see one colour, and the slow waves another. This is a very difficult question, for we have a great deal still to learn about the effect of light on the eye. But you can easily imagine that colour is to our eye much the same as music is to our ear. You know we can distinguish different notes when the air-waves play slowly or quickly upon the drum of the ear (as we shall see in Lecture VI) and somewhat in the same way the tiny waves of the ether play on the retina or curtain at the back of our eye, and make the nerves carry different messages to the brain: and the colour we see depends upon the number of waves which play upon the retina in a second.

Do you think we have now rightly answered the question – What is a sunbeam? We have seen that it is really a succession of tiny rapid waves, travelling from the sun to us across the invisible substance we call "ether", and keeping up a constant cannonade upon everything which comes in their way. We have also seen that, tiny as these waves are, they can still vary in size, so that one single sunbeam is made up of myriads of different-sized waves, which travel all together and make us see white light; unless for some reason they are scattered apart, so that we see them separately as red, green, blue, or yellow. How they are scattered, and many other secrets of the sun-waves, we cannot stop to consider not, but must pass on to ask -

What work do the sunbeams do for us?

They do two things – they give us light and heat. It is by means of them alone that we see anything. When the room was dark you could not distinguish the table, the chairs, or even the walls of the room. Why? Because they had no light-waves to send to your eye. But as the sunbeams began to pour in at the window, the waves played upon the things in the room, and when they hit them they bounded off them back to your eye, as a wave of the sea bounds back from a rock and strikes against a passing boat. Then, when they fell upon your eye, they entered it and excited the retina and the nerves, and the image of the chair or the table was carried to your brain. Look around at all the things in this room. Is it not strange to think that each one of them is sending these invisible messengers straight to your eye as you look at it; and that you see me, and distinguish me from the table, entirely by the kind of waves we each send to you?

Some substances send back hardly any waves of light, but let them all pass through them, and thus we cannot see them. A pane of clear glass, for instance, lets nearly all the light-waves pass through it, and therefore you often cannot see that the glass is there, because no light-messengers come back to you from it. Thus people have sometimes walked up against a glass door and broken it, not seeing it was there. Those substances are transparent which, for some reason unknown to us, allow the ether waves to pass through them without shaking the atoms of which the substance is made. In clear glass, for example, all the light-waves pass through without affecting the substance of the glass; while in a white wall the larger part of the rays are reflected back to your eye, and those which pass into the wall, by giving motion to its atoms lose their own vibrations.

Into polished shining metal the waves hardly enter at all, but are thrown back from the surface; and so a steel knife or a silver spoon are very bright, and are clearly seen. Quicksilver is put at the back of looking-glasses because it reflects so many waves. It not only sends back those which come from the sun, but those, too, which come from your face. So, when you see yourself in a looking-glass, the sun-waves have first played on your face and bounded off from it to the looking-glass; then, when they strike the looking-glass, they are thrown back again on to the retina of your eye, and you see your own face by means of the very waves you threw off from it an instant before.

But the reflected light-waves do more for us than this. They not only make us see things, but they make us see them in different colours. What, you will ask, is this too the work of the sunbeams? Certainly; for if the colour we see depends on the size of the waves which come back to us, then we must see things coloured differently according to the waves they send back. For instance, imagine a sunbeam playing on a leaf: part of its waves bound straight back from it to our eye and make us see the surface of the leaf, but the rest go right into the leaf itself, and there some of them are used up and kept prisoners. The red, orange, yellow, blue, and violet waves are all useful to the leaf, and it does not let them go again. But it cannot absorb the green waves, and so it throws them back, and they travel to your eye and make you see a green colour. So when you say a leaf is green, you mean that the leaf does not want the green waves of the sunbeam, but sends them back to you. In the same way the scarlet geranium rejects the red waves; this table sends back brown waves; a white tablecloth sends back nearly the whole of the waves, and a black coat scarcely any. This is why, when there is very little light in the room, you can see a white tablecloth while you would not be able to distinguish a black object, because the few faint rays that are there, are all sent back to you from a white surface.

Is it not curious to think that there is really no such thing as colour in the leaf, the table, the coat, or the geranium flower, but we see them of different colours because, for some reason, they send back only certain coloured waves to our eye?

Wherever you look, then, and whatever you see, all the beautiful tints, colours, lights, and shades around you are the work of the tiny sun-waves.

Again, light does a great deal of work when it falls upon plants. Those rays of light which are caught by the leaf are by no means idle; we shall see in Lecture VII that the leaf uses them to digest its food and make the sap on which the plant feeds.

We all know that a plant becomes pale and sickly if it has not sunlight, and the reason is, that without these light-waves it cannot get food out of the air, nor make the sap and juices which it needs. When you look at plants and trees growing in the beautiful meadows; at the fields of corn, and at the lovely landscape, you are looking on the work of the tiny waves of light, which never rest all through the day in helping to give life to every green thing that grows.

So far we have spoken only of light; but hold your hand in the sun and feel the heat of the sunbeams, and then consider if the waves of heat do not do work also. There are many waves in a sunbeam which move too slowly to make us see light when they hit our eye, but we can feel them as heat, though we cannot see them as light. The simplest way of feeling heat-waves is to hold a warm iron near your face. You know that no light comes from it, yet you can feel the heat-waves beating violently against your face and scorching it. Now there are many of these dark heat-rays in a sunbeam, and it is they which do most of the work in the world.

In the first place, as they come quivering to the earth, it is they which shake the water-drops apart, so that these are carried up in the air, as we shall see in the next lecture. And then remember, it is these drops, falling again as rain, which make the rivers and all the moving water on the earth. So also it is the heat-waves which make the air hot and light, and so cause it to rise and make winds and air-currents, and these again give rise to ocean-currents. It is these dark rays, again, which strike upon the land and give it the warmth which enables plants to grow. It is they also which keep up the warmth in our own bodies, both by coming to us directly from the sun, and also in a very roundabout way through plants. You will remember that plants use up rays of light and heat in growing; then either we eat the plants, or animals eat the plants and we eat the animals; and when we digest the food, that heat comes back in our bodies, which the plants first took from the sunbeam. Breathe upon your hand, and feel how hot your breath is; well, that heat which you feel, was once in a sunbeam, and has travelled from it through the food you have eaten, and has now been at work keeping up the heat of your body.

But there is still another way in which these plants may give out the heat-waves they have imprisoned. You will remember how we learnt in the first lecture that coal is made of plants, and that the heat they give out is the heat these plants once took in. Think how much work is done by burning coals. Not only are our houses warmed by coal fires and lighted by coal gas, but our steam-engines and machinery work entirely by water which has been turned into steam by the heat of coal and coke fire; and our steamboats travel all over the world by means of the same power. In the same way the oil of our lamps comes either from olives, which grow on trees; or from coal and the remains of plants and animals in the earth. Even our tallow candles are made of mutton fat, and sheep eat grass; as so, turn which way we will, we find that the light and heat on our earth, whether it comes from fires, or candles, or lamps, or gas, and whether it moves machinery, or drives a train, or propels a ship, is equally the work of the invisible waves of ether coming from the sun, which make what we call a sunbeam.

Lastly, there are still some hidden waves which we have not yet mentioned, which are not useful to us either as light or heat, and yet they are not idle.

Before I began this lecture, I put a piece of paper, which had been dipped in nitrate of silver, under a piece of glass; and between it and the glass I put a piece of lace. Look what the sun has been doing while I have been speaking. It has been breaking up the nitrate of silver on the paper and turning it into a deep brown substance; only where the threads of the lace were, and the sun could not touch the nitrate of silver, there the paper has remained light-coloured, and by this means I have a beautiful impression of the lace on the paper. I will now dip the impression into water in which some hyposulphite of soda is dissolved, and this will "fix" the picture, that is, prevent the sun acting upon it any more; then the picture will remain distinct, and I can pass it round to you all. Here, again, invisible waves have been at work, and this time neither as light nor as heat, but as chemical agents, and it is these waves which give us all our beautiful photographs. In any toyshop you can buy this prepared paper, and set the chemical waves at work to make pictures. Only you must remember to fix it in the solution afterwards, otherwise the chemical rays will go on working after you have taken the lace away, and all the paper will become brown and your picture will disappear.

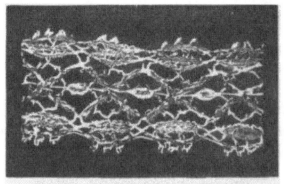

Piece of lace photographed during the lecture.

And now, tell me, may we not honestly say, that the invisible waves which make our sunbeams, are wonderful fairy messengers as they travel eternally and unceasingly across space, never resting, never tiring in doing the work of our world? Little as we have been able to learn about them in one short hour, do they not seem to you worth studying and worth thinking about, as we look at the beautiful results of their work? The ancient Greeks worshipped the sun, and condemned to death one of their greatest philosophers, named Anaxagoras, because he denied that it was a god. We can scarcely wonder at this when we see what the sun does for our world; but we know that it is a huge globe made of gases and fiery matter and not a god. We are grateful for the sun instead of to him, and surely we shall look at him with new interest, now that we can picture his tiny messengers, the sunbeams, flitting over all space, falling upon our earth, giving us light to see with, and beautiful colours to enjoy, warming the air and the earth, making the refreshing rain, and, in a word, filling the world with life and gladness.

Lesson 137

1. Today read the first part of chapter 3 of *The Fairy Land of Science*.
2. Choose a topic from your reading. Write or tell a topic sentence, or main idea sentence, for that topic.

Lecture III. The Aerial Ocean in Which We Live.

Did you ever sit on the bank of a river in some quiet spot where the water was deep and clear, and watch the fishes swimming lazily along? When I was a child this was one of my favourite occupations in the summertime on the banks of the Thames, and there was one question which often puzzled me greatly, as I watched the minnows and gudgeon gliding along through the water. Why should fishes live in something and be often buffeted about by waves and currents, while I and others lived on the top of the earth and not in anything? I do not remember ever asking anyone about this; and if I had, in those days people did not pay much attention to children's questions, and probably nobody would have told me, what I now tell you, that we do live in something quite as real and often quite as rough and stormy as the water in which the fishes swim. The something in which we live is air, and the reason that we do not perceive it, is that we are in it, and that it is a gas, and invisible to us; while we are above the water in which the fishes live, and it is a liquid which our eyes can perceive.

But let us suppose for a moment that a being, whose eyes were so made that he could see gases as we see liquids, was looking down from a distance upon our earth. He would see an ocean of air, or aerial ocean, all round the globe, with birds floating about in it, and people walking along the bottom, just as we see fish gliding along the bottom of a river. It is true, he would never see even the birds come near to the surface, for the highest- flying bird, the condor, never soars more than five miles from the ground, and our atmosphere, as we shall see, is at least 100 miles high. So he would call us all deep-air creatures, just as we talk of deep-sea animals; and if we can imagine that he fished in this air-ocean, and could pull one of us out of it into space, he would find that we should gasp and die just as fishes do when pulled out of the water.

He would also observe very curious things going on in our air-ocean; he would see large streams and currents of air, which we call winds, and which would appear to him as ocean-currents do to us, while near down to the earth he would see thick mists forming and then disappearing again, and these would be our clouds. From them he would see rain, hail and snow falling to the earth, and from time to time bright flashes would shoot across the air-ocean, which would be our lightning. Nay even the brilliant rainbow, the northern aurora borealis, and the falling stars, which seem to us so high up in space, would be seen by him near to our earth, and all within the aerial ocean.

But as we know of no such being living in space, who can tell us what takes place in our invisible air, and we cannot see it ourselves, we must try by experiments to see it with our imagination, though we cannot with our eyes.

First, then, can we discover what air is? At one time it was thought that it was a simple gas and could not be separated into more than one kind. But we are now going to make an experiment by which it has been shown that air is made of two gases mingled together, and that one of these gases, called oxygen, is used up when anything burns, while the other nitrogen is not used, and only serves to dilute the minute atoms of oxygen. I have here a glass bell-jar, with a cork fixed tightly in the neck, and I place the jar over a pan of water, while on the water floats a plate with a small piece of phosphorus upon it.

Phosphorus burning under a bell-jar (Roscoe).

You will see that by putting the bell-jar over the water, I have shut in a certain quantity of air, and my object now is to use up the oxygen out of this air and leave only nitrogen behind. To do this I must light the piece of phosphorus, for you will remember it is in burning that oxygen is used up. I will take the cork out, light the phosphorus, and cork up the jar again. See! as the phosphorus burns white fumes fill the jar. These fumes are phosphoric acid which is a substance made of phosphorous and the oxygen of the air together.

Now, phosphoric acid melts in water just as sugar does, and in a few minutes these fumes will disappear. They are beginning to melt already, and the water from the pan is rising up in the bell-jar. Why is this? Consider for a moment what we have done. First, the jar was full of air, that is, of mixed oxygen and nitrogen; then the phosphorus used up the oxygen making white fumes; afterwards, the water sucked up these fumes; and so, in the jar now nitrogen is the only gas left, and the water has risen up to fill all the rest of the space that was once taken up with oxygen.

We can easily prove that there is no oxygen now in the jar. I take out the cork and let a lighted taper down into the gas. If there were any oxygen the taper would burn, but you see it goes out directly proving that all the oxygen has been used up by the phosphorous. When this experiment is made very accurately, we find that for every pint of oxygen in air there are four pints of nitrogen, so that the active oxygen-atoms are scattered about, floating in the sleepy, inactive nitrogen.

It is these oxygen-atoms which we use up when we breathe. If I had put a mouse under the bell-jar, instead of the phosphorus, the water would have risen just the same, because the mouse would have breathed in the oxygen and used it up in its body, joining it to carbon and making a bad gas, carbonic acid, which would also melt in the water, and when all the oxygen was used, the mouse would have died.

Do you see now how foolish it is to live in rooms that are closely shut up, or to hide your head under the bedclothes when you sleep? You use up all the oxygen-atoms, and then there are none left for you to breathe; and besides this, you send out of your mouth bad fumes, though you cannot see them, and these, when you breathe them in again, poison you and make you ill.

Perhaps you will say, If oxygen is so useful, why is not the air made entirely of it? But think for a moment. If there was such an immense quantity of oxygen, how fearfully fast everything would burn! Our bodies would soon rise above fever heat from the quantity of oxygen we should take in, and all fires and lights would burn furiously. In fact, a flame once lighted would spread so rapidly that no power on earth could stop it, and everything would be destroyed. So the lazy nitrogen is very useful in keeping the oxygen-atoms apart; and we have time, even when a fire is very large and powerful, to put it out before it has drawn in more and more oxygen from the surrounding air. Often, if you can shut a fire into a closed space, as in a closely-shut room or the hold of a ship, it will go out, because it has used up all the oxygen in the air.

So, you see, we shall be right in picturing this invisible air all around us as a mixture of two gases. But when we examine ordinary air very carefully, we find small quantities of other gases in it, besides oxygen and nitrogen. First, there is carbonic acid gas. This is the bad gas which we give out of our mouths after we have burnt up the oxygen with the carbon of our bodies inside our lungs; and this carbonic acid is also given out from everything that burns. If only animals lived in the world, this gas would soon poison the air; but plants get hold of it, and in the sunshine they break it up again, as we shall see in Lecture VII, and use up the carbon, throwing the oxygen back into the air for us to use. Secondly, there are very small quantities of ammonia, or the gas which almost chokes you in smelling-salts, and which, when liquid, is commonly called "spirits of hartshorn." This ammonia is useful to plants, as we shall see by and by. Lastly, there is a great deal of water in the air, floating about as invisible vapour or water-dust, and this we shall speak of in the next lecture. Still, all these gases and vapours in the atmosphere are in very small quantities, and the bulk of the air is composed of oxygen and nitrogen.

Having now learned what air is, the next question which presents itself is, Why does it stay round our earth? You will remember we saw in the first lecture, that all the little atoms of a gas are trying to fly away from each other, so that if I turn on this gas-jet the atoms soon leave it, and reach you at the farther end of the room, and you can smell the gas. Why, then, do not all the atoms of oxygen and nitrogen fly away from our earth into space, and leave us without any air?

Ah! here you must look for another of our invisible forces. Have you forgotten our giant force, "gravitation," which draws things together from a distance? This force draws together the earth and the atoms of oxygen and nitrogen; and as the earth is very big and heavy, and the atoms of air are light and easily moved, they are drawn down to the earth and held there by gravitation. But for all that, the atmosphere does not leave off trying to fly away; it is always pressing upwards and outwards with all its might, while the earth is doing its best to hold it down.

The effect of this is, that near the earth, where the pull downward is very strong, the air-atoms are drawn very closely together, because gravitation gets the best of the struggle. But as we get farther and farther from the earth, the pull downward becomes weaker, and then the air-atoms spring farther apart, and the air becomes thinner. Suppose that the lines in this diagram represent layers of air. Near the earth we have to represent them as lying closely together, but as they recede from the earth they are also farther apart.

But the chief reason why the air is thicker or denser nearer the earth, is because the upper layers press it down. If you have a heap of papers lying one on the top of the other, you know that those at the bottom of the heap will be more closely pressed together than those above, and just the same is the case with the atoms of the air. Only there is this difference, if the papers have lain for some time, when you take the top ones off, the under ones remain close together. But it is not so with the air, because air is elastic, and the atoms are always trying to fly apart, so that directly you take away the pressure they spring up again as far as they can.

I have here an ordinary pop-gun. If I push the cork in very tight, and then force the piston slowly inwards, I can compress the air a good deal. Now I am forcing the atoms nearer and nearer together, but at last they rebel so strongly against being more crowded that the cork cannot resist their pressure. Out it flies, and the atoms spread themselves out comfortably again in the air all around them. Now, just as I pressed the air together in the pop-gun, so the atmosphere high up above the earth presses on the air below and keeps the atoms closely packed together. And in this case the atoms cannot force back the air above them as they did the cork in the pop-gun; they are obliged to submit to be pressed together.

Lesson 138

1. Today read the next section of chapter 3 of *The Fairy Land of Science*.
2. Choose a topic from your reading. Write or tell a topic sentence, or main idea sentence, for that topic.

Lecture III. The Aerial Ocean in Which We Live. Continued...

Even a short distance from the earth, however, at the top of a high mountain, the air becomes lighter, because it has less weight of atmosphere above it, and people who go up in balloons often have great difficulty in breathing, because the air is so thin and light. In 1804 a Frenchman, named Gay-Lussac, went up four miles and a half in a balloon, and brought down some air; and he found that it was much less heavy than the same quantity of air taken close down to the earth, showing that it was much thinner, or rarer, as it is called;* and when, in 1862, Mr. Glaisher and Mr. Coxwell went up five miles and a half, Mr. Glaisher's veins began to swell, and his head grew dizzy, and he fainted. The air was too thin for him to breathe enough in at a time, and it did not press heavily enough on the drums of his ears and the veins of his body. He would have died if Mr. Coxwell had not quickly let off some of the gas in the balloon, so that it sank down into denser air. (*100 cubic inches near the earth weighed 31 grains, while the same quantity taken at four and a half miles up in the air weighed only 12 grains, or two-fifths of the weight.)

And now comes another very interesting question. If the air gets less and less dense as it is farther from the earth, where does it stop altogether? We cannot go up to find out, because we should die long before we reached the limit; and for a long time we had to guess about how high the atmosphere probably was, and it was generally supposed not to be more than fifty miles. But lately, some curious bodies, which we should have never suspected would be useful to us in this way, have let us into the secret of the height of the atmosphere. These bodies are the meteors, or falling stars.

Most people, at one time or another, have seen what looks like a star shoot right across the sky, and disappear. On a clear starlight night you may often see one or more of these bright lights flash through the air; for one falls on an average in every twenty minutes, and on the nights of August

9th and November 13th there are numbers in one part of the sky. These bodies are not really stars; they are simply stones or lumps of metal flying through the air, and taking fire by clashing against the atoms of oxygen in it. There are great numbers of these masses moving round and round the sun, and when our earth comes across their path, as it does especially in August and November, they dash with such tremendous force through the atmosphere that they grow white-hot, and give out light, and then disappear, melted into vapour. Every now and then one falls to the earth before it is all melted away, and thus we learn that these stones contain tin, iron, sulphur, phosphorus, and other substances.

It is while these bodies are burning that they look to us like falling stars, and when we see them we know that they must be dashing against our atmosphere. Now if two people stand a certain known distance, say fifty miles, apart on the earth and observe these meteors and the direction in which they each see them fall, they can calculate (by means of the angle between the two directions) how high they are above them when they first see them, and at that moment they must have struck against the atmosphere, and even travelled some way through it, to become white-hot. In this way we have learnt that meteors burst into light at least 100 miles above the surface of the earth, and so the atmosphere must be more than 100 miles high.

A square inch of paper, as shown in the lecture.

Our next question is as to the weight of our aerial ocean. You will easily understand that all this air weighing down upon the earth must be very heavy, even though it grows lighter as it ascends. The atmosphere does, in fact, weigh down upon land at the level of the sea as much as if a 15-pound weight were put upon every square inch of land. This little piece of linen paper, which I am holding up, measures exactly a square inch, and as it lies on the table, it is bearing a weight of 15 lbs. on its surface. But how, then, comes it that I can lift it so easily? Why am I not conscious of the weight?

To understand this you must give all your attention, for it is important and at first not very easy to grasp. you must remember, in the first place, that the air is heavy because it is attracted to the earth, and in the second place, that since air is elastic all the atoms of it are pushing upwards against this gravitation. And so, at any point in air, as for instance the place where the paper now is as I hold it up, I feel no pressure because exactly as much as gravitation is pulling the air down, so much elasticity is resisting and pushing it up. So the pressure is equal upwards, downwards, and on all sides, and I can move the paper with equal ease any way.

Even if I lay the paper on the table this is still true, because there is always some air under it. If, however, I could get the air quite away from one side of the paper, then the pressure on the other side would show itself. I can do this by simply wetting the paper and letting it fall on the table, and the water will prevent any air from getting under it. Now see! if I try to lift it by the thread in the middle, I have great difficulty, because the whole 15 pounds' weight of the atmosphere is pressing it down. A still better way of making the experiment is with a piece of leather, such as the boys often amuse themselves with in the streets. This piece of leather has been well soaked. I drop it on the floor and see! it requires all my strength to pull it up. (In fastening the string to the leather the hole must be very small and the know as flat as possible, and it is even well to put a small piece of kid under the knot. When I first made this experiment, not having taken these precautions, it did not succeed well, owing to air getting in through the hole.) I now drop it on this stone weight, and so heavily is it pressed down upon it by the atmosphere that I can lift the weight without its breaking away from it.

Soaked leather lifting a stone paper-weight.

Have you ever tried to pick limpets off a rock? If so, you know how tight they cling. The limpet clings to the rock just in the same way as this leather does to the stone; the little animal exhausts the air inside it's shell, and then it is pressed against the rock by the whole weight of the air above.

Perhaps you will wonder how it is that if we have a weight of 15 lbs. pressing on every square inch of our bodies, it does not crush us. And, indeed, it amounts on the whole to a weight of about 15 tons upon the body of a grown man. It would crush us if it were not that there are gases and fluids inside our bodies which press outwards and balance the weight so that we do not feel it at all.

This is why Mr. Glaisher's veins swelled and he grew giddy in thin air. The gases and fluids inside his body were pressing outwards as much as when he was below, but the air outside did not press so heavily, and so all the natural condition of his body was disturbed.

I hope we now realize how heavily the air presses down upon our earth, but it is equally necessary to understand how, being elastic, it also presses upwards; and we can prove this by a simple experiment. I fill this tumbler with water, and keeping a piece of card firmly pressed against it, I turn the whole upside- down.

Inverted tumbler of water with card kept against it by atmospheric pressure.

When I now take my hand away you would naturally expect the card to fall, and the water to be spilt. But no! the card remains as if glued to the tumbler, kept there entirely by the air pressing upwards against it. (The engraver has drawn the tumbler only half full of water. The experiment will succeed quite as well in this way if the tumbler be turned over quickly, so that part of the air escapes between the tumbler and the card, and therefore the space above the water is occupied by air less dense than that outside.)

And now we are almost prepared to understand how we can weigh the invisible air. One more experiment first. I have here what is called a U tube, because it is shaped like a large U. I pour some water in it till it is about half full, and you will notice that the water stands at the same height in both arms of the tube, because the air presses on both surfaces alike. Putting my thumb on one end I tilt the tube carefully, so as to make the water run up to the end of one arm, and then turn it back again. But the water does not now return to its even position, it remains up in the arm on which my thumb rests.

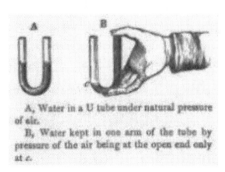

A, Water in a U tube under natural pressure of air.
B, Water kept in one arm of the tube by pressure of the air being at the open end only at c.

Why is this? Because my thumb keeps back the air from pressing at that end, and the whole weight of the atmosphere rests on the water at the other end. And so we learn that not only has the atmosphere real weight, but we can see the effects of this weight by making it balance a column of water or any other liquid. In the case of the wetted leather we felt the weight of the air, here we see its effects.

Lesson 139

1. Today read to the end of chapter 3 of *The Fairy Land of Science*.
2. Choose a topic from your reading. Write or tell a topic sentence, or main idea sentence, for that topic.

Lecture III.   The Aerial Ocean in Which We Live.   Continued…

Now when we wish to see the weight of the air we consult a barometer, which works really just in the same way as the water in this tube. An ordinary upright barometer is simply a straight tube of glass filled with mercury or quicksilver, and turned upside-down in a small cup of mercury. The tube is a little more than 30 inches long, and though it is quite full of mercury before it is turned up, yet directly it stands in the cup the mercury falls, till there is a height of about 30 inches between the surface of the mercury in the cup, and that of the mercury in the tube. As it falls it leaves an empty space above the mercury which is called a vacuum, because it has no air in it. Now, the mercury is under the same conditions as the water was in the U tube, there is no pressure upon it at the top of the tube, while there is a pressure of 15 lbs. upon it in the bowl, and therefore it remains held up in the tube.

Tube of mercury inverted in a
basin of mercury.

But why will it not remain more than 30 inches high in the tube? You must remember it is only kept up in the tube at all by the air which presses on the mercury in the cup. And that column of mercury now balances the pressure of the air outside, and presses down on the mercury in the cup at its mouth just as much as the air does on the rest. So this cup and tube act exactly like a pair of scales. The air outside is the thing to be weighed at one end as it presses on the mercury, the column answers to the leaden weight at the other end which tells you how heavy the air is. Now if the bore of this tube is made an inch square, then the 30 inches of mercury in it weigh exactly 15 lbs, and so we know that the weight of the air is 15 lbs. upon every square inch, but if the bore of the tube is only half a square inch, and therefore the 30 inches of mercury only weigh 7 1/2 lbs. instead of 15 lbs., the pressure of the atmosphere will also be halved, because it will only act upon half a square inch of surface, and for this reason it will make no difference to the height of the mercury whether the tube be broad or narrow.

Ordinary upright
barometer.
A, Wood covering
cup of mercury.
B, Hole through
which air acts.

But now suppose the atmosphere grows lighter, as it does when it has much damp in it. The barometer will show this at once, because there will be less weight on the mercury in the cup, therefore it will not keep the mercury pushed so high up in the tube. In other words, the mercury in the tube will fall.

Let us suppose that one day the air is so much lighter that it presses down only with a weight of 14 1/2 lbs. to the square inch instead of 15 lbs. Then the mercury would fall to 29 inches, because each inch is equal to the weight of half a pound. Now, when the air is damp and very full of water-vapour it is much lighter, and so when the barometer falls we expect rain. Sometimes, however, other causes make the air light, and then, although the barometer is low, no rain comes.

Again, if the air becomes heavier the mercury is pushed up above 30 to 31 inches, and in this way we are able to weigh the invisible air-ocean all over the world, and tell when it grows lighter or heavier. This then, is the secret of the barometer. We cannot speak of the thermometer today, but I should like to warn you in passing that it has nothing to do with the weight of the air, but only with heat, and acts in quite a different way.

And now we have been so long hunting out, testing and weighing our aerial ocean, that scarcely any time is left us to speak of its movements or the pleasant breezes which it makes for us in our country walks. Did you ever try to run races on a very windy day? Ah! then you feel the air strongly enough; how it beats against your face and chest, and blows down your throat so as to take your breath away; and what hard work it is to struggle against it! Stop for a moment and rest, and ask yourself, what is the wind? Why does it blow sometimes one way and sometimes another, and sometimes not at all?

Wind is nothing more than air moving across the surface of the earth, which as it passes along bends the tops of the trees, beats against the houses, pushes the ships along by their sails, turns the windmill, carries off the smoke from cities, whistles through the keyhole, and moans as it rushes down the valley. What makes the air restless? why should it not lie still all round the earth?

It is restless because, as you will remember, its atoms are kept pressed together near the earth by the weight of the air above, and they take every opportunity, when they can find more room, to spread out violently and rush into the vacant space, and this rush we call a wind.

Imagine a great number of active schoolboys all crowded into a room till they can scarcely move their arms and legs for the crush, and then suppose all at once a large door is opened. Will they not all come tumbling out pell-mell, one over the other, into the hall beyond, so that if you stood in their way you would most likely be knocked down? Well, just this happens to the air-atoms; when they find a space before them into which they can rush, they come on helter-skelter, with such force that you have great difficulty in standing against them, and catch hold of something to support you for fear you should be blown down.

But how come they to find any empty space to receive them? To answer this we must go back again to our little active invisible fairies the sunbeams. When the sun-waves come pouring down upon the earth they pass through the air almost without heating it. But not so with the ground; there they pass down only a short distance and then are thrown back again. And when these sun-waves come quivering back they force the atoms of the air near the earth apart and make it lighter; so that the air close to the surface of the heated ground becomes less heavy than the air above it, and rises just as a cork rises in water. You know that hot air rises in the chimney; for if you put a piece of lighted paper on the fire it is carried up by the draught of air, often even before it can ignite. Now just as the hot air rises from the fire, so it rises from the heated ground up into higher parts of the atmosphere. and as it rises it leaves only thin air behind it, and this cannot resist the strong cold air whose atoms are struggling and trying to get free, and they rush in and fill the space.

One of the simplest examples of wind is to be found at the seaside. there in the daytime the land gets hot under the sunshine, and heats the air, making it grow light and rise. Meanwhile the sunshine on the water goes down deeper, and so does not send back so many heat-waves into the air; consequently the air on the top of the water is cooler and heavier, and it rushes in from over the sea to fill up the space on the shore left by the warm air as it rises. This is why the seaside is so pleasant in hot weather. During the daytime a light sea-breeze nearly always sets in from the sea to the land.

When night comes, however, then the land loses its heat very quickly, because it has not stored it up and the land-air grows cold; but the sea, which has been hoarding the sun-waves down in its depths, now gives them up to the atmosphere above it, and the sea-air becomes warm and rises. For this reason it is now the turn of the cold air from the land to spread over the sea, and you have a land-breeze blowing off the shore.

Again, the reason why there are such steady winds, called the trade winds, blowing towards the equator, is that the sun is very hot at the equator, and hot air is always rising there and making room for colder air to rush in. We have not time to travel farther with the moving air, though its journeys are extremely interesting; but if, when you read about the trade and other winds, you will always picture to yourselves warm air made light by the heat rising up into space and cold air expanding and rushing in to fill its place, I can promise you that you will not find the study of aerial currents so dry as many people imagine it to be.

We are now able to form some picture of our aerial ocean. We can imagine the active atoms of oxygen floating in the sluggish nitrogen, and being used up in every candle-flame, gas-jet and fire, and in the breath of all living beings; and coming out again tied fast to atoms of carbon and making carbonic acid. Then we can turn to trees and plants, and see them tearing these two apart again, holding the carbon fast and sending the invisible atoms of oxygen bounding back again into the air, ready to recommence work. We can picture all these air-atoms, whether of oxygen or nitrogen, packed close together on the surface of the earth, and lying gradually farther and farther apart, as they have less weight above them, till they become so scattered that we can only detect them as they rub against the flying meteors which flash into light. We can feel this great weight of air pressing the limpet on to the rock; and we can see it pressing up the mercury in the barometer and so enabling us to measure its weight. Lastly, every breath of wind that blows past us tells us how this aerial ocean is always moving to and fro on the face of the earth; and if we think for a moment how much bad air and bad matter it must carry away, as it goes from crowded cities to be purified in the country, we can see how, in even this one way alone, it is a great blessing to us.

Yet even now we have not mentioned many of the beauties of our atmosphere. It is the tiny particles floating in the air which scatter the light of the sun so that it spreads over the whole country and into shady places. The sun's rays always travel straight forward; and in the moon, where there is no atmosphere, there is no light anywhere except just where the rays fall. But on our earth the sun-waves hit against the myriads of particles in the air and glide off them into the corners of the room or the recesses of a shady lane, and so we have light spread before us wherever we walk in the daytime, instead of those deep black shadows which we can see through a telescope on the face of the moon.

Again, it is electricity playing in the air-atoms which gives us the beautiful lightning and the grand aurora borealis, and even the twinkling of the starts is produced entirely by minute changes in the air. If it were not for our aerial ocean, the stars would stare at us sternly, instead of smiling with the pleasant twinkle-twinkle which we have all learned to love as little children.

All these questions, however, we must leave for the present; only I hope you will be eager to read about them wherever you can, and open your eyes to learn their secrets. For the present we must be content if we can even picture this wonderful ocean of gas spread round our earth, and some of the work it does for us.

We said in the last lecture that without the sunbeams the earth would be cold, dark, and frost-ridden. With sunbeams, but without air, it would indeed have burning heat, side by side with darkness and ice, but it could have no soft light. our planet might look beautiful to others, as the moon does to us, but it could have comparatively few beauties of its own. With the sunbeams and the air, we see it has much to make it beautiful. But a third worker is wanted before our planet can revel in activity and life. This worker is water; and in the next lecture we shall learn something of the beauty and the usefulness of the "drops of water" on their travels.

Lesson 140

1. Today read the first part of chapter 4 of *The Fairy Land of Science*.
2. Choose a topic from your reading. Write or tell a topic sentence, or main idea sentence, for that topic.

Lecture IV. A Drop Of Water On Its Travels

We are going to spend an hour to-day in following a drop of water on its travels. If I dip my finger in this basin of water and lift it up again, I bring with it a small glistening drop out of the body of water below, and hold it before you. Tell me, have you any idea where this drop has been? what changes it has undergone, and what work it has been doing during all the long ages that water has lain on the face of the earth? It is a drop now, but it was not so before I lifted it out of the basin; then it was part of a sheet of water, and will be so again if I let it fall. Again, if I were to put this basin on the stove till all the water had boiled away, where would my drop be then? Where would it go? What forms will it take before it reappears in the rain-cloud, the river, or the sparkling dew?

These are questions we are going to try to answer to-day; and first, before we can in the least understand how water travels, we must call to mind what we have learnt about the sunbeams and the air. We must have clearly pictured in our imagination those countless sun-waves which are for ever crossing space, and especially those larger and slower undulations, the dark heat-waves; for it is these, you will remember, which force the air-atoms apart and make the air light, and it is also these which are most busy in sending water on its travels. But not these alone. The sun-waves might shake the water-drops as much as they liked and turn them into invisible vapour, but they could not carry them over the earth if it were not for the winds and currents of that aerial ocean which bears the vapour on its bosom, and wafts it to different regions of the world.

Let us try to understand how these two invisible workers, the sun-waves and the air, deal with the drops of water. I have here a kettle boiling over a spirit-lamp, and I want you to follow minutely what is going on in it. First, in the flame of the lamp, atoms of the spirit drawn up from below are clashing with the oxygen-atoms in the air. This, as you know, causes heat-waves and light-waves to move rapidly all round the lamp. The light-waves cannot pass through the kettle, but the heat-waves can, and as they enter the water inside they agitate it violently. Quicker, and still more quickly, the particles of water near the bottom of the kettle move to and fro and are shaken apart; and as they become light they rise through the colder water letting another layer come down to be heated in its turn. The motion grows more and more violent, making the water hotter and hotter, till at last the particles of which it is composed fly asunder, and escape as invisible vapour. If this kettle were transparent you would not see any steam above the water, because it is in the form of an invisible gas. But as the steam comes out of the mouth of the kettle you see a cloud. Why is this? Because the vapour is chilled by coming out into the cold air, and its particles are drawn together again into tiny, tiny drops of water, to which Dr. Tyndall has given the suggestive name of water-dust. If you hold a plate over the steam you can catch these tiny drops, though they will run into one another almost as you are catching them.

The clouds you see floating in the sky are made of exactly the same kind of water-dust as the cloud from the kettle, and I wish to show you that this is also really the same as the invisible steam within the kettle. I will do so by an experiment suggested by Dr. Tyndall. Here is another spirit-lamp, which I will hold under the cloud of steam – see! the cloud disappears! As soon as the water-dust is heated the heat-waves scatter it again into invisible particles, which float away into the room. Even without the spirit-lamp, you can convince yourself that water-vapour may be invisible; for close to the mouth of the kettle you will see a short blank space before the cloud begins. In this space there must be steam, but it is still so hot that you cannot see it; and this proves that heat-waves can so shake water apart as to carry it away invisibly right before your eyes.

Now, although we never see any water travelling from our earth up into the skies, we know that it goes there, for it comes down again in rain, and so it must go up invisibly. But where does the heat come from which makes this water invisible? Not from below, as in the case of the kettle, but from above, pouring down from the sun. Wherever the sun-waves touch the rivers, ponds, lakes, seas, or fields of ice and snow upon our earth, they carry off invisible water-vapour. They dart down through the top layers of the water, and shake the water-particles forcibly apart; and in this case the drops fly asunder more easily and before they are so hot, because they are not kept down by a great weight of water above, as in the kettle, but find plenty of room to spread themselves out in the gaps between the air-atoms of the atmosphere.

Can you imagine these water-particles, just above any pond or lake, rising up and getting entangled among the air-atoms? They are very light, much lighter than the atmosphere; and so, when a great many of them are spread about in the air which lies just over the pond, they make it much lighter than the layer of air above, and so help it to rise, while the heavier layer of air comes down ready to take up more vapour.

In this way the sun-waves and the air carry off water everyday, and all day long, from the top of lakes, rivers, pools, springs, and seas, and even from the surface of ice and snow. Without any fuss or noise or sign of any kind, the water of our earth is being drawn up invisibly into the sky.

It has been calculated that in the Indian Ocean three-quarters of an inch of water is carried off from the surface of the sea in one day and night; so that as much as 22 feet, or a depth of water about twice the height of an ordinary room, is silently and invisibly lifted up from the whole surface of the ocean in one year. It is true this is one of the hottest parts of the earth, where the sun-waves are most active; but even in our own country many feet of water are drawn up in the summer-time.

What, then, becomes of all this water? Let us follow it as it struggles upwards to the sky. We see it in our imagination first carrying layer after layer of air up with it from the sea till it rises far above our heads and above the highest mountains. But now, call to mind what happens to the air as it recedes from the earth. Do you not remember that the air-atoms are always trying to fly apart, and are only kept pressed together by the weight of air above them? Well, so this water-laden air rises up, its particles, no longer so much pressed together, begin to separate, and as all work requires an expenditure of heat, the air becomes colder, and then you know at once what must happen to the invisible vapour, — it will form into tiny water-drops, like the steam from the kettle. And so, as the air rises and becomes colder, the vapour gathers into the visible masses, and we can see it hanging in the sky, and call it clouds. When these clouds are highest they are about ten miles from the earth, but when they are made of heavy drops and hang low down, they sometimes come within a mile of the ground.

Look up at the clouds as you go home, and think that the water of which they are made has all been drawn up invisibly through the air. Not, however, necessarily here in London, for we have already seen that air travels as wind all over the world, rushing in to fill spaces made by rising air wherever they occur, and so these clouds may be made of vapour collected in the Mediterranean, or in the Gulf of Mexico off the coast of America, or even, if the wind is from the north, of chilly particles gathered from the surface of Greenland ice and snow, and brought here by the moving currents of air. Only, of one thing we may be sure, that they come from the water of our earth.

Sometimes, if the air is warm, these water-particles may travel a long way without ever forming into clouds; and on a hot, cloudless day the air is often very full of invisible vapour. Then, if a cold wind comes sweeping along, high up in the sky, and chills this vapour, it forms into great bodies of water-dust clouds, and the sky is overcast. At other times clouds hang lazily in a bright sky, and these show us that just where they are the air is cold and turns the invisible vapour rising from the ground into visible water-dust, so that exactly in those spaces we see it as clouds. Such clouds form often on warm, still summer's day, and they are shaped like masses of wool, ending in a straight line below. They are not merely hanging in the sky, they are really resting upon a tall column of invisible vapour which stretches right up from the earth; and that straight line under the clouds marks the place where the air becomes cold enough to turn this

And now, suppose that while these or any other kind of clouds are overhead, there comes along either a very cold wind, or a wind full of vapour. As it passes through the clouds, it makes them very full of water, for, if it chills them, it makes the water-dust draw more closely together; or, if it brings a new load of water-dust, the air is fuller than it can hold. In either case a number of water-particles are set free, and our fairy force "cohesion" seizes upon them at once and forms them into large water-drops. Then they are much heavier than the air, and so they can float no longer, but down they come to the earth in a shower of rain.

There are other ways in which the air may be chilled, and rain made to fall, as, for example, when a wind laden with moisture strikes against the cold tops of mountains. Thus the Khasia Hills in India which face the Bay of Bengal, chill the air which crosses them on its way from the Indian Ocean. The wet winds are driven up the sides of the hills, the air expands, and the vapour is chilled, and forming into drops, falls in torrents of rain. Sir J. Hooker tells us that as much as 500 inches of rain fell in these hills in nine months. That is to say, if you could measure off all the ground over which the rain fell, and spread the whole nine months' rain over it, it would make a lake 500 inches, or more than 40 feet deep! You will not be surprised that the country on the other side of these hills gets hardly any rain, for all the water has been taken out of the air before it comes there. Again for example in England, the wind comes to Cumberland and Westmorland over the Atlantic, full of vapour, and as it strikes against the Pennine Hills it shakes off its watery load; so that the lake district is the most rainy in England, with the exception perhaps of Wales, where the high mountains have the same effect.

In this way, from different causes, the water of which the sun has robbed our rivers and seas, comes back to us, after it has travelled to various parts of the world, floating on the bosom of the air. But it does not always fall straight back into the rivers and seas again, a large part of it falls on the land, and has to trickle down slopes and into the earth, in order to get back to its natural home, and it is often caught on its way before it can reach the great waters.

Lesson 141
1. Today read the next part of chapter 4 of *The Fairy Land of Science*.
2. Choose a topic from your reading. Write or tell a topic sentence, or main idea sentence, for that topic.

Lecture IV.   A Drop Of Water On Its Travels.   Continued…

Go to any piece of ground which is left wild and untouched you will find it covered with grass weeds, and other plants; if you dig up a small plot you will find innumerable tiny roots creeping through the ground in every direction. Each of these roots has a sponge-like mouth by which the plant takes up water. Now, imagine rain-drops falling on this plot of ground and sinking into the earth. On every side they will find rootlets thirsting to drink them in, and they will be sucked up as if by tiny sponges, and drawn into the plants, and up the stems to the leaves. Here, as we shall see in Lecture VII, they are worked up into food for the plant, and only if the leaf has more water than it needs, some drops may escape at the tiny openings under the leaf, and be drawn up again by the sun-waves as invisible vapour into the air.

Again, much of the rain falls on hard rock and stone, where it cannot sink in, and then it lies in pools till it is shaken apart again into vapour and carried off in the air. Nor is it idle here, even before it is carried up to make clouds. We have to thank this invisible vapour in the air for protecting us from the burning heat of the sun by day and intolerable frost by night.

Let us for a moment imagine that we can see all that we know exists between us and the sun. First, we have the fine ether across which the sunbeams travel, beating down upon our earth with immense force, so that in the sandy desert they are like a burning fire. Then we have the coarser atmosphere of oxygen and nitrogen atoms hanging in this ether, and bending the minute sun-waves out of their direct path. But they do very little to hinder them on their way, and this is why in very dry countries the sun's heat is so intense. The rays beat down mercilessly, and nothing opposes them. Lastly, in damp countries we have the larger but still invisible particles of vapour hanging about among the air-atoms. Now, these watery particles, although they are very few (only about one twenty-fifth part of the whole atmosphere), do hinder the sun-waves. For they are very greedy of heat, and though the light-waves pass easily through them, they catch the heat-waves and use them to help themselves to expand. And so, when there is invisible vapour in the air, the sunbeams come to us deprived of some of their heat-waves, and we can remain in the sunshine without suffering from the heat.

This is how the water-vapour shields us by day, but by night it is still more useful. During the day our earth and the air near it have been storing up the heat which has been poured down on them, and at night, when the sun goes down, all this heat begins to escape again. Now, if there were no vapour in the air, this heat would rush back into space so rapidly that the ground would become cold and frozen even on a summer's night, and all but the most hardy plants would die. But the vapour which formed a veil against the sun in the day, now forms a still more powerful veil against the escape of the heat by night. It shuts in the heat-waves, and only allows them to make their way slowly upwards from the earth – thus producing for us the soft, balmy nights of summer and preventing all life being destroyed in the winter.

Perhaps you would scarcely imagine at first that it is this screen of vapour which determines whether or not we shall have dew upon the ground. Have you ever thought why dew forms, or what power has been at work scattering the sparkling drops upon the grass? Picture to yourself that it has been a very hot summer's day, and the ground and the grass have been well warmed, and that the sun goes down in a clear sky without any clouds. At once the heat-waves which have been stored up in the ground, bound back into the air, and here some are greedily absorbed by the vapour, while others make their way slowly upwards. The grass, especially, gives out these heat-waves very quickly, because the blades, being very thin, are almost all surface. In consequence of this they part with their heat more quickly than they can draw it up from the ground, and become cold. Now the air lying just above the grass is full of invisible vapour, and the cold of the blades, as it touches them, chills the water-particles, and they are no longer able to hold apart, but are drawn together into drops on the surface of the leaves.

We can easily make artificial dew for ourselves. I have here a bottle of ice which has been kept outside the window. When I bring it into the warm room a mist forms rapidly outside the bottle. This mist is composed of water-drops, drawn out of the air of the room, because the cold glass chilled the air all round it, so that it gave up its invisible water to form dew-drops. Just in this same way the cold blades of grass chill the air lying above them, and steal its vapour.

But try the experiment, some night when a heavy dew is expected, of spreading a thin piece of muslin over some part of the grass, supporting it at the four corners with pieces of stick so that it forms an awning. Though there may be plenty of dew on the grass all round, yet under this awning you will find scarcely any. The reason of this is that the muslin checks the heat-waves as they rise from the grass, and so the grass-blades are not chilled enough to draw together the water-drops on their surface. If you walk out early in the summer mornings and look at the fine cobwebs flung across the hedges, you will see plenty of drops on the cobwebs themselves sparkling like diamonds; but underneath on the leaves there will be none, for even the delicate cobweb has been strong enough to shut in the heat-waves and keep the leaves warm.

Again, if you walk off the grass on to the gravel path, you find no dew there. Why is this? Because the stones of the gravel can draw up heat from the earth below as fast as they give it out, and so they are never cold enough to chill the air which touches them. On a cloudy night also you will often find little or no dew even on the grass. The reason of this is that the clouds give back heat to the earth, and so the grass does not become chilled enough to draw the water-drops together on its surface. But after a hot, dry day, when the plants are thirsty and there is little hope of rain to refresh them, then they are able in the evening to draw the little drops from the air and drink them in before the rising sun comes again to carry them away.

But our rain-drop undergoes other changes more strange than these. Till now we have been imagining it to travel only where the temperature is moderate enough for it to remain in a liquid state as water. But suppose that when it is drawn up into the air it meets with such a cold blast as to bring it to the freezing point. If it falls into this blast when it is already a drop, then it will freeze into a hailstone, and often on a hot summer's day we may have a severe hailstorm, because the rain-drops have crossed a bitterly cold wind as they were falling, and have been frozen into round drops of ice.

But if the water-vapour reaches the freezing air while it is still an invisible gas, and before it has been drawn into a drop, then its history is very different. The ordinary force of cohesion has then no power over the particles to make them into watery globes, but its place is taken by the fairy process of "crystallization," and they are formed into beautiful white flakes, to fall in a snow-shower. I want you to picture this process to yourselves, for if once you can take an interest in the wonderful power of nature to build up crystals, you will be astonished how often you will meet with instances of it, and what pleasure it will add to your life.

The particles of nearly all substances, when left free and not hurried, can build themselves into crystal forms. If you melt salt in water and then let all the water evaporate slowly, you will get salt-crystals; — beautiful cubes of transparent salt all built on the same pattern. The same is true of sugar; and if you will look at the spikes of an ordinary stick of sugar-candy, such as I have here, you will see the kind of crystals which sugar forms. You may even pick out such shapes as these from the common crystallized brown sugar in the sugar basin, or see them with a magnifying glass on a lump of white sugar.

A piece of sugar-candy, photographed of the natural size.

But it is not only easily melted substances such as sugar and salt which form crystals. The beautiful stalactite grottos are all made of crystals of lime. Diamonds are crystals of carbon, made inside the earth. Rock-crystals, which you know probably under the name of Irish diamonds, are crystallized quartz; and so, with slightly different colourings, are agates, opals, jasper, onyx, cairngorms, and many other precious stones. Iron, copper, gold, and sulphur, when melted and cooled slowly build themselves into crystals, each of their own peculiar form, and we see that there is here a wonderful order, such as we should never have dreamt of, if we had not proved it. If you possess a microscope you may watch the growth of crystals yourself by melting some common powdered nitre in a little water till you find that no more will melt in it. Then put a few drops of this water on a warm glass slide and place it under the microscope. As the drops dry you will see the long transparent needles of nitre forming on the glass, and notice how regularly these crystals grow, not by taking food inside like living beings, but by adding particle to particle on the outside evenly and regularly.

Can we form any idea why the crystals build themselves up so systematically? Dr. Tyndall says we can, and I hope by the help of these small bar magnets to show you how he explains it. These little pieces of steel, which I hope you can see lying on this white cardboard, have been rubbed along a magnet until they have become magnets themselves, and I can attract and lift up a needle with any one of them. But if I try to lift one bar with another, I can only do it by bringing certain ends together. I have tied a piece of red cotton round one end of each of the magnets, and if I bring two red ends together they will not cling together but roll apart. If, on the contrary, I put a red end against an end where there is not cotton, then the two bars cling together.

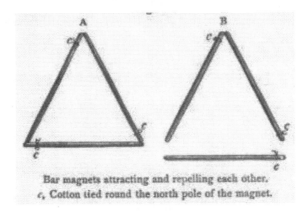

Bar magnets attracting and repelling each other.
c, Cotton tied round the north pole of the magnet.

This is because every magnet has two poles or points which are exactly opposite in character, and to distinguish them one is called the positive pole and the other the negative pole. Now when I bring two red ends, that is, two positive poles together, they drive each other away. See! the magnet I am not holding runs away from the other. But if I bring a red end and a black end, that is, a positive and a negative end together, then they are attracted and cling. I will make a triangle (A, Fig. 21) in which a black end and a red end always come together, and you see the triangle holds together. But now if I take off the lower bar and turn it so that two red ends and two black ends come together, then this bar actually rolls back from the others down the cardboard. If I were to break these bars into a thousand pieces, each piece would still have two poles, and if they were scattered about near each other in such a way that they were quite free to move, they would arrange themselves always so two different poles came together.

Lesson 142

1. Today read the rest of chapter 4 of *The Fairy Land of Science*.
2. Choose a topic from your reading. Write or tell a topic sentence, or main idea sentence, for that topic.

Lecture IV.   A Drop Of Water On Its Travels.   Continued…

Now picture to yourselves that all the particles of those substances which form crystals have poles like our magnets, then you can imagine that when the heat which held them apart is withdrawn and the particles come very near together, they will arrange themselves according to the attraction of their poles and so build up regular and beautiful patterns.

So, if we could travel up to the clouds where this fairy power of crystallization is at work, we should find the particles of water-vapour in a freezing atmosphere being built up into minute solid crystals of snow. If you go out after a snow-shower and search carefully, you will see that the snow-flakes are not mere lumps of frozen water, but beautiful six-pointed crystal stars, so white and pure that when we want to speak of anything being spotlessly white, you say that it is "white as snow." Some of these crystals are simply flat slabs with six sides, others are stars with six rods or spikes springing from the centre, others with six spikes each formed like a delicate fern.

Snow-crystals.

No less than a thousand different forms of delicate crystals have been found among snowflakes, but though there is such a great variety, yet they are all built on the six-sided and six-pointed plan, and are all rendered dazzlingly white by the reflection of the light from the faces of the crystals and the tiny air-bubbles built up within them. This, you see, is why, when the snow melts, you have only a little dirty water in your hand; the crystals are gone and there are no more air-bubbles held prisoners to act as looking-glasses to the light. Hoar-frost is also made up of tiny water-crystals, and is nothing more than frozen dew hanging on the blades of grass and from the trees.

But how about ice? Here, you will say, is frozen water, and yet we see no crystals, only a clear transparent mass. Here, again, Dr. Tyndall helps us. He says (and as I have proved it true, so may you for yourselves, if you will) that if you take a magnifying glass, and look down on the surface of ice on a sunny day, you will see a number of dark, six-sided stars, looking like flattened flowers, and in the centre of each a bright spot. These flowers, which are seen when the ice is melting, are our old friends the crystal stars turning into water, and the bright spot in the middle is a bubble of empty space, left because the watery flower does not fill up as much room as the ice of the crystal star did.

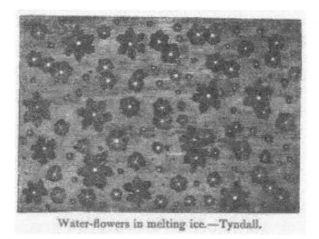

Water-flowers in melting ice.—Tyndall.

And this leads us to notice that ice always takes up more room than water, and that this is the reason why our water-pipes burst in severe frosts; for as the water freezes it expands with great force, and the pipe is cracked, and then when the thaw comes on, and the water melts again, it pours through the crack it has made.

It is not difficult to understand why ice should take more room; for we know that if we were to try to arrange bricks end to end in star-like shapes, we must leave some spaces between, and could not pack them so closely as if they lay side by side. And so, when this giant force of crystallization constrains the atoms of frozen water to grow into star-like forms, the solid mass must fill more room than the liquid water, and when the star melts, this space reveals itself to us in the bright spot of the centre.

We have now seen our drop of water under all its various forms of invisible gas, visible steam, cloud, dew, hoar-frost, snow, and ice, and we have only time shortly to see it on its travels, not merely up and down, as hitherto, but round the world.

We must first go to the sea as the distillery, or the place from which water is drawn up invisibly, in its purest state, into the air; and we must go chiefly to the seas of the tropics, because here the sun shines most directly all the year round, sending heat-waves to shake the water-particles asunder. It has been found by experiment that, in order to turn 1 lb. of water into vapour, as much heat must be used as is required to melt 5 lbs. of iron; and if you consider for a moment how difficult iron is to melt, and how we can keep an iron poker in a hot fire and yet it remains solid, this will help you to realize how much heat the sun must pour down in order to carry off such a constant supply of vapour from the tropical seas.

Now, when all this vapour is drawn up into the air, we know that some of it will form into clouds as it gets chilled high up in the sky, and then it will pour down again in those tremendous floods of rain which occur in the tropics.

But the sun and air will not let it all fall down at once, and the winds which are blowing from the equator to the poles carry large masses of it away with them. Then, as you know, it will depend on many things how far this vapour is carried. Some of it, chilled by cold blasts, or by striking on cold mountain tops, as it travels northwards, will fall in rain in Europe and Asia, while that which travels southwards may fall in South America, Australia, or New Zealand, or be carried over the sea to the South Pole. Wherever it falls on the land as rain, and is not used by plants, it will do one of two things; either it will run down in streams and form brooks and rivers, and so at last find its way back to the sea, or it will sink deep in the earth till it comes upon some hard rock through which it cannot get, and then, being hard pressed by the water coming on behind, it will rise up again through cracks, and come to the surface as a spring. These springs, again, feed rivers, sometimes above-ground, sometimes for long distances under-ground; but one way or another at last the whole drains back into the sea.

But if the vapour travels on till it reaches high mountains in cooler lands, such as the Alps of Switzerland; or is carried to the poles and to such countries as Greenland or the Antarctic Continent, then it will come down as snow, forming immense snow-fields. And here a curious change takes place in it. If you make an ordinary snowball and work it firmly together, it becomes very hard, and if you then press it forcibly into a mould you can turn it into transparent ice. And in the same way the snow which falls in Greenland and on the high mountains of Switzerland becomes very firmly pressed together, as it slides down into the valleys. It is like a crowd of people passing from a broad thoroughfare into a narrow street. As the valley grows narrower and narrower the great mass of snow in front cannot move down quickly, while more and more is piled up by the snowfall behind, and the crowd and crush grow denser and denser. In this way the snow is pressed together till the air that was hidden in its crystals, and which gave it its beautiful whiteness, is all pressed out, and the snow-crystals themselves are squeezed into one solid mass of pure, transparent ice.

Then we have what is called a "glacier," or river of ice, and this solid river comes creeping down till, in Greenland, it reaches the edge of the sea. There it is pushed over the brink of the land, and large pieces snap off, and we have "icebergs." These icebergs – made, remember, of the same water which was first draw up from the tropics – float on the wide sea, and melting in its warm currents, topple over and over. (A floating iceberg must have about eight times as much ice under the water as it has above, and therefore, when the lower part melts in a warm current, the iceberg loses its balance and tilts over, so as to rearrange itself round the centre of gravity.) till they disappear and mix with the water, to be carried back again to the warm ocean from which they first started. In Switzerland the glaciers cannot reach the sea, but they move down into the valleys till they come to a warmer region, and there the end of the glacier melts, and flows away in a stream. The Rhone and many other rivers are fed by the glaciers of the Alps; and as these rivers flow into the sea, our drop of water again finds its way back to its home.

But when it joins itself in this way to its companions, from whom it was parted for a time, does it come back clear and transparent as it left them? From the iceberg it does indeed return pure and clear; for the fairy Crystallization will have no impurities, not even salt, in her ice-crystals, and so as they melt they give back nothing but pure water to the sea. Yet even icebergs bring down earth and stones frozen into the bottom of the ice, and so they feed the sea with mud.

But the drops of water in rivers are by no means as pure as when they rose up into the sky. We shall see in the next lecture how rivers carry down not only sand and mud all along their course, but even solid matter such as salt, lime, iron, and flint, dissolved in the clear water, just as sugar is dissolved, without our being able to see it. The water, too, which has sunk down into the earth, takes up much matter as it travels along. You all know that the water you drink from a spring is very different from rain-water, and you will often find a hard crust at the bottom of kettles and in boilers, which is formed of the carbonate of lime which is driven out of the clear water when it is boiled. The water has become "hard" in consequence of having picked up and dissolved the carbonate of lime on its way through the earth, just in the same way as water would become sweet if you poured it through a sugar-cask. You will also have heard of iron-springs, sulphur-springs, and salt-springs, which come out of the earth, even if you have never tasted any of them, and the water of all these springs finds its way back at last to the sea.

And now, can you understand why sea-water should taste salty and bitter? Every drop of water which flows from the earth to the sea carries something with it. Generally, there is so little of any substance in the water that we cannot taste it, and we call it pure water; but the purest of spring or river-water has always some solid matter dissolved in it, and all this goes to the sea. Now, when the sun-waves come to take the water out of the sea again, they will have nothing but the pure water itself; and so all these salts and carbonates and other solid substances are left behind, and we taste them in sea-water.

Some day, when you are at the seaside, take some extra water and set it on the hob till a great deal has simmered gently away, and the liquid is very thick. Then take a drop of this liquid, and examine it under a microscope. As it dries up gradually, you will see a number of crystals forming, some square – and these will be crystals of ordinary salt; some oblong – these will be crystals of gypsum or alabaster; and others of various shapes. Then, when you see how much matter from the land is contained in sea-water, you will no longer wonder that the sea is salty; on the contrary, you will ask, Why does it not grow saltier every year?

The answer to this scarcely belongs to our history of a drop of water, but I must just suggest it to you. In the sea are numbers of soft-bodied animals, like the jelly animals which form the coral, which require hard material for their shells or the solid branches on which they live, and they are greedily watching for these atoms of lime, of flint, or magnesia, and of other substances brought down into the sea. It is with lime and magnesia that the tiny chalk-builders form their beautiful shells, and the coral animals their skeletons, while another class of builders use the flint; and when these creatures die, their remains go to form fresh land at the bottom of the sea; and so, though the earth is being washed away by the rivers and springs it is being built up again, out of the same materials, in the depths of the great ocean.

And now we have reached the end of the travels of our drop of water. We have seen it drawn up by the fairy "heat," invisible into the sky; there fairy "cohesion" seized it and formed it into water-drops and the giant, "gravitation," pulled it down again to the earth. Or, if it rose to freezing regions, the fairy of "crystallization" built it up into snow-crystals, again to fall to the earth, and either to be melted back into water by heat, or to slide down the valleys by force of gravitation, till it became squeezed into ice. We have detected it, when invisible, forming a veil round our earth, and keeping off the intense heat of the sun's rays by day, or shutting it in by night. We have seen it chilled by the blades of grass, forming sparkling dew-drops or crystals of hoar-frost, glistening in the early morning sun; and we have seen it in the dark underground, being drunk up greedily by the roots of plants. We have started with it from the tropics, and travelled over land and sea, watching it forming rivers, or flowing underground in springs, or moving onwards to the high mountains or the poles, and coming back again in glaciers and icebergs. Through all this, while it is being carried hither and thither by invisible power, we find no trace of its becoming worn out, or likely to rest from its labours. Ever onwards it goes, up and down, and round and round the world, taking many forms, and performing many wonderful feats. We have seen some of the work that it does, in refreshing the air, feeding the plants, giving us clear, sparkling water to drink, and carrying matter to the sea; but besides this, it does a wonderful work in altering all the face of our earth. This work we shall consider in the next lecture, on "The two great Sculptors – Water and Ice."

Lesson 143

1. Today read the first part of chapter 5 of *The Fairy Land of Science*.
2. Choose a topic from your reading. Write or tell a topic sentence, or main idea sentence, for that topic.

Lecture V. The Two Great Sculptors – Water And Ice.

In our last lecture we saw that water can exist in three forms:— 1st, as an invisible vapour; 2nd, as liquid water; 3rd, as solid snow and ice.

To-day we are going to take the two last of these forms, water and ice, and speak of them as sculptors.

To understand why they deserve this name we must first consider what the work of a sculptor is. If you go into a statuary yard you will find there large blocks of granite, marble, and other kinds of stone, hewn roughly into different shapes; but if you pass into the studio, where the sculptor himself is at work you will find beautiful statues, more or less finished; and you will see that out of rough blocks of stone he has been able to cut images which look like living forms. You can even see by their faces whether they are intended to be sad, or thoughtful, or gay, and by their attitude whether they are writhing in pain, or dancing with joy, or resting peacefully. How has all this history been worked out from the shapeless stone? It has been done by the sculptor's chisel. A piece chipped off here, a wrinkle cut there, a smooth surface rounded off in another place, so as to give a gentle curve; all these touches gradually shape the figure and mould it out of the rough stone, first into a rude shape and afterwards, by delicate strokes, into the form of a living being.

Now, just in the same way as the wrinkles and curves of a statue are cut by the sculptor's chisel, so the hills and valleys, the steep slopes and gentle curves on the face of our earth, giving it all its beauty, and the varied landscapes we love so well, have been cut out by water and ice passing over them. It is true that some of the greater wrinkles of the earth, the lofty mountains, and the high masses of land which rise above the sea have been caused by earthquakes and shrinking of the earth. We shall not speak of these to-day, but put them aside as belonging to the rough work of the statuary yard. But when once these large masses are put ready for water to work upon, then all the rest of the rugged wrinkles and gentle slopes which make the country so beautiful are due to water and ice, and for this reason I have called them "sculptors."

Go for a walk in the country, or notice the landscape as you travel on a railway journey. You pass by hills and through valleys, through narrow steep gorges cut in hard rock, or through wild ravines up the sides of which you can hardly scramble. Then you come to grassy slopes and to smooth plains across which you can look for miles without seeing a hill; or, when you arrive at the seashore, you clamber into caves and grottos, and along dark narrow passages leading from one bay to another. All these – hills, valleys, gorges, ravines, slopes, plains, caves, grottos, and rocky shores – have been cut out by the water. Day by day and year by year, while everything seems to us to remain the same, this industrious sculptor is chipping away, a few grains here, a corner there, a large mass in another place, till he gives to the country its own peculiar scenery, just as the human sculptor gives expression to his statue.

Our work to-day will consist in trying to form some idea of the way in which water thus carves out the surface of the earth, and we will begin by seeing how much can be done by our old friends the rain-drops before they become running streams.

Everyone must have noticed that whenever rain falls on soft ground it makes small round holes in which it collects, and then sinks into the ground, forcing its way between the grains of earth. But you would hardly think that the beautiful pillars have been made entirely in this way by rain beating upon and soaking into the ground.

Earth-pillars near Botzen, in the Tyrol.
(Adapted from Lyell's 'Principles.')

Where these pillars stand there was once a solid mass of clay and stones, into which the rain-drops crept, loosening the earthly particles; and then when the sun dried the earth again cracks were formed, so that the next shower loosened it still more, and carried some of the mud down into the valley below. But here and there large stones were buried in the clay, and where this happened the rain could not penetrate, and the stones became the tops of tall pillars of clay, washed into shape by the rain beating on its sides, but escaping the general destruction of the rest of the mud. In this way the whole valley has been carved out into fine pillars, some still having capping-stones, while others have lost them, and these last will soon be washed away. We have no such valleys of earth-pillars here in England, but you may sometimes see tiny pillars under bridges where the drippings have washed away the earth between the pebbles, and such small examples which you can observe for yourselves are quite as instructive as more important ones.

Another way in which rain changes the surface of the earth is by sinking down through loose soil from the top of a cliff to a depth of many feet till it comes to solid rock, and then lying spread over a wide apace. Here it makes a kind of watery mud, which is a very unsafe foundation for the hill of earth above it, and so after a time the whole mass slips down and makes a fresh piece of land at the foot of the cliff. If you have ever been at the Isle of Wight you will have seen an undulating strip of ground, called the Undercliff, at Ventnor and other places, stretching all along the sea below the high cliffs. This land was once at the top of the cliff, and came down by succession of landslips such as we have been describing. A very great landslip of this kind happened in the memory of living people, at Lyme Regis, in Dorsetshire, in the year 1839.

You will easily see how in forming earth-pillars and causing landslips rain changes the face of the country, but these are only rare effects of water. It is when the rain collects in brooks and forms rivers that it is most busy in sculpturing the land. Look out some day into the road or the garden where the ground slopes a little, and watch what happens during a shower of rain. First the rain-drops run together in every little hollow of the ground, then the water begins to flow along any ruts or channels it can find, lying here and there in pools, but always making its way gradually down the slope. Meanwhile from other parts of the ground little rills are coming, and these all meet in some larger ruts where the ground is lowest, making one great stream, which at last empties itself into the gutter or an area, or finds its way down some grating.

Now just this, which we can watch whenever a heavy shower of rain comes down on the road, happens also all over the world. Up in the mountains, where there is always a great deal of rain, little rills gather and fall over the mountain sides, meeting in some stream below. Then, as this stream flows on, it is fed by many runnels of water, which come from all parts of the country, trickling along ruts, and flowing in small brooks and rivulets down the gentle slope of the land till they reach the big stream, which at last is important enough to be called a river. Sometimes this river comes to a large hollow in the land and there the water gathers and forms a lake; but still at the lower end of this lake out it comes again, forming a new river, and growing and growing by receiving fresh streams until at last it reaches the sea.

The River Thames, which you all know, and whose course you will find clearly described in Mr. Huxley's 'Physiography,' drains in this way no less than one-seventh of the whole of England. All the rain which falls in Berkshire, Oxfordshire, Middlesex, Hertfordshire, Surrey, the north of Wiltshire and north-west of Kent, the south of Buckinghamshire and of Gloucestershire, finds its way into the Thames; making an area of 6160 square miles over which every rivulet and brook trickle down to the one great river, which bears them to the ocean. And so with every other area of land in the world there is some one channel towards which the ground on all sides slopes gently down, and into this channel all the water will run, on its way to the sea.

But what has this to do with sculpture or cutting out of valleys? If you will only take a glass of water out of any river, and let it stand for some hours, you will soon answer this question for yourself. For you will find that even from river water which looks quite clear, a thin layer of mud will fall to the bottom of the glass, and if you take the water when the river is swollen and muddy you will get quite a thick deposit. This shows that the brooks, the streams, and the rivers wash away the land as they flow over it and carry it from the mountains down to the valleys, and from the valleys away out into the sea.

But besides earthly matter, which we can see, there is much matter dissolved in the water of rivers (as we mentioned in the last lecture), and this we cannot see.

If you use water which comes out of a chalk country you will find that after a time the kettle in which you have been in the habit of boiling this water has a hard crust on its bottom and sides, and this crust is made of chalk or carbonate of lime, which the water took out of the rocks when it was passing through them. Professor Bischoff has calculated that the river Rhine carries past Bonn every year enough carbonate of lime dissolved in its water to make 332,000 million oyster-shells, and that if all these shells were built into a cube it would measure 560 feet.

Imagine to yourselves the whole of St. Paul's churchyard filled with oyster-shells, built up in a large square till they reached half as high again as the top of the cathedral, then you will have some idea of the amount of chalk carried invisibly past Bonn in the water of the Rhine every year.

Since all this matter, whether brought down as mud or dissolved, comes from one part of the land to be carried elsewhere or out to sea, it is clear that some gaps and hollows must be left in the places from which it is taken. Let us see how these gaps are made. Have you ever clambered up the mountainside, or even up one of those small ravines in the hillside, which have generally a little stream trickling through them? If so, you must have noticed the number of pebbles, large and small, lying in patches here and there in the stream, and many pieces of broken rock, which are often scattered along the sides of the ravine; and how, as you climb, the path grows steeper, and the rocks become rugged and stick out in strange shapes.

The history of this ravine will tell us a great deal about the carving of water. Once it was nothing more than a little furrow in the hillside down which the rain found its way in a thin thread-like stream. But by and by, as the stream carried down some of the earth, and the furrow grew deeper and wider, the sides began to crumble when the sun dried up the rain which had soaked in. Then in winter, when the sides of the hill were moist with the autumn rains, frost came and turned the water to ice, and so made the cracks still larger, and the swollen steam rushing down, caught the loose pieces of rock and washed them down into its bed. Here they were rolled over and over, and grated against each other, and were ground away till they became rounded pebbles; while the grit which was rubbed off them was carried farther down by the stream. And so in time this became a little valley, and as the stream cut it deeper and deeper, there was room to clamber along the sides of it, and ferns and mosses began to cover the naked stone, and small trees rooted themselves along the banks, and this beautiful little nook sprang up on the hill-side entirely by the sculpturing of water.

Lesson 144

1. Today read the next part of chapter 5 of *The Fairy Land of Science*.
2. Choose a topic from your reading. Write or tell a topic sentence, or main idea sentence, for that topic.

Lecture V. The Two Great Sculptors – Water And Ice. Continued…

Shall you not feel a fresh interest in all the little valleys, ravines, and gorges you meet with in the country, if you can picture them being formed in this way year by year? There are many curious differences in them which you can study for yourselves. Some will be smooth, broad valleys and here the rocks have been soft and easily worn, and water trickling down the sides of the first valley has cut other channels so as to make smaller valleys running across it. In other places there will be narrow ravines, and here the rocks have been hard, so that they did not wear away gradually, but broke off and fell in blocks, leaving high cliffs on each side. In some places you will come to a beautiful waterfall, where the water has tumbled over a steep cliff, and then eaten its way back, just like a saw cutting through a piece of wood.

There are two things in particular to notice in a waterfall like this. First, how the water and spray dash against the bottom of the cliff down which it falls, and grind the small pebbles against the rock. In this way the bottom of the cliff is undermined, and so great pieces tumble down from time to time, and keep the fall upright instead of its being sloped away at the top, and becoming a mere steam. Secondly, you may often see curious cup-shaped holes, called "pot-holes," in the rocks on the sides of a waterfall, and these also are concerned in its formation. In these holes you will generally find two or three small pebbles, and you have here a beautiful example of how water uses stones to grind away the face of the earth. These holes are made entirely by the falling water eddying round and round in a small hollow of the rock, and grinding the pebbles which it has brought down, against the bottom and sides of this hollow, just as you grind round a pestle in a mortar. By degrees the hole grows deeper and deeper and though the first pebbles are probably ground down to powder, others fall in, and so in time there is a great hole perforated right through, helping to make the rock break and fall away.

In this and other ways the water works its way back in a surprising manner. The Isle of Wight gives us some good instances of this; Alum Bay Chine and the celebrated Blackgang Chine have been entirely cut out by waterfalls. But the best know and most remarkable example is the Niagara Falls, in America. Here, the River Niagara first wanders through a flat country, and then reaches the great Lake Erie in a hollow of the plain. After that, it flows gently down for about fifteen miles, and then the slope becomes greater and it rushes on to the Falls of Niagara. These falls are not nearly so high as many people imagine, being only 165 feet, or about half the height of St. Paul's Cathedral, but they are 2700 feet or nearly half-a-mile wide, and no less than 670,000 tons of water fall over them every minute, making magnificent clouds of spray.

Sir Charles Lyell, when he was at Niagara, came to the conclusion that, taking one year with another, these falls eat back the cliff at the rate of about one foot a year, as you can easily imagine they would do, when you think with what force the water must dash against the bottom of the falls. In this way a deep cleft has been cut right back from Queenstown for a distance of seven miles, to the place where the falls are now. This helps us a little to understand how very slowly and gradually water cuts its way; for if a foot a year is about the average of the waste of the rock, it will have taken more than thirty-five thousand years for that channel of seven miles to be made.

But even this chasm cut by the falls of Niagara is nothing compared with the canyons of Colarado. Canyon is a Spanish word for a rocky gorge, and these gorges are indeed so grand, that if we had not seen in other places what water can do, we should never have been able to believe that it could have cut out these gigantic chasms. For more than three hundred miles the River Colorado, coming down from the Rocky Mountains, has eaten its way through a country made of granite and hard beds of limestone and sandstone, and it has cut down straight through these rocks, leaving walls from half-a-mile to a mile high, standing straight up from it. The cliffs of the Great Canyon, as it is called, stretch up for more than a mile above the river which flows in the gorge below! Fancy yourselves for a moment in a boat on this river, as shown in Figure 27, and looking up at these gigantic walls of rock towering above you. Even half-way up them, a man, if he could get there, would be so small you could not see him without a telescope; while the opening at the top between the two walls would seem so narrow at such an immense distance that the sky above would have the appearance of nothing more than a narrow streak of blue. Yet these huge chasms have not been made by any violent breaking apart of the rocks or convulsion of an earthquake. No, they have been gradually, silently, and steadily cut through by the river which now glides quietly in the wider chasms, or rushes rapidly through the narrow gorges at their feet.

"No description," says Lieutenant Ives, one of the first explorers of this river, "can convey the idea of the varied and majestic grandeur of this peerless waterway. Wherever the river turns, the entire panorama changes. Stately facades, august cathedrals, amphitheatres, rotundas, castellated walls, and rows of time-stained ruins, surmounted by every form of tower, minaret, dome and spire, have been moulded from the cyclopean masses of rock that form the mighty defile." Who will say, after this, that water is not the grandest of all sculptors, as it cuts through hundreds of miles of rock, forming such magnificent granite groups, not only unsurpassed but unequalled by any of the works of man?

But we must not look upon water only as a cutting instrument, for it does more than merely carve out land in one place, it also carries it away and lays it down elsewhere; and in this it is more like a modeller in clay, who smooths off the material from one part of his figure to put it upon another.

Running water is not only always carrying away mud, but at the same time laying it down here and there wherever it flows. When a torrent brings down stones and gravel from the mountains, it will depend on the size and weight of the pieces how long they will be in falling through the water. If you take a handful of gravel and throw it into a glass full of water, you will notice that the stones in it will fall to the bottom at once, the grit and coarse sand will take longer in sinking, and lastly, the fine sand will be an hour or two in settling down, so that the water becomes clear. Now, suppose that this gravel were sinking in the water of a river. The stones would be buoyed up as long as the river was very full and flowed very quickly, but they would drop through sooner than the coarse sand. The coarse sand in its turn would begin to sink as the river flowed more slowly, and would reach the bottom while the fine sand was still borne on. Lastly, the fine sand would sink through very, very slowly, and only settle in comparatively still water.

From this it will happen that stones will generally lie near to the bottom of torrents at the foot of the banks from which they fall, while the gravel will be carried on by the stream after it leaves the mountains. This too, however, will be laid down when the river comes into a more level country and runs more slowly. Or it may be left together with the finer mud in a lake, as in the lake of

Geneva, into which the Rhone flows laden with mud and comes out at the other end clear and pure. But if no lake lies in the way the finer earth will still travel on, and the river will take up more and more as it flows, till at last it will leave this too on the plains across which it moves sluggishly along, or will deposit it at its mouth when it joins the sea.

You all know the history of the Nile; how, when the rains fall very heavily in March and April in the mountains of Abyssinia, the river comes rushing down and brings with it a load of mud which it spreads out over the Nile valley in Egypt. This annual layer of mud is so thin that it takes a thousand years for it to become 2 or 3 feet thick; but besides that which falls in the valley a great deal is taken to the mouth of the river and there forms new land, making what is called the "Delta" of the Nile. Alexandria, Rosetta, and Damietta, are towns which are all built on land made of Nile mud which was carried down ages and ages ago, and which has now become firm and hard like the rest of the country. You will easily remember other deltas mentioned in books, and all these are made of the mud carried down from the land to the sea. The delta of the Ganges and Brahmapootra in India, is actually as large as the whole of England and Wales, (58,311 square miles.) and the River Mississippi in America drains such a large tract of country that its delta grows, Mr. Geikie tells us, at the rate of 86 yards in year.

All this new land laid down in Egypt, in India, in America, and in other places, is the work of water. Even on the Thames you may see mud-banks, as at Gravesend, which are made of earth brought from the interior of England. But at the mouth of the Thames the sea washes up very strongly every tide, and so it carries most of the mud away and prevents a delta growing up there. If you will look about when you are at the seaside, and notice wherever a stream flows down into the sea, you may even see little miniature deltas being formed there, though the sea generally washes them away again in a few hours, unless the place is well sheltered.

This, then, is what becomes of the earth carried down by rivers. Either on plains, or in lakes, or in the sea, it falls down to form new land. But what becomes of the dissolved chalk and other substances? We have seen that a great deal of it is used by river and sea animals to build their shells and skeletons, and some of it is left on the surface of the ground by springs when the water evaporates. It is this carbonate of lime which forms a hard crust over anything upon which it may happen to be deposited, and then these things are called "petrified."

But it is in the caves and hollows of the earth that this dissolved matter is built up into the most beautiful forms. If you have ever been to Buxton in Derbyshire, you will probably have visited a cavern called Poole's Cavern, not far from there, which when you enter it looks as if it were built up entirely of rods of beautiful transparent white glass, hanging from the ceiling, from the walls, or rising up from the floor. In this cavern, and many others like it,(See the picture at the head of the lecture.) water comes dripping through the roof, and as it falls carbonate of lime forms itself into a thin, white film on the roof, often making a complete circle, and then, as the water drips from it day by day, it goes on growing and growing till it forms a long needle-shaped or tube-shaped rod, hanging like an icicle. These rods are called stalactites, and they are so beautiful, as their minute crystals glisten when a light is taken into the cavern, that one of them near Tenby is called the "Fairy Chamber." Meanwhile, the water which drips on to the floor also leaves some carbonate of lime where it falls, and this forms a pillar, growing up towards the roof, and often the hanging stalactites and the rising pillars (called stalagmites) meet in the middle and form one column. And thus we see that underground, as well as aboveground, water moulds beautiful forms in the crust of the earth. At Adelsberg, near Trieste, there is a magnificent stalactite grotto made of a number of chambers one following another, with a river flowing through them; and the famous Mammoth Cave of Kentucky, more than ten miles long, is another example of these wonderful limestone caverns.

Lesson 145

1. Today read the last part of chapter 5 of *The Fairy Land of Science*.
2. Choose a topic from your reading. Write or tell a topic sentence, or main idea sentence, for that topic.

Lecture V. The Two Great Sculptors – Water And Ice. Continued...

But we have not yet spoken of the sea, and this surely is not idle in altering the shape of the land. Even the waves themselves in a storm wash against the cliffs and bring down stones and pieces of rock on to the shore below. And they help to make cracks and holes in the cliffs, for as they dash with force against them they compress the air which lies in the joints of the stone and cause it to force the rock apart, and so larger cracks are made and the cliff is ready to crumble.

It is, however, the stones and sand and pieces of rock lying at the foot of the cliff which are most active in wearing it away. Have you never watched the waves breaking upon a beach in a heavy storm? How they catch up the stones and hurl them down again, grinding them against each other! At high tide in such a storm these stones are thrown against the foot of the cliff, and each blow does something towards knocking away part of the rock, till at last, after many storms, the cliff is undermined and large pieces fall down. These pieces are in their turn ground down to pebbles which serve to batter against the remaining rock.

Professor Geikie tells us that the waves beat in a storm against the Bell Rock Lighthouse with as much force as if you dashed a weight of 3 tons against every square inch of the rock, and Stevenson found stones of 2 tons' weight which had been thrown during storms right over the ledge of the lighthouse. Think what force there must be in waves which can lift up such a rock and throw it, and such force as this beats upon our sea-coasts and eats away the land.

Cliffs off Arbroath, showing the waste of the shore.

[That] is a sketch on the shores of Arbroath which I made some years ago. You will not find it difficult to picture to yourselves how the sea has eaten away these cliffs till some of the strongest pieces which have resisted the waves stand out by themselves in the sea. That cave in the left-hand corner ends in a narrow dark passage from which you come out on the other side of the rocks into another bay. Such caves as these are made chiefly by the force of the waves and the air, bringing down pieces of rock from under the cliff and so making a cavity, and then as the waves roll these pieces over and over and grind them against the sides, the hole is made larger. There are many places on the English coast where large pieces of the road are destroyed by the crumbling down of cliffs when they have been undermined by caverns such as these.

Thus, you see, the whole of the beautiful scenery of the sea – the shores, the steep cliffs, the quiet bays, the creeks and caverns – are all the work of the "sculptor" water; and he works best where the rocks are hardest, for there they offer him a good stout wall to batter, whereas in places where the ground is soft it washes down into a gradual gentle slope, and so the waves come flowing smoothly in and have no power to eat away the shore.

And now, what has ice got to do with the sculpturing of the land? First, we must remember how much the frost does in breaking up the ground. The farmers know this, and always plough after a frost, because the moisture, freezing in the ground, has broken up the clods, and done half their work for them.

But this is not the chief work of ice. You will remember how we learnt in our last lecture that snow, when it falls on the mountains, gradually slides down into the valleys, and is pressed together by the gathering snow behind until it becomes moulded into a solid river of ice. In Greenland and in Norway there are enormous ice-rivers or glaciers, and even in Switzerland some of them are very large. The Aletsch glacier, in the Alps, is fifteen miles long, and some are even longer than this. They move very slowly – on an average about 20 to 27 inches in the centre, and 13 to 19 inches at the sides every twenty-four hours, in the summer and autumn. How they move, we cannot stop to discuss now; but if you will take a slab of thin ice and rest it upon its two ends only, you can prove to yourself that ice does bend, for in a few hours you will find that its own weight has drawn it down in the centre, so as to form a curve. This will help you to picture to yourselves how glaciers can adapt themselves to the windings of the valley, creeping slowly onwards until they come down to a point where the air is warm enough to melt them, and then the ice flows away in a stream of water. It is very curious to see the number of little rills running down the great masses of ice at the glacier's mouth, bringing down with them gravel, and every now and then a large stone, which falls splashing into the stream below. If you look at the glacier in the Frontispiece, you will see that these stones come from those long lines of stones and boulders stretching along the sides and centre of the glacier. It is easy to understand where the stones at the side come from; for we have seen that damp and frost cause pieces to break off the surface of the rocks, and it is natural that these pieces should roll down the steep sides of the mountains on to the glacier. But the middle row requires some explanation. Look to the back of the picture, and you will see that this line of stones is made of two side rows, which come from the valleys above. Two glaciers, you see, have there joined into one, and so made a heap of stones all along their line of junction.

These stones are being continually, though slowly, conveyed by the glacier, from all the mountains along its sides, down to the place where it melts. Here it lets them fall, and they are gradually piled

241

up till they form great walls of stone, which are called moraines. Some of the moraines left by the larger glaciers of olden time, in the country near Turin, form high hills, rising up even to 1500 feet.

Therefore, if ice did no more than carry these stone blocks, it would alter the face of the country; but it does much more than this. As the glacier moves along, it often cracks for a considerable way across its surface, and this crack widens and widens, until at last it becomes a great gaping chasm, or crevasse as it is called, so that you can look down it right to the bottom of the glacier. Into these crevasses large blocks of rock fall, and when the chasm is closed again as the ice presses on, these masses are frozen firmly into the bottom of the glacier, much in the same way as a steel cutter is fixed in the bottom of a plane. And they do just the same kind of work; for as the glacier slides down the valley, they scratch and grind the rocks underneath them, rubbing themselves away, it is true, but also scraping away the ground over which they move. In this way the glacier becomes a cutting instrument, and carves out the valleys deeper and deeper as it passes through them.

You may always know where a glacier has been, even if no trace of ice remains; for you will see rocks with scratches along them which have been cut by these stones; and even where the rocks have not been ground away, you will find them rounded, showing that the glacier-plane has been over them. These rounded rocks are called "roches moutonnees," because at the distance they look like sheep lying down.

You have only to look at the stream flowing from the mouth of a glacier to see what a quantity of soil it has ground off from the bottom of the valley; for the water is thick, and coloured a deep yellow by the mud it carries. This mud soon reaches the rivers into which the streams run; and such rivers as the Rhone and the Rhine are thick with matter brought down from the Alps. The Rhone leaves this mud in the Lake of Geneva, flowing out at the other end quite clear and pure. A mile and a half of land has been formed at the head of the lake since the time of the Romans by the mud thus brought down from the mountains.

Thus we see that ice, like water, is always busy carving out the surface of the earth, and sending down material to make new land elsewhere. We know that in past ages the glaciers were much larger than they are in our time; for we find traces of them over large parts of Switzerland where glaciers do not now exist, and huge blocks which could only have been carried by ice, and which are called "erratic blocks," some of them as big as cottages, have been left scattered over all the northern part of Europe. These blocks were a great puzzle to scientific men till, in 1840, Professor Agassiz showed that they must have been brought by ice all the way from Norway and Russia.

In those ancient days, there were even glaciers in England; for in Cumberland and in Wales you may see their work, in scratched and rounded rocks, and the moraines they have left. Llanberis Pass, so famous for its beauty, is covered with ice-scratches, and blocks are scattered all over the sides of the valley. There is one block high up on the right-hand slope of the valley, as you enter from the Beddgelert side, which is exactly poised upon another block, so that it rocks to and fro. It must have been left thus balanced when the ice melted round it. You may easily see that these blocks were carried by ice, and not by water, because their edges are sharp, whereas if they had been rolled in water, they would have been smoothed down.

We cannot here go into the history of that great Glacial Period long ago, when large fields of ice covered all the north of England; but when you read it for yourselves and understand the changes on the earth's surface which we can see being made by ice now, then such grand scenery as the rugged valleys of Wales, with large angular stone blocks scattered over them, will tell you a wonderful story of the ice of bygone times.

And now we have touched lightly on the chief ways in which water and ice carve out the surface of the earth. We have seen that rain, rivers, springs, the waves of the sea, frost, and glaciers all do their part in chiselling out ravines and valleys, and in producing rugged peaks or undulating plains – here cutting through rocks so as to form precipitous cliffs, there laying down new land to add to the flat country – in one place grinding stones to powder, in others piling them up in gigantic ridges. We cannot go a step into the country without seeing the work of water around us; every little gully and ravine tells us that the sculpture is going on; every stream, with its burden of visible or invisible matter, reminds us that some earth is being taken away and carried to a new spot. In our little lives we see indeed but the very small changes, but by these we learn how greater ones have been brought about, and how we owe the outline of all our beautiful scenery, with its hills and valleys, its mountains and plains, its cliffs and caverns, its quiet nooks and its grand rugged precipices, to the work of the "Two great sculptors, Water and Ice."

Lesson 146

1. Today read the first part of chapter 6 of *The Fairy Land of Science*.
2. Choose a topic from your reading. Write or tell a topic sentence, or main idea sentence, for that topic.
3. Pay attention to how information is presented.

Lecture VI. The Voices Of Nature And How We Hear Them

We have reached to-day the middle point of our course, and here we will make a new start. All the wonderful histories which we have been studying in the last five lectures have had little or nothing to do with living creatures. The sunbeams would strike on our earth, the air would move restlessly to and fro, the water-drops would rise and fall, the valleys and ravines would still be cut out by rivers , if there were no such thing as life upon the earth. But without living things there could be none of the beauty which these changes bring about. Without plants, the sunbeams, the air and the water would be quite unable to clothe the bare rocks, and without animals and man they could not produce light, or sound, or feeling of any kind.

In the next five lectures, however, we are going to learn something of the use living creatures make of the earth; and to-day we will begin by studying one of the ways in which we are affected by the changes of nature, and hear her voice.

We are all so accustomed to trust to our sight to guide us in most of our actions, and to think of things as we see them, that we often forget how very much we owe to sound. And yet Nature speaks to us so much by her gentle, her touching, or her awful sounds, that the life of a deaf person is even more hard to bear than that of a blind one.

Have you ever amused yourself with trying how many different sounds you can distinguish if you listen at an open window in a busy street? You will probably be able to recognize easily the jolting of the heavy wagon or dray, the rumble of the omnibus, the smooth roll of the private carriage and the rattle of the light butcher's cart; and even while you are listening for these, the crack of the carter's whip, the cry of the costermonger at his stall, and the voices of the passers-by will strike upon you ear. Then if you give still more close attention you will hear the doors open and shut along the street, the footsteps of the passengers, the scraping of the shovel of the mud-carts; nay, if he happen to stand near, you may even hear the jingling of the shoeblack's pence as he plays pitch and toss upon the pavement. If you think for a moment, does it not seem wonderful that you should hear all these sounds so that you can recognize each one distinctly while all the rest are going on around you?

But suppose you go into the quiet country. Surely there will be silence there. Try some day and prove it for yourself, lie down on the grass in a sheltered nook and listen attentively. If there be ever so little wind stirring you will hear it rustling gently through the trees; or even if there is not this, it will be strange if you do not hear some wandering gnat buzzing, or some busy bee humming as it moves from flower to flower. Then a grasshopper will set up a chirp within a few yards of you, or, if all living creatures are silent, a brook not far off may be flowing along with a rippling musical sound. These and a hundred other noises you will hear in the most quiet country spot; the lowing of the cattle, the song of the birds, the squeak of the field-mouse, the croak of the frog, mingling with the sound of the woodman's axe in the distance, or the dash of some river torrent. And beside these quiet sounds, there are still other occasional voices of nature which speak to us from time to time. The howling of the tempestuous wind, the roar of the sea-waves in a storm, the crash of thunder, and the mighty noise of the falling avalanche; such sounds as these tell us how great and terrible nature can be.

Now, has it ever occurred to you to think what sounds is, and how it is that we hear all these things? Strange as it may seem, if there were no creature that could hear upon the earth, there would be no such thing as sound, though all these movements in nature were going on just as they are now.

Try and grasp this thoroughly, for it is difficult at first to make people believe it. Suppose you were stone-deaf, there would be no such thing as sound to you. A heavy hammer falling on an anvil would indeed shake the air violently, but since this air when it reached your ear would find a useless instrument, it could not play upon it. And it is this play on the drum of your ear and the nerves within it speaking to your brain which make sound. Therefore, if all creatures on or around the earth were without ears or nerves of hearing, there would be no instrument on which to play, and consequently there would be no such thing as sound. This proves that two things are needed in order that we may hear. First, the outside movement which plays on our hearing instrument; and, secondly, the hearing instrument itself.

First, then, let us try to understand what happens outside our ears. Take a poker and tie a piece of string to it, and holding the ends of the string to your ears, strike the poker against the fender. You will hear a very loud sound, for the blow will set all the particles of the poker quivering, and this movement will pass right along the string to the drum of your ear and play upon it.

Now take the string away from you ears, and hold it with your teeth. Stop your ears tight, and strike the poker once more against the fender. You will hear the sound quite as loudly and clearly as you did before, but this time the drum of your ear has not been agitated. How, then, has the sound been produced? In this case, the quivering movement has passed through your teeth into the bones of your hear, and from them into the nerves, and so produced sound in your brain. And now, as a final experiment, fasten the string to the mantelpiece, and hit it again against the fender. How much feebler the sound is this time, and how much sooner it stops! Yet still it reaches you, for the movement has come this time across the air to the drums of your ear.

Here we are back again in the land of invisible workers! We have all been listening and hearing ever since we were babies, but have we ever made any picture to ourselves of how sound comes to us right across a room or a field, when we stand at one end and the person who calls is at the other?

Since we have studied the "aerial ocean," we know that the air filling the space between us, though invisible, is something very real, and now all we have to do is to understand exactly how the movement crosses this air.

This we shall do most readily by means of an experiment made by Dr. Tyndall in his lectures on Sound. I have here a number of boxwood balls resting in a wooden tray which has a bell hung at the end of it. I am going to take the end ball and roll it sharply against the rest, and then I want you to notice carefully what happens. See! the ball at the other end has flown off and hit the bell, so that you hear it ring. Yet the other balls remain where they were before. Why is this? It is because each of the balls, as it was knocked forwards, had one in front of it to stop it and make it bound back again, but the last one was free to move on. When I threw this ball from my hand against the others, the one in front of it moved, and hitting the third ball, bounded back again; the third did the same to the fourth, the fourth to the fifth, and so on to the end of the line. Each ball thus came back to its place, but it passed the shock on to the last ball, and the ball to the bell. If I now put the balls close up to the bell, and repeat the experiment, you still hear the sound, for the last ball shakes the bell as if it were a ball in front of it.

Now imagine these balls to be atoms of air, and the bell your ear. If I clap my hands and so hit the air in front of them, each air-atom hits the next just as the balls did, and though it comes back to its place, it passes the shock on along the whole line to the atom touching the drum of your ear, and so you receive a blow. But a curious thing happens in the air which you cannot notice in the balls. You must remember that air is elastic, just as if there were springs between the atoms as in the diagram, Fig. 31, and so when any shock knocks the atoms forward, several of them can be crowded together before they push on those in front. Then, as soon as they have passed the shock on, they rebound and begin to separate again, and so swing to and fro till they come to rest. Meanwhile the second set will go through just the same movements, and will spring apart as soon as they have passed the shock on to a third set, and so you will have one set of crowded atoms and one set of separated atoms alternately all along the line, and the same set will never be crowded two instants together.

You may see an excellent example of this in a luggage train in a railway station, when the trucks are left to bump each other till they stop. You will see three or four trucks knock together, then they will pass the shock on to the four in front, while they themselves bound back and separate as far as their chains will let them: the next four trucks will do the same, and so a kind of wave of crowded trucks passes on to the end of the train, and they bump to and fro till the whole comes to a standstill. Try to imagine a movement like this going on in the line of air-atoms, the drum of your ear being at the end. Those which are crowded together at that end will hit on the drum of your ear and drive the membrane which covers it inwards; then instantly the wave will change, these atoms will bound back, and the membrane will recover itself again, but only to receive a second blow as the atoms are driven forwards again, and so the membrane will be driven in and out till the air has settled down.

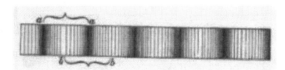

This you see is quite different to the waves of light which moves in crests and hollows. Indeed, it is not what we usually understand by a wave at all, but a set of crowdings and partings of atoms of air which follow each other rapidly across the air. A crowding of atoms is called a condensation, and a parting is called a rarefaction, and when we speak of the length of a wave of sound, we mean the distance between two condensations, or between two rarefactions.

Although each atom of air moves a very little way forwards and then back, yet, as a long row of atoms may be crowded together before they begin to part, a wave is often very long. When a man talks in an ordinary bass voice, he makes sound-waves from 8 to 12 feet long; a woman's voice makes shorter waves, from 2 to 4 feet long, and consequently the tone is higher, as we shall presently explain.

Lesson 147

1. Today read the next part of chapter 6 of *The Fairy Land of Science*.
2. Choose a topic from your reading. Write or tell a topic sentence, or main idea sentence, for that topic.

Lecture VI The Voices Of Nature And How We Hear Them Continued…

And now I hope that some one is anxious to ask why, when I clap my hands, anyone behind me or at the side, can hear it as well or nearly as well as you who are in front. This is because I give a shock to the air all round my hands, and waves go out on all sides, making as it were gloves of crowdings and partings widening and widening away from the clap as circles widen on a pond. Thus the waves travel behind me, above me, and on all sides, until they hit the walls, the ceiling, and the floor of the room, and wherever you happen to be, they hit upon your ear.

If you can picture to yourself these waves spreading out in all directions, you will easily see why sound grows fainter at the distance. Just close round my hands when I clap them, there is a small quantity of air, and so the shock I give it is very violent, but as the sound-waves spread on all sides they have more and more air to move, and so the air-atoms are shaken less violently and strike with less force on your ear.

If we can prevent the sound-wave from spreading, then the sound is not weakened. The Frenchman Biot found that a low whisper could be heard distinctly for a distance of half a mile through a tube, because the waves could not spread beyond the small column of air. But unless you speak into a small space of some kind, you cannot prevent the waves going out from you in all directions.

Try and imagine that you see these waves spreading all round me now and hitting on your ears as they pass, then on the ears of those behind you, and on and on in widening globes till they reach the wall. What will happen when they get there? If the wall were thin, as a wooden partition is, they would shake it, and it again would shake the air on the other side, and so anyone in the next room would have the sound of my voice brought to their ear.

But something more will happen. In any case the sound-waves hitting against the wall will bound back from it just as a ball bounds back when thrown against anything, and so another set of sound-waves reflected from the wall will come back across the room. If these waves come to your ear so quickly that they mix with direct waves, they help to make the sound louder in this room than you would in the open air, for the "Ha" from my mouth and a second "Ha" from the wall come to your ear so instantaneously that they make one sound. This is why you can often hear better at the far end of a church when you stand against a screen or a wall, then when you are half-way up the building nearer to the speaker, because near the wall the reflected waves strike strongly on your ear and make the sound louder.

Sometimes, when the sound comes from a great explosion, these reflected waves are so strong that they are able to break glass. In the explosion of gunpowder in St. John's Wood, many houses in the back streets had their windows broken; for the sound-waves bounded off at angles from the walls and struck back upon them.

Now suppose the wall were so far behind you that the reflected sound-waves only hit upon your ear after those coming straight from me had died away; then you would hear the sound twice, "Ha" from me and "Ha" from the wall, and here you have an echo, "Ha, ha." In order for this to happen in ordinary air, you must be standing at least 56 feet away from the point from which the waves are reflected, for then the second blow will come one-tenth of a second after the first one, and that is long enough for you to feel them separately.* Miss C. A. Martineau tells a story of a dog which was terribly frightened by an echo. Thinking another dog was barking, he ran forward to meet him, and was very much astonished, when, as he came nearer the wall, the echo ceased. I myself once knew a case of this kind, and my dog, when he could find no enemy, ran back barking, till he was a certain distance off, and then the echo of course began again. He grew so furious at last that we had great difficulty in preventing him from flying at a strange man who happened to be passing at the time. (*Sound travels 1120 feet in a second, in air of ordinary temperature, and therefore 112 feet in the tenth of a second. Therefore the journey of 56 feet beyond you to reach the wall and 56 feet to return, will occupy the sound-wave one-tenth of a second and separate the two sounds.)

Sometimes, in the mountains, walls of rock rise at some distance one behind another, and then each one will send back its echo a little later than the rock before it, so that the "Ha" which you give will come back as a peal of laughter. There is an echo in Woodstock Park which repeats the word twenty times. Again sometimes, as in the Alps, the sound-waves coming back rebound from mountain to mountain and are driven backwards and forwards, becoming fainter and fainter till they die away; these echoes are very beautiful.

If you are now able to picture to yourselves one set of waves going to the wall, and another set returning and crossing them, you will be ready to understand something of that very difficult question, How is it that we can hear many different sounds at one time and tell them apart?

Have you ever watched the sea when its surface is much ruffled, and noticed how, besides the big waves of the tide, there are numberless smaller ripples made by the wind blowing the surface of the water, or the oars of a boat dipping in it, or even rain-drops falling? If you have done this you will have seen that all these waves and ripples cross each other, and you can follow any one ripple with you eye as it goes on its way undisturbed by the rest. Or you may make beautiful crossing and recrossing ripples on a pond by throwing in two stones at a little distance from each other, and here too you can follow any one wave on to the edge of the pond.

Now just in this way the waves of sound, in their manner of moving, cross and recross each other. You will remember too, that different sounds make waves of different lengths, just as the tide makes a long wave and the rain-drops tiny ones. Therefore each sound falls with its own peculiar wave upon your ear, and you can listen to that particular wave just as you look at one particular ripple, and then the sound becomes clear to you.

All this is what is going on outside your ear, but what is happening in your ear itself? How do these blows of the air speak to your brain? By means of the following diagram, we will try to understand roughly our beautiful hearing instrument, the ear.

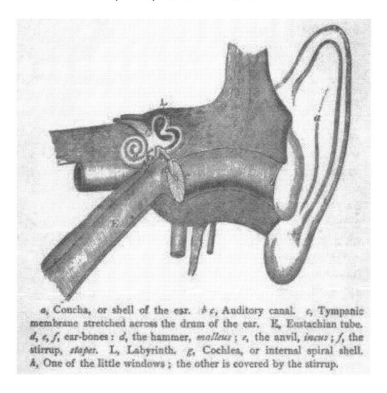

a, Concha, or shell of the ear. *b c*, Auditory canal. *c*, Tympanic membrane stretched across the drum of the ear. E, Eustachian tube. *d, e, f*, ear-bones : *d*, the hammer, *malleus* ; *e*, the anvil, *incus* ; *f*, the stirrup, *stapes*. L, Labyrinth. *g*, Cochlea, or internal spiral shell. *h*, One of the little windows ; the other is covered by the stirrup.

First, I want you to notice how beautifully the outside shell, or concha as it is called, is curved round so that any movement of the air coming to it from the front is caught in it and reflected into the hole of the ear. Put your finger round your ear and feel how the gristly part is curved towards the front of your head. This concha makes a curve much like the curve a deaf man makes with his hand behind his ear to catch the sound. Animals often have to raise their ears to catch the sound well, but ours stand always ready. When the air-waves have passed in at the hole of your ear, they move all the air in the passage, which is called the auditory, or hearing, canal. This canal is lined with little hairs to keep out insects and dust, and the wax which collects in it serves the same purpose. But if too much wax collects, it prevents the air from playing well upon the drum, and therefore makes you deaf. Across the end of this canal, a membrane or skin called the tympanum is stretched, like the parchment over the head of a drum, and it is this membrane which moves to and fro as the air-waves strike on it. A violent box on the ear will sometimes break this delicate membrane, or injure it, and therefore it is very wrong to hit a person violently on the ear.

On the other side of this membrane, inside the ear, there is air, which fills the whole of the inner chamber and the tube, which runs down into the throat behind the nose, and is called the Eustachian tube after the man who discovered it. This tube is closed at the end by a valve which opens and shuts. If you breathe out strongly, and then shut your mouth and swallow, you will hear a little "click" in your ear. This is because in swallowing you draw the air out of the Eustachian tube and so draw in the membrane, which clicks as it goes back again. But unless you do this the tube and the whole chamber cavity behind the membrane remains full of air.

Now, as this membrane is driven to and fro by the sound-waves, it naturally shakes the air in the cavity behind it, and it also sets moving three most curious little bones. The first of the bones is fastened to the middle of the drumhead so that it moves to and fro every time this membrane quivers. The head of this bone fits into a hole in the next bone, the anvil, and is fastened to it by muscles, so as to drag it along with it; but, the muscles being elastic, it can draw back a little from the anvil, and so give it a blow each time it comes back. This anvil is in its turn very firmly fixed to the little bone, shaped like a stirrup, which you see at the end of the chain.

This stirrup rests upon a curious body which looks in the diagram like a snail-shell with tubes coming out of it. This body, which is called the labyrinth, is made of bone, but it has two little windows in it, one covered only by a membrane, while the other has the head of the stirrup resting upon it.

Now, with a little attention you will understand that when the air in the canal shakes the drumhead to and fro, this membrane must drag with it the hammer, the anvil, and the stirrup. Each time the drum goes in, the hammer will hit the anvil, and drive the stirrup against the little window; every time it goes out it will draw the hammer, the anvil, and the stirrup out again, ready for another blow. Thus the stirrup is always playing upon this little window. Meanwhile, inside the bony labyrinth there is a fluid like water, and along the little passages are very fine hairs, which wave to and fro like reeds; and whenever the stirrup hits at the little window, the fluid moves these hairs to and fro, and they irritate the ends of a nerve, and this nerve carries the message to your brain. There are also some curious little stones called otoliths, lying in some parts of this fluid, and they, by their rolling to and fro, probably keep up the motion and prolong the sound.

You must not imagine we have explained here the many intricacies which occur in the ear; I can only hope to give you a rough idea of it, so that you may picture to yourselves the air-waves moving backwards and forward in the canal of your ear, then the tympanum vibrating to and fro, the hammer hitting the anvil, the stirrup knocking at the little window, the fluid waving the fine hairs and rolling the tiny stones, the ends of the nerve quivering, and then (how we know not) the brain hearing the message.

Is not this wonderful, going on as it does at every sound you hear? And yet this is not all, for inside that curled part of the labyrinth, which looks like a snail-shell and is called the cochlea, there is a most wonderful apparatus of more than three thousand fine stretched filaments or threads, and these act like the strings of a harp, and make you hear different tones. If you go near to a harp or a piano, and sing any particular note very loudly, you will hear this note sounding in the instrument, because you will set just that particular string quivering, which gives the note you sang. The air-waves set going by your voice touch that string, because it can quiver in time with them, while none of the other strings can do so. Now, just in the same way the tiny instrument of three thousand strings in your ear, which is called Corti's organ, vibrates to the air-waves, one thread to one set of waves, and another to another, and according to the fibre that quivers, will be the sound you hear. Here then at last, we see how nature speaks to us. All the movements going on outside, however violent and varied they may be, cannot of themselves make sound. But here, in the little space behind the drum of our ear, the air-waves are sorted and sent on to our brain, where they speak to us as sound.

Lesson 148

1. Today read the last part of chapter 6 of *The Fairy Land of Science*.
2. Choose a topic from your reading. Write or tell a topic sentence, or main idea sentence, for that topic.

Lecture VI. The Voices Of Nature And How We Hear Them. Continued...

But why then do we not hear all sounds as music? Why are some mere noise, and others clear musical notes? This depends entirely upon whether the sound-waves come quickly and regularly, or by an irregular succession of shocks. For example, when a load of stones is being shot out of a cart, you hear only a long, continuous noise, because the stones fall irregularly, some quicker, some slower, here a number together, and there two or three stragglers by themselves; each of these different shocks comes to your ear and makes a confused, noisy sound. But if you run a stick very quickly along a paling, you will hear a sound very like a musical note. This is because the rods of the paling are all at equal distances one from another, and so the shocks fall quickly one after another at regular intervals upon your ear. Any quick and regular succession of sounds makes a note, even though it may be an ugly one. The squeak of a slate pencil along a slate, and the shriek of a railway whistle are not pleasant, but they are real notes which you could copy on a violin.

I have here a simple apparatus which I have had made to show you that rapid and regular shocks produce a natural musical note. This wheel is milled at the edge like a shilling, and when I turn it rapidly so that it strikes against the edge of the card fixed behind it, the notches strike in rapid succession, and produce a musical sound. We can also prove by this experiment that the quicker the blows are, the higher the note will be. I pull the string gently at first, and then quicker and quicker, and you will notice that the note grows sharper and sharper, till the movement begins to slacken, when the note goes down again. This is because the more rapidly the air is hit, the shorter are the waves it makes, and short waves give a high note.

Let us examine this with two tuning-forks. I strike one, and it sounds D, the third space in the treble; I strike the other, and it sounds G, the first leger line, five notes above the C. I have drawn on this diagram, an imaginary picture of these two sets of waves. You see that the G fork makes three waves, while the C fork makes only two. Why is this? Because the prong of the G fork moves three times backwards and forwards while the prong of the C fork only moves twice; therefore the G fork does not crowd so many atoms together before it draws back, and the waves are shorter. These two notes, C and G, are a fifth of an octave apart; if we had two forks, of which one went twice as fast as the other, making four waves while the other made two, then that note would be an octave higher.

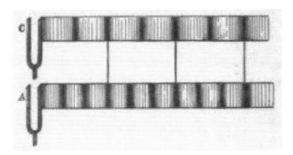

So we see that all the sounds we hear, – the warning noises which keep us from harm, the beautiful musical notes with all the tunes and harmonies that delight us, even the power of hearing the voices of those we love, and learning from one another that which each can tell, – all these depend upon the invisible waves of air, even as the pleasures of light depend on the waves of ether. It is by these sound-waves that nature speaks to us, and in all her movements there is a reason why her voice is sharp or tender, loud or gentle, awful or loving. Take for instance the brook we spoke of at the beginning of the lecture. Why does it sing so sweetly, while the wide deep river makes no noise? Because the little brook eddies and purls round the stones, hitting them as it passes; sometimes the water falls down a large stone, and strikes against the water below; or sometimes it grates the little pebbles together as they lie in its bed. Each of these blows makes a small globe of sound-waves, which spread and spread till they fall on your ear, and because they fall quickly and regularly, they make a low, musical note. We might almost fancy that the brook wished to show how joyfully it flows along, recalling Shelley's beautiful lines:-

> Sometimes it fell
> Among the moss with hollow harmony,
> Dark and profound; now on the polished stones
> It danced; like childhood laughing as it went.

The broad deep river, on the contrary, makes none of these cascades and commotions. The only places against which it rubs are the banks and the bottom; and here you can sometimes hear it grating the particles of sand against each other if you listen very carefully. But there is another reason why falling water makes a sound, and often even a loud roaring noise in the cataract and in the breaking waves of the sea. You do not only hear the water dashing against the rocky ledges or on the beach, you also hear the bursting of innumerable little bladders of air which are contained in the water. As each of these bladders is dashed on the ground, it explodes and sends sound-waves

252

to your ear. Listen to the sea some day when the waves are high and stormy, and you cannot fail to be struck by the irregular bursts of sound.

The waves, however, do not only roar as they dash on the ground; have you never noticed how they seem to scream as they draw back down the beach? Tennyson calls it,

The scream of the madden'd beach dragged down by the wave;

and it is caused by the stones grating against each other as the waves drag them down. Dr. Tyndall tells us that it is possible to know the size of the stones by the kind of noise they make. If they are large, it is a confused noise, when smaller, a kind of scream; while a gravelly beach will produce a mere hiss.

Who could be dull by the side of a brook, a waterfall, or the sea, while he can listen for sounds like these, and picture to himself how they are being made? You may discover a number of other causes of sound made by water, if you once pay attention to them.

Nor is it only water that sings to us. Listen to the wind, how sweetly it sighs among the leaves. There we hear it, because it rubs the leaves together, and they produce the sound-waves. But walk against the wind some day and you can hear it whistling in your own ear, striking against the curved cup, and then setting up a succession of waves in the hearing canal of the ear itself.

Why should it sound in one particular tone when all kinds of sound-waves must be surging about in the disturbed air?

This glass jar will answer our question roughly. If I strike my tuning-fork and hold it over the jar, you cannot hear it, because the sound is feeble, but if I fill the jar gently with water, when the water rises to a certain point you will hear a loud clear note, because the waves of air in the jar are exactly the right length to answer to the note of the fork. If I now blow across the mouth of the jar you hear the same note, showing that a cavity of a particular length will only sound to the waves which fit it. Do you see now the reason why pan-pipes give different sounds, or even the hole at the end of a common key when you blow across it? Here is a subject you will find very interesting if you will read about it, for I can only just suggest it to you here. But now you will see that the canal of your ear also answers only to certain waves, and so the wind sings in your ear with a real if not a musical note.

Again, on a windy night have you not heard the wind sounding a wild, sad note down a valley? Why do you think it sounds so much louder and more musical here than when it is blowing across the plain? Because air in the valley will only answer to a certain set of waves, and, like the pan-pipe, gives a particular note as the wind blows across it, and these waves go up and down the valley in regular pulses, making a wild howl. You may hear the same in the chimney, or in the keyhole; all these are waves set up in the hole across which the wind blows. Even the music in the shell which you hold to your ear is made by the air in the shell pulsating to and fro. And how do you think it is set going? By the throbbing of the veins in your own ear, which causes the air in the shell to vibrate.

Another grand voice of nature is the thunder. People often have a vague idea that thunder is produced by the clouds knocking together, which is very absurd, if you remember that clouds are but water-dust. The most probable explanation of thunder is much more beautiful than this. You will remember from Lecture III that heat forces the air-atoms apart. Now, when a flash of lightning crosses the sky it suddenly expands the air all round it as it passes, so that globe after globe of sound-waves is formed at every point across which the lightning travels. Now light, you remember, travels so wonderfully rapidly (192,000 miles in a second) that a flash of lightning is seen by us and is over in a second, even when it is two or three miles long. But sound comes slowly, taking five seconds to travel half a mile, and so all the sound-waves at each point of the two or three miles fall on our ear one after the other, and make the rolling thunder. Sometimes the roll is made even longer by the echo, as the sound-waves are reflected to and fro by the clouds on their road; and in the mountains we know how the peals echo and re-echo till they die away.

We might fill up far more than an hour in speaking of those voices which come to us as nature is at work. Think of the patter of the rain, how each drop as it hits the pavement sends circles of sound-waves out on all sides; or the loud report which falls on the ear of the Alpine traveller as the glacier cracks on its way down the valley; or the mighty boom of the avalanche as the snow slides in huge masses off the side of the lofty mountain. Each and all of these create their sound-waves, large or small, loud or feeble, which make their way to your ear, and become converted into sound.

We have, however, only time now just to glance at life-sounds, of which there are so many around us. Do you know why we hear a buzzing, as the gnat, the bee, or the cockchafer fly past? Not by the beating of their wings against the air, as many people imagine, and as is really the case with humming birds, but by the scraping of the under-part of their hard wings against the edges of their hind legs, which are toothed like a saw. The more rapidly their wings move the stronger the grating sound becomes, and you will now see why in hot, thirsty weather the buzzing of the gnat is so loud, for the more thirsty and the more eager he becomes, the wilder his movements will be.

Some insects, like the drone-fly (Eristalis tenax), force the air through the tiny air-passages in their sides, and as these passages are closed by little plates, the plates vibrate to and fro and make sound-waves. Again, what are those curious sounds you may hear sometimes if you rest your head on a trunk in the forest? They are made by the timber-boring beetles, which saw the wood with their jaws and make a noise in the world, even though they have no voice.

All these life-sounds are made by creatures which do not sing or speak; but the sweetest sounds of all in the woods are the voices of the birds. All voice-sounds are made by two elastic bands or cushions, called vocal chords, stretched across the end of the tube or windpipe through which we breathe, and as we send the air through them we tighten or loosen them as we will, and so make them vibrate quickly or slowly and make sound-waves of different lengths. But if you will try some day in the woods you will find that a bird can beat you over and over again in the length of his note; when you are out of breath and forced to stop he will go on with his merry trill as fresh and clear as if he had only just begun. This is because birds can draw air into the whole of their body, and they have a large stock laid up in the folds of their windpipe, and besides this the air-chamber behind their elastic bands or vocal chords has two compartments where we have only one, and the second compartment has special muscles by which they can open and shut it, and so prolong the trill.

Only think what a rapid succession of waves must quiver through the air as a tiny lark agitates his little throat and pours forth a volume of song! The next time you are in the country in the spring, spend half an hour listening to him, and try and picture to yourself how that little being is moving all the atmosphere round him. Then dream for a little while about sound, what it is, how marvellously it works outside in the world, and inside in your ear and brain; and then, when you go back to work again, you will hardly deny that it is well worth while to listen sometimes to the voices of nature and ponder how it is that we hear them.

Lesson 149

1. Today read the first part of chapter 7 of *The Fairy Land of Science*.
2. Choose a topic from your reading. Write or tell a topic sentence, or main idea sentence, for that topic.

Lecture VII. The Life Of A Primrose.

When the dreary days of winter and the early damp days of spring are passing away, and the warm bright sunshine has begun to pour down upon the grassy paths of the wood, who does not love to go out and bring home posies of violets, and bluebells, and primroses? We wander from one plant to another picking a flower here and a bud there, as they nestle among the green leaves, and we make our rooms sweet and gay with the tender and lovely blossoms. But tell me, did you ever stop to think, as you added flower after flower to your nosegay, how the plants which bear them have been building up their green leaves and their fragile buds during the last few weeks? If you had visited the same spot a month before, a few of last year's leaves, withered and dead, would have been all that you would have found. And now the whole wood is carpeted with delicate green leaves, with nodding bluebells, and pale-yellow primroses, as if a fairy had touched the ground and covered it with fresh young life. And our fairies have been at work here; the fairy "Life," of whom we know so little, though we love her so well and rejoice in the beautiful forms she can produce; the fairy sunbeams with their invisible influence kissing the tiny shoots and warming them into vigour and activity; the gentle rain-drops, the balmy air, all these have been working, while you or I passed heedlessly by; and now we come and gather the flowers they have made, and too often forget to wonder how these lovely forms have sprung up around us.

Our work during the next hour will be to consider this question. You were asked last week to bring with you to-day a primrose-flower, or a whole plant if possible, in order the better to follow out with me the "Life of a Primrose." (To enjoy this lecture, the reader ought to have, if possible, a primrose-flower, an almond soaked for a few minutes in hot water, and a piece of orange.) This is a very different kind of subject from those of our former lectures. There we took world- wide histories; we travelled up to the sun, or round the earth, or into the air; now I only ask you to fix your attention on one little plant, and inquire into its history.

There is a beautiful little poem by Tennyson, which says:

> Flower in the crannied wall,
> I pluck you out of the crannies;
> Hold you here, root and all, in my hand,
> Little flower; but if I could understand
> What you are, root and all, and all in all,
> I should know what God and man is.

We cannot learn all about this little flower, but we can learn enough to understand that it has a real separate life of its own, well worth knowing. For a plant is born, breathes, sleeps, feeds, and digests just as truly as an animal does, though in a different way. It works hard both for itself to get its food, and for others in making the air pure and fit for animals to breathe. It often lays by provision for the winter. It sends young plants out, as parents send their children, to fight for themselves in the world; and then, after living sometimes to a good old age, it dies, and leaves its place to others.

We will try to follow out something of this life to-day; and first, we will begin with the seed.

I have here a packet of primrose-seeds, but they are so small that we cannot examine them; so I have also had given to each one of you an almond-kernel, which is the seed of the almond- tree, and which has been soaked, so that it splits in half easily. From this we can learn about seeds in general, and then apply it to the primrose.

Half an almond,
showing the
plantlet.

a, rudiment of
stem. b, begin-
ning of root.

If you peel the two skins off your almond-seed (the thick, brown, outside skin, and the thin, transparent one under it), the two halves of the almond will slip apart quite easily. One of these halves will have a small dent at the pointed end, while in the other half you will see a little lump, which fitted into the dent when the two halves were joined. This little lump is a young plant, and the two halves of the almond are the seed leaves which hold the plantlet, and feed it till it can feed itself. The rounded end of the plantlet (b) sticking out of the almond, is the beginning of the root, while the other end (a) will in time become the stem. If you look carefully, you will see two little points at this end, which are the tips of future leaves. Only think how minute this plantlet must be in a primrose, where the whole seed is scarcely larger than a grain of sand! Yet in this tiny plantlet lies hid the life of the future plant.

When a seed falls into the ground, so long as the earth is cold and dry, it lies like a person in a trance, as if it were dead; but as soon as the warm, damp spring comes, and the busy little sun-waves pierce down into the earth, they wake up the plantlet and make it bestir itself. They agitate to and fro the particles of matter in this tiny body, and cause them to seek out for other particles to seize and join to themselves.

But these new particles cannot come in at the roots, for the seed has none; nor through the leaves, for they have not yet grown up; and so the plantlet begins by helping itself to the store of food laid up in the thick seed-leaves in which it is buried. Here it finds starch, oils, sugar, and substances called albuminoids, — the sticky matter which you notice in wheat-grains when you chew them is one of the albuminoids. This food is all ready for the plantlet to use, and it sucks it in, and works itself into a young plant with tiny roots at one end, and a growing shoot, with leaves, at the other.

But how does it grow? What makes it become larger? To answer this you must look at the second thing I asked you to bring – a piece of orange. If you take the skin off a piece of orange, you will see inside a number of long-shaped transparent bags, full of juice. These we call cells, and the flesh of all plants and animals is made up of cells like these, only of various shapes. In the pith of elder they are round, large, and easily seen; in the stalks of plants they are long, and lap over each other,

257

so as to give the stalk strength to stand upright. Sometimes many cells growing one on the top of the other break into one tube and make vessels. But whether large or small, they are all bags growing one against the other.

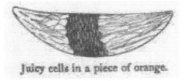

Juicy cells in a piece of orange.

In the orange-pulp these cells contain only sweet juice, but in other parts of the orange-tree or any other plant they contain a sticky substance with little grains in it. This substance is called "protoplasm," or the first form of life, for it is alive and active, and under a microscope you may see in a living plant streams of the little grains moving about in the cells.

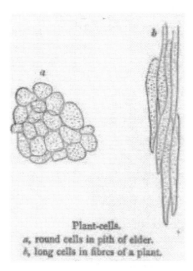

Plant-cells.
a, round cells in pith of elder.
b, long cells in fibres of a plant.

Now we are prepared to explain how our plant grows. Imagine the tiny primrose plantlet to be made up of cells filled with active living protoplasm, which drinks in starch and other food from the seed-leaves. In this way each cell will grow too full for its skin, and then the protoplasm divides into two parts and builds up a wall between them, and so one cell becomes two. Each of these two cells again breaks up into two more, and so the plant grows larger and larger, till by the time it has used up all the food in the seed-leaves, it has sent roots covered with fine hairs downwards into the earth, and a shoot with beginnings of leaves up into the air.

Sometimes the seed-leaves themselves come above the ground, as in the mustard-plant, and sometimes they are left empty behind, while the plantlet shoots through them.

And now the plant can no longer afford to be idle and live on prepared food. It must work for itself. Until now it has been taking in the same kind of food that you and I do; for we too find many seeds very pleasant to eat and useful to nourish us. But now this store is exhausted. Upon what then is the plant to live? It is cleverer than we are in this, for while we cannot live unless we have food which has once been alive, plants can feed upon gases and water and mineral matter only. Think over the substances you can eat or drink, and you will find they are nearly all made of things which have been alive: meat, vegetables, bread, beer, wine, milk; all these are made from living matter, and though you do take in such things as water and salt, and even iron and phosphorus, these would be quite useless if you did not eat and drink prepared food which your body can work into living matter.

But the plant as soon as it has roots and leaves begins to make living matter out of matter that has never been alive. Through all the little hairs of its roots it sucks in water, and in this water are dissolved more or less of the salts of ammonia, phosphorus, sulphur, iron, lime, magnesia, and even silica, or flint. In all kinds of earth there is some iron, and we shall see presently that this is very important to the plant.

Suppose, then, that our primrose has begun to drink in water at its roots. How is it to get this water up into the stem and leaves, seeing that the whole plant is made of closed bags or cells? It does it in a very curious way, which you can prove for yourselves. Whenever two fluids, one thicker than the other, such as treacle and water for example, are only separated by a skin or any porous substance, they will always mix, the thinner one oozing through the skin into the thicker one. If you tie a piece of bladder over a glass tube, fill the tube half-full of treacle, and then let the covered end rest in a bottle of water, in a few hours the water will get in to the treacle and the mixture will rise up in the tube till it flows over the top. Now, the saps and juices of plants are thicker than water, so, directly the water enters the cells at the root it oozes up into the cells above, and mixes with the sap. Then the matter in those cells becomes thinner than in the cells above, so it too oozes up, and in this way cell by cell the water is pumped up into the leaves.

Lesson 150

1. Today read the next part of chapter 7 of *The Fairy Land of Science*.
2. Choose a topic from your reading. Write or tell a topic sentence, or main idea sentence, for that topic.

Lecture VII. The Life Of A Primrose. Continued…

When it gets there it finds our old friends the sun-beams hard at work. If you have ever tried to grow a plant in a cellar, you will know that in the dark its leaves remain white and sickly. It is only in the sunlight that a beautiful delicate green tint is given to them, and you will remember from Lecture II that this green tint shows that the leaf has used all the sun-waves except those which make you see green; but why should it do this only when it has grown up in the sunshine?

The reason is this: when the sunbeam darts into the leaf and sets all its particles quivering, it divides the protoplasm into two kinds, collected into different cells. One of these remains white, but the other kind, near the surface, is altered by the sunlight and by the help of the iron brought in by the water. This particular kind of protoplasm, which is called "chlorophyll," will have nothing to do with the green waves and throws them back, so that every little grain of this protoplasm looks green and gives the leaf its green colour.

It is these little green cells that by the help of the sun-waves digest the food of the plant and turn the water and gases into useful sap and juices. We saw in Lecture III that when we breathe-in air, we use up the oxygen in it and send back out of our mouths carbonic acid, which is a gas made of oxygen and carbon.

Now, every living things wants carbon to feed upon, but plants cannot take it in by itself, because carbon is solid (the blacklead in your pencils is pure carbon), and a plant cannot eat, it can only drink-in fluids and gases. Here the little green cells help it out of its difficulty. They take in or absorb out of the air carbonic acid gas which we have given out of our mouths and then by the help of the sun-waves they tear the carbon and oxygen apart. Most of the oxygen they throw back into the air for us to use, but the carbon they keep.

Oxygen-bubbles rising from laurel-leaves in water.

If you will take some fresh laurel-leaves and put them into a tumbler of water turned upside-down in a saucer of water, and set the tumbler in the sunshine, you will soon see little bright bubbles rising up and clinging to the glass. These are bubbles of oxygen gas, and they tell you that they have been set free by the green cells which have torn from them the carbon of the carbonic acid in the water.

But what becomes of the carbon? And what use is made of the water which we have kept waiting all this time in the leaves? Water, you already know, is made of hydrogen and oxygen, but perhaps you will be surprised when I tell you that starch, sugar, and oil, which we get from plants, are nothing more than hydrogen and oxygen in different quantities joined to carbon.

Carbon rising up from white sugar.

It is very difficult at first to picture such a black thing as carbon making part of delicate leaves and beautiful flowers, and still more of pure white sugar. But we can make an experiment by which we can draw the hydrogen and oxygen out of common loaf sugar, and then you will see the carbon stand out in all its blackness. I have here a plate with a heap of white sugar in it. I pour upon it first some hot water to melt and warm it, and then some strong sulphuric acid. This acid does nothing more than simply draw the hydrogen and oxygen out. See! in a few moments a black mass of carbon begins to rise, all of which has come out of the white sugar you saw just now. (The common dilute sulphuric acid of commerce is not strong enough for this experiment, but pure sulphuric acid can be secured from any chemist. Great care must be taken in using it, as it burns everything it touches.) You see, then, that from the whitest substance in plants we can get this black carbon; and in truth, one-half of the dry part of every plant is composed of it.

Now look at my plant again, and tell me if we have not already found a curious history? Fancy that you see the water creeping in at the roots, oozing up from cell to cell till it reaches the leaves, and there meeting the carbon which has just come out of the air, and being worked up with it by the sun-waves into starch, or sugar, or oils.

But meanwhile, how is new protoplasm to be formed? for without this active substance none of the work can go on. Here comes into use a lazy gas we spoke of in Lecture III. There we thought that nitrogen was of no use except to float oxygen in the air, but here we shall find it very useful. So far, as we know, plants cannot take up nitrogen out of the air, but they can get it out of the ammonia which the water brings in at their roots.

Ammonia, you will remember, is a strong-smelling gas, made of hydrogen and nitrogen, and which is often almost stifling near a manure-heap. When you manure a plant you help it to get this ammonia, but at any time it gets some from the soil and also from the rain-drops which bring it down in the air. Out of this ammonia the plant takes the nitrogen and works it up with the three elements, carbon, oxygen, and hydrogen, to make the substances called albuminoids, which form a large part of the food of the plant, and it is these albuminoids which go to make protoplasm. You will notice that while the starch and other substances are only made of three elements, the active protoplasm is made of these three added to a fourth, nitrogen, and it also contains phosphorus and sulphur.

And so hour after hour and day after day our primrose goes on pumping up water and ammonia from its roots to its leaves, drinking in carbonic acid from the air, and using the sun-waves to work them all up into food to be sent to all parts of its body. In this way these leaves act, you see, as the stomach of the plant, and digest its food.

Sometimes more water is drawn up into the leaves than can be used, and then the leaf opens thousands of little mouths in the skin of its under surface, which let the drops out just as drops of perspiration ooze through our skin when we are overheated. These little mouths, which are called stomates are made of two flattened cells, fitting against each other. When the air is damp and the plant has too much water these lie open and let it out, but when the air is dry, and the plant wants to keep as much water as it can, then they are closely shut. There are as many as a hundred thousand of these mouths under one apple-leaf, so you may imagine how small they often are.

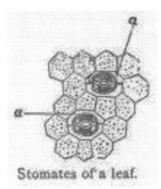

Stomates of a leaf.

Plants which only live one year, such as mignonette, the sweet pea, and the poppy, take in just enough food to supply their daily wants and to make the seeds we shall speak of presently. Then, as soon as their seeds are ripe their roots begin to shrivel, and water is no longer carried up. The green cells can no longer get food to digest, and they themselves are broken up by the sunbeams and turn yellow, and the plant dies.

But many plants are more industrious than the stock and mignonette, and lay by store for another year, and our primrose is one of these. Look at this thick solid mass below the primrose leaves, out of which the roots spring. (See the plant in the foreground of the heading of the lecture.) This is really the stem of the primrose hidden underground, and all the starch, albuminoids, &c., which the plant can spare as it grows, are sent down into this underground stem and stored up there, to lie quietly in the ground through the long winter, and then when the warm spring comes this stem begins to send out leaves for a new plant.

We have now seen how a plant springs up, feeds itself, grows, stores up food, withers, and dies; but we have said nothing yet about its beautiful flowers or how it forms its seeds. If we look down close to the bottom of the leaves in a primrose root in spring-time, we shall always find three or four little green buds nestling in among the leaves, and day by day we may see the stalk of these buds lengthening till they reach up into the open sunshine, and then the flower opens and shows its beautiful pale-yellow crown.

We all know that seeds are formed in the flower, and that the seeds are necessary to grow into new plants. But do we know the history of how they are formed, or what is the use of the different parts of the bud? Let us examine them all, and then I think you will agree with me that this is not the least wonderful part of the plant.

Lesson 151

1. Today read the last part of chapter 7 of *The Fairy Land of Science*.
2. Choose a topic from your reading. Write or tell a topic sentence, or main idea sentence, for that topic.

Lecture VII. The Life Of A Primrose. Continued…

Remember that the seed is the one important thing and then notice how the flower protects it. First, look at the outside green covering, which we call the calyx. See how closely it fits in the bud, so that no insects can creep in to gnaw the flower, nor any harm come to it from cold or blight. Then, when the calyx opens, notice that the yellow leaves which form the crown or corolla, are each alternate with one of the calyx leaves, so that anything which got past the first covering would be stopped by the second. Lastly, when the delicate corolla has opened out, look at those curious yellow bags just at the top of the tube. What is their use?

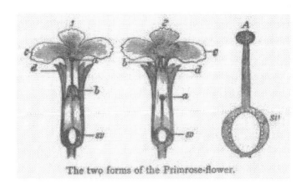

The two forms of the Primrose-flower.

But I fancy I see two or three little questioning faces which seem to say, "I see no yellow bags at the top of the tube." Well, I cannot tell whether you can or not in the specimen you have in your hand; for one of the most curious things about primrose flowers is, that some of them have these yellow bags at the top of the tube and some of them hidden down right in the middle. But this I can tell you: those of you who have got no yellow bags at the top will have a round knob there (I a, Fig. 43), and will find the yellow bags (b) buried in the tube. Those, on the other hand, who have the yellow bags at the top will find the knob (a) half-way down the tube.

Now for the use of these yellow bags, which are called the anthers of the stamens, the stalk on which they grow being called the filament or thread. If you can manage to split them open you will find that they have a yellow powder in them, called pollen, the same as the powder which sticks to your nose when you put it into a lily; and if you look with a magnifying glass at the little green knob in the centre of the flower, you will probably see some of this yellow dust sticking on it. We will leave it there for a time, and examine the body called the pistil, to which the knob belongs. Pull off the yellow corolla (which will come off quite easily), and turn back the green leaves. You will then see that the knob stands on the top of a column, and at the bottom of this column there is a round ball (sv), which is a vessel for holding the seeds. In this diagram I have drawn the whole of this curious ball and column as if cut in half, so that we may see what is in it. In the middle of the ball, in a cluster, there are a number of round transparent little bodies, looking something like round green orange-cells full of juice. They are really cells full of protoplasm, with one little dark spot in each of them, which by-and-by is to make our little plantlet that we found in the seed.

"These, then, are seeds," you will say. Not yet; they are only ovules, or little bodies which may become seeds. If they were left as they are they would all wither and die. But those little grains of pollen, which we saw sticking to the knob at the top, are coming down to help them. As soon as these yellow grains touch the sticky knob or stigma, as it is called, they throw out tubes, which grow down the column until they reach the ovules. In each one of these they find a tiny hole, and into this they creep, and then they pour into the ovule all the protoplasm from the pollen-grain which is sticking above, and this enables it to grow into a real seed, with a tiny plantlet inside.

This is how the plant forms its seed to bring up new little ones next year, while the leaves and the roots are at work preparing the necessary food. Think sometimes when you walk in the woods, how hard at work the little plants and big trees are, all around you. You breathe in the nice fresh oxygen they have been throwing out, and little think that it is they who are making the country so fresh and pleasant, and that while they look as if they were doing nothing but enjoying the bright sunshine, they are really fulfilling their part in the world by the help of this sunshine; earning their food from the ground working it up; turning their leaves where they can best get light (and in this it is chiefly the violet sun-waves that help them), growing, even at night, by making new cells out of the food they have taken in the day; storing up for the winter; putting out their flowers and making their seeds, and all the while smiling so pleasantly in quiet nooks and sunny dells that it makes us glad to see them.

But why should the primroses have such golden crowns? plain green ones would protect the seed quite as well. Ah! now we come to a secret well worth knowing. Look at the two primrose flowers, and tell me how you think the dust gets on to the top of the sticky knob or stigma. No. 2 seems easy enough to explain, for it looks as if the pollen could fall down easily from the stamens on to the knob, but it cannot fall up, as it would have to do in No. 1. Now the curious truth is, as Mr. Darwin has shown, that neither of these flowers can get the dust easily for themselves, but of the two No. 1 has the least difficulty.

Look at a withered primrose, and see how it holds its head down, and after a little while the yellow crown falls off. It is just about as it is falling that the anthers or bags of stamens burst open, and then, they are dragged over the knob and some of the grains stick there. But in the other form of primrose, No. 2, when the flower falls off, the stamens do not come near the knob, so it has no chance of getting any pollen; and while the primrose is upright the tube is so narrow that the dust does not easily fall. But, as I have said, neither kind gets it very easily, nor is it good for them if they do. The seeds are much stronger and better if the dust or pollen of one flower is carried away and left on the knob or stigma of another flower; and the only way this can be done is by insects flying from one flower to another and carrying the dust on their legs and bodies.

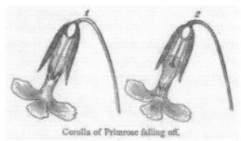

Corolla of Primrose falling off.

If you suck the end of the tube of the primrose flower you will find it tastes sweet, because a drop of honey has been lying there. When the insects go in to get this honey, they brush themselves against the yellow dust-bags, and some of the dust sticks to them, and then when they go to the next flower they rub it off on to its sticky knob.

Look at [the diagrams] and you will see at once that if an insect goes into No. 1 and the pollen sticks to him, when he goes into No. 2 just that part of his body on which the pollen is will touch the knob; and so the flowers become what we call "crossed," that is, the pollen-dust of the one feeds the ovule of the other. And just the same thing will happen if he flies from No. 2 to No. 1. There the dust will be just in the position to touch the knob which sticks out of the flower.

Therefore, we can see clearly that it is good for the primrose that bees and other insects should come to it, and anything it can do to entice them will be useful. Now, do you not think that when an insect once knew that the pale-yellow crown showed where honey was to be found, he would soon spy these crowns out as he flew along? or if they were behind a hedge, and he could not see them, would not the sweet scent tell him where to come and look for them? And so we see that the pretty sweet-scented corolla is not only delightful for us to look at and to smell, but it is really very useful in helping the primrose to make strong healthy seeds out of which the young plants are to grow next year.

And now let us see what we have learnt. We began with a tiny seed, though we did not then know how this seed had been made. We saw the plantlet buried in it, and learnt how it fed at first on prepared food, but soon began to make living matter for itself out of gases taken from the water through the cells to its stomach – the leaves! And how marvellously the sun-waves entering there formed the little green granules, and then helped them to make food and living protoplasm! At this point we might have gone further, and studied how the fibres and all the different vessels of the plant are formed, and a wondrous history it would have been. But it was too long for one hour's lecture, and you must read it for yourselves in books on botany. We had to pass on to the flower, and learn the use of the covering leaves, the gaily coloured crown attracting the insects, the dust-bags holding the pollen, the little ovules each with the germ of a new plantlet, lying hidden in the seed-vessel, waiting for the pollen-grains to grow down to them. Lastly, when the pollen crept in at the tiny opening we learnt that the ovule had now all it wanted to grow into a perfect seed.

And so we came back to a primrose seed, the point from which we started; and we have a history of our primrose from its birth to the day when its leaves and flowers wither away and it dies down for the winter.

But what fairies are they which have been at work here? First, the busy little fairy Life in the active protoplasm; and secondly, the sun-waves. We have seen that it was by the help of the sunbeams that the green granules were made, and the water, carbonic acid, and nitrogen worked up into the living plant. And in doing this work the sun-waves were caught and their strength used up, so that they could no longer quiver back into space. But are they gone for ever? So long as the leaves or the stem or the root of the plant remain they are gone, but when those are destroyed we can get them back again. Take a handful of dry withered plants and light them with a match, then as the leaves burn and are turned back again to carbonic acid, nitrogen, and water, our sunbeams come back again in the flame and heat.

And the life of the plant? What is it, and why is this protoplasm always active and busy? I cannot tell you. Study as we may, the life of the tiny plant is as much a mystery as your life and mine. It came, like all things, from the bosom of the Great Father, but we cannot tell how it came nor what it is. We can see the active grains moving under the microscope, but we cannot see the power that moves them. We only know it is a power given to the plant, as to you and to me, to enable it to live its life, and to do its useful work in the world.

Lesson 152

1. Today read the first part of chapter 8 of *The Fairy Land of Science*.
2. Choose a topic from your reading. Write or tell a topic sentence, or main idea sentence, for that topic.

Lecture VIII The History Of A Piece Of Coal

I have here a piece of coal (Fig. 45), which, though it has been cut with some care so as to have a smooth face, is really in no other way different from any ordinary lump which you can pick for yourself out of the coal-scuttle. Our work to-day is to relate the history of this black lump; to learn what it is, what it has been, and what it will be.

Fig. 45.

Piece of coal.
a, Smooth face, showing laminæ or thin layers.

It looks uninteresting enough at first sight, and yet if we examine it closely we shall find some questions to ask even about its appearance. Look at the smooth face of this specimen and see if you can explain those fine lines which run across so close together as to look like the edges of the leaves of a book. Try to break a piece of coal, and you will find that it will split much more easily along those lines than across the other way of the lump; and if you wish to light a fire quickly you should always put this lined face downwards so that the heat can force its way up through these cracks and gradually split up the block. Then again if you break the coal carefully along one of these lines you will find a fine film of charcoal lying in the crack, and you will begin to suspect that this black coal must have been built up in very thin layers, with a kind of black dust between them.

The next thing you will call to mind is that this coal burns and gives flame and heat, and that this means that in some way sunbeams are imprisoned in it; lastly, this will lead you to think of plants, and how they work up the strength of the sunbeams into their leaves, and hide black carbon in even the purest and whitest substance they contain.

Is coal made of burnt plants, then? Not burnt ones, for if so it would not burn again; but you may have read how the makers of charcoal take wood and bake it without letting it burn, and then it turns black and will afterwards make a very good fire; and so you will see that it is probable that our piece of coal is made of plants which have been baked and altered, but which have still much sunbeam strength bottled up in them, which can be set free as they burn.

If you will take an imaginary journey with me to a coal-pit near Newcastle, which I visited many years ago, you will see that we have very good evidence that coal is made of plants, for in all coal-mines we find remains of them at every step we take.

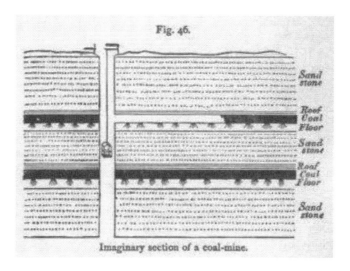

Imaginary section of a coal-mine.

Let us imagine that we have put on old clothes which will not spoil, and have stepped into the iron basket (see Fig. 46) called by the miners a cage, and are being let down the shaft to the gallery where the miners are at work. Most of them will probably be in the gallery b, because a great deal of the coal in a has been already taken out. But we will stop in a because there we can see a great deal of the roof and the floor. When we land on the floor of the gallery we shall find ourselves in a kind of tunnel with railway lines laid along it and trucks laden with coal coming towards the cage to be drawn up, while empty ones are running back to be loaded where the miners are at work. Taking lamps in our hands and keeping out of the way of the trucks, we will first throw the light on the roof, which is made of shale or hardened clay.

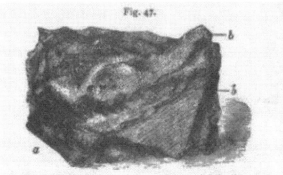

A piece of shale with impressions of ferns and Calamite stems.

We shall not have gone many yards before we see impressions of plants in the shale, like those in this specimen (Fig. 47), which was taken out of a coal-mine at Neath in Glamorganshire, a few days ago, and sent up for this lecture. You will recognize at once the marks of ferns (a), for they look like those you gather in the hedges of an ordinary country lane, and that long striped branch (b) does not look unlike a reed, and indeed it is something of this kind, as we shall see by-and-by. You will find plenty of these impressions of plants as you go along the gallery and look up at the roof, and with them there will be others with spotted stems, or with stems having a curious diamond pattern upon them, and many ferns of various kinds.

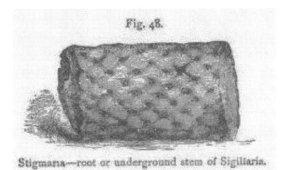

Stigmaria—root or underground stem of Sigillaria.

Next look down at your feet and examine the floor. You will not have to search long before you will almost certainly find a piece of stone like that represented in Fig. 48, which has also come from Neath Colliery. This fossil, which is the cast of a piece of a plant, puzzled those who found it for a very long time. At last, however, Mr. Binney found the specimen growing to the bottom of the trunk of one of the fossil trees with spotted stems, called Sigillaria; and so proved that this curious pitted stone is a piece of fossil root, or rather underground stem, like that which we found in the primrose, and that the little pits or dents in it are scars where the rootlets once were given off.

Whole masses of these root-stems, with ribbon-like roots lying scattered near them, are found buried in the layer of clay called the underclay which makes the floor of the coal, and they prove to us that this underclay must have been once the ground in which the roots of the coal-plants grew. You will feel still more sure of this when you find that there is not only one straight gallery of coal, but that galleries branch out right and left, and that everywhere you find the coal lying like a sandwich between the floor and the roof, showing that quite a large piece of country must be covered by these remains of plants all rooted in the underclay.

But how about the coal itself? It seems likely, when we find roots below and leaves and stems above, that the middle is made of plants, but can we prove it? We shall see presently that it has been so crushed and altered by being buried deep in the ground that the traces of leaves have almost been destroyed, though people who are used to examining with the microscope, can see the crushed remains of plants in thin slices of coal.

But fortunately for us, perfect pieces of plants have been preserved even in the coal-bed itself. Do you remember our learning in Lecture IV, that water with lime in it petrifies things, that is, leaves carbonate of lime to fill up grain by grain the fibres of an animal or plant as the living matter decays, and so keeps an exact representation of the object?

Now, it so happens that in a coal-bed at South Ouram, near Halifax, as well as in some other places, carbonate of lime trickled in before the plants were turned into coal, and made some round nodules in the plant-bed, which look like cannon- balls. Afterwards, when all the rest of the bed was turned into coal, these round balls remained crystallized, and by cutting thin transparent slices across the nodule we can distinctly see the leaves and stems and curious little round bodies which make up the coal. Several such sections may be seen at the British Museum, and when we compare these fragments of plants with those which we find above and below the coal-bed, we find that they agree, thus proving that coal is made of plants, and of those plants whose roots grew in the clay floor, while their heads reached up far above where the roof now is.

The next question is, what kind of plants were these? Have we anything like them living in the world now? You might perhaps think that it would be impossible to decide this question from mere petrified pieces of plants.

Lesson 153

1. Today read the next part of chapter 8 of *The Fairy Land of Science*.
2. Choose a topic from your reading. Write or tell a topic sentence, or main idea sentence, for that topic.

Lecture VIII. The History Of A Piece Of Coal. Continued...

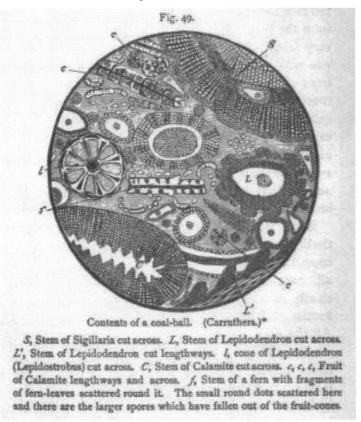

Fig. 49.

Contents of a coal-ball. (Carruthers.)*

S, Stem of Sigillaria cut across. *L*, Stem of Lepidodendron cut across. *L'*, Stem of Lepidodendron cut lengthways. *l*, cone of Lepidodendron (Lepidostrobus) cut across. *C*, Stem of Calamite cut across. *c, c, c*, Fruit of Calamite lengthways and across. *f*, Stem of a fern with fragments of fern-leaves scattered round it. The small round dots scattered here and there are the larger spores which have fallen out of the fruit-cones.

But many men have spent their whole lives in deciphering all the fragments that could be found, and though the section given in Fig. 49 may look to you quite incomprehensible, yet a botanist can reed it as we read a book. For example, at S and L, where stems are cut across, he can learn exactly how they were build up inside, and compare them with the stems of living plants, while the fruits cc and the little round spores lying near them, tell him their history as well as if he had gathered them from the tree. In this way we have learnt to know very fairly what the plants of the coal were like, and you will be surprised when I tell you that the huge trees of the coal-forests, of which we sometimes find trunks in the coal-mines from ten to fifty feet long are only represented on the earth now by small insignificant plants, scarcely ever more than two feet, and often not many inches high.

Fig. 50.

Selaginella selaginoides.
Species of club-moss bearing two
kinds of spores.

Have you ever seen the little club moss or Lycopodium which grows all over England, but chiefly in the north, on heaths and mountains? At the end of each of its branches it bears a cone made of scaly leaves; and fixed to the inside of each of these leaves is a case called a sporangium, full of little spores or moss-seeds, as we may call them, though they are not exactly like true seeds. In one of these club-mosses called Selaginella, the cases near the bottom of the cone contain large spores, while those near the top contain a powdery dust. These spores are full of resin, and they are collected on the Continent for making artificial lightning in the theatres, because they flare when lighted.

Now this little Selaginella is of all living plants the one most like some of the gigantic trees of the coal-forests. If you look at this picture of a coal-forest (Fig. 51), you will find it difficult perhaps to believe that those great trees, with diamond markings all up the trunk, hanging over from the right to the left of the picture, and covering all the top with their boughs, could be in any way relations of the little Selaginella; yet we find branches of them in the beds above the coal, bearing cones larger but just like Selaginella cones; and what is most curious, the spores in these cones are of exactly the same kind and not any larger than those of the club-mosses.

These trees are called by botanists Lepidodendrons, or scaly trees; there are numbers of them in all coal-mines, and one trunk has been found 49 feet long. Their branches were divided in a curious forked manner and bore cones at the ends. The spores which fell from these cones are found flattened in the coal, and they may be seen scattered about in the coal-ball.

Fig. 51.—A Forest of the Coal Period.

Another famous tree which grew in the coal-forests was the one whose roots we found in the floor or underclay of the coal. It has been called Sigillaria, because it has marks like seals (sigillum, a seal) all up the trunk, due to the scars left by the leaves when they fell from the tree. You will see the Sigillarias on the left-hand side of the coal-forest picture, having those curious tufts of leaves springing out of them at the top. Their stems make up a great deal of the coal, and the bark of their trunks is often found in the clays above, squeezed flat in lengths of 30, 60, or 70 feet. Sometimes, instead of being flat the bark is still in the shape of a trunk, and the interior is filled with sand; and then the trunk is very heavy, and if the miners do not prop the roof up well it falls down and kills those beneath it. Stigmaria is the root of the Sigillaria, and is found in the clays below the coal. Botanists are not yet quite certain about the seed-cases of this tree, but Mr. Carruthers believes that they grew inside the base of the leaves, as they do in the quillwort, a small plant which grows at the bottom of our mountain lakes.

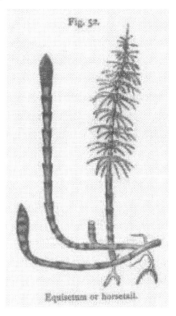

Equisetum or horsetail.

But what is that curious reed-like stem we found in the piece of shale (see Fig. 47)? That stem is very important, for it belonged to a plant called a Calamite, which, as we shall see presently, helped to sift the earth away from the coal and keep it pure. This plant was a near relation of the "horsetail," or Equisetum, which grows in our marshes; only, just as in the case of the other trees, it was enormously larger, being often 20 feet high, whereas the little Equisetum, Fig. 52, is seldom more than a foot, and never more than 4 feet high in England, though in tropical South America they are much higher. Still, if you have ever gathered "horsetails," you will see at once that those trees in the foreground of the picture (Fig. 51), with leaves arranged in stars round the branches, are only larger copies of the little marsh-plants; and the seed-vessels of the two plants are almost exactly the same.

These great trees, the Lepidodendrons, the Sigillarias, and the Calamites, together with large tree-ferns, are the chief plants that we know of in the coal-forests. It seems very strange at first that they should have been so large when their descendants are now so small, but if you look at our chief plants and trees now, you will find that nearly all of them bear flowers, and this is a great advantage to them, because it tempts the insects to bring them the pollen-dust, as we saw in the last lecture.

Now the Lipidodendrons and their companions had no true flowers, but only these seed-cases which we have mentioned; but as there were no flowering plants in their time, and they had the ground all to themselves, they grew fine and large. By-and-by, however, when the flowering plants came in, these began to crowd out the old giants of the coal-forests, so that they dwindled and dwindled from century to century till their great-great-grandchildren, thousands of generations after, only lift up their tiny heads in marshes and on heaths, and tell us that they were big once upon a time.

And indeed they must have been magnificent in those olden days, when they grew thick and tall in the lonely marshes where plants and trees were the chief inhabitants. We find no traces in the clay-beds of the coal to lead us to suppose that men lived in those days, nor lions, nor tigers, nor even birds to fly among the trees; but these grand forests were almost silent, except when a huge animal something like a gigantic newt or frog went croaking through the marsh, or a kind of grasshopper chirruped on the land. But these forms of life were few and far between, compared to the huge trees and tangled masses of ferns and reeds which covered the whole ground, or were reflected in the bosom of the large pools and lakes round about which they grew.

And now, if you have some idea of the plants and trees of the coal, it is time to ask how these plants became buried in the earth and made pure coal, instead of decaying away and leaving behind only a mixture of earth and leaves?

To answer this question, I must ask you to take another journey with me across the Atlantic to the shores of America, and to land at Norfolk in Virginia, because there we can see a state of things something like the marshes of the coal-forests. All round about Norfolk the land is low, flat, and marshy, and to the south of the town, stretching far away into North Carolina, is a large, desolate swamp, no less than forty miles long and twenty-five broad. The whole place is one enormous quagmire, overgrown with water-plants and trees. The soil is as black as ink from the old, dead leaves, grasses, roots, and stems which lie in it; and so soft, that everything would sink into it, if it were not for the matted roots of the mosses, ferns, and other plants which bind it together. You may dig down for ten or fifteen feet, and find nothing but peat made of the remains of plants which have lived and died there in succession for ages and ages, while the black trunks of the fallen trees lie here and there, gradually being covered up by the dead plants.

The whole place is so still, gloomy, and desolate, that it goes by the name of the "Great Dismal Swamp," and you see we have here what might well be the beginning of a bed of coal; for we know that peat when dried becomes firm and makes an excellent fire, and that if it were pressed till it was hard and solid it would not be unlike coal. If, then, we can explain how this peaty bed has been kept pure from earth, we shall be able to understand how a coal-bed may have been formed, even though the plants and trees which grow in this swamp are different from those which grew in the coal-forests.

The explanation is not difficult; streams flow constantly, or rather ooze into the Great Dismal Swamp from the land that lies to the west, but instead of bringing mud in with them as rivers bring to the sea, they bring only clear, pure water, because, as they filter for miles through the dense jungle of reeds, ferns, and shrubs which grow round the marsh, all the earth is sifted out and left behind. In this way the spongy mass of dead plants remains free from earthy grains, while the water and the shade of the thick forest of trees prevent the leaves, stems, etc., from being decomposed by the air and sun. And so year after year as the plants die they leave their remains for other plants to take root in, and the peaty mass grows thicker and thicker, while tall cedar trees and evergreens live and die in these vast, swampy forests, and being in loose ground are easily blown down by the wind, and leave their trunks to be covered up by the growing moss and weeds.

Lesson 154

1. Today read the last part of chapter 8 of *The Fairy Land of Science*.
2. Choose a topic from your reading. Write or tell a topic sentence, or main idea sentence, for that topic.

Lecture VIII. The History Of A Piece Of Coal. Continued…

Now we know that there were plenty of ferns and of large Calamites growing thickly together in the coal-forests, for we find their remains everywhere in the clay, so we can easily picture to ourselves how the dense jungle formed by these plants would fringe the coal-swamp, as the present plants do the Great Dismal Swamp, and would keep out all earthy matter, so that year after year the plants would die and form a thick bed of peat, afterwards to become coal.

The next thing we have to account for is the bed of shale or hardened clay covering over the coal. Now we know that from time to time land has gone slowly up and down on our globe so as in some places to carry the dry ground under the sea, and in others to raise the sea-bed above the water. Let us suppose, then, that the great Dismal Swamp was gradually to sink down so that the sea washed over it and killed the reeds and shrubs. Then the streams from the west would not be sifted any longer but would bring down mud, and leave it, as in the delta of the Nile or Mississippi, to make a layer over the dead plants. You will easily understand that this mud would have many pieces of dead trees and plants in it, which were stifled and died as it covered them over; and thus the remains would be preserved like those which we find now in the roof of the coal-galleries.

But still there are the thick sandstones in the coal-mine to be explained. How did they come there? To explain them, we must suppose that the ground went on sinking till the sea covered the whole place where once the swamp had been, and then sea-sand would be thrown down over the clay and gradually pressed down by the weight of new sand above, till it formed solid sandstone and our coal-bed became buried deeper and deeper in the earth.

At last, after long ages, when the thick mass of sandstones above the bed b (Fig. 46) had been laid down, the sinking must have stopped and the land have risen a little, so that the sea was driven back; and then the rivers would bring down earth again and make another clay-bed. Then a new forest would spring up, the ferns, Calamites, Lepidodendrons, and Sigillarias would gradually form another jungle, and many hundred of feet above the buried coal-bed b, a second bed of peat and vegetable matter would begin to accumulate to form the coal-bed a.

Such is the history of how the coal which we now dig out of the depths of the earth once grew as beautiful plants on the surface. We cannot tell exactly all the ground over which these forests grew in England, because some of the coal they made has been carried away since by rivers and cut down by the waves of the sea, but we can say that wherever there is coal now, there they must have been then.

Try and picture to yourselves that on the east coast of Northumberland and Durham, where all is now black with coal-dust, and grimy with the smoke of furnaces; and where the noise of hammers and steam-engines, and of carts and trucks hurrying to and fro, makes the country re-echo with the sound of labour; there ages ago in the silent swamp shaded with monster trees, one thin layer of plants after another was formed, year after year, to become the coal we now value so much. In Lancashire, busy Lancashire, the same thing was happening, and even in the middle of Yorkshire and Derbyshire the sea must have come up and washed a silent shore where a vast forest spread out over at least 700 or 800 square miles. In Stafford-shire, too, which is now almost the middle of England, another small coal-field tells the same story, while in South Wales the deep coal-mines and number of coal-seams remind us how for centuries and centuries forests must have flourished and have disappeared over and over again under the sand of the sea.

But what is it that has changed these beds of dead plants into hard, stony coal? In the first place you must remember they have been pressed down under an enormous weight of rocks above them. We can learn something about this even from our common lead pencils. At one time the graphite or pure carbon, of which the blacklead (as we wrongly call it) of our pencils is made, was dug solid out of the earth. but so much has now been used that they are obliged to collect the graphite dust, and press it under a heavy weight, and this makes such solid pieces that they can cut them into leads for ordinary cedar pencils.

Now the pressure which we can exert by machinery is absolutely nothing compared to the weight of all those hundreds of feet of solid rock which lie over the coal-beds, and which has pressed them down for thousands and perhaps millions of years; and besides this, we know that parts of the inside of the earth are very hot, and many of the rocks in which coal is found are altered by heat. So we can picture to ourselves that the coal was not only squeezed into a solid mass, but often much of the oil and gas which were in the leaves of the plants was driven out by heat, and the whole baked, as it were, into one substance. The difference between coal which flames and coal which burns only with a red heat, is chiefly that one has been baked and crushed more than the other. Coal which flames has still got in it the tar and the gas and the oils which the plant stored up in its leaves, and these when they escape again give back the sunbeams in a bright flame. The hard stone coal, on the contrary, has lost a great part of these oils, and only carbon remains, which seizes hold of the oxygen of the air and burns without flame. Coke is pure carbon, which we make artificially by driving out the oils and gases from coal, and the gas we burn is part of what is driven out.

We can easily make coal-gas here in this room. I have brought a tobacco-pipe, the bowl of which is filled with a little powdered coal, and the broad end cemented up with Stourbridge clay. When we place this bowl over a spirit-lamp and make it very hot, the gas is driven out at the narrow end of the pipe and lights easily (see Fig. 53). This is the way all our gas is made, only that furnaces are used to bake the coal in, and the gas is passed into large reservoirs till it is wanted for use.

Fig. 53.

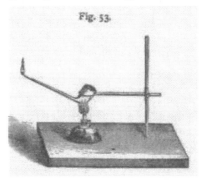

276

You will find it difficult at first to understand how coal can be so full of oil and tar and gases, until you have tried to think over how much of all these there is in plants, and especially in seeds – think of the oils of almonds, of lavender, of cloves, and of caraways; and the oils of turpentine which we get from the pines, and out of which tar is made. When you remember these and many more, and also how the seeds of the club-moss now are largely charged with oil, you will easily imagine that the large masses of coal-plants which have been pressed together and broken and crushed, would give out a great deal of oil which, when made very hot, rises up as gas. You may often yourself see tar oozing out of the lumps of coal in a fire, and making little black bubbles which burst and burn. It is from this tar that James Young first made the paraffin oil we burn in our lamps, and the spirit benzoline comes from the same source.

From benzoline, again, we get a liquid called aniline, from which are made so many of our beautiful dyes – mauve, magenta, and violet; and what is still more curious, the bitter almonds, pear-drops, and many other sweets which children like so well, are actually flavoured by essences which come out of coal-tar. Thus from coal we get not only nearly all our heat and our light, but beautiful colours and pleasant flavours. We spoke just now of the plants of the coal as being without beautiful flowers, and yet we see that long, long after their death they give us lovely colours and tints as beautiful as any in flower-world now.

Think, then, how much we owe to these plants which lived and died so long ago! If they had been able to reason, perhaps they might have said that they did not seem of much use in the world. They had no pretty flowers, and there was no one to admire their beautiful green foliage except a few croaking reptiles, and little crickets and grasshoppers; and they lived and died all on one spot, generation after generation, without seeming to do much good to anything or anybody. Then they were covered up and put out of sight, and down in the dark earth they were pressed all out of shape and lost their beauty and became only black, hard coal. There they lay for centuries and centuries, and thousands and thousands of years, and still no one seemed to want them.

At last, one day, long, long after man had been living on the earth, and had been burning wood for fires, and so gradually using up the trees in the forests, it was discovered that this black stone would burn, and from that time coal has been becoming every day more and more useful. Without it not only should we have been without warmth in our houses, or light in our streets when the stock of forest-wood was used up; but we could never have melted large quantities of iron-stone and extracted the iron. We have proof of this in Sussex. The whole country is full of iron-stone, and the railings of St. Paul's churchyard are made of Sussex iron. Iron-foundries were at work there as long as there was wood enough to supply them, but gradually the works fell into disuse, and the last furnace was put out in the year 1809. So now, because there is no coal in Sussex, the iron lies idle, while in the North, where the iron-stone is near the coal-mines, hundreds of tons are melted out every day.

Again, without coal we could have had no engines of any kind, and consequently no large manufactories of cotton goods, linen goods, or cutlery. In fact, almost everything we use could only have been made with difficulty and in small quantities; and even if we could have made them it would have been impossible to have sent them so quickly all over the world without coal, for we could have had no railways or steamships, but must have carried all goods along canals, and by slow sailing vessels. We ourselves must have taken days to perform journeys now made in a few hours, and months to reach our colonies.

In consequence of this we should have remained a very poor people. Without manufactories and industries we should have had to live chiefly by tilling the ground, and everyone being obliged to toil for daily bread, there would have been much less time or opportunity for anyone to study science, or literature, or history, or to provide themselves with comforts and refinements of life.

All this then, those plants and trees of the far-off ages, which seemed to lead such useless lives, have done and are doing for us. There are many people in the world who complain that life is dull, that they do not see the use of it, and that there seems no work specially for them to do. I would advise such people, whether they are grown up or little children, to read the story of the plants which form the coal. These saw no results during their own short existences, they only lived and enjoyed the bright sunshine, and did their work, and were content. And now thousands, probably millions, of years after they lived and died, England owes her greatness, and we much of our happiness and comfort, to the sunbeams which those plants wove into their lives.

They burst forth again in our fires, in our brilliant lights, and in our engines, and do the greater part of our work; teaching us

> That nothing walks with aimless feet
> That not one life shall be destroyed,
> Or cast as rubbish to the void,
> When God hath made the pile complete.
> *In Memoriam*

Lesson 155

1. Today read the first part of chapter 9 of *The Fairy Land of Science*.
2. Choose a topic from your reading. Write or tell a topic sentence, or main idea sentence, for that topic.

Lecture IX. Bees in the Hive.

I am going to ask you to visit with me to-day one of the most wonderful cities with no human beings in it, and yet it is densely populated, for such a city may contain from twenty thousand to sixty thousand inhabitants. In it you will find streets, but no pavements, for the inhabitants walk along the walls of the houses; while in the houses you will see no windows, for each house just fits its owner, and the door is the only opening in it. Though made without hands these houses are most evenly and regularly built in tiers one above the other; and here and there a few royal palaces, larger and more spacious than the rest, catch the eye conspicuously as they stand out at the corners of the streets.

Some of the ordinary houses are used to live in, while others serve as storehouses where food is laid up in the summer to feed the inhabitants during the winter, when they are not allowed to go outside the walls. Not that the gates are ever shut: that is not necessary, for in this wonderful city each citizen follows the laws; going out when it is time to go out, coming home at proper hours, and staying at home when it is his or her duty. And in the winter, when it is very cold outside, the inhabitants, having no fires, keep themselves warm within the city by clustering together, and never venturing out of doors.

One single queen reigns over the whole of this numerous population, and you might perhaps fancy that, having so many subjects to work for her and wait upon her, she would do nothing but amuse herself. On the contrary, she too obeys the laws laid down for her guidance, and never, except on one or two state occasions, goes out of the city, but works as hard as the rest in performing her own royal duties.

From sunrise to sunset, whenever the weather is fine, all is life, activity, and bustle in this busy city. Though the gates are so narrow that two inhabitants can only just pass each other on their way through them, yet thousands go in and out every hour of the day; some bringing in materials to build new houses, others food and provisions to store up for the winter; and while all appears confusion and disorder among this rapidly moving throng, yet in reality each has her own work to do, and perfect order reigns over the whole.

Even if you did not already know from the title of the lecture what city this is that I am describing, you would no doubt guess that it is a beehive. For where in the whole world, except indeed upon an anthill, can we find so busy, so industrious, or so orderly a community as among the bees? More than a hundred years ago, a blind naturalist, Francois Huber, set himself to study the habits of these wonderful insects and with the help of his wife and an intelligent manservant managed to learn most of their secrets. Before his time all naturalists had failed in watching bees, because if they put them in hives with glass windows, the bees, not liking the light, closed up the windows with cement before they began to work. But Huber invented a hive which he could open and close at will, putting a glass hive inside it, and by this means he was able to surprise the bees at their work. Thanks to his studies, and to those of other naturalists who have followed in his steps, we now know almost as much about the home of bees as we do about our own; and if we follow out to-day the building of a bee-city and the life of its inhabitants, I think you will acknowledge that they are a wonderful community, and that it is a great compliment to anyone to say that he or she is "as busy as a bee."

In order to begin at the beginning of the story, let us suppose that we go into a country garden one fine morning in May when the sun is shining brightly overhead, and that we see hanging from the bough of an old apple-tree a black object which looks very much like a large plum-pudding. On approaching it, however, we see that it is a large cluster or swarm of bees clinging to each other by their legs; each bee with its two fore-legs clinging to the two hinder legs of the one above it. In this way as many as 20,000 bees may be clinging together, and yet they hang so freely that a bee, even from quite the centre of the swarm, can disengage herself from her neighbours and pass through to the outside of the cluster whenever she wishes.

If these bees were left to themselves, they would find a home after a time in a hollow tree, or under the roof of a house, or in some other cavity, and begin to build their honeycomb there. But as we do not wish to lose their honey we will bring a hive, and, holding it under the swarm, shake the bough gently so that the bees fall into it, and cling to the sides as we turn it over on a piece of clean linen, on the stand where the hive is to be.

And now let us suppose that we are able to watch what is going on in the hive. Before five minutes are over the industrious little insects have begun to disperse and to make arrangements in their new home. A number (perhaps about two thousand) of large, lumbering bees of a darker colour than the rest, will it is true, wander aimlessly about the hive, and wait for the others to feed them and house them; but these are the drones, or male bees (3, Fig. 54), who never do any work except during one or two days in their whole lives. But the smaller working bees (1, Fig. 54) begin to be busy at once. Some fly off in search of honey.

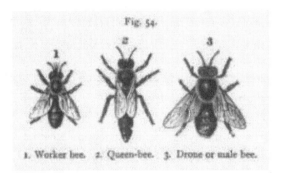

Fig. 54.

1. Worker bee. 2. Queen-bee. 3. Drone or male bee.

Others walk carefully all round the inside of the hive to see if there are any cracks in it; and if there are, they go off to the horse-chestnut trees, poplars, hollyhocks, or other plants which have sticky buds, and gather a kind of gum called "propolis," with which they cement the cracks and make them air-tight. Others again, cluster round one bee (2, Fig. 54) blacker than the rest and having a longer body and shorter wings; for this is the queen-bee, the mother of the hive, and she must be watched and tended.

But the largest number begin to hang in a cluster from the roof just as they did from the bough of the apple tree. What are they doing there? Watch for a little while and you will soon see one bee come out from among its companions and settle on the top of the inside of the hive, turning herself round and round, so as to push the other bees back, and to make a space in which she can work. Then she will begin to pick at the under part of her body with her fore-legs, and will bring a scale of wax from a curious sort of pocket under her abdomen. Holding this wax in her claws, she will bite it with her hard, pointed upper jaws, which move to and fro sideways like a pair of pincers, then, moistening it with her tongue into a kind of paste, she will draw it out like a ribbon and plaster it on the top of the hive.

After that she will take another piece; for she has eight of these little wax-pockets, and she will go on till they are all exhausted. Then she will fly away out of the hive, leaving a small lump on the hive ceiling or on the bar stretched across it; then her place will be taken by another bee who will go through the same manoeuvres. This bee will be followed by another, and another, till a large wall of wax has been built, hanging from the bar of the hive as in Fig. 55, only that it will not yet have cells fashioned in it.

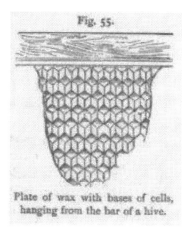

Fig. 55.

Plate of wax with bases of cells, hanging from the bar of a hive.

Meanwhile the bees which have been gathering honey out of doors begin to come back laden. But they cannot store their honey, for there are no cells made yet to put it in; neither can they build combs with the rest, for they have no wax in their wax-pockets. So they just go and hang quietly on to the other bees, and there they remain for twenty-four hours, during which time they digest the honey they have gathered, and part of it forms wax and oozes out from the scales under their body. Then they are prepared to join the others at work and plaster wax on to the hive.

And now, as soon as a rough lump of wax is ready, another set of bees come to do their work. These are called the nursing bees, because they prepare the cells and feed the young ones. One of these bees, standing on the roof of the hive, begins to force her head into the wax, biting with her jaws and moving her head to and fro. Soon she has made the beginning of a round hollow, and then she passes on to make another, while a second bee takes her place and enlarges the first one. As many as twenty bees will be employed in this way, one after another, upon each hole before it is large enough for the base of a cell.

Lesson 156

1. Today read the next part of chapter 9 of *The Fairy Land of Science*.
2. Choose a topic from your reading. Write or tell a topic sentence, or main idea sentence, for that topic.

Lecture IX. Bees in the Hive. Continued…

Meanwhile another set of nursing bees have been working just in the same way on the other side of the wax, and so a series of hollows are made back to back all over the comb. Then the bees form the walls of the cells and soon a number of six-sided tubes, about half an inch deep, stand all along each side of the comb ready to receive honey or bee-eggs.

You can see the shape of these cells in c,d, Fig. 56, and notice how closely they fit into each other. Even the ends are so shaped that, as they lie back to back, the bottom of one cell (B, Fig. 56) fits into the space between the ends of three cells meeting it from the opposite side (A, Fig. 56), while they fit into the spaces around it. Upon this plan the clever little bees fill every atom of space, use the least possible quantity of wax, and make the cells lie so closely together that the whole comb is kept warm when the young bees are in it.

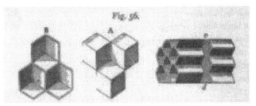

There are some kinds of bees who do not live in hives, but each one builds a home of its own. These bees – such as the upholsterer bee, which digs a hole in the earth and lines it with flowers and leaves, and the mason bee, which builds in walls – do not make six-sided cells, but round ones, for room is no object to them. But nature has gradually taught the little hive-bee to build its cells more and more closely, till they fit perfectly within each other. If you make a number of round holes close together in a soft substance, and then squeeze the substance evenly from all sides, the rounds will gradually take a six-sided form, showing that this is the closest shape into which they can be compressed. Although the bee does not know this, yet as gnaws away every bit of wax that can be spared she brings the holes into this shape.

As soon as one comb is finished, the bees begin another by the side of it, leaving a narrow lane between, just broad enough for two bees to pass back to back as they crawl along, and so the work goes on till the hive is full of combs.

As soon, however, as a length of about five or six inches of the first comb has been made into cells, the bees which are bringing home honey no longer hang to make it into wax, but begin to store it in the cells. We all know where the bees go to fetch their honey, and how, when a bee settles on a flower, she thrusts into it her small tongue-like proboscis, which is really a lengthened under-lip, and sucks out the drop of honey. This she swallows, passing it down her throat into a honey-bag or first stomach, which lies between her throat and her real stomach, and when she gets back to the hive she can empty this bag and pass honey back through her mouth again into the honey-cells.

But if you watch bees carefully, especially in the spring-time, you will find that they carry off something else besides honey. Early in the morning, when the dew is on the ground, or later in the day, in moist shady places, you may see a bee rubbing itself against a flower, or biting those bags of yellow dust or pollen which we mentioned in Lecture VII. When she has covered herself with pollen, she will brush it off with her feet, and, bringing it to her mouth, she will moisten and roll it into a little ball, and then pass it back from the first pair of legs to the second and so to the third or hinder pair. Here she will pack it into a little hairy groove called a "basket" in the joint of one of the hind legs, where you may see it, looking like a swelled joint, as she hovers among the flowers. She often fills both hind legs in this way, and when she arrives back at the hive the nursing bees take the lumps form her, and eat it themselves, or mix it with honey to feed the young bees; or, when they have any to spare, store it away in old honey-cells to be used by-and-by. This is the dark, bitter stuff called "bee- bread" which you often find in a honeycomb, especially in a comb which has been filled late in the summer.

When the bee has been relieved of the bee-bread she goes off to one of the clean cells in the new comb, and, standing on the edge, throws up the honey from the honey-bag into the cell. One cell will hold the contents of many honey-bags, and so the busy little workers have to work all day filling cell after cell, in which the honey lies uncovered, being too thick and sticky to flow out, and is used for daily food – unless there is any to spare, and then they close up the cells with wax to keep for the winter.

Meanwhile, a day or two after the bees have settled in the hive, the queen-bee begins to get very restless. She goes outside the hive and hovers about a little while, and then comes in again, and though generally the bees all look very closely after her to keep her indoors, yet now they let her do as she likes. Again she goes out, and again back, and then, at last, she soars up into the air and flies away. But she is not allowed to go alone. All the drones of the hive rise up after her, forming a guard of honour to follow her wherever she goes.

In about half-an-hour she comes back again, and then the working bees all gather round her, knowing that now she will remain quietly in the hive and spend all her time in laying eggs; for it is the queen-bee who lays all the eggs in the hive. This she begins to do about two days after her flight. There are now many cells ready besides those filled with honey; and, escorted by several bees, the queen-bee goes to one of these, and, putting her head into it remains there a second as if she were examining whether it would make a good home for the young bee. Then, coming out, she turns round and lays a small, oval, bluish-white egg in the cell. After this she takes no more notice of it, but goes on to the next cell and the next, doing the same thing, and laying eggs in all the empty cells equally on both sides of the comb. She goes on so quickly that she sometimes lays as many as 200 eggs in one day.

Then the work of the nursing bees begins. In two or three days each egg has become a tiny maggot or larva, and the nursing bees put into its cell a mixture of pollen and honey which they have prepared in their own mouths, thus making a kind of sweet bath in which the larva lies. In five or six days the larva grows so fat upon this that it nearly fills the cell, and then the bees seal up the mouth of the cell with a thin cover of wax, made of little rings and with a tiny hole in the centre.

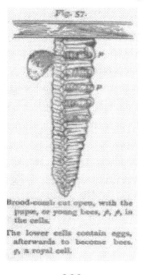

Fig. 57.

Brood-comb cut open, with the pupæ, or young bees, *A, A,* in the cells.
The lower cells contain eggs, afterwards to become bees. *p,* a royal cell.

As soon as the larva is covered in, it begins to give out from its under-lip a whitish, silken film, made of two threads of silk glued together, and with this it spins a covering or cocoon all round itself, and so it remains for about ten days more. At last, just twenty-one days after the egg was laid, the young bee is quite perfect, lying in the cell as in Fig. 57, and she begins to eat her way through the cocoon and through the waxen lid, and scrambles out of her cell. Then the nurses come again to her, stroke her wings and feed her for twenty-four hours, and after that she is quite ready to begin work, and flies out to gather honey and pollen like the rest of the workers.

By this time the number of working bees in the hive is becoming very great, and the storing of honey and pollen-dust goes on very quickly. Even the empty cells which the young bees have left are cleaned out by the nurses and filled with honey; and this honey is darker than that stored in clean cells, and which we always call "virgin honey" because it is so pure and clear.

At last, after six weeks, the queen leaves off laying worker- eggs, and begins to lay, in some rather larger cells, eggs from which drones, or male bees, will grow up in about twenty days. Meanwhile the worker-bees have been building on the edge of the cones some very curious cells (q, Fig. 57) which look like thimbles hanging with the open side upwards, and about every three days the queen stops in laying drone-eggs and goes to put an egg in one of these cells. Notice that she waits three days between each of these peculiar layings, because we shall see presently that there is a good reason for her doing so.

Lesson 157

1. Today read the next part of chapter 9 of *The Fairy Land of Science.*
2. Choose a topic from your reading. Write or tell a topic sentence, or main idea sentence, for that topic.

Lecture IX. Bees in the Hive. Continued...

The nursing bees take great care of these eggs, and instead of putting ordinary food into the cell, they fill it with a sweet, pungent jelly, for this larva is to become a princess and a future queen bee. Curiously enough, it seems to be the peculiar food and the size of the cell which makes the larva grow into a mother-bee which can lay eggs, for if a hive has the misfortune to lose its queen, they take one of the ordinary worker-larvae and put it into a royal cell and feed it with jelly, and it becomes a queen-bee. As soon as the princess is shut in like the others, she begins to spin her cocoon, but she does not quite close it as the other bees do, but leaves a hole at the top.

At the end of sixteen days after the first royal egg was laid, the eldest princess begins to try to eat her way out of her cell, and about this time the old queen becomes very uneasy, and wanders about distractedly. The reason of this is that there can never be two queen-bees in one hive, and the queen knows that her daughter will soon be coming out of her cradle and will try to turn her off her throne. So, not wishing to have to fight for her kingdom, she makes up her mind to seek a new home and take a number of her subjects with her. If you watch the hive about this time you will notice many of the bees clustering together after they have brought in their honey, and hanging patiently, in order to have plenty of wax ready to use when they start, while the queen keeps a sharp look-out for a bright, sunny day, on which they can swarm: for bees will never swarm on a wet or doubtful day if they can possibly help it, and we can easily understand why, when we consider how the rain would clog their wings and spoil the wax under their bodies.

Meanwhile the young princess grows very impatient, and tries to get out of her cell, but the worker-bees drive her back, for they know there would be a terrible fight if the two queens met. So they close up the hole she has made with fresh wax after having put in some food for her to live upon till she is released.

At last a suitable day arrives, and about ten or eleven o'clock in the morning the old queen leaves the hive, taking with her about 2000 drones and from 12,000 to 20,000 worker-bees, which fly a little way clustering round her till she alights on the bough of some tree, and then they form a compact swarm ready for a new hive or to find a home of their own.

Leaving them to go their way, we will now return to the old hive. Here the liberated princess is reigning in all her glory; the worker-bees crowd round her, watch over her, and feed her as though they could not do enough to show her honour. But still she is not happy. She is restless, and runs about as if looking for an enemy, and she tries to get at the remaining royal cells where the other young princesses are still shut in. But the workers will not let her touch them, and at last she stands still and begins to beat the air with her wings and to tremble all over, moving more and more quickly, till she makes quite a loud, piping noise.

Hark! What is that note answering her? It is a low, hoarse sound, and it comes from the cell of the next eldest princess. Now we see why the young queen has been so restless. She knows her sister will soon come out, and the louder and stronger the sound becomes within the cell, the sooner she knows the fight will have to begin. And so she makes up her mind to follow her mother's example and to lead off a second swarm. But she cannot always stop to choose a fine day, for her sister is growing very strong and may come out of her cell before she is off. And so the second, or after swarm, gets ready and goes away. And this explains why princesses' eggs are laid a few days apart, for if they were laid all on the same day, there would be no time for one princess to go off with a swarm before the other came out of her cell. Sometimes, when the workers are not watchful enough, two queens do meet, and then they fight till one is killed; or sometimes they both go off with the same swarm without finding each other out. But this only delays the fight till they get into the new hive; sooner or later one must be killed.

And now a third queen begins to reign in the old hive, and she is just as restless as the preceding ones, for there are still more princesses to be born. But this time, if no new swarm wants to start, the workers do not try to protect the royal cells. The young queen darts at the first she sees, gnaws a hole with her jaws, and, thrusting in her sting through the hole in the cocoon, kills the young bee while it is still a prisoner. She then goes to the next, and the next, and never rests till all the young princesses are destroyed. Then she is contented, for she knows no other queen will come to dethrone her. After a few days she takes her flight in the air with the drones, and comes home to settle down in the hive for the winter.

Then a very curious scene takes place. The drones are no more use, for the queen will not fly out again, and these idle bees will never do any work in the hive. So the worker-bees begin to kill them, falling upon them, and stinging them to death, and as the drones have no stings they cannot defend themselves, and in a few days there is not a drone, nor even a drone-egg, left in the hive. This massacre seems very sad to us, since the poor drones have never done any harm beyond being hopelessly idle. But it is less sad when we know that they could not live many weeks, even if they were not attacked, and, with winter coming, the bees cannot afford to feed useless mouths, so a quick death is probably happier for them than starvation.

And now all the remaining inhabitants of the hive settle down to feeding the young bees and laying in the winter's store. It is at this time, after they have been toiling and saving, that we come and take their honey; and from a well-stocked hive we may even take 30 lbs. without starving the industrious little inhabitants. But then we must often feed them in return and give them sweet syrup in the late autumn and the next early spring when they cannot find any flowers.

Although the hive has now become comparatively quiet and the work goes on without excitement, yet every single bee is employed in some way, either out of doors or about the hive. Besides the honey collectors and the nurses, a certain number of bees are told off to ventilate the hive. You will easily understand that where so many insects are packed closely together the heat will become very great, and the air impure and unwholesome. And the bees have no windows that they can open to let in fresh air, so they are obliged to fan it in from the one opening of the hive. The way in which they do this is very interesting. Some of the bees stand close to the entrance, with their faces towards it, and opening their wings, so as to make them into fans, they wave them to and fro, producing a current of air. Behind these bees, and all over the floor of the hive, there stand others, this time with their backs towards the entrance, and fan in the same manner, and in this way air is sent into all the passages.

Another set of bees clean out the cells after the young bees are born, and make them fit to receive honey, while others guard the entrance of the hive to keep away the destructive wax-moth, which tries to lay its eggs in the comb so that its young ones may feed on the honey. All industrious people have to guard their property against thieves and vagabonds, and the bees have many intruders, such as wasps and snails and slugs, which creep in whenever they get a chance. If they succeed in escaping the sentinel bees, then a fight takes place within the hive, and the invader is stung to death.

Sometimes, however, after they have killed the enemy, the bees cannot get rid of his body, for a snail or slug is too heavy to be easily moved, and yet it would make the hive very unhealthy to allow it to remain. In this dilemma the ingenious little bees fetch the gummy "propolis" from the plant-buds and cement the intruder all over, thus embalming his body and preventing it from decaying.

And so the life of this wonderful city goes on. Building, harvesting, storing, nursing, ventilating and cleaning from morn till night, the little worker-bee lives for about eight months, and in that time has done quite her share of work in the world. Only the young bees, born late in the season, live on till the next year to work in the spring. The queen-bee lives longer, probably about two years, and then she too dies, after having had a family of many thousands of children.

We have already pointed out that in our fairy-land of nature all things work together so as to bring order out of apparent confusion. But though we should naturally expect winds and currents, rivers and clouds, and even plants to follow fixed laws, we should scarcely have looked for such regularity in the life of the active, independent busy bee. Yet we see that she, too, has her own appointed work to do, and does it regularly and in an orderly manner. In this lecture we have been speaking entirely of the bee within the hive, and noticing how marvellously her instincts guide her in her daily life. But within the last few years we have learnt that she performs a most curious and wonderful work in the world outside her home and that we owe to her not only the sweet honey to eat, but even in a great degree the beauty and gay colours of the flowers which she visits when collecting it. This work will form the subject of our next lecture, and while we love the little bee for her constant industry, patience, and order within the hive, we shall, I think, marvel at the wonderful law of nature which guides her in her unconscious mission of love among the flowers which grow around it.

Lesson 158

1. You have just one chapter left to read!
2. Read the first part of chapter 10 of *The Fairy Land of Science*.
3. Choose a topic from your reading. Write or tell a topic sentence, or main idea sentence, for that topic.

Lecture X Bees And Flowers

Whatever thoughts each one of you may have brought to the lecture to-day, I want you to throw them all aside and fancy yourself to be in a pretty country garden on a hot summer's morning. Perhaps you have been walking, or reading, or playing, but it is getting too hot now to do anything; and so you have chosen the shadiest nook under the old walnut-tree, close to the flower-bed on the lawn, and would almost like to go to sleep if it were not too early in the day.

As you lie there thinking of nothing in particular, except how pleasant it is to be idle now and then, you notice a gentle buzzing close to you, and you see that on the flower-bed close by, several bees are working busily among the flowers. They do not seem to mind the heat, nor to wish to rest; and they fly so lightly and look so happy over their work that it does not tire you to look at them.

That great humble-bee takes it leisurely enough as she goes lumbering along, poking her head into the larkspurs, and remaining so long in each you might almost think she had fallen asleep. The brown hive-bee on the other hand, moves busily and quickly among the stocks, sweet peas, and mignonette. She is evidently out on active duty, and means to get all she can from each flower, so as to carry a good load back to the hive. In some blossoms she does not stay a moment, but draws her head back directly she has popped it in, as if to say "No honey there." But over the full blossoms she lingers a little, and then scrambles out again with her drop of honey, and goes off to seek more in the next flower.

Let us watch her a little more closely. There are plenty of different plants growing in the flower-bed, but, curiously enough, she does not go first to one kind and then to another; but keeps to one, perhaps the mignonette, the whole time till she flies away. Rouse yourself up to follow her, and you will see she takes her way back to the hive. She may perhaps stop to visit a stray plant of mignonette on her way, but no other flower will tempt her till she has taken her load home.

Then when she comes back again she may perhaps go to another kind of flower, such as the sweet peas, for instance, and keep to them during the next journey, but it is more likely that she will be true to her old friend the mignonette for the whole day.

We all know why she makes so many journeys between the garden and the hive, and that she is collecting drops of honey from each flower, and carrying it to be stored up in the honeycomb for winter's food. How she stores it, and how she also gathers pollen-dust for her bee-bread, we saw in the last lecture; to-day we will follow her in her work among the flowers, and see, while they are so useful to her, what she is doing for them in return.

We have already learnt from the life of a primrose that plants can make better and stronger seeds when they can get pollen-dust from another plant, than when they are obliged to use that which grows in the same flower; but I am sure you will be very much surprised to hear that the more we study flowers the more we find that their colours, their scent, and their curious shapes are all so many baits and traps set by nature to entice insects to come to the flowers, and carry this pollen-dust from one to the other.

So far as we know, it is entirely for this purpose that the plants form honey in different parts of the flower, sometimes in little bags or glands, as in the petals of the buttercup flower, sometimes in clear drops, as in the tube of the honeysuckle. This food they prepare for the insects, and then they have all sorts of contrivances to entice them to come and fetch it.

You will remember that the plants of the coal had no bright or conspicuous flowers. Now we can understand why this was, for there were no flying insects at that time to carry the pollen- dust from flower to flower, and therefore there was no need of coloured flowers to attract them. But little by little, as flies, butterflies, moths and bees began to live in the world, flowers too began to appear, and plants hung out these gay-coloured signs, as much as to say, "Come to me, and I will give you honey if you will bring me pollen-dust in exchange, so that my seeds may grow healthy and strong."

We cannot stop to inquire to-day how this all gradually came about, and how the flowers gradually put on gay colours and curious shapes to tempt the insects to visit them; but we will learn something about the way they attract them now, and how you may see it for yourselves if you keep your eyes open.

For example, if you watch the different kinds of grasses, sedges and rushes, which have such tiny flowers that you can scarcely see them, you will find that no insects visit them. Neither will you ever find bees buzzing round oak-trees, nut-trees, willows, elms or birches. But on the pretty and sweet-smelling apple-blossoms, or the strongly scented lime-trees, you will find bees, wasps, and plenty of other insects.

The reason of this is that grasses, sedges, rushes, nut-trees, willow, and the others we have mentioned, have all of them a great deal of pollen-dust, and as the wind blows them to and fro, it wafts the dust from one flower to another, and so these plants do not want the insects, and it is not worth their while to give out honey, or to have gaudy or sweet-scented flowers to attract them.

But wherever you see bright or conspicuous flowers you may be quite sure that the plants want the bees or some other winged insect to come and carry their pollen for them. Snowdrops hanging their white heads among their green leaves, crocuses with their violet and yellow flowers, the gaudy poppy, the large-flowered hollyhock or the sunflower, the flaunting dandelion, the pretty pink willow-herb, the clustered blossoms of the mustard and turnip flowers, the bright blue forget-me-not and the delicate little yellow trefoil, all these are visited by insects, which easily catch sight of them as they pass by and hasten to sip their honey.

Sir John Lubbock has shown that bees are not only attracted by bright colours, but that they even know one colour from another. He put some honey on slips of glass with coloured papers under them, and when he had accustomed the bees to find the honey always on the blue glass, he washed this glass clean, and put the honey on the red glass instead. Now if the bees had followed only the smell of the honey, they would have flown to the red glass, but they did not. They went first to the blue glass, expecting to find the honey on the usual colour, and it was only when they were disappointed that they went off to the red.

Is it not beautiful to think that the bright pleasant colours we love so much in flowers, are not only ornamental, but that they are useful and doing their part in keeping up healthy life in our world?

Neither must we forget what sweet scents can do. Have you never noticed the delicious smell which comes from beds of mignonette, thyme, rosemary, mint, or sweet alyssum, from the small hidden bunches of laurustinus blossom, or from the tiny flowers of the privet? These plants have found another way of attracting the insects; they have no need of bright colours, for their scent is quite as true and certain a guide. You will be surprised if you once begin to count them up, how many white and dull or dark-looking flowers are sweet-scented, while gaudy flowers, such as tulip, foxglove and hollyhock, have little or no scent. And then, just as in the world we find some people who have everything to attract others to them, beauty and gentleness, cleverness, kindliness, and loving sympathy, so we find some flowers, like the beautiful lily, the lovely rose, and the delicate hyacinth, which have colour and scent and graceful shapes all combined.

Lesson 159

1. Read the next part of chapter 10 of *The Fairy Land of Science*.
2. Choose a topic from your reading. Write or tell a topic sentence, or main idea sentence, for that topic.

Lecture X. Bees And Flowers. Continued…

But we are not yet nearly at an end of the contrivances of flowers to secure the visits of insects. Have you not observed that different flowers open and close at different times? The daisy receives its name day's eye, because it opens at sunrise and closes at sunset, while the evening primrose (Aenothera biennis) and the night campion (Silene noctiflora) spread out their flowers just as the daisy is going to bed.

What do you think is the reason of this? If you go near a bed of evening primroses just when the sun is setting, you will soon be able to guess, for they will then give out such a sweet scent that you will not doubt for a moment that they are calling the evening moths to come and visit them. The daisy opens by day, because it is visited by day insects, but those particular moths which can carry the pollen-dust of the evening primrose, fly only by night, and if this flower opened by day other insects might steal its honey, while they would not be the right size or shape to touch its pollen-bags and carry the dust.

It is the same if you pass by a honeysuckle in the evening; you will be surprised how much stronger its scent is than in the day-time. This is because the sphinx hawk-moth is the favourite visitor of that flower, and comes at nightfall, guided by the strong scent, to suck out the honey with its long proboscis, and carry the pollen-dust.

Again, some flowers close whenever rain is coming. The pimpernel (Anagallis arvensis) is one of these, hence its name of the "Shepherd's Weather-glass." This little flower closes, no doubt, to prevent its pollen-dust being washed away, for it has no honey; while other flowers do it to protect the drop of honey at the bottom of their corolla. Look at the daisies for example when a storm is coming on; as the sky grows dark and heavy, you will see them shrink up and close till the sun shines again. They do this because in each of the little yellow florets in the centre of the flower there is a drop of honey which would be quite spoiled if it were washed by the rain.

And now you will see why cup-shaped flowers so often droop their heads – think of the harebell, the snowdrop, the lily-of-the-valley, the campanula, and a host of others; how pretty they look with their bells hanging so modestly from the slender stalk! They are bending down to protect the honey-glands within them, for if the cup became full of rain or dew the honey would be useless, and the insects would cease to visit them.

But it is not only necessary that the flowers should keep their honey for the insects, they also have to take care and keep it for the right kind of insect. Ants are in many cases great enemies to them, for they like honey as much as bees and butterflies do, yet you will easily see that they are so small that if they creep into a flower they pass the anthers without rubbing against them, and so take the honey without doing any good to the plant. Therefore we find numberless contrivances for keeping the ants and other creeping insects away. Look for example at the hairy stalk of the primrose flower;

those little hairs are like a forest to a tiny ant, and they protect the flower from his visits. The Spanish catchfly (Silene otites), on the other hand, has a smooth, but very gummy stem, and on this the insects stick, if they try to climb. Slugs and snails too will often attack and bite flowers, unless they are kept away by thorns and bristles, such as we find on the teazel and the burdock. And so we are gradually learning that everything which a plant does has its meaning, if we can only find it out, and that even very insignificant hair has its own proper use, and when we are once aware of this a flower-garden may become quite a new world to us if we open our eyes to all that is going on in it.

But as we cannot wander among many plants to-day, let us take a few which the bees visit, and see how they contrive not to give up their honey without getting help in return. We will start with the blue wood-geranium, because from it we first began to learn the use of insects to flowers.

More than a hundred years ago a young German botanist, Christian Conrad Sprengel, noticed some soft hairs growing in the centre of this flower, just round the stamens, and he was so sure that every part of a plant is useful, that he set himself to find out what these hairs meant. He soon discovered that they protected some small honey-bags at the base of the stamens, and kept the rain from washing the honey away, just as our eyebrows prevent the perspiration on our faces from running into our eyes. This led him to notice that plants take great care to keep their honey for insects, and by degrees he proved that they did this in order to tempt the insects to visit them and carry off their pollen.

The first thing to notice in this little geranium flower is that the purple lines which ornament it all point directly to the place where the honey lies at the bottom of the stamens, and actually serve to lead the bee to the honey; and this is true of the veins and marking of nearly all flowers except of those which open by night, and in these they would be useless, for the insects would not see them.

Fig. 58.

Geranium sylvaticum, the Wood Geranium.

When the geranium first opens, all its ten stamens are lying flat on the corolla or coloured crown, as in the left-hand flower in Fig. 58, and then the bee cannot get at the honey. But in a short time five stamens begin to raise themselves and cling round the stigma or knob at the top of the seed-vessel, as in the middle flower. Now you would think they would leave their dust there. But no! the stigma is closed up so tight that the dust cannot get on to the sticky part. Now, however, the bee can get at the honey-glands on the outside of the raised stamens; and as he sucks it, his back touches the anthers or dust-bags, and he carries off the pollen. Then, as soon as all their dust is gone, these five stamens fall down, and the other five spring up. Still, however, the stigma remains closed, and the pollen of these stamens, too, may be carried away to another flower. At last these five also fall down, and then, and not till then, the stigma opens and lays out its five sticky points, as you may see in the right-hand flower, Fig. 58.

But its own pollen is all gone, how then will it get any? It will get it from some bee who has just taken it from another and younger flower; and thus you see the blossom is prevented from using its own pollen, and made to use that of another blossom, so that its seeds may grow healthy and strong.

The garden nasturtium, into whose blossom we saw the humble-bee poling his head, takes still more care of its pollen-dust. It hides its honey down at the end of its long spur, and only sends out one stamen at a time instead of five like the geranium; and then, when all the stamens have had their turn, the sticky knob comes out last for pollen from another flower.

Fig. 59.

Flower of the Dead-Nettle (*Lamium album*).
1, Whole. 2, Cut in half.
f, Fringe of hairs protecting honey at base. s, Stigma.
a, Anthers of stamens. l, Lip of flower.

All this you may see for yourselves if you find geraniums* in the hedges, and nasturtiums in you garden. But even if you have not these, you may learn the history of another flower quite as curious, and which you can find in any field or lane even near London. The common dead-nettle (Fig. 59) takes a great deal of trouble in order that the bee may carry off its pollen. When you have found one of these plants, take a flower from the ring all round the stalk and tear it gently open, so that you can see down its throat. There, just at the very bottom, you will find a thick fringe of hairs, and you will guess at once that these are to protect a drop of honey below. Little insects which would creep into the flower and rob it of its honey without touching the anthers of the stamens cannot get past these hairs, and so the drop is kept till the bee comes to fetch it. (*The scarlet and other bright geraniums of our flower-gardens are not true geraniums, but pelargoniums. You may, however, watch all these peculiarities in them if you cannot procure the true wild geranium.)

Lesson 160

1. Read the next part of chapter 10 of *The Fairy Land of Science*.
2. Choose a topic from your reading. Write or tell a topic sentence, or main idea sentence, for that topic.

Lecture X. Bees And Flowers.   Continued...

Now look for the stamens; there are four of them, two long and two short, and they are quite hidden under the hood which forms the top of the flower. How will the bee touch them? If you were to watch one, you would find that when the bee alights on the broad lip and thrusts her head down the tube, she first of all knocks her back against the little forked tip. This is the sticky stigma, and she leaves there any dust she has brought from another flower; then, as she must push far in to reach the honey, before she comes out again has carried away the yellow powder on her back, ready to give it to the next flower.

Do you remember how we noticed at the beginning of the lecture that a bee always likes to visit the same kind of plant in one journey? You see now that this is very useful to the flowers. If the bee went from a dead-nettle to a geranium, the dust would be lost, for it would be of no use to any other plant but a dead-nettle. But since the bee likes to get the same kind of honey each journey, she goes to the same kind of flowers, and places the pollen-dust just where it is wanted.

There is another flower, called the Salvia, which belongs to the same family as our dead-nettle, and I think you will agree with me that its way of dusting the bee's back is most clever. The Salvia (Fig. 60) is shaped just like the dead-nettle, with a hood and a broad lip, but instead of four stamens it has only two, the other two being shrivelled up. The two that are left have a very strange shape, for the stalk or filament of the stamen is very short, while the anther, which is in most flowers two little bags stuck together, has here grown out into a long thread, with a little dust-bag at one end only.

In 1, Fig. 60, you only see one of these stems, because the flower is cut in half, but in the whole flower, one stands on each side just within the lip. Now, when the bee puts her head into the tube to reach the honey, she passes right between these two swinging anthers, and knocking against the end pushes it before her and so brings the dust-bag plump down on her back, scattering the dust there! you can easily try this by thrusting a pencil into any Salvia flower, and you will see the anther fall.

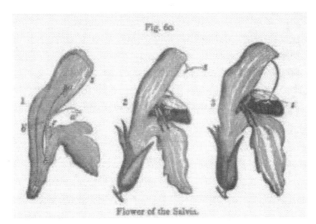

Fig. 60.

Flower of the Salvia.

You will notice that all this time the bee does not touch the sticky stigma which hangs high above her, but after the anthers are empty and shrivelled the stalk of the stigma grows longer, and it falls lower down. By-and-by another bee, having pollen on her back, comes to look for honey, and as she goes into No. 3, she rubs against the stigma and leaves upon it the dust from another flower.

Tell me, has not the Salvia, while remaining so much the same shape as the dead-nettle, devised a wonderful contrivance to make use of the visits of the bee?

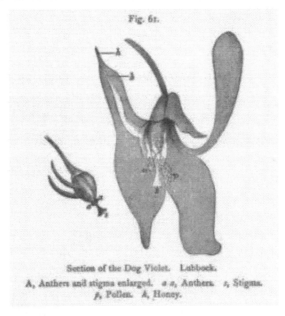

Fig. 61.

Section of the Dog Violet. Lubbock.
A, Anthers and stigma enlarged. *a a*, Anthers. *s*, Stigma.
p, Pollen. *h*, Honey.

The common sweet violet (Viola odorata) or the dog violet (Viola canina), which you can gather in any meadow, give up their pollen-dust in quite a different way from the Salvia, and yet it is equally ingenious. Everyone has noticed what an irregular shape this flower has, and that one of its purple petals has a curious spur sticking out behind. In the tip of this spur and in the spur of the stamen lying in it the violet hides its honey, and to reach it the bee must press past the curious ring of orange-tipped bodies in the middle of the flower. These bodies are the anthers, Fig. 61, which

294

fit tightly round the stigma, so that when the pollen-dust, which is very dry, comes out of the bags, it remains shut in by the tips as if in a box. Two of these stamens have spurs which lie in the coloured spur of the flower, and have honey at the end of them. Now, when the bee shakes the end of the stigma, it parts the ring of anthers, and the fine dust falls through upon the insect.

Let us see for a moment how wonderfully this flower is arranged to bring about the carrying of the pollen, as Sprengel pointed out years ago. In the first place, it hangs on a thin stalk, and bends its head down so that the rain cannot come near the honey in the spur, and also so that the pollen-dust falls forward into the front of the little box made by the closed anthers. Then the pollen is quite dry, instead of being sticky as in most plants. This is in order that it may fall easily through the cracks. Then the style or stalk of the stigma is very thin and its tip very broad, so that it quivers easily when the bee touches it, and so shakes the anthers apart, while the anthers themselves fold over to make the box, and yet not so tightly but that the dust can fall through when they are shaken. Lastly, if you look at the veins of the flower, you will find that they all point towards the spur where the honey is to be found, so that when the sweet smell of the flower has brought the bee, she cannot fail to go in at the right place.

Two more flowers still I want us to examine together, and then I hope you will care to look at every flower you meet, to try and see what insects visit it, and how its pollen-dust is carried. These two flowers are the common Bird's-foot trefoil (Lotus corniculatus) and the Early Orchis (Orchis mascula), which you may find in almost any moist meadow in the spring and early summer.

The Bird's-foot trefoil, Fig. 62, you will find almost anywhere all through the summer, and you will know it from other flowers very like it by its leaf, which is not a true trefoil, for behind the three usual leaflets of the clover and the shamrock leaf, it has two small leaflets near the stalk. The flower, you will notice, is shaped very like the flower of a pea, and indeed it belongs to the same family, called the Papilionaceae or butterfly family, because the flowers look something like an insect flying.

Lesson 161

1. Read the next part of chapter 10 of *The Fairy Land of Science*.
2. Choose a topic from your reading. Write or tell a topic sentence, or main idea sentence, for that topic.

Lecture X. Bees And Flowers. Continued…

In all these flowers the top petal stands up like a flag to catch the eye of the insect, and for this reason botanists call it the "standard". Below it are two side-petals called the "wings," and if you pick these off you will find that the remaining two petals are joined together at the tip in a shape like the keel of a boat. For this reason they are called the "keel". Notice as we pass that these two last petals have in them a curious little hollow or depression, and if you look inside the "wings" you will notice a little knob that fits into this hollow, and so locks the two together. We shall see by-and-by that this is important.

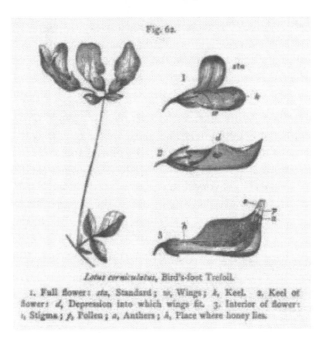

Fig. 62.

Lotus corniculatus, Bird's-foot Trefoil.

1. Full flower: *sta*, Standard; *w*, Wings; *k*, Keel. 2. Keel of flower: *d*, Depression into which wings fit. 3. Interior of flower: *s*, Stigma; *p*, Pollen; *a*, Anthers; *h*, Place where honey lies.

Next let us look at the half-flower when it is cut open, and see what there is inside. There are ten stamens in all, enclosed with the stigma in the keel; nine are joined together and one is by itself. The anthers of five of these stamens burst open while the flower is still a bud, but the other stamens go on growing, and push the pollen-dust, which is very moist and sticky, right up into the tip of the keel. Here you see it lies right round the stigma, but as we saw before in the geranium, the stigma is not ripe and sticky yet, and so it does not use the pollen grains.

Now suppose that a bee comes to the flower. The honey she has to fetch lies inside the tube, and the one stamen being loose she is able to get her proboscis in. But if she is to be of any use to the flower she must uncover the pollen-dust. See how cunningly the flower has contrived this. In order to put her head into the tube the bee must stand upon the wings, and her weight bends them down. but they are locked to the keel by the knob fitting in the hole, and so the keel is pushed down too, and the sticky pollen-dust is uncovered and comes right against the stomach of the bee and sticks there! As soon as she has done feeding and flies away, up go the wings and the keel with them, covering up any pollen that remains ready for next time. Then when the bee goes to another flower, as she touches the stigma as well as the pollen, she leaves some of the foreign dust upon it, and the flower uses that rather than its own, because it is better for its seeds. If however no bee happens to come to one of these flowers, after a time the stigma becomes sticky and it uses its own pollen: and this is perhaps one reason why the bird's-foot trefoil is so very common, because it can do its own work if the bee does not help it.

Now we come lastly to the Orchis flower. Mr. Darwin has written a whole book on the many curious and wonderful ways in which orchids tempt bees and other insects to fertilize them. We can only take the simplest, but I think you will say that even this blossom is more like a conjuror's box than you would have supposed it possible that a flower could be.

Let us examine it closely. It has six deep-red covering leaves, Fig. 62, three belonging to the calyx or outer cup, and three belonging to the corolla or crown of the flower; but all six are coloured alike, except that the large on in front, called the "lip", has spots and lines upon it which will suggest to you at once that they point to the honey.

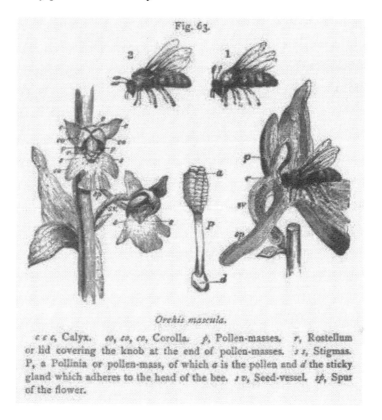

Fig. 63.

Orchis mascula.

c c c, Calyx. *co, co, co,* Corolla. *p,* Pollen-masses. *r,* Rostellum or lid covering the knob at the end of pollen-masses. *s s,* Stigmas. P, a Pollinia or pollen-mass, of which *a* is the pollen and *d* the sticky gland which adheres to the head of the bee. *s v,* Seed-vessel. *sp,* Spur of the flower.

But where are the anthers, and where is the stigma? Look just under the arch made by those three bending flower-leaves, and there you will see two small slits, and in these some little club-shaped bodies, which you can pick out with the point of a needle. One of these enlarged is shown. It is composed of sticky grains of pollen held together by fine threads on the top of a thin stalk; and at the bottom of the stalk there is a little round body. This is all that you will find to represent the stamens of the flower. When these masses of pollen, or pollinia as they are called, are within the flower, the knob at the bottom is covered by a little lid, shutting them in like the lid of a box, and just below this lid you will see two yellowish lumps, which are very sticky. These are the top of the stigma, and they are just above the seed-vessel, which you can see in the lowest flower in the picture.

Now let us see how this flower gives up its pollen. When a bee comes to look for honey in the orchis, she alights on the lip, and guided by the lines makes straight for the opening just in front of the stigmas. Putting her head into this opening she pushes down into the spur, where by biting the inside skin she gets some juicy sap. Notice that she has to bite, which takes time.

You will see at once that she must touch the stigmas in going in, and so give them any pollen she has on her head. but she also touches the little lid and it flies instantly open, bringing the glands at the end of the pollen-masses against her head. These glands are moist and sticky, and while she is gnawing the inside of the spur they dry a little and cling to her head and she brings them out with her. Darwin once caught a bee with as many as sixteen of these pollen-masses clinging to her head.

But if the bee went into the next flower with these pollinia sticking upright, she would simply put them into the same slits in the next flower, she would not touch them against the stigma. Nature, however, has provided against this. As the bee flies along, the glands sticking to its head dry more and more, and as they dry they curl up and drag the pollen-masses down, so that instead of standing upright, as in 1, Fig. 63, they point forwards, as in 2.

And now, when the bee goes into the next flower, she will thrust them right against the sticky stigmas, and as they cling there the fine threads which hold the grains together break away, and the flower is fertilized.

If you will gather some of these orchids during your next spring walk in the woods, and will put a pencil down the tube to represent the head of the bee you may see the little box open, and the two pollen-masses cling to the pencil. Then if you draw it out you may see them gradually bend forwards, and by thrusting your pencil into the next flower you may see the grains of pollen break away, and you will have followed out the work of a bee.

Lesson 162
1. Read the last part of chapter 10 of *The Fairy Land of Science*.
2. Choose a topic from your reading. Write or tell a topic sentence, or main idea sentence, for that topic.

Lecture X. Bees And Flowers. Continued…

Do not such wonderful contrivances as these make us long to know and understand all the hidden work that is going on around us among the flowers, the insects, and all forms of life? I have been able to tell you but very little, but I can promise you that the more you examine, the more you will find marvellous histories such as these in simple field-flowers.

Long as we have known how useful honey was to the bee, and how it could only get it from flowers, yet it was not till quite lately that we have learned to follow out Sprengel's suggestion, and to trace the use which the bee is to the flower. But now that we have once had our eyes opened, every flower teaches us something new, and we find that each plant adapts itself in a most wonderful way to the insects which visit it, both so as to provide them with honey, and at the same time to make them unconsciously do it good service.

And so we learn that even among insects and flowers, those who do most for others, receive most in return. The bee and the flower do not either of them reason about the matter, they only go on living their little lives as nature guides them, helping and improving each other. Think for a moment how it would be, if a plant used up all its sap for its own life, and did not give up any to make the drop of honey in its flower. The bees would soon find out that these particular flowers were not worth visiting, and the flower would not get its pollen-dust carried, and would have to do its own work and grow weakly and small. Or suppose on the other hand that the bee bit a hole in the bottom of the flower, and so got at the honey, as indeed they sometimes do; then she would not carry the pollen-dust, and so would not keep up the healthy strong flowers which make her daily food.

But this, as you see, is not the rule. On the contrary, the flower feeds the bee, and the bee quite unconsciously helps the flower to make its healthy seed. Nay more; when you are able to read all that has been written on this subject, you will find that we have good reason to think that the flowerless plants of the Coal Period have gradually put on the beautiful colours, sweet scent, and graceful shapes of our present flowers, in consequence of the necessity of attracting insects, and thus we owe our lovely flowers to the mutual kindliness of plants and insects.

And is there nothing beyond this? Surely there is. Flowers and insects, as we have seen, act without thought or knowledge of what they are doing; but the law of mutual help which guides them is the same which bids you and me be kind and good to all those around us, if we would lead useful and happy lives. And when we see that the Great Power which rules over our universe makes each work for the good of all, even in such humble things as bees and flowers; and that beauty and loveliness come out of the struggle and striving of all living things; then, if our own life be sometimes difficult, and the struggle hard to bear, we learn from the flowers that the best way to meet our troubles is to lay up our little drop of honey for others, sure that when they come to sip it they will, even if unconsciously, give us new vigour and courage in return.

And now we have arrived at the end of those subjects which we selected out of the Fairy-land of Science. You must not for a moment imagine, however, that we have in any way exhausted our fairy domain; on the contrary, we have scarcely explored even the outskirts of it. The "History of a Grain of Salt," "A Butterfly's Life," or "The Labours of an Ant," would introduce us to fairies and wonders quite as interesting as those of which we have spoken in these Lectures. While "A Flash of Lightning," "An Explosion in a Coal-mine," or "The Eruption of a Volcano," would bring us into the presence of terrible giants known and dreaded from time immemorial.

But at least we have passed through the gates, and have learnt that there is a world of wonder which we may visit if we will; and that it lies quite close to us, hidden in every dewdrop and gust of wind, in every brook and valley, in every little plant or animal. We have only to stretch out our hand and touch them with the wand of inquiry, and they will answer us and reveal the fairy forces which guide and govern them; and thus pleasant and happy thoughts may be conjured up at any time, wherever we find ourselves, by simply calling upon nature's fairies and asking them to speak to us. Is it not strange, then, that people should pass them by so often without a thought, and be content to grow up ignorant of all the wonderful powers ever active in the world around them?

Neither is it pleasure alone which we gain by a study of nature. We cannot examine even a tiny sunbeam, and picture the minute waves of which it is composed, travelling incessantly from the sun, without being filled with wonder and awe at the marvellous activity and power displayed in the infinitely small as well as in the infinitely great things of the universe. We cannot become familiar with the facts of gravitation, cohesion, or crystallization, without realizing that the laws of nature are fixed, orderly, and constant, and will repay us with failure or success according as we act ignorantly or wisely; and thus we shall begin to be afraid of leading careless, useless, and idle lives. We cannot watch the working of the fairy "life" in the primrose or the bee, without learning that living beings as well as inanimate things are governed by these same laws of nature; nor can we contemplate the mutual adaptation of bees and flowers without acknowledging that it teaches the truth that those succeed best in life who, whether consciously or unconsciously, do their best for others.

And so our wanderings in the Fairy-land of Science will not be wasted, for we shall learn how to guide our own lives, while we cannot fail to see that the forces of nature, whether they are apparently mechanical, as in gravitation or heat; or intelligent, as in living beings, are one and all the voice of the Great Creator, and speak to us of His Nature and His Will.

The End.

Lesson 163

1. Let's review the parts of a story.
    - The plot of a story is how the main character solves his problem. The story begins when the problem is introduced. The story ends when the problem is solved.
    - The setting is where and when the story takes place.
    - The main character is who the story is about.
    - The theme is why the story was told. What's the point of the story?
2. Choose a book you have read and tell its main character, setting, plot, and theme.

Lesson 164

1. An inference is an educated guess based on what you have read. If I said that I was headed out to lunch, maybe you could infer that I was hungry. If you called and asked if I could come over, and I said that I was headed out to the dance class, you could infer that I was busy with something else and couldn't come now.
2. Make an inference based on this sentence. (Answers)
    - I heard a pattering across the floor, so I flicked on the light and then let out a shriek!
    - What do you think happened based on the clues? Make an inference.
3. Make an inference based on this sentence. (Answers)
    - After spending the afternoon hanging up the lights only to have a dark house, he regretted buying the light strands at the dollar store.
4. Make an inference based on this sentence. (Answers)
    - She thanked her mom for dinner and then tried to look as if she were politely wiping her mouth with her napkin as she spat out her bite into it.

Lesson 165

1. Write a synonym, or word with similar meaning, for each of the following words.
   - agitate, diffuse, acquaintance, dilate, keen, subdue, tumultuous

Lesson 166

1. As you round out the year, we'll read a little more, just for fun. Keep reading for fun always, even if it's a little kid book. Sometimes they are the best! Here's another story by Mark Twain, "The Million Pound Banknote." Read the first part of the story.

When I was twenty-seven years old, I worked in San Francisco for a mining broker. I was an expert in all the details of buying and selling stock. I was alone in the world, but I was intelligent and people thought well of me. So with these two things, I felt that I would soon be rich, and I was happy enough with that.

My time was my own after work. On Saturdays I was in the habit of putting that time into a little boat which I took sailing. One day I went too far out to sea, and was lost. Just as night fell, and I had almost lost hope, I was picked up by a small ship which was going to London. It was a long and stormy journey, and they made me work as a sailor to pay for my trip. When I stepped ashore in London my clothes were ragged and worn out, and I had only a dollar in my pocket. This money gave me somewhere to stay, and food to eat for twenty-four hours. During the next twenty-four hours I went without food and shelter.

About ten o'clock on the following morning, I was tired and hungry. In Portland Place, a child dropped a delicious big pear on the road after he had taken just one bite. I stopped, of course, and stared at that muddy pear as if it was treasure. My mouth watered for it, my stomach desired it, my whole body begged for the pear. But every time I made a move to get it someone saw what I was doing. Of course I straightened up then, and looked bored, and pretended that I hadn't even been thinking about the pear. This kept happening and happening, and I still couldn't get the pear

I was getting desperate enough to take the pear despite all the shame of people watching me do it. But then a window behind me opened, and a gentleman spoke to me, saying 'Step in here, please'.

A well-dressed servant let me into the house. He took me to a richly-decorated room where a couple of elderly gentlemen were sitting. They sent away the servant, and made me sit down. They had just finished their breakfast. The sight of the food which was left over was almost too much for me. I could hardly think clearly in front of that food, but I was not asked to try any of it, so there was nothing I could do.

Now, something had been happening a little earlier. I didn't know about it until many days afterwards, but I will tell you about it now. A few days before, those two old brothers had been having a pretty hot argument. They had ended up agreeing to decide who was right by a bet, which is the English way of settling everything.

You will remember that the Bank of England once printed two banknotes of a million pounds each. These were to be used in a business deal with a foreign country. For some reason only one of these banknotes had been used. The other was still the vaults of the Bank.

Well, the brothers were having a chat, and they started to wonder what would happen to a completely honest and intelligent stranger who was in London with no friends, and with no money but that million-pound bank-note, and no way to explain why he had that bank-note with him. Brother A said he would starve to death; Brother B said he wouldn't.

Brother A said he couldn't take the banknote to a bank because he would be arrested at once. So they went on arguing till Brother B said he would bet twenty thousand pounds that the man would live thirty days, at least, on that million, and keep out of jail as well. Brother A accepted the bet. Brother B went down to the Bank and bought that note. Then the brother dictated a letter, which one of his clerks wrote out in a beautiful round handwriting. After that the two brothers sat looking out of the window all day. They were looking for the right man to give the letter and bank-note to.

They saw many honest people go past, but they were not intelligent enough. Other people were intelligent, but they not were honest enough. Many people were honest and intelligent, but they were not poor enough. If they were poor enough, they were not strangers in London. There was always something wrong, until I came along. However the brothers agreed that I was exactly what they were looking for; so they had chosen me without arguing about it. And now here I was, waiting to find out why they wanted to see me.

The brothers began to ask me questions about myself, and soon they knew my story. Finally, they told me that I was the man they had been looking for. I said I was very pleased, and asked why they were looking for someone. One of the brothers handed me an envelope, and said I would find the explanation inside. I started to open it, but he told me not to do that. Instead I should take the letter back to the place where I was staying. I should read it carefully, and think about what I would do next.

I was puzzled. I wanted to find out more, but now they didn't want to talk to me. So I went out of the house, feeling hurt and insulted. It seemed that the two men had been having some kind of stupid joke with me. Yet I had to put up with it, because I was too poor and hungry to be able to get angry about insults from rich and powerful people.

I would have picked up the pear now and eaten it in front of everybody, but now it was gone. I had lost the pear because I had been called into the house. This made me even more upset with those two men. As soon as I was out of sight of the house I opened my envelope, and saw that there was money inside! I started to think differently about those people, I can tell you!

Lesson 167

1. Read the next section of "The Million Pound Banknote."

I did not lose a moment. I pushed the money into my vest pocket, and ran to the nearest cheap eating house. Well, how I ate! At last I couldn't hold any more food. Then I took out my money and unfolded it. I had one glimpse and I nearly fainted. It was a million pounds. That was five million dollars! It made me giddy to think about it.

I was so astonished that I must have sat there for almost a minute blinking at the banknote. When I remembered where I was, the first thing I noticed was the landlord. He had seen the banknote, and it seemed as though the sight had turned him to stone. He was worshipping the banknote with all his body and soul, but he couldn't move a hand or foot. At that moment I knew what I should do. It was the only logical thing I could do. I passed the note to him, and said carelessly 'Give me the change, please.'

Then he came back to normal. He made a thousand apologies for not being able to give me so much change. I couldn't get him to touch the banknote. He wanted to look at it all the time. He couldn't seem to get enough of looking at it, but he would not touch it. It was as if it was something too precious for his poor human hands to touch. I said 'I am sorry if this is a bit of a problem for you, but I must insist. Please change it, I haven't anything else.'

But he said that wasn't important. He was quite happy to let the small amount be paid another time. I said I might not be in his neighborhood again for a long time. But he said it didn't matter, he could wait. Also, I could have anything I wanted, any time I chose, and just pay him back whenever I was ready. He said he wasn't afraid to trust a rich gentleman like me, just because I had a sense of humour and liked to make a joke with people in the way I was dressed.

By this time another customer was entering, and the landlord hinted to me to put the banknote out of sight. He bowed at me all the way to the door. Then I went straight to that house and those brothers. I wanted to correct the mistake which had been made before the police started hunting for me to correct the mistake as well. I was pretty nervous; in fact, I was pretty badly frightened. Of course, there was no way that it was my fault. But I knew people well enough to know that if they find they've given a beggar a million-pound banknote when they thought it was one pound, they will be furious with him instead of being upset that they did not look properly, as they should have done.

As I approached the house I began to worry less. All was quiet there, which made me feel sure the huge mistake had not been discovered yet. I rang the doorbell. The same servant appeared. I asked for those gentlemen whom I had talked to earlier.

'They are gone.' He said this in the slightly rude, cold way of that type of servant.

'Gone? Gone where?'

'On a journey.'

'They have gone to the Continent. I cannot say what road they are taking. They said they would be back next month.'

'A month! Oh, this is awful! You must tell me how to send a message to them. It's extremely important. Also I must see someone else in their family at once. There's been a very big mistake. When they find out what has happened they'll be back before night. Will you tell them I've been here? I will keep coming back here until the mistake is put right, and they needn't be afraid.'

'They said you would be here in an hour to make inquiries. I must tell you there is no problem, they'll be here on time and expect you.'

So I had to give up and go away. It was all a big puzzle! I felt as though I was going mad. What did the servant mean when he said they would be here 'on time'? I remembered the letter that was in the envelope with the banknote. Maybe that would explain. I took the letter out and read it. This is what it said:

> *You look as though you are an intelligent and honest man. We get the idea that you are poor and a stranger in London. You will find some money in this envelope. You can have it for thirty days, without interest. Come back to this house at the end of the month. I have made a bet. If I win it you shall have any employment that I can give you. That is, any job that you know how to do and can do well.*

There was no signature on the letter, no address, and no date. Well, here was a strange situation to be in! You know what had gone on before all this, but I did not. It was just a deep, dark puzzle to me. I hadn't the least idea what was going on. I did not know whether harm was meant to me or kindness. I went into a park, and sat down to try to think it out. I needed to work out the best thing to do.

At the end of an hour this is what I had decided. Maybe those men want something good for me, maybe they do not. There is no way to decide which is correct – so let it go. They are up to some game, or scheme, or experiment, of some kind. There is no way to know what it is – let it go. There's a bet on me. But I have no way to find out what the bet is – let it go. That finishes with the things I do not know about. All the rest is solid, and may be put into place with certainty. I can ask the Bank of England to put this banknote into the account of the man it belongs to. They'll do it, for they know him, although I don't. But they will ask me how I came to have the banknote with me. If I tell the truth, they'll put me in the asylum, and a lie will get me into jail.

The same thing will happen if I try to put the money in a bank somewhere or to borrow money on it. I have got to carry this great burden around until those men come back, whether I want to or not. It is useless to me, as useless as a handful of ashes. Yet I must take care of it, and watch over it, while I beg for my living. I couldn't give it away if I tried. No honest man would accept it or any robber want anything to do with it.

Lesson 168

1. Read the next section of "The Million Pound Banknote."

Those brothers are safe. Even if I lose their banknote, or burn it, they are still safe. They can stop payment, and the Bank will return the money to them. But in the meantime I've got to suffer for a month without getting anything from it. But if I help to win that bet, whatever that bet is, they promised me that I would get a job. That would be good. Men like the brothers would be able to give me very good employment.

I started to think a lot about that job. My hopes began to rise high. I was sure that the salary would be large. It would begin in a month; after that I should be all right. Pretty soon I was feeling very happy again. By this time I was walking around the streets once more. The sight of a tailor's shop gave me a strong desire to get out of the rags I was wearing. I wanted to be properly dressed once more. Could I afford it? No; I had nothing in the world but a million pounds.

So I made myself go past the shop. But soon I came back again. I was feeling very tempted by the idea of getting a suit. I must have passed that shop six times while I struggled with temptation. At last I gave in; I had to. I asked in the shop if they had a badly-fitting suit that no-one wanted. The fellow I spoke to nodded his head towards another fellow, and gave me no answer. I went to the fellow, and he pointed to another fellow, and still no-one spoke to me.

I waited till this other fellow had finished what he was doing. He then took me into a back room, and went through a pile of rejected suits. He selected the rattiest one for me, but I put it on. It didn't fit, and wasn't in any way attractive. But it was a new suit, and I very much wanted to have it; so I didn't complain.

I said, very politely 'It would be a big help to me if you could wait some days for the money. I am not carrying any small change on me.'

The fellow's face showed that he did not believe I could pay for the suit. He said 'Oh, you haven't any small change? Well, of course not, I didn't expect it. I'd only expect gentlemen like you to carry large change.'

This made me rather annoyed. So I said 'My friend, you shouldn't always judge a stranger by the clothes he wears. I am quite able to pay for this suit. I simply thought that it would be inconvenient for you to have to give change from a large banknote.'

His behaviour changed a bit when he heard that. But he still acted as though he was much better than I was. He said 'I didn't mean any particular harm. But if we are criticizing each other, I might say that you have no reason to think that we can't give change for any note that you are carrying around. You are wrong, because we can.'

I handed the note to him, and said 'Oh, all right then; I apologize.'

He smiled and took the banknote. He had one of those large smiles which goes all around the face. There are folds in it, and it curves, and it looks like where you have thrown a brick into a pond. Then when he looked quickly at the banknote this smile froze solid. His face turned yellow, and the smile looked like those wavy, worm-like spreads of lava which have hardened on the side of Mount Vesuvius.

I never before saw a smile which froze into place like that. The man stood there holding the bill, and looking like that until the shop owner came over to see what was the matter. He said, briskly: 'Well, what's up? What's the trouble? What does the customer still need? Come on; get him his change, Tod; get him his change.'

Tod replied 'Get him his change! It's easy to say, Sir; but look at the bill yourself.' The owner took a look at the banknote and whistled under his breath with a lot of feeling. Then he dived for the pile of rejected clothing. He began to throw the clothes around, all the time talking excitedly to himself;

'Sell an eccentric millionaire such a terrible suit as that! Tod's a fool – a born fool. He is always doing something like this. He pushes every millionaire away from this place, because he can't tell a millionaire from a tramp, and never could. Ah, here's the thing I am after. Please get those things off, Sir, and throw them in the fire.'

'Please put on this shirt and this suit for me. It's just right, exactly right. It is not showy, but rich and modest. It was made for a foreign prince – you may know him. His name is His Serene Highness the Hospodar of Halifax. He had to leave the suit with us and order something suitable for a funeral instead. His mother was going to die – but she didn't. That's all right; things can't always happen the way we – that is, the way they – there! The trousers are all right, they fit you perfectly, Sir. Now the waistcoat; aha, right again! And the coat; look at that, now! Perfect – the whole thing! In all my time as a tailor I have never seen something fit so well.'

I said that I was very pleased.

'Quite right, Sir, quite right. I have to say it will do as a temporary suit for you. But wait. When we have measured you, we will make something even better. Come, Tod, take a book and pen; get busy. Length of leg, 32 inches.' And so on. Before I could say a word he had measured me, and was giving orders for me to get dress-suits, morning suits, shirts, and all sorts of clothing.

When I got a chance I said: 'But, my dear Sir, I can't order these things. I don't know when I can pay you unless you give me change for the banknote.'

'Don't know! Weak words, Sir, weak words. For ever – that's right, Sir. I can wait for ever. Tod, rush these things through, and send them to the gentleman's address without wasting time. Let the less important customers wait.'

Lesson 169

1. Read the next section of "The Million Pound Banknote."

'You are quite right, sir, quite right. One moment – let me show you out of the shop, sir. There – good day, sir, good day.'

Well, don't you see what was going to happen after that? I simply started buying whatever I wanted, and asking for change. Within a week I had everything I needed to be comfortable. I stayed at an expensive private hotel in Hanover Square. I ate my dinners there, but for breakfast I kept going to Harris's humble eating place, the place where I had got my first meal on my million-pound banknote. Thanks to me, things were going well for Harris. The news had got out that the foreign crazy man who carried million-pound bills in his pocket always ate at the place. That was enough. From being a poor, struggling, little business that did not make much money, Harris' eating place had become famous, and overcrowded with customers.

Harris was so grateful that kept lending me money, and would not let me say no. So, I was a poor man who had money to spend. I lived like the rich and the great. I judged that sooner or later things were going to go wrong; but I was in this mess now, and I had to swim across it or drown.

You see, I thought that disaster had to happen eventually. This was the serious side, the sober side, yes, the tragic side, of a situation which would otherwise have been completely ridiculous. In the dark of the night, the tragedy part was always in my mind. It was always warning and always worrying me and so I moaned and turned around in my bed, and sleep was hard to find. But in the cheerful daylight the tragedy disappeared, and I walked on air. I was so happy that I felt almost drunk with it.

You can't blame me for being happy. I had become rather well-known in the biggest city in the world. This stopped me from thinking clearly about things. You could not buy a newspaper, English, Scottish, or Irish, without reading one or more stories about the 'vest-pocket million-pounder' and things I had done or said.

At first, when the newspapers mentioned me, I was at the bottom of the gossip column. Next, I was listed above the lower aristocracy, and next above the barons. It went on and on. As my reputation increased I was mentioned earlier and earlier in the gossip column, until I reached as high as it was possible to go. There I stayed, being mentioned above all aristocrats but the royal family, and above all churchmen apart from the top one in all England. But I knew that although I was well-known, I had not earned my fame.

Then came the greatest moment of all – the official recognition, so to speak. *Punch* magazine showed a cartoon of me! In a single instant this changed me from someone who was notorious to someone who was famous! Yes, my name and reputation were secure now; my place was established. I might be still joked about, but with respect, not rudely. I could be smiled at, but not laughed at. The time for that had gone by. *Punch* had pictured me dressed in rags, bargaining with a Beefeater for the Tower of London. Well, you can imagine how this affected a young fellow like me. No-one had ever taken notice of me before, and now suddenly I couldn't say anything that didn't catch on and get repeated everywhere.

When I left the house I kept overhearing people telling each other, 'There he goes; that's him!' I couldn't eat breakfast without a crowd watching me; couldn't appear at the opera without being watched by a thousand opera glasses. Why, I just swam in glory all day long – that is all I can say about it.

You know, I even kept my old suit of rags. Every now and then I went out in them. I enjoyed the old pleasure of buying something unimportant and being insulted, and then showing the person insulting me the million-pound banknote. But I couldn't keep that up. The illustrated papers made the suit well-known. Now when I went out in it I was recognized at once and a crowd followed me. If I tried to buy something the man would offer me his whole shop on credit before I could even pull my note on him.

When I had been famous for about ten days I went to do my duty to my country. That is to say, I visited the American ambassador. He received me with enthusiasm, but complained that I had been slow in coming to him. He said that there was only one way to get his forgiveness. One of his guests for his dinner-party that night had been taken ill, and I should take the vacant place. I said I would, and we started talking. It turned out that he and my father had been friends while boys at school. Later they were students together at Yale University, and had always been warm friends until my father's death.

So then he required me to visit him at his house any time I was free, and of course I was very happy to do this. In fact, I was more than willing; I was glad. When the crash came, he might somehow be able to save me from total destruction. I didn't know how, but I hoped that he might think of a way. I didn't dare to tell him everything, because it had all become so complicated. I did wish that I might have been able to come to him before I started this strange life in London.

No, I couldn't tell him now. I was in too deep. That is, too deep to tell my new friend about the bet. However, I did not think things were completely out of control. Because you see, even though I was borrowing money, I was being very careful – that is, I was not spending more than my salary. Of course, I couldn't know what my salary was going to be. However I had a good enough idea. If I won the bet I could choose any job which that rich old gentleman could give me. Of course I would have to be good at the job, but I would be – I hadn't any doubt about that.

Lesson 170

1. Read the next section of "The Million Pound Banknote."

I didn't worry about the bet. I had always been lucky. I estimated that I would be paid six hundred to a thousand pounds a year. Let us say that I might earn six hundred for the first year, and this would go up year by year, until I showed that I was worth a thousand a year. At present I only owed money for my first year's salary. Everybody had been trying to lend me money but I had always made up an excuse so that I did not need to take it. I only actually owed £300. The other £300 was money which I had used to buy things and for my food and a place to stay.

I believed that the money from my second year's salary would get me through the rest of the month – and I intended to make very sure that I went on being cautious and economical. When the month was over my employer would be back from his journey. Then I would be all right once more. I would immediately give up my next two years' salary to people whom I owed money, and get right down to my work.

It was a lovely dinner-party of fourteen. These were the Duke and Duchess of Shoreditch, and their daughter the Lady Anne-Grace-Eleanor-Celeste-and-so-forth-de-Bohun, the Earl and Countess of Newgate, Viscount Cheapside, Lord and Lady Blatherskite, There were also some men and women who were not aristocrats and the ambassador and his wife and daughter. The daughter had a friend who was visiting her, an English girl who was twenty-two years old. Her name was Portia Langham and I fell in love with her in two minutes. And she fell in love with me – I could see it clearly.

There was also another guest, an American – but I shall say more of this later. People were still outside the dining room, sharpening their appetites for dinner and giving icy looks to those who arrived late. The servant announced that a Mr. Lloyd Hastings had arrived. As soon as he had finished being polite to his host, Hastings saw me. He came straight over with his hand stretched out in greeting; then he stopped just before he shook my hand. He said, with an embarrassed look:

'I beg your pardon, sir, I thought I knew you. Are you the – the …'.

'Vest-pocket monster? I am, indeed. Don't be afraid to call me by my nickname; I'm used to it.'

'Well, well, this is a surprise. Once or twice I've seen your name together with that nickname. I never thought that you could be the Henry Adams people were talking about. Just six months ago you were working for Blake Hopkins in San Francisco. You also used to work nights on a second job, helping me arrange and check the papers and statistics on the Gould and Curry Mine Extension. I am amazed that you are in London, and a millionaire, and a huge celebrity! Why, it's like a fairy story. I just can't believe it; can't comprehend it. Give me a minute, because my head is spinning.'

'The fact is, Lloyd, that things are about the same for both you and I. I can't really understand it myself.'

'Dear me, it is amazing, isn't it? Why just three months ago we went to the What Cheer restaurant – went there at two in the morning. We had a meal and coffee because we had been working hard for six hours over those papers. I tried to persuade you to come to London with me. I offered to get you permission to be away from your job and pay all your expenses, and give you something extra if I succeeded in making the sale. You would not listen to me. You said I wouldn't succeed, and you couldn't afford to lose business and it would take you a long time to get the hang of things again when you got back home. And yet here you are. How odd it all is! How did it happen that you came after all, and whatever gave you this incredible start?'

'Oh, just an accident. It's a long story – a romance, one may say. I'll tell you all about it, but only at the end of this month. But how is your business going?'

His cheerfulness vanished like a breath, and he said with a sigh: 'You were a true prophet, Hal, a true prophet. I wish I hadn't come. I don't want to talk about it.'

'But I want to hear the whole story, every word.'

'I'm so grateful! Just to find someone who is interested in me and what I am doing. After what has happened to me here here – Lord! I could go down on my knees for it!' He gripped my hand hard, and straightened himself up. He was all right and cheerful after that, so then we got ready for the dinner – which didn't happen.

'No; the usual thing happened. This always happens with that horrible and annoying English system – no-one could decide who was the most important person there, so there was no dinner. Englishmen always eat dinner before they go out to dinner, because they know that this might happen. But nobody ever warns the stranger, and so he walks placidly into the trap. Of course, nobody was hurt this time, because we had all eaten dinner already. None of us were new to this except Hastings, and when Hastings was invited by the Ambassador he was told that because of this the English custom there would not be any dinner.

Because it is usual to act as though dinner will happen, everybody took a lady and we went down to the dining-room. There the usual problems began. The Duke of Shoreditch wanted to sit at the head of the table, saying that he was more important than the Ambassador, but I refused to let him have his way.

Lesson 171

1. Read the next section of "The Million Pound Banknote."

I said that in the gossip column I came before all dukes who were not relatives of the king. Therefore I should go first on this occasion. The question couldn't be settled, of course, no matter how much we argued about it – and we did argue. So we all went back to the drawing-room again and ate lunch – for lunch you get a plate of sardines and a strawberry, and you stand together and eat that.

For lunch the question of who goes first is not so difficult. The two most important people toss a coin. The one that wins is the first to start eating his strawberry, and the loser gets the shilling. The next two toss a coin, then the next two, and so on. After lunch, card tables were brought out, and we all played cribbage. We bet sixpence a game. The English never play any game for amusement. They won't play if they can't win something or lose something, but they don't care if they win or lose.

We had a lovely time. Certainly two of us had a lovely time – and those two were Miss Langham and I. I was so bewitched by her that I couldn't keep score if the points went too high. When I won a game I never noticed and just started again. I would have lost every game, only the girl was the same. You see she was just as bewitched as I. So neither of us ever completed a game. But we didn't bother to wonder why we didn't; we just knew we were happy, and didn't want to know anything else, and didn't want to be interrupted.

And I told her – I did, indeed – told her I loved her. Well, she blushed until her hair turned red. But she liked it; she said she did. Oh, there was never such an evening! Every time I marked the score I added a little message; every time she scored she replied to it. I couldn't even say 'Two for this' without adding, 'My, how sweet you do look!' and she would say, 'Two, four, and a pair are eight – oh, do you think so?'. Then she would peep at me from under her eyelashes, you know, and try to look all sweet. Oh, it was just too wonderful!

Well, I was perfectly honest and I told her everything. I said that I hadn't any money at all. All I had was the million-pound note she'd heard so much about, and that note didn't belong to me. That made her curious. Talking quietly I told her the whole story right from the start. It nearly killed her with laughing. I couldn't see what made her laugh, but there it was. Every half-minute some new detail would make her laugh again, and I would have to stop for as much as a minute and a half to give her a chance to stop laughing. She laughed so much she could hardly stand – yes, she did; I never saw anything like it.

I never before saw a painful story – a story of a person's troubles and worries and fears – make someone laugh like that. So I loved her even more, seeing she could be so cheerful when there wasn't anything to be cheerful about. I joked that I might soon need that kind of wife the way my future looked. I told her that of course, we should have to wait a couple of years, till I could pay off my debts with my salary. She joked back that she didn't mind that, only she hoped I would be as careful as possible with the money. I must try not to spend any of our third year's pay.

Then she began to get a little worried, and wondered if we were making a mistake. So she decided my salary for the first year should be higher than before. This was good sense, though it made me feel a little less sure than I had been that everything would work as we planned. However it gave me a good business idea, and told it to her without trying to hide anything.

'Portia, dear, would you mind going with me on the day when I confront those old gentlemen?'

She looked a little worried about this, but said 'N-o; if my being with you would make you happier. But – do you think that it would be good manners for me to come?'

'No, I don't think that it would – in fact, I'm afraid it wouldn't. But, you see, it's just so very important that-'

'Then I'll go anyway, whether it's good manners or not,' she said, with a beautiful and generous enthusiasm. 'Oh, I shall be so happy to think I'm helping you!'

'You won't just be helping – you'll be doing it all. You're beautiful and so lovely that no-one can argue with you. With you there I can increase our salary till I break those good old fellows, and they'll never have the heart to struggle.'

Oh! You should have seen the blush on her face, and the shine in her happy eyes!

She said 'It is wicked to say nice things that you know are not true! What you say is wrong, but I'll still go with you. Maybe then you will see that other people don't see things the way you do. That will teach you a lesson'

Was I less worried after that? Did I think that everything would go well? You may judge by this fact: right then and there I decided that I would ask for a salary of twelve hundred pounds for the first year. But I didn't tell her; I saved it for a surprise. All the way home I was so happy I couldn't think properly. I heard Hastings talking, but did not hear a word. When he and I entered my parlor, he brought me down to earth. He was amazed by my many comforts and luxuries.

'Let me just stand here for a little while and look at everything. Dear me! it's a palace – it's just a palace! And in it everything anybody could want, including a warm coal fire and supper standing ready. Henry, it doesn't just make me realize how rich you are; it makes me realize, it makes me completely understand, how poor I am – how poor, and how miserable, how defeated and crushed!'

This language really upset me. It scared me right out of my dreams. Again I remembered that I was standing on a half-inch crust, and there was a volcano underneath.

Lesson 172

1. Read the next section of "The Million Pound Banknote."

I had been dreaming without knowing it. In fact I had been dreaming for a while now, but I hadn't allowed myself to know it. But now – oh, dear! I remembered that I owed a lot of money. I had not a cent in the world, and a lovely girl's happiness or sadness depended on me. There was nothing in my future but a salary which I might never get! Oh, I was ruined past hope! Nothing could save me!

As I thought these things, Hastings said 'Henry, just the left-over bits of your daily income would–'

'Oh, my daily income! Here, drink down this Scotch, and cheer up. Or, no – you're hungry; sit down and-'

'Not a bite for me; I'm not hungry. I can't eat these days, but I'll drink with you till I drop. Come!'

'I'm with you! Ready? Here we go! Now then, Lloyd, tell your story while I prepare the drinks.'

'Why? I mean, do you want to hear it over again? Henry, you alarm me. Didn't I tell you the whole story on the way here?'

'I'm afraid I did not hear a word of it.'

'Henry, this is a serious thing. It troubles me. What did you have to drink at the ambassador's?'

Then I suddenly realized what had happened, and I admitted it like a man.

'I was not listening, because at the ambassador's, I took the dearest girl in this world into my heart.'

So then he came over with a rush, and we shook hands, and shook, and shook till our hands ached. He was not angry with me for not having heard a story which had lasted while we walked three miles. He just sat down, like the patient, good fellow that he was, and told his story all over again.

In brief his story was this. Lloyd had come to England with what he thought was a grand opportunity. He had the chance to sell the new part of the Gould and Curry Mine. He had to give a million dollars to the people who had found that part, and if he sold for more than a million dollars, he could keep the rest.

He had worked hard. He had talked to anyone who might help him. He had tried everything possible without being dishonest. Now he had spent nearly all the money he had in the world. Still he had not been able to get a single capitalist to listen to him, and his money would run out at the end of the month. In a word, he was ruined. Then he jumped up and cried out:

'Henry, you can save me! You can save me, and you're the only man in the universe that can. Will you do it? Won't you do it? Give me a million dollars and pay for my journey home and you can sell the mine extension instead! Please don't, don't refuse!'

I was in a kind of agony. I was just about to say, 'Lloyd, I also have no money. I don't have a penny, and I am in debt!' But then a white-hot idea came flaming through my head. I gripped my jaws together, and calmed myself down until I was as cold as a capitalist. When I spoke, I was all business and completely in control of myself

'I will save you. But I will do it in a way that would be fair to you. You have worked hard, and taken many chances. I don't need to buy mines. In a busy place like London I can keep my money moving without buying anything. It's what I do, all the time. Here is what I'll do for you. I know all about that mine, of course. I know it is very valuable, and if anybody asks me I will swear that is the truth. In a fortnight you will sell all your shares for three million cash by using my name as much as you like. We'll share out the money you get.'

Do you know, he was so mad with joy that he would have danced on the furniture until he had smashed it to little pieces? He would have broken everything in the place, if I hadn't tripped him up and tied him. Then he lay there, perfectly happy, saying,

'I may use your name! Your name – think of it! Man, crowds of these rich Londoners will come to buy, they'll fight for those shares! I've got my life in order, it's all sorted out, and I'll never forget you as long as I live!'

In less than twenty-four hours all London was talking! I hadn't anything to do, day after day, but sit at home and say to everyone who asked 'Yes; I told him to use my name. I know the man, and I know the mine. The man is completely honest and reliable, and the mine is worth much more money than he asks for it.'

In the meantime I spent all my evenings at the ambassador's with Portia. I didn't say a word to her about the mine; I saved it for a surprise. We talked about my salary; never anything but salary and love; sometimes love, sometimes salary, sometimes love and salary together. The ambassador's wife and daughter took great interest in our little love affair. They kept finding clever ways for us to be alone together. And they kept the ambassador in the dark so he had no idea what was going on. Well, it was just lovely of them!

When at last the month had finished, I had a million dollars in my bank account in the London and County Bank. Hastings had the same. I dressed in my best clothes and drove by the house in Portland Place. I judged by the look of the house that the people I wanted were home again. Therefore I went on to the ambassador's and got my precious Portia. We returned to Portland place, talking salary with all our might. She was excited and worried, and it made her more beautiful than I could stand.

Lesson 173

1. Finish reading "The Million Pound Banknote."

'My dear, you look so beautiful that it would be criminal for me to accept a salary of under three thousand a year.' I said. 'Don't you be afraid. Just keep on looking like that, and trust me. It will all come out right.'

As it happened, I had to keep encouraging her to be brave for the whole journey. She wanted me to accept a lower salary, and kept saying 'Henry, Henry, you'll ruin us! Oh, please remember that if we ask for too much we may get no salary at all. Then what will happen to us? We have no way in the world to make any money.'

We were shown into the room by that same servant as before. There they were, the two old gentlemen. Of course, they were surprised to see my wonderful Portia with me, but I said: 'It's all right, gentlemen; she is my future wife. I am ready to report.'

And I introduced them to her, and told Portia their names. It didn't surprise them that I knew who they were. They knew I would have discovered that. They seated us, and were very polite to me. They did their best to stop Portia from feeling embarrassed, and made her feel as comfortable as they could. Then one of them said 'Now we can decide the bet which my brother Abel and I made. If you have won for me, you shall have any job I can offer you. Do you have the million-pound note?'

When I handed the banknote to him he shouted 'I've won!'. He slapped Abel on the back. 'Now what do you say, brother?'

Abel replied 'I say he did survive. Now I've lost twenty thousand pounds. I never would have believed it.'

'I've even more to tell you,' I said. 'It is a rather long story. I want to visit you soon, and tell you all about the whole month. I promise you that it's worth hearing what I have to say. In the meantime, take a look at this. It is a bank account with £200,000 in it. The money is mine. I earned it by being careful how I used that banknote you let me borrow. And I only tried to buy small, unimportant things with it.'

But now it was Portia's turn to be surprised. Her eyes were spread wide, and she said 'Henry, is that really your money? Have you been fibbing to me?'

'I have indeed, dearie. But you'll forgive me, I know.'

She pouted, and pretended to look serious. She said 'Don't you be so sure. You are a naughty thing to hide the truth from me like that!'

'Oh, you'll soon stop being upset, sweetheart, it was only in fun, you know. Come, let's be going.'

'But wait, wait! The job, you know. I want to give you the job,' said my man.

'Well,' I said, 'I'm just as grateful as I can be, but really I don't want one.'

'But you can choose the very best one I can give you.'

'Thanks again, with all my heart; but I don't even want that one.'

'Henry, I'm ashamed of you. You haven't thanked the good gentleman properly. May I do it for you?'

'Indeed, you shall, dear, if you can do better. Let us see you try.'

She walked to my man and got up in his lap. Then she put her arm round his neck, and kissed him right on the mouth. The two old gentlemen shouted with laughter. I was so astonished and confused that I could not move a muscle.

Portia said 'Papa, he has said he wouldn't take any job you can give him; and I feel just as bad about it as –'

'My darling, is that your papa?'

'Yes; he's my step-father, and the dearest one ever. You understand now, don't you, why I laughed when you told me everything at the ambassador's? You did not know that he was my relative. Papa's and Uncle Abel's little plan was giving you so much worry and trouble!'

Of course, I now had something else to say. Without any fooling I went right to the important thing.

'Oh, my dearest dear sir, I was wrong about what I said before. You have got a job available that I want. Son-in-law.'

'Well, well, well! But you know, you haven't ever done that job before. So of course, you can't give a reference that shows that you can do the job well, and so – '

'Let me try – oh, I beg you, do please! Just test me for thirty or forty years, and if-'

'Oh, well, all right. You are not asking for much, so take her away.'

Are the two of us happy? There are not enough words in the entire dictionary to describe it. A day or two after that, London got the whole story of my month's adventure with that bank-note, and how the adventure ended. Did London talk, and have a good time? Yes.

Portia's papa gave back that friendly and very useful banknote to the Bank of England. Then the Bank cancelled it and presented it to him. Portia's papa gave that banknote to us at our wedding. Ever since then it has always hung in its frame in the most important place in our home.

That banknote gave me my Portia. Without it I could not have remained in London. I would never have visited the ambassador, and never would have met her. And so I always say, 'Yes, that banknote's a million-pounder, as you see. But it was only ever used once to buy something, and then what it was used to buy was worth ten times as much.'

The End

Lesson 174

1. Read the first few pages of "A Christmas Dream and How it Came True."

A CHRISTMAS DREAM, AND HOW IT CAME TRUE
By Louisa May Alcott

"I'm so tired of Christmas I wish there never would be another one!" exclaimed a discontented-looking little girl, as she sat idly watching her mother arrange a pile of gifts two days before they were to be given.

"Why, Effie, what a dreadful thing to say! You are as bad as old Scrooge; and I'm afraid something will happen to you, as it did to him, if you don't care for dear Christmas," answered mamma, almost dropping the silver horn she was filling with delicious candies.

"Who was Scrooge? What happened to him?" asked Effie, with a glimmer of interest in her listless face, as she picked out the sourest lemon-drop she could find; for nothing sweet suited her just then.

"He was one of Dickens's best people, and you can read the charming story some day. He hated Christmas until a strange dream showed him how dear and beautiful it was, and made a better man of him."

"I shall read it; for I like dreams, and have a great many curious ones myself. But they don't keep me from being tired of Christmas," said Effie, poking discontentedly among the sweeties for something worth eating.

"Why are you tired of what should be the happiest time of all the year?" asked mamma, anxiously.

"Perhaps I shouldn't be if I had something new. But it is always the same, and there isn't any more surprise about it. I always find heaps of goodies in my stocking. Don't like some of them, and soon get tired of those I do like. We always have a great dinner, and I eat too much, and feel ill next day. Then there is a Christmas tree somewhere, with a doll on top, or a stupid old Santa Claus, and children dancing and screaming over bonbons and toys that break, and shiny things that are of no use. Really, mamma, I've had so many Christmases all alike that I don't think I can bear another one." And Effie laid herself flat on the sofa, as if the mere idea was too much for her.

Her mother laughed at her despair, but was sorry to see her little girl so discontented, when she had everything to make her happy, and had known but ten Christmas days.

"Suppose we don't give you any presents at all—how would that suit you?" asked mamma, anxious to please her spoiled child.

"I should like one large and splendid one, and one dear little one, to remember some very nice person by," said Effie, who was a fanciful little body, full of odd whims and notions, which her friends loved to gratify, regardless of time, trouble, or money; for she was the last of three little girls, and very dear to all the family.

"Well, my darling, I will see what I can do to please you, and not say a word until all is ready. If I could only get a new idea to start with!" And mamma went on tying up her pretty bundles with a thoughtful face, while Effie strolled to the window to watch the rain that kept her in-doors and made her dismal.

"Seems to me poor children have better times than rich ones. I can't go out, and there is a girl about my age splashing along, with out any maid to fuss about rubbers and cloaks and umbrellas and colds. I wish I was a beggar-girl."

"Would you like to be hungry, cold, and ragged, to beg all day, and sleep on an ash-heap at night?" asked mamma, wondering what would come next.

"Cinderella did, and had a nice time in the end. This girl out here has a basket of scraps on her arm, and a big old shawl all round her, and doesn't seem to care a bit, though the water runs out of the toes of her boots. She goes paddling' along, laughing at the rain, and eating a cold potato as if it tasted nicer than the chicken and ice-cream I had for dinner. Yes, I do think poor children are happier than rich ones."

"So do I, sometimes. At the Orphan Asylum today I saw two dozen merry little souls who have no parents, no home, and no hope of Christmas beyond a stick of candy or a cake. I wish you had been there to see how happy they were, playing with the old toys some richer children had sent them."

"You may give them all mine; I'm so tired of them I never want to see them again," said Effie, turning from the window to the pretty baby-house full of everything a child's heart could desire.

"I will, and let you begin again with something you will not tire of, if I can only find it." And mamma knit her brows trying to discover some grand surprise for this child who didn't care for Christmas.

Nothing more was said then; and wandering off to the library, Effie found "A Christmas Carol," and, curling herself up in the sofa corner, read it all before tea. Some of it she did not understand; but she laughed and cried over many parts of the charming story, and felt better without knowing why.

All the evening she thought of poor Tiny Tim, Mrs. Cratchit with the pudding, and the stout old gentleman who danced so gayly that "his legs twinkled in the air." Presently bed-time arrived.

"Come now, and toast your feet," said Effie's nurse, "while I do your pretty hair and tell stories."

"I'll have a fairy tale tonight, a very interesting one," commanded Effie, as she put on her blue silk wrapper and little furlined slippers to sit before the fire and have her long curls brushed.

So Nursey told her best tales; and when at last the child lay down under her lace curtains, her head was fun of a curious jumble of Christmas elves, poor children, snow-storms, sugar-plums, and surprises. So it is no wonder that she dreamed all night; and this was the dream, which she never quite forgot.

She found herself sitting on a stone, in the middle of a great field, all alone. The snow was falling fast, a bitter wind whistled by, and night was coming on. She felt hungry, cold, and tired, and did not know where to go nor what to do.

"I wanted to be a beggar-girl, and now I am one; but I don't like it, and wish somebody would come and take care of me. I don't know who I am, and I think I must be lost," thought Effie, with the curious interest one takes in one's self in dreams.

But the more she thought about it, the more bewildered she felt. Faster fell the snow, colder blew the wind, darker grew the night; and poor Effie made up her mind that she was quite forgotten and left to freeze alone. The tears were chilled on her cheeks, her feet felt like icicles, and her heart died within her, so hungry, frightened, and forlorn was she. Laying her head on her knees, she gave herself up for lost, and sat there with the great flakes fast turning her to a little white mound, when suddenly the sound of music reached her, and starting up, she looked and listened with all her eyes and ears.

Far away a dim light shone, and a voice was heard singing. She tried to run toward the welcome glimmer, but could not stir, and stood like a small statue of expectation while the light drew nearer, and the sweet words of the song grew clearer.

From our happy home
Through the world we roam
One week in all the year,
Making winter spring
With the joy we bring
For Christmas-tide is here.

Now the eastern star
Shines from afar
To light the poorest home;
Hearts warmer grow,
Gifts freely flow,
For Christmas-tide has come.

Now gay trees rise
Before young eyes,
Abloom with tempting cheer;
Blithe voices sing.
And blithe bells ring,
For Christmas-tide is here.

Oh, happy chime,
Oh, blessed time,
That draws us all so near!
'Welcome, dear day,'
All creatures say,
For Christmas-tide is here.

Lesson 175

1. Read the next few pages of "A Christmas Dream and How it Came True."

A Christmas Dream, And How It Came True – Continued...

A child's voice sang, a child's hand carried the little candle; and in the circle of soft light it shed, Effie saw a pretty child coming to her through the night and snow. A rosy, smiling creature, wrapped in white fur, with a wreath of green and scarlet holly on its shining hair, the magic candle in one hand, and the other outstretched as if to shower gifts and warmly press all other hands.

Effie forgot to speak as this bright vision came nearer, leaving no trace of footsteps in the snow, only lighting the way with its little candle, and filling the air with the music of its song. "Dear child, you are lost, and I have come to find you," said the stranger, taking Effie's cold hands in his, with a smile like sunshine, while every holly berry glowed like a little fire.

"Do you know me?" asked Effie, feeling no fear, but a great gladness, at his coming.

"I know all children, and go to find them; for this is my holiday, and I gather them from all parts of the world to be merry with me once a year."

"Are you an angel?" asked Effie, looking for the wings.

"No; I am a Christmas spirit, and live with my mates in a pleasant place, getting ready for our holiday, when we are let out to roam about the world, helping to make this a happy time for all who will let us in. Will you come and see how we work?"

"I will go anywhere with you. Don't leave me again," cried Effie, gladly.

"First I will make you comfortable. That is what we love to do. You are cold, and you shall be warm; hungry, and I will feed you; sorrowful, and I will make you gay."

With a wave of his candle all three miracles were wrought—for the snowflakes turned to a white fur cloak and hood on Effie's head and shoulders; a bowl of hot soup came sailing to her lips, and vanished when she had eagerly drunk the last drop; and suddenly the dismal field changed to a new world so full of wonders that all her troubles were forgotten in a minute.

Bells were ringing so merrily that it was hard to keep from dancing. Green garlands hung on the walls, and every tree was a Christmas tree full of toys, and blazing with candles that never went out.

In one place many little spirits sewed like mad on warm clothes, turning off work faster than any sewing-machine ever invented, and great piles were made ready to be sent to poor people. Other busy creatures packed money into purses, and wrote checks which they sent flying away on the wind—a lovely kind of snow-storm to fall into a world below full of poverty.

Older and graver spirits were looking over piles of little books, in which the records of the past year were kept, telling how different people had spent it, and what sort of gifts they deserved. Some got peace, some disappointment, some remorse and sorrow, some great joy and hope. The rich had generous thoughts sent them; the poor, gratitude and contentment. Children had more love and duty to parents; and parents renewed patience, wisdom, and satisfaction for and in their children. No one was forgotten.

"Please tell me what splendid place this is?" asked Effie, as soon as she could collect her wits after the first look at all these astonishing things.

"This is the Christmas world; and here we work all the year round, never tired of getting ready for the happy day. See, these are the saints just setting off, for some have far to go, and the children must not be disappointed."

As he spoke the spirit pointed to four gates, out of which four great sleighs were just driving, laden with toys, while a jolly old Santa Claus sat in the middle of each, drawing on his mittens and tucking up his wraps for a long cold drive.

"Why, I thought there was only one Santa Claus, and even he was a humbug," cried Effie, astonished at the sight.

"Never give up your faith in the sweet old stories, even after you come to see that they are only the pleasant shadow of a lovely truth."

Just then the sleighs went off with a great jingling of bells and pattering of reindeer hoofs, while all the spirits gave a cheer that was heard in the lower world, where people said, "Hear the stars sing."

"I never will say there isn't any Santa Claus again. Now, show me more."

"You will like to see this place, I think, and may learn something here perhaps."

The spirit smiled as he led the way to a little door, through which Effie peeped into a world of dolls. Baby-houses were in full blast, with dolls of all sorts going on like live people. Waxen ladies sat in their parlors elegantly dressed; black dolls cooked in the kitchens; nurses walked out with the bits of dollies; and the streets were full of tin soldiers marching, wooden horses prancing, express wagons rumbling, and little men hurrying to and fro. Shops were there, and tiny people buying legs of mutton, pounds of tea, mites of clothes, and everything dolls use or wear or want.

But presently she saw that in some ways the dolls improved upon the manners and customs of human beings, and she watched eagerly to learn why they did these things. A fine Paris doll driving in her carriage took up a black worsted Dinah who was hobbling along with a basket of clean clothes, and carried her to her journey's end, as if it were the proper thing to do. Another interesting china lady took off her comfortable red cloak and put it round a poor wooden creature done up in a paper shift, and so badly painted that its face would have sent some babies into fits.

"Seems to me I once knew a rich girl who didn't give her things to poor girls. I wish I could remember who she was, and tell her to be as kind as that china doll," said Effie, much touched at the sweet way the pretty creature wrapped up the poor fright, and then ran off in her little gray gown to buy a shiny fowl stuck on a wooden platter for her invalid mother's dinner.

"We recall these things to people's minds by dreams. I think the girl you speak of won't forget this one." And the spirit smiled, as if he enjoyed some joke which she did not see.

A little bell rang as she looked, and away scampered the children into the red-and-green school-house with the roof that lifted up, so one could see how nicely they sat at their desks with mites of books, or drew on the inch-square blackboards with crumbs of chalk.

"They know their lessons very well, and are as still as mice. We make a great racket at our school, and get bad marks every day. I shall tell the girls they had better mind what they do, or their dolls will be better scholars than they are," said Effie, much impressed, as she peeped in and saw no rod in the hand of the little mistress, who looked up and shook her head at the intruder, as if begging her to go away before the order of the school was disturbed.

Effie retired at once, but could not resist one look in at the window of a fine mansion, where the family were at dinner, the children behaved so well at table, and never grumbled a bit when their mamma said they could not have any more fruit.

"Now, show me something else," she said, as they came again to the low door that led out of Doll-land.

"You have seen how we prepare for Christmas; let me show you where we love best to send our good and happy gifts," answered the spirit, giving her his hand again.

"I know. I've seen ever so many," began Effie, thinking of her own Christmases.

"No, you have never seen what I will show you. Come away, and remember what you see tonight." Like a flash that bright world vanished, and Effie found herself in a part of the city she had never seen before. It was far away from the gayer places, where every store was brilliant with lights and full of pretty things, and every house wore a festival air, while people hurried to and fro with merry greetings.

Lesson 176

1. Read the next few pages of "A Christmas Dream and How it Came True."

A Christmas Dream, And How It Came True – Continued...

It was down among the dingy streets where the poor lived, and where there was no making ready for Christmas.

Hungry women looked in at the shabby shops, longing to buy meat and bread, but empty pockets forbade. Tipsy men drank up their wages in the barrooms; and in many cold dark chambers little children huddled under the thick blankets, trying to forget their misery in sleep.

No nice dinners filled the air with savory smells, no gay trees dropped toys and bonbons into eager hands, no little stockings hung in rows beside the chimney-piece ready to be filled, no happy sounds of music, gay voices, and dancing feet were heard; and there were no signs of Christmas anywhere.

"Don't they have any in this place?" asked Effie, shivering, as she held fast the spirit's hand, following where he led her.

"We come to bring it. Let me show you our best workers." And the spirit pointed to some sweet-faced men and women who came stealing into the poor houses, working such beautiful miracles that Effie could only stand and watch.

Some slipped money into the empty pockets, and sent the happy mothers to buy all the comforts they needed; others led the drunken men out of temptation, and took them home to find safer pleasures there. Fires were kindled on cold hearths, tables spread as if by magic, and warm clothes wrapped round shivering limbs. Flowers suddenly bloomed in the chambers of the sick; old people found themselves remembered; sad hearts were consoled by a tender word, and wicked ones softened by the story of Him who forgave all sin.

But the sweetest work was for the children; and Effie held her breath to watch these human fairies hang up and fill the little stockings without which a child's Christmas is not perfect, putting in things that once she would have thought very humble presents, but which now seemed beautiful and precious because these poor babies had nothing.

"That is so beautiful! I wish I could make merry Christmas as these good people do, and be loved and thanked as they are," said Effie, softly, as she watched the busy men and women do their work and steal away without thinking of any reward but their own satisfaction.

"You can if you will. I have shown you the way. Try it, and see how happy your own holiday will be hereafter."

As he spoke, the spirit seemed to put his arms about her, and vanished with a kiss.

"Oh, stay and show me more!" cried Effie, trying to hold him fast.

"Darling, wake up, and tell me why you are smiling in your sleep," said a voice in her ear; and opening her eyes, there was mamma bending over her, and morning sunshine streaming into the room.

"Are they all gone? Did you hear the bells? Wasn't it splendid?" she asked, rubbing her eyes, and looking about her for the pretty child who was so real and sweet.

"You have been dreaming at a great rate—talking in your sleep, laughing, and clapping your hands as if you were cheering some one. Tell me what was so splendid," said mamma, smoothing the tumbled hair and lifting up the sleepy head.

Then, while she was being dressed, Effie told her dream, and Nursey thought it very wonderful; but mamma smiled to see how curiously things the child had thought, read, heard, and seen through the day were mixed up in her sleep.

"The spirit said I could work lovely miracles if I tried; but I don't know how to begin, for I have no magic candle to make feasts appear, and light up groves of Christmas trees, as he did," said Effie, sorrowfully.

"Yes, you have. We will do it! We will do it!" And clapping her hands, mamma suddenly began to dance all over the room as if she had lost her wits.

"How? how? You must tell me, mamma," cried Effie, dancing after her, and ready to believe anything possible when she remembered the adventures of the past night.

"I've got it! I've got it!—the new idea. A splendid one, if I can only carry it out!" And mamma waltzed the little girl round till her curls flew wildly in the air, while Nursey laughed as if she would die.

"Tell me! tell me!" shrieked Effie.

"No, no; it is a surprise—a grand surprise for Christmas day!" sung mamma, evidently charmed with her happy thought. "Now, come to breakfast; for we must work like bees if we want to play spirits tomorrow. You and Nursey will go out shopping, and get heaps of things, while I arrange matters behind the scenes."

They were running downstairs as mamma spoke, and Effie called out breathlessly—- .

"It won't be a surprise; for I know you are going to ask some poor children here, and have a tree or something. It won't be like my dream; for they had ever so many trees, and more children than we can find anywhere."

"There will be no tree, no party, no dinner, in this house at all, and no presents for you. Won't that be a surprise?" And mamma laughed at Effie's bewildered face.

"Do it. I shall like it, I think; and I won't ask any questions, so it will all burst upon me when the time comes," she said; and she ate her breakfast thoughtfully, for this really would be a new sort of Christmas.

All that morning Effie trotted after Nursey in and out of shops, buying dozens of barking dogs, woolly lambs, and squeaking birds; tiny tea-sets, gay picture-books, mittens and hoods, dolls and candy. Parcel after parcel was sent home; but when Effie returned she saw no trace of them, though she peeped everywhere. Nursey chuckled, but wouldn't give a hint, and went out again in the afternoon with a long list of more things to buy; while Effie wandered forlornly about the house, missing the usual merry stir that went before the Christmas dinner and the evening fun.

As for mamma, she was quite invisible all day, and came in at night so tired that she could only lie on the sofa to rest, smiling as if some very pleasant thought made her happy in spite of weariness.

"Is the surprise going on all right?" asked Effie, anxiously; for it seemed an immense time to wait till another evening came.

"Beautifully! better than I expected; for several of my good friends are helping, or I couldn't have done as I wish. I know you will like it, dear, and long remember this new way of making Christmas merry."

Mamma gave her a very tender kiss, and Effie went to bed. The next day was a very strange one; for when she woke there was no stocking to examine, no pile of gifts under her napkin, no one said, "Merry Christmas!" to her, and the dinner was just as usual to her. Mamma vanished again, and Nursey kept wiping her eyes and saying: "The dear things! It's the prettiest idea I ever heard of. No one but your blessed ma could have done it."

"Do stop, Nursey, or I shall go crazy because I don't know the secret!" cried Effie, more than once; and she kept her eye on the clock, for at seven in the evening the surprise was to come off.

The longed-for hour arrived at last, and the child was too excited to ask questions when Nursey put on her cloak and hood, led her to the carriage, and they drove away, leaving their house the one dark and silent one in the row.

"I feel like the girls in the fairy tales who are led off to strange places and see fine things," said Effie, in a whisper, as they jingled through the gay streets.

"Ah, my deary, it is like a fairy tale, I do assure you, and you will see finer things than most children will tonight. Steady, now, and do just as I tell you, and don't say one word whatever you see," answered Nursey, quite quivering with excitement as she patted a large box in her lap, and nodded and laughed with twinkling eyes.

They drove into a dark yard, and Effie was led through a back door to a little room, where Nursey coolly proceeded to take off not only her cloak and hood but her dress and shoes also.

Lesson 177

1. Finish reading "A Christmas Dream and How it Came True."

A Christmas Dream, And How It Came True – Continued...

Effie stared and bit her lips, but kept still until out of the box came a little white fur coat and boots, a wreath of holly leaves and berries, and a candle with a frill of gold paper round it. A long "Oh!" escaped her then; and when she was dressed and saw herself in the glass, she started back, exclaiming, "Why, Nursey, I look like the spirit in my dream!"

"So you do; and that's the part you are to play, my pretty! Now whist, while I blind your eyes and put you in your place."

"Shall I be afraid?" whispered Effie, full of wonder; for as they went out she heard the sound of many voices, the tramp of many feet, and, in spite of the bandage, was sure a great light shone upon her when she stopped.

"You needn't be; I shall stand close by, and your ma will be there."

After the handkerchief was tied about her eyes, Nursey led Effie up some steps, and placed her on a high platform, where something like leaves touched her head, and the soft snap of lamps seemed to fill the air.

Music began as soon as Nursey clapped her hands, the voices outside sounded nearer, and the tramp was evidently coming up the stairs.

"Now, my precious, look and see how you and your dear ma have made a merry Christmas for them that needed it!"

Off went the bandage; and for a minute Effie really did think she was asleep again, for she actually stood in "a grove of Christmas trees," all gay and shining as in her vision. Twelve on a side, in two rows down the room, stood the little pines, each on its low table; and behind Effie a taller one rose to the roof, hung with wreaths of popcorn, apples, oranges, horns of candy, and cakes of all sorts, from sugary hearts to gingerbread Jumbos. On the smaller trees she saw many of her own discarded toys and those Nursey bought, as well as heaps that seemed to have rained down straight from that delightful Christmas country where she felt as if she was again.

"How splendid! Who is it for? What is that noise? Where is mamma?" cried Effie, pale with pleasure and surprise, as she stood looking down the brilliant little street from her high place.

Before Nursey could answer, the doors at the lower end flew open, and in marched twenty-four little blue-gowned orphan girls, singing sweetly, until amazement changed the song to cries of joy and wonder as the shining spectacle appeared. While they stood staring with round eyes at the wilderness of pretty things about them, mamma stepped up beside Effie, and holding her hand fast to give her courage, told the story of the dream in a few simple words, ending in this way: "So my little girl wanted to be a Christmas spirit too, and make this a happy day for those who had not as many pleasures and comforts as she has. She likes surprises, and we planned this for you all. She shall play the good fairy, and give each of you something from this tree, after which everyone will find her own name on a small tree, and can go to enjoy it in her own way. March by, my dears, and let us fill your hands."

Nobody told them to do it, but all the hands were clapped heartily before a single child stirred; then one by one they came to look up wonderingly at the pretty giver of the feast as she leaned down to offer them great yellow oranges, red apples, bunches of grapes, bonbons, and cakes, till all were gone, and a double row of smiling faces turned toward her as the children filed back to their places in the orderly way they had been taught.

Then each was led to her own tree by the good ladies who had helped. mamma with all their hearts; and the happy hubbub that arose would have satisfied even Santa Claus himself—shrieks of joy, dances of delight, laughter and tears (for some tender little things could not bear so much pleasure at once, and sobbed with mouths full of candy and hands full of toys). How they ran to show one another the new treasures! how they peeped and tasted, pulled and pinched, until the air was full of queer noises, the floor covered with papers, and the little trees left bare of all but candles!

"I don't think heaven can be any gooder than this," sighed one small girl, as she looked about her in a blissful maze, holding her full apron with one hand, while she luxuriously carried sugar-plums to her mouth with the other.

"Is that a truly angel up there?" asked another, fascinated by the little white figure with the wreath on its shining hair, who in some mysterious way had been the cause of all this merry-making.

"I wish I dared to go and kiss her for this splendid party," said a lame child, leaning on her crutch, as she stood near the steps, wondering how it seemed to sit in a mother's lap, as Effie was doing, while she watched the happy scene before her.

Effie heard her, and remembering Tiny Tim, ran down and put her arms about the pale child, kissing the wistful face, as she said sweetly, "You may; but mamma deserves the thanks. She did it all; I only dreamed about it."

Lame Katy felt as if "a truly angel" was embracing her, and could only stammer out her thanks, while the other children ran to see the pretty spirit, and touch her soft dress, until she stood in a crowd of blue gowns laughing as they held up their gifts for her to see and admire.

Mamma leaned down and whispered one word to the older girls; and suddenly they all took hands to dance round Effie, singing as they skipped.

It was a pretty sight, and the ladies found it hard to break up the happy revel; but it was late for small people, and too much fun is a mistake. So the girls fell into line, and marched before Effie and mamma again, to say good-night with such grateful little faces that the eyes of those who looked grew dim with tears. Mamma kissed every one; and many a hungry childish heart felt as if the touch of those tender lips was their best gift. Effie shook so many small hands that her own tingled; and when Katy came she pressed a small doll into Effie's hand, whispering, "You didn't have a single present, and we had lots. Do keep that; it's the prettiest thing I got."

"I will," answered Effie, and held it fast until the last smiling face was gone, the surprise all over, and she safe in her own bed, too tired and happy for anything but sleep.

"Mamma, it was a beautiful surprise, and I thank you so much! I don't see how you ever did it; but I like it best of all the Christmases I ever had, and mean to make one every year. I had my splendid big present, and here is the dear little one to keep for love of poor Katy; so even that part of my wish came true."

And Effie fell asleep with a happy smile on her lips, her one humble gift still in her hand, and a new love for Christmas in her heart that never changed through a long life spent in doing good.

Lesson 178

1. Read the first part of "The Sounding of the Call."

THE SOUNDING OF THE CALL
(From *The Call of the Wild*)
By Jack London

Thrown into the hard life of the frozen north of America, Buck has learnt to fight for his survival. Rough treatment by the men who drive the sleighs and the savagery of the other dogs has almost turned him into a wild animal. Now, only the love of John Thornton, his master, keeps him from joining a wolf pack.

Spring came on once more, and at the end of all their wandering they found, not the Lost Cabin, but a shallow place in a broad valley where the gold showed like yellow butter across the bottom of the washing-pan. They sought no farther. Each day they worked earned them thousands of dollars in clean dust and nuggets, and they worked every day. The gold was sacked in moosehide bags, fifty pounds to the bag, and piled like so much firewood outside the spruce-bough lodge. Like giants they toiled, days flashing on the heels of days like dreams as they heaped the treasure up.

There was nothing for the dogs to do, save the hauling in of meat now and again that Thornton killed, and Buck spent long hours musing by the fire. The vision of the short-legged hairy man came to him more frequently, now that there was little work to be done; and often, blinking by the fire, Buck wandered with him in that other world which he remembered.

The salient thing of this other world seemed fear. When he watched the hairy man sleeping by the fire, head between his knees and hands clasped above, Buck saw that he slept restlessly, with many starts and awakenings, at which times he would peer fearfully into the darkness and fling more wood upon the fire. Did they walk by the beach of a sea, where the hairy man gathered shell-fish and ate them as he gathered, it was with eyes that roved everywhere for hidden danger and with legs prepared to run like the wind at its first appearance. Through the forest they crept noiselessly,

Buck at the hairy man's heels; and they were alert and vigilant, the pair of them, ears twitching and moving and nostrils quivering, for the man heard and smelled as keenly as Buck. The hairy man could spring up into the trees and travel ahead as fast as on the ground, swinging by the arms from limb to limb, sometimes a dozen feet apart, letting go and catching, never falling, never missing his grip. In fact, he seemed as much at home among the trees as on the ground; and Buck had memories of nights of vigil spent beneath trees wherein the hairy man roosted, holding on tightly as he slept.

And closely akin to the visions of the hairy man was the call still sounding in the depths of the forest. It filled him with a great unrest and strange desires. It caused him to feel a vague, sweet gladness, and he was aware of wild yearnings and stirrings for he knew not what. Sometimes he pursued the call into the forest, looking for it as though it were a tangible thing, barking softly or defiantly, as the mood might dictate. He would thrust his nose into the cool wood moss, or into the black soil where long grasses grew, and snort with joy at the fat earth smells; or he would crouch for hours, as if in concealment, behind fungus-covered trunks of fallen trees, wide-eyed and wide-eared to all that moved and sounded about him. It might be, lying thus, that he hoped to surprise this call he could not understand. But he did not know why he did these various things. He was impelled to do them, and did not reason about them at all.

Irresistible impulses seized him. He would by lying in camp, dozing lazily in the heat of the day, when suddenly his head would lift and his ears cock up, intent and listening, and he would spring to his feet and dash away, and on and on, for hours, through the forest aisles and across the open spaces where the men bunched. He loved to run down dry watercourses, and to creep up and spy upon the bird life in the woods. For a day at a time he would lie in the underbrush where he could watch the partridges drumming and strutting up and down. But especially he loved to run in the dim twilight of the summer midnights, listening to the subdued and sleepy murmurs of the forest, reading signs and sounds as man may read a book, and seeking for the mysterious something that called—called, waking or sleeping, at all times, for him to come.

One night he sprang from sleep with a start, eager-eyed, nostrils quivering and scenting, his mane bristling in recurrent waves. From the forest came the call (or one note of it, for the call was many noted), distinct and definite as never before—a long-drawn howl, like, yet unlike, any noise made by husky dog. And he knew it, in the old familiar way, as a sound heard before. He sprang through the sleeping camp and in swift silence dashed through the woods. As he drew closer to the cry he went more slowly, with caution every moment, till he came to an open place among the trees, and looking out saw, erect on haunches, with nose pointed to the sky, a long, lean, timber wolf.

He had made no noise, yet it ceased from its howling and tried to sense his presence. Buck stalked into the open, half crouching, body gathered compactly together, tail straight and stiff, feet falling with unwonted care. Every movement advertised commingled threatening and overture of friendliness. It was the menacing truce that marks the meeting of wild beasts that prey. But the wolf fled at sight of him. He followed, with wild leapings, in a frenzy to overtake. He ran him into a blind channel, in the bed of the creek, where a timber jam barred the way. The wolf whirled about, pivoting on his hind legs after the fashion of Joe and of all cornered husky dogs, snarling and bristling, clipping his teeth together in a continuous and rapid succession of snaps.

Buck did not attack, but circled him about and hedged him in with friendly advances. The wolf was suspicious and afraid; for Buck made three of him in weight, while his head barely reached Buck's shoulder. Watching his chance, he darted away, and the chase was resumed. Time and again he was cornered, and the thing repeated, though he was in poor condition or Buck could not so easily have overtaken him. He would run till Buck's head was even with his flank, when he would whirl around at bay, only to dash away again at the first opportunity.

But in the end Buck's pertinacity was rewarded; for the wolf, finding that no harm was intended, finally sniffed noses with him. Then they became friendly, and played about in the nervous, half-coy way with which fierce beasts belie their fierceness. After some time of this the wolf started off at an easy lope in a manner that plainly showed he was going somewhere. He made it clear to Buck that he was to come, and they ran side by side through the sombre twilight, straight up the creek bed, into the gorge from which it issued, and across the bleak divide where it took its rise.

On the opposite slope of the watershed they came down into a level country where were great stretches of forest and many streams, and through these great stretches they ran steadily, hour after hour, the sun rising higher and the day growing warmer. Buck was wildly glad. He knew he was at last answering the call, running by the side of his wood brother towards the place from where they surely came. Old memories were coming upon him fast, and he was stirring to them as of old he stirred to the realities of which they were the shadows. He had done this thing before, somewhere in that other and dimly remembered world, and he was doing it again, now, running free in the open, the unpacked earth underfoot, the wide sky overhead.

They stopped by a running stream to drink, and, stopping, Buck remembered John Thornton. He sat down. The wolf started on towards the place from where the call surely came, then returned to him, sniffing noses and making actions as though to encourage him. But Buck turned about and started slowly on the back track. For the better part of an hour the wild brother ran by his side, whining softly. Then he sat down, pointed his nose upward, and howled. It was a mournful howl, and as Buck held steadily on his way he heard it grow faint and fainter until it was lost in the distance.

John Thornton was eating his dinner when Buck dashed into camp and sprang upon him in a frenzy of affection, overturning him, scrambling upon him, licking his face, biting his hand—'playing the general tomfool,' as John Thornton characterized it, the while he shook Buck back and forth and cursed him lovingly.

For two days and nights Buck never left camp, never let Thornton out of his sight. He followed him about at his work, watched him while he ate, saw him into his blankets at night and out of them in the morning. But after two days the call of the forest began to sound more imperiously than ever. Buck's restlessness came back on him, and he was haunted by recollections of the wild brother, and of the smiling land beyond the divide and the run side by side through the wide forest stretches. Once again he took to wandering in the woods, but the wild brother came no more; and though he listened through long vigils, the mournful howl was never raised.

He began to sleep out at night, staying away from camp for days at a time; and once he crossed the divide at the head of the creek and went down into the land of timber and streams. There he wandered for a week, seeking vainly for fresh sign of the wild brother, killing his meat as he travelled and travelling with the long easy lope that seems never to tire. He fished for salmon in a broad stream that emptied somewhere into the sea, and by this stream he killed a large black bear, blinded by the mosquitoes while likewise fishing, and raging through the forest helpless and terrible. Even so, it was a hard fight, and it aroused the last latent remnants of Buck's ferocity. And two days later, when he returned to his kill and found a dozen wolverenes quarrelling over the spoil, he scattered them like chaff; and those that fled left two behind who would quarrel no more.

The blood-longing became stronger than ever before. He was a killer, a thing that preyed, living on the things that lived, unaided, alone, by virtue of his own strength and prowess, surviving triumphantly in a hostile environment where only the strong survived. Because of all this he became possessed of a great pride in himself, which communicated itself like a contagion to his physical being. It advertised itself in all his movements, was apparent in the play of every muscle, spoke plainly as speech in the way he carried himself, and made his glorious furry coat if anything more glorious. But for the stray brown of his muzzle and above his eyes, and for the splash of white hair that ran midmost down his chest, he might well have been mistaken for a gigantic wolf, larger than the largest of the breed. From his St. Bernard father he had inherited size and weight, but it was his shepherd mother who had given shape to that size and weight. His muzzle was the long wolf muzzle, save that it was larger than the muzzle of any wolf; and his head, somewhat broader, was the wolf head on a massive scale.

His cunning was wolf cunning, and wild cunning; his intelligence, shepherd intelligence and St. Bernard intelligence; and all this, plus an experience gained in the fiercest of schools, made him as formidable a creature as any that roamed the wild

Lesson 179

1. Read the next section of "The Sounding of the Call."

The Sounding of the Call – Continued...

A carnivorous animal, living on a straight meat diet, he was in full flower, at the high tide of his life, overspilling with vigour and virility. When Thornton passed a caressing hand along his back, a snapping and crackling followed the hand, each hair discharging its pent magnetism at the contact. Every part, brain and body, nerve tissue and fibre, was keyed to the most exquisite pitch; and between all the parts there was a perfect equilibrium or adjustment. To sights and sounds and events which required action, he responded with lightning-like rapidity. Quickly as a husky dog could leap to defend from attack or to attack, he could leap twice as quickly. He saw the movement, or heard sound, and responded in less time than another dog required to compass the mere seeing or hearing. He perceived and determined and responded in the same instant. In point of fact the three actions of perceiving, determining, and responding were sequential; but so infinitesimal were the intervals of time between them that they appeared simultaneous. His muscles were surcharged with vitality, and snapped into play sharply, like steel springs. Life streamed through him in splendid flood, glad and rampant, until it seemed that it would burst him asunder in sheer ecstasy and pour forth generously over the world.

'Never was there such a dog,' said John Thornton one day, as the partners watched Buck marching out of camp.

'When he was made, the mould was broke,' said Pete.

'Py jingo! I t'ink so mineself,' Hans affirmed.

They saw him marching out of camp, but they did not see the instant and terrible transformation which took place as soon as he was within the secrecy of the forest. He no longer marched. At once he became a thing of the wild, stealing along softly, cat-footed, a passing shadow that appeared and disappeared among the shadows. He knew how to take advantage of every cover, to crawl on his belly like a snake, and like a snake to leap and strike. He could take a ptarmigan from its nest, kill a rabbit as it slept, and snap in mid-air the little chipmunks fleeing a second too late for the trees. Fish, in open pools, were not too quick for him; nor were beaver, mending their dams, too wary. He killed to eat, not from wantonness; but he preferred to eat what he killed himself. So a lurking humour ran through his deeds, and it was his delight to steal upon the squirrels, and, when he had all but had them, to let them go, chattering in mortal fear to the tree-tops.

As the fall of the year came on, the moose appeared in greater abundance, moving slowly down to meet the winter in the lower and less rigorous valleys. Buck had already dragged down a stray part-grown calf; but he wished strongly for larger and more formidable quarry, and he came upon it one day on the divide at the head of the creek. A band of twenty moose had crossed over from the land of streams and timber, and chief among them was a great bull. He was in a savage temper, and, standing over six feet from the ground, was as formidable an antagonist as even Buck could desire. Back and forth the bull tossed his great palmated antlers, branching to fourteen points and embracing seven feet within the tips. His small eyes burned with a vicious and bitter light, while he roared with fury at sight of Buck.

From the bull's side, just forward of the flank, protruded a feathered arrowend, which accounted for his savageness. Guided by that instinct which came from the old hunting days of the primordial world, Buck proceeded to cut the bull out from the herd. It was no slight task. He would bark and dance about in front of the bull, just out of reach of the great antlers and of the terrible splay hoofs which could have stamped his life out with a single blow. Unable to turn his back on the fanged danger and go on, the bull would be driven into paroxysms of rage. At such moments he charged Buck, who retreated craftily, luring him on by a simulated inability to escape. But when he was thus separated from his fellows two or three of the younger bulls would charge back upon Buck and enable the wounded bull to rejoin the herd.

There is a patience of the wild—dogged, tireless, persistent as life itself—that holds motionless for endless hours the spider in its web, the snake in its coils, the panther in its ambuscade; this patience belongs peculiarly to life when it hunts its living food; and it belonged to Buck as he clung to the flank of the herd, retarding its march, irritating the young bulls, worrying the cows with their half-grown calves, and driving the wounded bull mad with helpless rage.

For half a day this continued. Buck multiplied himself, attacking from all sides, enveloping the herd in a whirlwind of menace, cutting out his victim as fast as it could rejoin its mates, wearing out the patience of creatures preyed upon, which is a lesser patience than that of creatures preying.

As the day wore along and the sun dropped to its bed in the north-west (the darkness had come back and the fall nights were six hours long), the young bulls retraced their steps more and more reluctantly to the aid of their beset leader. The down-coming winter was harrying them on to the lower levels, and it seemed they could never shake off this tireless creature that held them back. Besides, it was not the life of the herd, or of the young bulls that was threatened. The life of only one member was demanded, which was a remoter interest than their lives, and in the end they were content to pay the toll.

As twilight fell the old bull stood with lowered head, watching his mates—the cows he had known, the calves he had fathered, the bulls he had mastered —as they shambled on at a rapid pace through the fading night. He could not follow, for before his nose leaped the merciless fanged terror that would not let him go. Three hundredweight more than half a ton he weighed; he had lived a long, strong life, full of fight and struggle, and at the end he faced death at the teeth of a creature whose head did not reach beyond his great knuckled knees.

From then on, night and day, Buck never left his prey, never gave it a moment's rest, never permitted it to browse the leaves of trees or the shoots of young birch and willow. Nor did he give the wounded bull opportunity to slake his burning thirst in the slender trickling streams they crossed. Often, in desperation, he burst into long stretches of flight. At such times Buck did not attempt to stay him, but loped easily at his heels, satisfied with the way the game was played, lying down when the moose stood still, attacking him fiercely when he strove to eat or drink.

The great head drooped more and more under its tree of horns, and the shambling trot grew weak and weaker. He took to standing for long periods, with nose to the ground and dejected ears dropped limply; and Buck found more time in which to get water for himself and in which to rest. At such moments, panting with red lolling tongue and with eyes fixed upon the big bull, it appeared to Buck that a change was coming over the face of things. He could feel a new stir in the land. As the moose were coming into the land, other kinds of life were coming in. Forest and stream and air seemed palpitant with their presence. The news of it was borne in upon him, not by sight, or sound, or smell, but by some other and subtler sense. He heard nothing, saw nothing, yet knew that the land was somehow different; that through it strange things were afoot and ranging; and he resolved to investigate after he had finished the business in hand.

At last, at the end of the fourth day, he pulled the great moose down. For a day and a night he remained by the kill, eating and sleeping, turn and turn about. Then, rested, refreshed and strong, he turned his face towards camp and John Thornton. He broke into the long easy lope, and went on, hour after hour, never at loss for the tangled way, heading straight home through strange country with a certitude of direction that put man and his magnetic needle to shame.

As he held on he became more and more conscious of the new stir in the land. There was life abroad in it different from the life which had been there throughout the summer. No longer was this fact borne upon him in some subtle, mysterious way. The birds talked of it, the squirrels chattered about it, the very breeze whispered of it. Several times he stopped and drew in the fresh morning air in great sniffs, reading a message which made him leap on with greater speed. He was oppressed with a sense of calamity happening, if it were not calamity already happened; and as he crossed the last watershed and dropped down into the valley towards camp, he proceeded with greater caution.

Three miles away he came upon a fresh trail that sent his neck hair rippling and bristling. It led straight towards camp and John Thornton. Buck hurried on, swiftly and stealthily, every nerve straining and tense, alert to the multitudinous details which told a story—all but the end.

Lesson 180

1. Finish reading "The Sounding of the Call."

The Sounding of the Call – Continued...

His nose gave him a varying description of the passage of life on the heels of which he was travelling. He remarked the pregnant silence of the forest. The bird life had flitted. The squirrels were in hiding. One only he saw—a sleek grey fellow, flattened against a grey dead limb so that he seemed a part of it, a woody excrescence upon the wood itself.

As Buck slid along with the obscureness of a gliding shadow, his nose was jerked suddenly to the side as though a positive force had gripped and pulled it. He followed the new scent into a thicket and found Nig. He was lying on his side, dead where he had dragged himself, an arrow protruding, head and feathers, from either side of his body.

A hundred yards farther on, Buck came upon one of the sled-dogs Thornton had bought in Dawson. This dog was thrashing about in a death-struggle, directly on the trail, and Buck passed around him without stopping. From the camp came the faint sound of many voices, rising and falling in a sing-song chant. Bellying forward to the edge of the clearing, he found Hans, lying on his face; feathered with arrows like a porcupine. At the same instant Buck peered out where the spruce-bough lodge had been and saw what made his hair leap straight up on his neck and shoulders. A gust of overpowering rage swept over him. He did not know that he growled, but he growled aloud with a terrible ferocity. For the last time in his life he allowed passion to usurp cunning and reason, and it was because of his great love for John Thornton that he lost his head.

The Yeehats were dancing about the wreckage of the spruce-bough when they heard a fearful roaring and saw rushing upon them an animal the like of which they had never seen before. It was Buck, a live hurricane of fury, hurling himself upon them in a frenzy to destroy. He sprang at the foremost man (it was the chief of the Yeehats), ripping the throat wide open till the rent jugular spouted a fountain of blood. He did not pause to worry the victim, but ripped in passing, with the next bound tearing wide the throat of a second man. There was no withstanding him. He plunged about in their very midst, tearing, rending, destroying, in constant and terrific motion which defied the arrows they discharged at him. In fact, so inconceivably rapid were his movements, and so closely were the Indians tangled together, that they shot one another with the arrows; and one young hunter, hurling a spear at Buck in mid-air, drove it through the chest of another hunter with such force that the point broke through the skin of the back and stood out beyond. Then a panic seized the Yeehats, and they fled in terror to the woods, proclaiming as they fled the advent of the Evil Spirit.

And truly Buck was the Fiend incarnate, raging at their heels and dragging them down like deer as they raced through the trees. It was a fateful day for the Yeehats. They scattered far and wide over the country, and it was not till a week later that the last of the survivors gathered together in a lower valley and counted their losses. As for Buck, wearying of the pursuit, he returned to the desolated camp. He found Pete where he had been killed in his blankets in the first moment of surprise. Thornton's desperate struggle was fresh-written on the earth, and Buck scented every detail of it down to the edge of a deep pool.

By the edge, head and fore feet in the water, lay Skeet, faithful to the last. The pool itself, muddy and discoloured from the sluice boxes, effectually hid what it contained, and it contained John Thornton; for Buck followed his trace into the water, from which no trace led away.

All day Buck brooded by the pool or roamed restlessly about the camp. Death, as a cessation of movement, as a passing out and away from the lives of the living, he knew, and he knew John Thornton was dead. It left a great void in him, somewhat akin to hunger, but a void which ached and ached, and which food could not fill. At times, when he paused to contemplate the carcasses of the Yeehats, he forgot the pain of it; and at such times he was aware of a great pride in himself— a pride greater than any he had yet experienced. He had killed man, the noblest game of all, and he had killed in the face of the law of club and fang. He sniffed the bodies curiously. They had died so easily. It was harder to kill a husky dog than them. They were no match at all, were it not for their arrows and spears and clubs. Thenceforward he would be unafraid of them except when they bore in their hands, arrows, spears, and clubs.

Night came on, and a full moon rose high over the trees into the sky, lighting the land till it lay bathed in ghostly day. And with the coming of the night, brooding and mourning by the pool, Buck became alive to a stirring of the new life in the forest other than that which the Yeehats had made. He stood up, listening and scenting. From far away drifted a faint, sharp yelp, followed by a chorus of similar sharp yelps. As the moments passed the yelps grew closer and louder. Again Buck knew them as things heard in that other world which persisted in his memory. He walked to the centre of the open space and listened. It was the call, the many-noted call, sounding more luringly and compellingly than ever before. And as never before, he was ready to obey. John Thornton was dead. The last tie was broken. Man and the claims of man no longer bound him.

Hunting their living meat, as the Yeehats were hunting it, on the flanks of the migrating moose, the wolf pack had at last crossed over from the land of streams and timber and invaded Buck's valley. Into the clearing where the moonlight streamed, they poured in a silvery flood; and in the centre of the clearing stood Buck, motionless as a statue, waiting their coming. They were awed, so still and large he stood, and a moment's pause fell, till the boldest one leaped straight for him. Like a flash Buck struck, breaking the neck. Then he stood, without movement, as before, the stricken wolf rolling in agony behind him. Three others tried it in sharp succession; and one after the other they drew back, streaming blood from slashed throats or shoulders.

This was sufficient to fling the whole pack forward pell-mell, crowded together, blocked and confused by its eagerness to pull down the prey. Buck's marvellous quickness and agility stood him in good stead. Pivoting on his hind legs, and snapping and gashing, he was everywhere at once, presenting a front which was apparently unbroken so swiftly did he whirl and guard from side to side. But to prevent them from getting behind him, he was forced back, down past the pool and into the creek bed, till he brought up against a high gravel bank. He worked along to a right angle in the bank which the men had made in the course of mining, and in this angle he came to bay, protected on three sides and with nothing to do but face the front.

And so well did he face it, that at the end of half an hour the wolves drew back discomfited. The tongues of all were out and lolling, the white fangs showing cruelly white in the moonlight. Some were lying down with heads raised and ears pricked forward; others stood on their feet, watching him; and still others were lapping water from the pool. One wolf, long and lean and grey, advanced cautiously, in a friendly manner, and Buck recognized the wild brother with whom he had run for a night and a day. He was whining softly, and, as Buck whined, they touched noses.

Then an old wolf, gaunt and battle-scarred, came forward. Buck writhed his lips into the preliminary of a snarl, but sniffed noses with him. Whereupon the old wolf sat down, pointed nose at the moon, and broke out the long wolf howl. The others sat down and howled. And now the call came to Buck in unmistakable accents. He, too, sat down and howled. This over, he came out of his angle and the pack crowded around him, sniffing in half-friendly, half savage manner. The leaders lifted the yelp of the pack and sprang away into the woods. The wolves swung in behind, yelping in chorus. And Buck ran with them, side by side with the wild brother, yelping as he ran.

And here may well end the story of Buck. The years were not many when the Yeehats noted a change in the breed of timber wolves; for some were seen with splashes of brown on head and muzzle, and with a rift of white centring down the chest. But more remarkable than this, the Yeehats tell of a Ghost Dog that runs at the head of the pack. They are afraid of this Ghost Dog, for it has cunning greater than they, stealing from their camps in fierce winters, robbing their traps, slaying their dogs, and defying their bravest hunters.

Nay, the tale grows worse. Hunters there are who fail to return to the camp, and hunters there have been whom their tribesmen found with their throats slashed cruelly open and with wolf prints about them in the snow greater than the prints of any wolf. Each fall, when the Yeehats follow the movement of the moose, there is a certain valley which they never enter. And women there are who become sad when the word goes over the fire of how the Evil Spirit came to select that valley for an abiding-place.

In the summers there is one visitor, however, to that valley, of which the Yeehats do not know. It is a great, gloriously coated wolf, like, and yet unlike, all other wolves. He crosses alone from the smiling timber land and comes down into an open space among the trees. Here a yellow stream flows from rotted moose-hide sacks and sinks into the ground, with long grasses growing through it and vegetable mould overrunning it and hiding its yellow from the sun; and here he muses for a time, howling once, long and mournfully, ere he departs.

But he is not always alone. When the long winter nights come on and the wolves follow their meat into the lower valleys, he may be seen running at the head of the pack through the pale moonlight or glimmering borealis, leaping gigantic above his fellows, his great throat a-bellow as he sings a song of the young world, which is the song of the pack.

ANSWERS

Lesson 101

5. "Two inseparable friends, Jack and Jill's bond is tested by a serious sledding accident." (from http://www.online-literature.com/alcott/jack_and_jill/)

Vocabulary 1H, 2I, 3J, 4A, 5B, 6E, 7C, 8D, 9G, 10F

Lesson 103

It usually takes twenty-one days for bones to knit. Young ones make quick work of it.

Lesson 104

1. Write to each other over telegraph.

2. "Frank's was full of books, maps, machinery, chemical messes, and geometrical drawings, which adorned the walls like intricate cobwebs."

3. "A delicious couch was there, with Frank reposing in its depths, half hidden under several folios which he was consulting for a history of the steam-engine, the subject of his next composition."

Vocabulary, answers will vary: weary-energized, drowsy-alert, sorrow-joy, resent-good will, kindness-meanness, sympathy-offended, lull-excite, soothing-aggravating

Lesson 106

He was ubiquitous. He must have traveled extensively to make it seem like he had been everywhere. Or do you think some folks might be lying, saying the president had been to their home/inn?

Lesson 107

3. Jill cries when she is frustrated; Jack gets mad and kicks.

Vocabulary 1C, 2F, 3A, 4G, 5D, 6H, 7E, 8B

Lesson 164

2. A mouse was running across the floor.

3. The lights didn't work.

4. She didn't like the dinner.

Lesson 165

1. agitate-annoy, diffuse-disperse, acquaintance-friend, dilate-widen, keen-eager, subdue-quieten, tumultuous-uproarious (answers will vary)

ABOUT
Easy Peasy All-in-One Homeschool

Easy Peasy All-in-One Homeschool is a free, complete online homeschool curriculum. There are 180 days of ready-to-go lessons for every level and every subject. It's created for your children to work as independently as you want them to. Preschool through high school is available as well as courses ranging from English, math, science and history to art, music, computer, physical education and health. A daily Bible lesson is offered as well. The mission of Easy Peasy is to enable those to homeschool who otherwise thought they couldn't.

Made in the USA
Coppell, TX
01 May 2024

31904400R00188